'At last, an original big history of British politics in the last 100 years.'

Sir Anthony Seldon, biographer of prime ministers and co-author of
The Impossible Office?

'A fascinating exploration of how politicians come to think the unthinkable, *The Death of Consensus* is essential reading for our age of permacrisis.'

Helen Lewis, author of *Difficult Women: A History of Feminism in 11 Fights*

'Phil Tinline is exceptionally clever, and this fascinating book makes us rethink the British, our government and how we want to be governed. His grasp of the detail and sweep of politics is astonishing, his central idea completely original. He makes us look at familiar faces and events with new clarity, as though we've remembered to clean our glasses. Plus, he makes it fun.'

Miranda Sawyer, journalist and broadcaster

'This is an epiphany of a book and everyone should read it, urgently. If you want to understand the state we're in and how we got here, you'll find no better guide than Phil Tinline. Intelligent, incredibly well-informed and utterly compelling.'

Manveen Rana, host of *Stories of our Times*, Times Radio

'A bracing and highly accessible account of the three most shape-shifting phases in Britain's modern political history.'

David Kynaston, author of *Austerity Britain*; *Family Britain*; and *Modernity Britain*

'A much-needed, nuanced and compelling account. Tinline brilliantly challenges the way we view the past and inspires us to take a fresh look.'

Steve Richards, author of *The Prime Ministers We Never Had*

'An account of modern Britain unlike any other. Tinline's portrait of people and ideas is witty, affectionate and angry, reintroducing us to a place we thought we knew, but which looks fresh through his eyes.'

Rana Mitter, historian and Vice-President of the British Academy

'Admirers of Phil Tinline's radio programmes are in for a treat. Here in proper portion size is his trademark fast-paced history of political ideas, studded with stories about Barbara Castle and Keith Joseph. Delicious.'

Aditya Chakrabortty, Senior Economics Commentator, *The Guardian*

'This perceptive and sharply insightful book will change how you think about consensus itself—let alone how it is established and retained. It's a riveting new lens through which to reassess some key moments from the last century.'

James Ball, Global Editor, The Bureau of Investigative Journalism

THE DEATH OF CONSENSUS

PHIL TINLINE

The Death of Consensus

100 Years of British Political Nightmares

HURST & COMPANY, LONDON

First published in the United Kingdom in 2022 by
C. Hurst & Co. (Publishers) Ltd.,
New Wing, Somerset House, Strand, London, WC2R 1LA
© Phil Tinline, 2022
All rights reserved.
Printed in Great Britain by Bell and Bain Ltd, Glasgow

Distributed in the United States, Canada and Latin America by
Oxford University Press, 198 Madison Avenue, New York, NY 10016,
United States of America.

A Cataloguing-in-Publication data record for this book
is available from the British Library.

This book is printed using paper from registered sustainable
and managed sources.

ISBN: 9781787386907

www.hurstpublishers.com

For my parents

CONTENTS

CONTENTS

INTRODUCTION

CONSENSUS AND NIGHTMARE

In 2008, the Crash sent cracks running through the foundations of the free-market thinking that had long dominated British politics. Ever since, we have been living through shocks and crises. From the 2011 riots, to the Brexit wars, to the grind of the pandemic, Britain has seemed trapped between watching the old order collapse, and waiting for another to be born. The public have often been divided; democratic institutions have come under terrible strain. A decade of hung parliaments and short-lived governments ended with the general election of December 2019, which delivered the first large parliamentary majority since 2005—but then came Covid-19, and a whole new array of challenges to the old certainties. After years of trying, no one has yet managed to lead us to a settled new consensus.

But was there ever really a 'consensus' in British politics? The term is most often used with 'post-war' tacked before it, to describe the years from the Labour election victory in 1945, to the turmoil of the 1970s and the rise of Thatcherism. The Conservative governments of the 1950s, however grudgingly, accepted much of the model built by Labour. But the period that began in 1945 did not utterly transform British society, with everyone in the country suddenly invested in an entirely new set of ideas. Nor did 1979 bring a total reversal of the ways Britain had been governed since the end of the war. The idea of 'consensus' became prominent in scholarship in the 1970s, but since then, it has often been challenged, in useful and necessary ways. 'Consensus' is not, for instance, a particularly helpful way to understand the development of the 'welfare state', which had its origins long before 1945, and was not scrapped after 1979. Too often, 'consensus' is used as a glib generalisation, smoothing important political fights from the collective memory. Yet the idea of consensus is also remarkably tenacious, not least because it appears to shape the thinking of many politicians.

No one could seriously think that politics is ever somehow harmonious. The most the political establishment can ever manage is a relatively high degree of compromise—a relative absence of agony. A period of consensus might best be defined as one where there is agreement, at least, on what to reject.[1] Modern Britain's past periods of consensus have centred on a shared understanding, whatever the differences between the political parties, that something was unthinkable: budget deficits, mass unemployment, inflation, strikes. These were the limits that shaped the politically possible. Those who accepted them did so for very different motives: for some, it was belief, sympathy, or the scars of personal experience; for others, just building a political career. And these periods of consensus were more of a strained compromise for one party than another. This meant they could only hold for so long.

So I want to use this idea, of consensus based on something unthinkable, to make sense of how the long-fixed boundaries of what is politically possible can start to move. Specifically, I want to explore how all of this is shaped by the fears, memories and imaginations of politicians—along with journalists, novelists, playwrights, screenwriters, policy advisers, and many others. To do this, we need a second idea: the political nightmare.

The word 'nightmare' is useful here partly because, like 'consensus', politicians use it so readily; but also because it is ambiguous. It encompasses fears based on past disasters, and fears based only on possible future ones; threats that are actually present, and possibilities that exist only in the imagination. They are sometimes passionate expressions of fear, or strategic warnings, or cynical scare stories, but all of these—everything I classify as a 'nightmare'—is a prospect that is both vividly present in politicians' minds, and somehow intolerable. It could be hyperinflation. National bankruptcy. Mass unemployment. Fascist dictatorship, total war, or Nazi invasion. Socialist dictatorship, or trade union tyranny. Or mass racial strife, violent anarchy, a police state, a catastrophic no-deal Brexit, the thwarting of a referendum, or the closing down of parliamentary democracy. This book is the story of how, no matter whether they are based on memories, precedents or imagined fears, these nightmares have hemmed politicians in, and shaped what they thought they could and could not do.

Whether they appear in speeches, government papers or diaries, or plays, novels and television scripts, these 'unthinkables' allow us to recapture what many once feared a near-future Britain would look like. When these nightmares failed to come true, they were easily forgotten; but recovering them can help us understand how consensus breaks and changes. So this is not simply a story about what happened. It is about the fears that did not happen, but significantly shaped what did.

Since Britain became a mass democracy in 1918,[2] there have been two broad periods before our own which, I want to suggest, have witnessed the death of a political consensus. We'll take these one by one.

The consensus whose death we'll trace in Part One had long roots in orthodox Victorian economics. We'll start with how it hit a huge financial crisis in 1931. Then we'll trace the fourteen-year struggle that followed, until a new consensus was secured in the wake of the Second World War.

In Part Two, we'll explore how that post-war consensus began to break down in the industrial strife of the late 1960s—and how politicians repeatedly struggled to remake the old compromise with the unions, until Thatcherism overwhelmed them.

Then, in Part Three, we'll follow what has happened since the consensus established by Margaret Thatcher was riddled with fissures by the 2008 Crash. This, of course, is still unfolding, so our story here is more provisional. And each of these three periods is very different. But within each of them, I think a process is discernible. Stripped down to essentials, it might run something like this:

There is a political consensus, based on a taboo: some nightmarish thing that must not be allowed to happen. Perhaps it is happening in another country, or has happened in our own past. The taboo enables the development of what you might call a 'concentration of power', a group whose interests it protects.

The death of consensus begins when a crisis strikes, and the existing solutions no longer seem to work. At this point, the existing system can only be kept going with a blatant assertion of dominance by those holding that concentrated power, forcing people to choose whether they still support it. Those for whom the crisis is a worse nightmare try to fight the concentration of power, but it's a hopeless struggle. While the old nightmare prevails, it blocks politicians from trying anything radically new.

Opposition to the concentration of power eventually puts the taboo under intolerable pressure, but even then it proves impossible to dislodge, precisely because it is secured in place by fear. This impasse plunges politics into flux and crisis, as the realisation that the old ways no longer work edges closer to the heart of power, yet every alternative still seems unthinkable. Every road leads to a nightmare.

Amid all this, leaders struggle to reinvent the consensus model—their only safe option. But this cannot last. More and more people decide that one of those alternatives might actually be worse than the existing taboo, the old nightmare still governing the limits of politics.

Finally, through a new crisis, or a shift in public mood, the breakpoint comes. With the old taboo no longer protecting it, the old concentration of power is exposed to a much more effective challenge. Leaders still hemmed in by the old fears start to look weak and out of time, next to the once-marginal figures who step forward to fight them, break the taboo, and take power.

The incoming leaders have a new story to tell about what has gone so terribly wrong, and about the weakness—and treachery—of the old leaders. This marks a sharp break with the past. The way through to a new democratic consensus at last becomes clear: it comes once enough people accept the newly dominant nightmare, the new 'thing to which we must never go back'.

Of course, it doesn't happen exactly this way. There is no precise template, and none of this is to suggest that history is somehow circular. These steps have not necessarily happened in exactly this order. Sometimes they have happened more than once. One major difference is that in 1931–45, the breakpoint was caused by an external threat (Nazi attack, and war), whereas in 1968–85, it sprang from internal conflict (between government and trade unions). It is hardly surprising, however, that societies move through periods of relative consensus and relative crisis, rather as economies move through phases of growth and recession. Nor is it so strange that this process, as it has played out across Britain's first century of mass democracy, does show some consistent patterns, which may help us understand our current predicaments. To trace how all this played out in messy reality, let's try looking at British democracy from a fresh angle.

We will track a series of people who played a major role as leading politicians in the 1970s: Labour's Harold Wilson, Barbara Castle and Michael Foot, and Conservatives Quintin Hogg (Lord Hailsham), Keith Joseph and Edward Heath.

But we will meet them first as youngsters in the 1930s, as they participated in that process of consensus change; at first from the margins, and then more decisively. We will see how they were shaped by the process too—particularly through their relationship with the nightmare of mass unemployment.

So, as we follow the story of consensus from 1931 to 1945, we will trace a series of remarkable connections, from the teenage Harold Wilson's reverence for the Labour defector Philip Snowden, to the far-left political debuts of the twenty-something Barbara Castle and Michael Foot, at the side of the upper-class firebrand Sir Stafford Cripps. We will move from the student Keith Joseph's encounter with Yorkshire miners to the young Edward Heath and Quintin Hogg fighting over appeasement.

Only then will we jump forwards to the 1960s and 1970s, to trace how memories of the unemployment nightmare of the 1930s shaped these individuals' actions in the governments they ran. We'll follow the increasingly desperate attempts by Wilson, Castle, Foot and even Heath to reinvent and rescue the old consensus, and Keith Joseph's effort to replace it.

Finally, we will jump again, to the period from the 2008 Crash, via the travails of the Big Society, Red Tories and Blue Labour, through the Brexit wars, to Covid and 'levelling up'. And as we do so, we'll trace what the 1930s and the 1970s can tell us about today's struggles and nightmares—about our own experience of the death of consensus, and what might be coming next.

PART ONE

1931–45

1

STARVATION AND RUIN

1931

Late in 1971, British politics found itself troubled by ghosts. The total number of people out of work in the United Kingdom had been rising for a while, and now it was creeping closer and closer to the miserably symbolic figure of 1 million. This was not how things were meant to be.

On the first Tuesday in October, the Leader of the Opposition stood up to speak at his party's annual conference in Brighton. 'For the first time since the Thirties,' claimed Harold Wilson, 'it is anger, it is fear that dominate the nation's life.' Eight years earlier, on the verge of power, Wilson had promised to build a white-hot technological future. Now, the foundations of his political life were falling away. So he opened an old wound.

The unemployment level, Wilson charged, was now 'far above any figure which has been accepted at any time, by any political party, since the war, since the nation resolved never again to return to the dismal and divided Thirties.' The blame lay with the Conservative Prime Minister and his 'obsession with a free market policy'. Wilson told the delegates that Britain had the highest unemployment of any industrialised nation and asked: 'Proud of that, Mr Heath?'

Harold Wilson was often seen as too clever by half: a statistician turned strategist, forever dodging, plotting, second-guessing. Some contend that unemployment was heading for a million by the early 1970s as a consequence of earlier deflationary budgeting by Wilson's then chancellor, Roy Jenkins. Nevertheless, if Wilson was making a political calculation that afternoon, it was that this abstract figure, a million unemployed, meant something personal—not only to his party conference, but to voters across the country. That this word, 'million', threatened the unthinkable: the flooding back of a nightmare they'd thought had ebbed forever. And however cynical he was, there are reasons to think that Wilson might have meant what he was saying; reasons rooted in a time before his life was so successful and secure.

Many of the leading politicians of the 1970s were forged by their experiences in the 1930s—even that alleged hard man of the free market, Edward Heath. The residual fear of a return to mass unemployment had underpinned British politics for decades. When the number of people out of work finally did reach a million, what would Heath do then?

But let's begin with Harold Wilson, and how those old fears had marked him, perhaps more deeply than any other front-rank politician of the time. 'Do they not realise,' he asked the delegates before him in Brighton, 'that for the man who is unemployed, for his wife as she shops to make limited ends meet, for his anxious family, the unemployment percentage is not a statistic; it's not 3.6 per cent seasonally corrected, or 8 or 10 per cent? It is, for him, for them, 100 per cent.'

* * *

The Right Honourable Harold Wilson MP, Her Majesty's Prime Minister of the United Kingdom of Great Britain and Northern Ireland from 1964 to 1970, had come a very long way from the drab corner of Yorkshire where he'd grown up with his big sister Marjorie and his frugal, Sunday School teacher parents. His astonishing career took off after he won a place at the University of Oxford in 1934. But he almost never made it.

Milnsbridge was a cramped little industrial town in the Colne Valley, near Huddersfield. Even in the 1960s, when Wilson went back for a by-election campaign, one newspaper called it a 'black valley', living 'in the shadow of the nineteenth century'. When he knew it as a child, Milnsbridge had a cinema, a few shops and pubs, a lot of chapels and, each morning and evening, crowds of workers pouring into and out of the factories and mills to turn out woollen textiles.[1] In September 1930, Harold was fourteen, and he did what he loved best: he escaped onto the moors for a Scout camp. There, a quest for custard nearly killed him. He bought some milk from a local farm, which gave him typhoid. Harold was taken to Meltham's Isolation Hospital. The medical consensus of the time was that the only cure was to starve the guilty microbes—that meant being fed nothing but milk and water. Some people would be killed not by the disease, but the cure.

Harold's father, Herbert, was an industrial chemist. He had trained at Manchester Technical School, but he had not done as well in his career as he thought he could have, had he only had the chance to go to university. Now his hopes were invested in his son, who was meant to be in the fourth year of a scholarship place at Royds Hall Grammar School. Each morning before work, and after work each evening, Herbert rang the hospital from a call box for news of his boy. Eleven other people had caught typhoid from the toxic milk; while Harold was in hospital, six of them died. Wilson biographer Leslie Smith reported that the family found this drawn-out crisis a 'nightmare of anxiety', distressing to talk about even thirty years later.[2]

Harold was still in hospital for Christmas. When he was finally allowed home, on 2 January 1931, he weighed four and a half stone. He had not been back long when he heard his parents whispering behind their bedroom door: 'Shall we tell him?' The secret they revealed, later that day, was not how close Harold had come to never coming home; they kept that to themselves. It was that, just a few days after he had heard his boy was beginning to improve,[3] Herbert had lost his job.

One nightmare of anxiety seeped into the next. Harold was told the secret, but it was made clear that unemployment was a matter of shame, not to be mentioned beyond the family. Herbert had been laid off with a month's salary, a month earlier. His care with money now came into its own: his savings would need to last them for as long as it took to find new work.

In 1931, there were many Herbert Wilsons. In the wake of the First World War, as international trade declined, British industry was losing its dominance of world markets to rising competitors. For much of the 1920s, 1 million workers were unemployed.

11

Then, in 1929, the American banking system crashed, triggering devastating international crisis. The reigning economic orthodoxy promised that trade would naturally recover, but in the course of 1930, unemployment in Britain—already at unprecedented highs for a decade—did not fall. It leapt. That meant the government had to borrow more and more to pay out in unemployment benefit. Not for the last time, a long-reliable economic model was not working any more.

By December 1930, as Harold lay starving in hospital, unemployment, which had already reached 1.5 million at the start of the year, hit 2.5 million. That figure excluded the tens of thousands of professionals without unemployment insurance, such as clerks, office managers, engineers, architects, and chemists like Herbert. Later, at Harold's Huddersfield grammar school, one boy would have to leave before he could sit his exams, because his father had lost his job.

Who could help the unemployed fathers of Colne Valley? Given that the Wilsons' MP was Philip Snowden, Chancellor of the Exchequer in the minority Labour government, they might have had reason for optimism. But Snowden instead took a devastating decision, in a desperate bid to defend the reigning economic consensus. To understand why, we need to trace how that consensus had emerged, and how Snowden had come to embody the fear that shaped it.

* * *

Philip Snowden was born in Yorkshire in 1864, and had been Colne Valley's MP since 1922. He loved the place: from its air, fresh from having 'swept over wide regions of moor and heather', to the people who lived in 'the stone cottages on the bleak and rugged hillsides', to the area's proud radical history.[4] At the end of the nineteenth century, as a frail but fiery young political preacher, he had evangelised for socialism in the Valley's scattered towns, denouncing the miseries that capitalism and greed and materialism had foisted on working people. This was 'ethical' socialism, distilled from Yorkshire's Nonconformist Christianity, driven by the vision of building the kingdom of heaven on Earth. Snowden preached 'salvation in the common life', promising a 'New Jerusalem'.[5] In 1900, Snowden became one of the founding leaders of the Labour Party. But—crucially for Herbert Wilson and the millions like him—beneath Snowden's socialism lay older political strata: a bedrock of strict economic orthodoxy.

He had grown up in a remote Yorkshire mill village with his poor weaver father, a Radical Liberal who followed the Victorian creed of self-help. This John Snowden practised by saving all he could at the Yorkshire Penny Bank, to keep his son in school beyond the standard leaving age of 10. Philip held to the three commandments inherited from his father, and from the great Victorian Chancellor of the Exchequer, William Gladstone:

First, thou shalt balance the budget. Snowden grew up understanding that borrowing, like gambling, was evil.

Second, thou shalt not thwart trade with tariffs. Free trade had powered the astounding success of the Victorian economy, making import-derived food and clothing affordable for the poor.

Third, thou shalt make paper money exchangeable, at a fixed price, for gold. The 'gold standard' ensured that free trade worked, and that money remained sound.

There were other imperatives too. Taxes should be kept low. Trade unions were to be respected, but not allowed too much power. Snowden was driven by a moralistic fury at the way working people were treated, but he did not want to see capitalism smashed by strikes or revolution. Stick fast to the orthodoxy, Snowden believed, and in time an evolving capitalism could be nurtured into socialism, funded by tax revenue.

As British politics emerged transformed from the First World War, Snowden—as Labour's leading voice on economics—was to play a crucial role. The 1918 extension of the vote, to most women over 30 who owned property or were married to a property-owner, and to all working men, made democratic politics into a clash between the classes. The Liberal Prime Minister David Lloyd George kept spending high, promising a better world for working people. Amid a post-war boom, newly powerful unions led successful strikes on pay. But the middle classes found themselves with higher taxes, scraping to keep up appearances, living in dread of the unpayable bill. The Treasury, unnerved by the way Victorian economic orthodoxy had been abandoned to pay for the war, began to push for it to be re-imposed. In 1920, interest rates were raised to 7 per cent; taxes and public spending were cut. Lloyd George's grandiose promises shrank like slashed balloons. A mines dispute ended in a swingeing pay cut; unemployment rose. This was the workers' nightmare: on Armistice Day 1921, thousands of jobless veterans, some wearing pawn tickets like medals, marched to the Cenotaph to lay a wreath which read: 'From the living victims—the unemployed—to our dead comrades, who died in vain.'[6]

But the middle classes could soon point to a counter-nightmare: the terrible consequences of profligate government. In 1923, Germany fell into a whirlpool of hyperinflation. Multi-million-mark banknotes became worthless almost as soon as they were printed. The desperate middle classes ended up selling their Steinways, then themselves.[7]

Caught between these two sides and their conflicting nightmares, many feared that Britain was heading for a devastating battle for power. The Conservative leader, Stanley Baldwin, worried that 'great consolidations of capital managed by small concentrated groups' were facing off against 'great organizations of Labour'. In the long shadow of the 1917 Bolshevik Revolution in Russia, he feared that mass democracy could break down. In 1922, he had helped force Lloyd George, a dangerously 'dynamic force', out of power; now he set about presenting himself as the embodiment of democratic compromise. At one point, he closed a parliamentary oration on industrial relations by saying: 'Give peace in our time, O Lord.'[8] This prayer for consensus was published, and sold half a million copies in three months.

Baldwin was a Conservative who shared Philip Snowden's concern for the working classes; crucially, Snowden was a socialist whose overriding nightmare was inflation. He saw it as a threat not just to the middle classes but to ordinary workers, warning in 1920 that Britain's post-war borrowing threatened 'national bankruptcy.'[9] In 1924, Labour formed its first, short-lived government, and Snowden became the first socialist Chancellor of the Exchequer. Far from bringing on the revolution, he advanced the return to orthodoxy, setting in train the process of returning sterling to the gold standard, in part to ward off inflation. Back in power at the end of the year, Baldwin's Conservatives finished the job. But the return to gold over-valued the pound and raised the price of exports, leading to wage cuts, even higher unemployment, a miners' strike, and, in May 1926, the long-anticipated general strike. The head of the railwaymen's union warned Baldwin that if the government tried to break the strike, it could bring on a revolutionary 'nightmare'.[10]

The Prime Minister took a moderate approach, while Snowden stayed pointedly quiet. When the TUC ended the general strike after only a week, the miners were left to limp on to defeat, and the Victorian consensus cohered again, in updated form. On the one hand, the workers had made some gains: there would be no more use of wage cuts to restore profits, and the TUC General Council took to meeting progressive industrialists for consensus-building talks. On the other hand, the 'immense organised power' of the trade unions was constrained by new legislation.[11] So the old commandments of economic orthodoxy remained in place, suffused with conciliatory mood music. While Baldwin soothed his grumbling right wing, Snowden preached the necessity of controlling spending to the discontented unions. In 1927, he told the TUC General Council that expanding credit or the currency to boost demand was an invitation to disaster: 'The microbe of inflation is always in the atmosphere'.[12] And, like medical orthodoxy, economic orthodoxy said that the cure was to starve the microbes. If inflation threatened, the British economy would need to go on a milk-and-water diet of spending cuts and higher taxes.

* * *

All of this meant that, back as chancellor again in 1931, Snowden was convinced that the only way to tackle the rocketing expense of unemployment benefit was still to try to bring about recovery through austerity. But this was doing nothing to help his constituents—not least Herbert Wilson, 'thrown out of my job,' as he remembered, 'just like an old newspaper.'[13]

His son had recovered from typhoid, and from his milk-and-water hospital diet. But Snowden's austere prescription for the economy was not just starving the microbes of unorthodoxy: it was starving

15

Herbert Wilson's capacity to provide for his family. 'That such a thing could happen,' Harold would later recall, 'frightened me more than any other single thing.'[14] He had read about the unemployed feeling 'unwanted and useless'.[15] Now it was happening to his dad.

'The adjustment, not only of the wage- or salary-earner and his wife, but also of the children in a house struck by unemployment, is hard to describe,' he remembered. 'I shall never really know how the family survived ... Our food became more simple, although my mother always managed to keep me adequately fed.'[16] Worn-out clothes were not always replaced. When Herbert and his friends talked politics, young Harold paid attention. Back at school, he started following the unfolding economic crisis, and the central role being played by his boyhood hero, the family's MP, Philip Snowden.

On 11 February 1931, Snowden addressed a silent House of Commons: 'I say with all the seriousness that I can command that the national position is so grave that drastic and disagreeable measures will have to be taken if Budget equilibrium is to be maintained and if industrial progress is to be made'.

He was still adhering faithfully to economic orthodoxy, even as unemployment rose and rose, and his cherished vision of a better life for working men and women was sliding away. 'Schemes involving heavy expenditure, however desirable they may be,' he warned, 'will have to wait until prosperity returns.' Throughout his forty years of active politics, the chancellor told the House, 'my only object has been to improve the lot of the toiling millions. That is still my aim and my object, and, if I ask for some temporary suspension, some temporary sacrifice, it is because I believe that that is necessary in order to make future progress possible.'[17]

Orthodoxy said that the economy reached equilibrium at full employment. Stick to the rules, and trade will recover. But that was not what was actually happening. The more trade dropped away and global prices fell, the more workers were laid off; the less revenue reached the Treasury—and the more it had to pay out in benefit. Round and round, in a vicious circle. Snowden, however, thought breaking from the orthodoxy would set a vicious circle spinning in the opposite direction, bringing uncontrollable inflation. Something had to give.

The chancellor was caught between those demanding hikes in government spending and those demanding it be cut. He knew proposals for cuts 'would meet with violent opposition' from those who had got used to progressive increases in spending on the social services. He faced MPs' anger and dismay. His Labour colleagues, he thought, felt 'that their old foundations had been swept from under them.'[18] But that was true of Snowden too. Was there any other way through?

* * *

Up in the Strangers' Gallery during that Commons debate sat the novelist Aldous Huxley, 36, peering down in despair at the politicians 'twaddling' below.[19] During the 1931 crisis, Huxley became one of a growing number of the great and good who were so frightened of economic collapse that they began to contemplate embracing once-unthinkable ideas to avoid it: a turn to an extreme form of planned economy, abandoning democracy. In October 1930, Huxley had been invited to see the impact of the slump in the Durham coalfield. In nearby Middlesbrough, he found the streets filled with the 'slow interminable procession' of the unemployed: 'Dead men walking ... aimlessly and in silence.'[20] He admonished rich Londoners to go and see the human reality for themselves. In the same month as Snowden's cuts-or-chaos speech to the Commons, Huxley visited the huge Imperial Chemical Industries plant at Billingham, on Teesside. There he found a 'triumphant embodiment of particular planning': a quarter-mile of steel towers, pipe bridges and turbines like 'softly purring monsters'. It was 'one of those ordered universes which exist ... in the midst of the larger world of planless incoherence.'[21] Was this a viable alternative both to the terrifying mess he had seen in Durham, and to Snowden's nightmares of ruinous inflation?

Later in 1931, Huxley attended the inaugural meeting of a group anxious to find a different way through the gathering crisis: Political and Economic Planning (PEP), whose founders saw politicians' failure to prepare an immediate National Plan as 'a major national danger'.[22] Huxley applauded their calls for drastic measures, including the elimination of needless competition between companies. As Snowden battled to save the old orthodoxy, Huxley grew sick of the 'whorish old slut' that democracy had become.[23]

He was so desperate for radical action to stave off the collapse of the economy that he called for a dictatorship to push through a PEP-style plan, overriding politicians by force.

By May, Huxley was hard at work on his novel *Brave New World*. It began as a satire on Californian consumerism, but under the pressure of the crisis, it became a sketch of a totally planned economy. For all the novel's sex, drugs and entertainment, its future 'World State' has no brands or commercial competition, and new inventions are suppressed to preserve stability. As the state slogan has it, 'everyone works for everyone else'. This, we discover, is because the World State was created in the wake of war, economic crisis and the feared death of civilisation. After 'the great Economic Collapse', as Mustapha Mond explains, 'There was a choice between World Control and destruction.' Mond is 'Western European Controller', and was named after Sir Alfred Mond of ICI, owner of the Teesside plant that had left such an impression on Huxley.

On the day he finished the novel, Huxley wrote to his father in praise of the Soviets' Five-Year Plan. Yet, much as Huxley appears to have decided that a total state was better than total chaos, *Brave New World* is still a dystopia. 'Unorthodoxy,' one conformist official counsels another, 'strikes at Society itself'.[24] The novel's title became an instant catchphrase, used by commentators to attack not only the European dictatorships of the 1930s but also British socialists' planning, and Roosevelt's New Deal. Huxley's struggle to write *Brave New World* served to show how hard it was to imagine a tolerable alternative to Snowden and his orthodox cuts. It may have been set 600 years in the future, but—as one critic put it—it was of course 'a nightmare of the present'.[25]

* * *

Was there a way forward that could avoid all of these nightmares: inflation-driven chaos, a planners' dictatorship, worsening the misery of the unemployed? On Monday 27 April, Snowden was back at the Despatch Box to deliver the Budget statement. Scanning the packed chamber, the staunch old guardian of economic orthodoxy found himself facing political rivals who thought the only way out of the crisis was to jettison one element or another of the beleaguered beliefs inherited from the Victorians.

Perhaps Britain could abandon that old shibboleth, free trade? Debate had raged over this for decades, and now, along with spending cuts, this was the solution proposed by the two Midlands industrialists facing Snowden from the Opposition front bench. Stanley Baldwin and his shadow chancellor Neville Chamberlain argued that tariffs on imports would bolster British industry. Or could the Treasury abandon its obsession with balanced budgets? Among the Liberals sat the former Prime Minister, Lloyd George, whose 1929 platform, *We Can Conquer Unemployment*, had proposed a loan-funded emergency programme of public works. Or could the government try... socialism? Over to Snowden's right, along the Labour benches, sat Frank Wise of the affiliated Independent Labour Party—now a more hotly radical outfit than when Snowden had helped to found it forty years earlier. Wise would tell Snowden to face the fact that 'in industry and in finance the old methods are breaking down.'[26]

Or, at last, what if the unemployment problem was now so urgent that all of this had to be tried at once? The young politician who advocated a wholesale abandonment of orthodoxy, with much more emphasis on the domestic economy than international trade, had been one of the chancellor's front-bench colleagues until May 1930. But, after months of seeing his ideas blocked by Snowden and others, Sir Oswald Mosley had resigned in frustration. In February 1931, when Snowden insisted that 'some temporary sacrifice' was unavoidable, Mosley had scoffed: 'These suggestions to put the nation in bed on a starvation diet are the suggestions of an old woman in a fright.'[27] Less than a month later, he broke from Labour to set up the New Party, demanding that unemployment should be tackled on an 'emergency war footing'.[28]

There was a single figure hovering behind the various risky proposals advanced by Lloyd George, Wise and Mosley: the Treasury heretic, Lucifer to Snowden's Gabriel, John Maynard Keynes. In some ways, Keynes and Snowden sprang from similar soil: they were the sons of Liberal Nonconformist families, knew the Treasury well, and thought poverty was a great evil. But where Snowden hated gambling and saw borrowing as another sin, Keynes enjoyed playing the markets and was ready to take risks and break rules. This made him much more likely to respond to crisis by rethinking.

Keynes' case was that the economy no longer reached equilibrium at full employment, as the orthodoxy claimed. Even in the 1920s, unemployment was at around 10 per cent. The economy was stuck in a rut, business 'weighed down in timidity'.[29] It needed a jolt. From September 1930, he had been pressing into service the idea of the 'multiplier', to attack the belief that public spending on public works simply deprived business of money they could turn into profit. Interest rates should be lowered to stimulate investment. He had also challenged the wisdom of returning to the gold standard, saying it would force down prices—and wages, which would require 'the deliberate intensification of unemployment'.[30]

Support for Keynes' ideas was detectable among businessmen and industrialists, who would have welcomed cheaper interest rates, and even from a former Liberal chancellor, Reginald McKenna. But those willing to consider a break from orthodoxy had no powerbase or shared programme. To Snowden, all these ideas were unthinkable.

* * *

Six weeks after the April Budget, creditors started pulling their money out of the City. The huge costs of unemployment benefit were pushing the government deeper into deficit. Confidence in the pound began to spiral. The Bank of England raised the interest rate to 3.5 per cent. A report commissioned by Snowden forecast a terrifying deficit for the next financial year of £120 million, which might drive up inflation to the point where sterling was forced off gold. This prediction made the crisis of confidence markedly worse. Treasury officials warned the chancellor that 'the gold exodus is unprecedented', and that, 'Unless we take such steps as are open to us to rectify the situation, there is a real danger of our being driven off the gold standard.'[31] In desperation, advisers invoked again and again the nightmare that would follow: inflation and the dislocation of global finance. The Bank of England borrowed £50 million from the Bank of France and the US Federal Reserve, but it was not enough. In one week, the Bank of England lost a quarter of its gold reserves to withdrawals. On 30 July, it raised the interest rate again, to 4.5 per cent, but this did nothing to stop the loss of gold. Around this time, the Bank's highly strung Governor, Sir Montagu Norman, collapsed—rather like investors' confidence in sterling. Rather like their money, he left the country to recuperate.

The Labour Prime Minister, Ramsay MacDonald, sought an alternative view—from Keynes. On 5 August Keynes replied that to make deflation effective by 'bringing incomes down to the level of prices' in isolation would be 'a most gross perversion of social justice'. For the gold standard, he judged, 'the game is up'.[32] MacDonald had Keynes and social injustice in one ear; in the other, Snowden and economic collapse. He retreated to his home in Scotland, but on 7 August, as the Bank's reserves of gold and foreign exchange drained away, Snowden wrote to warn him that 'the point of exhaustion will come very soon with disastrous consequences ... Three millions of unemployed is certain in the near future and four millions next year is not out of the question.' They were close to exhausting the government's borrowing power, and failing to secure additional loans would be 'an admission of national bankruptcy.' They were 'perilously near' to 'utter chaos'.[33] MacDonald hurried back to London, to be told by Snowden and the Bank of England that the only way to restore confidence was to balance the budget within a fortnight. This meant cutting unemployment benefit, which was also necessary to instil sufficient confidence in foreign creditors. This would stop the run on the pound, and convince American banks to lend the government enough money to pull it through its immediate crisis.

Over the course of the next five days, from Wednesday 19 to Sunday 23 August, the Labour Cabinet and their trade union allies put themselves through an intensive run of meetings to find a compromise between heaping more suffering onto the backs of the unemployed, and the threat of economic chaos. But there was no such compromise. They had to choose. And this—a choice between nightmares—is how a consensus begins to die.

The first meeting ran for almost twelve hours. Ministers accepted that running an ongoing deficit, which would force the pound off gold, remained unthinkable. They began a desperate search for another way of balancing the books and restoring confidence, through 'common sacrifice',[34] without penalising the unemployed and government workers. Some pushed for tax rises. But because Labour had no majority, they would need the support of either the

21

Conservatives or the Liberals to get the necessary legislation through Parliament. And all the while, both those parties were pushing for fewer tax rises and more cuts. Snowden, backed by MacDonald, insisted to the Cabinet again and again that they had no choice but to cut unemployment benefit.

The next morning, against Snowden's wishes, a Cabinet committee trooped to Transport House, to consult the party's National Executive Committee, and the General Council of the TUC. MacDonald pleaded that 'unless the outward drain of gold could be arrested unemployment might rise over 5,000,000'.[35] But the General Council struggled to stop the coming deflation: they wanted tax rises,[36] and public works to relieve unemployment, and looser monetary policy. MacDonald saw the unions' stance as 'practically a declaration of war'.[37]

On the Friday, another drawn-out discussion won half the Cabinet round to accepting the benefit cuts—but only half. Snowden met representatives from the Bank of England, which needed fresh loans from America and France to support the pound. The current cuts offer was no good: to the foreign creditors, the burden on British industry from unemployment insurance costs looked like a threat to the security of their loans.

When the Cabinet met again the following morning, MacDonald warned them that the financial situation 'had undergone further deterioration'. Snowden said the choice was the full cuts, or defeat in a Commons vote. If getting the cuts through, preserving the orthodoxy and warding off the nightmare meant destroying the Labour Party, then so be it. If he was forced to choose between 'retaining the Labour Movement in its present form and reducing the standard of living of the workmen by 50% which would be the effect of departing from the Gold Standard, he knew where his duty would lie.'[38] But the question for his colleagues was whether they believed Snowden's scenario, or thought that cutting unemployment benefit would be even worse.

The Cabinet met yet again on Saturday afternoon, and again on Sunday night. MacDonald continued to press the nightmare scenario, even as he conceded that he knew cutting unemployment benefit was the 'negation of everything that the Labour Party stood for'.[39] They needed to line up the backing of banks in the United

States, which would lend the money to save the gold standard; and the support of the Opposition, which would help him vote through the cuts. When the cable finally came through from New York to say that the loan would be forthcoming if Cabinet approved the benefit cuts, MacDonald insisted that it had to be a unanimous decision. But nine ministers held out. Next morning, out of nowhere, MacDonald told Cabinet that he was forming an emergency administration, a 'National' government, with the Conservatives and the Liberals. Philip Snowden was one of a handful of Labour ministers who followed him.

In Colne Valley, Snowden's socialist supporters were stunned. Why had he betrayed them? Harold Wilson followed the crisis, and the shocking actions of his boyhood hero. According to Leslie Smith, Harold's grandfather broke down in tears. Even before the split, Snowden had done nothing for Herbert Wilson, still out of work after nine months. While the family waited and waited for good news, Harold concentrated ever harder on his studies. But as Herbert's savings drained away, the family made plans for Harold to leave school at sixteen. Instead of university, he would have to go to work in his uncle's umbrella factory.

Snowden had been forced to choose between his deepest economic beliefs and the socialism of the party he had helped to found. His belief that coming off the gold standard would generate a collapse that would be even worse for workers than the cuts had driven him to abandon his party. The crisis had forced the creation, in the new National Government, of a formal coalition, dedicated to shoring up the orthodoxy. The new administration's blatant requisitioning of the word 'national' reflected Baldwin's strategy of isolating hardliners and claiming the moderate middle, equated to the national interest.

But something else had happened too—something that would eventually prove to matter more. Even in the face of extreme crisis, Snowden's nightmare had been rejected by nine Cabinet ministers, with the backing of the TUC leadership. They had effectively decided that worsening the suffering of the unemployed was unthinkable. More unthinkable, even, than the risk of economic collapse. This act of heresy, however hopeless, was the start of a years-long struggle to transform what was politically possible.

23

Not that that was how it felt at the time, however. The crisis had exposed their enemy: the power of finance, in the Treasury and the banks. This now appeared to have broken the government and thrown Labour MPs unceremoniously back onto the Opposition benches; the prospects of defeating it seemed slight indeed. The veteran socialist intellectual Beatrice Webb, whose husband Sidney had been one of those Labour ministers, was convinced that American and British financiers had overthrown the government, and that this was 'an open declaration, without any disguise, of Capitalist Dictatorship'.[40] In its attempts to end the nightmare of mass unemployment, the left had come up against a new nightmare, which it now, somehow, had to defeat.

* * *

For the new government, the overriding nightmares remained inflation, and falling off the gold standard. When Parliament resumed in September, Snowden—still chancellor—introduced the new coalition's benefit cuts in an emergency Budget, which drew noisy objections from the new Labour Opposition, and an ovation from the government benches. When one Labour MP asked, 'What is the use of democracy?', one of Snowden's new Liberal colleagues, Walter Runciman, denounced such fevered Labour talk about bankers undermining democracy, and invoked the German hyperinflation of 1923, which he had personally watched unfold. It was wrong, Runciman insisted, to imagine that 'nothing could happen here such as happened on the Continent.' Frank Wise of the Independent Labour Party had also witnessed the hyperinflation in Berlin, but dismissed all this as scare-mongering. Britain in 1931 was quite different from Germany in 1923, he argued; a controlled devaluation was not dangerous, and MPs should listen to Keynes, who said the problem was barriers to investment. But Sir Henry Page Croft—a hard-right Conservative MP and yet another spectator at the Weimar economic freak show—was terrified of seeing the same in Britain. 'It has been a positive nightmare to me,' he lamented, 'to see the steam-roller coming along, threatening such disasters to our country.'[41]

After Snowden's drawn-out struggle to push his cuts through the party's resistance, the same measures now sailed through with support from the new government's handsome majority, laid on by his Liberal and Conservative allies. £85 million in loans was duly provided by the banks in Paris and New York. Parliament also approved sweeping powers to allow the National Government to make emergency spending cuts by ministerial fiat, or Orders in Council. But now they had to enact the 10 per cent cuts to unemployment benefit, and introduce a household means test. This sent inspectors into the homes of the long-term unemployed to assess their eligibility for transitional payments. Within a year, 180,000 people had lost their benefits. Because income was assessed on a household basis, this forced some young people and pensioners out of family homes, because their earnings or pensions would have taken the household over the limit. When a peer laughed at Aneurin Bevan for denouncing this, the young Welsh miner turned Labour MP offered to wipe the grin off the Noble Lord's face. The punishing of one family member for the income of another, and the indignity of means test inspectors intruding into struggling homes, hunting for any saleable assets, provoked lasting hatred.

The government also reduced the pay of its workers, from teachers to the military, which would soon have more immediate, and ironic, consequences. The Royal Navy was one of the great guarantors of Britain's long dominance of global trade; but when news of the pay cuts broke among sailors, they mutinied. And, when reports of such unheard-of unrest reached foreign investors in London, they took flight, and started pulling out their money all over again. On Wednesday 16 September, the Bank of England lost £5 million, just as Keynes was telling MPs that the cuts to benefits, wages and public works were 'dreadful errors'.[42] Next day, the Bank of England spent another £10 million. The financiers in New York and Paris had had enough. There would be no more loans.

On the Friday, the Prime Minister was summoned back from Chequers to be told by Treasury and Bank officials that the game was up. They could not keep going. Sterling would have to come off gold. Here it finally was: the nightmare Snowden had fought so hard to hold back. As he had warned his local Labour Party, falling off the gold standard would mean 'irretrievable disaster ... catastrophe ... the certain loss of all I have fought for.'[43]

And yet, when the news broke, there was no panic. No deluge. No German-style hyperinflation apocalypse. No one had to take their salary home in a wheelbarrow. The British middle classes did not end up in desperation, selling their possessions then prostituting themselves. The pound dropped somewhat in value, from \$4.86 to \$3.90 by the end of September—but it did not collapse. The working classes, the cause that had always driven Snowden's career, did not find it any harder to afford food.

Orthodoxy is held in place in part by the dead weight of intellectual habit. In his memoirs, one senior Treasury official was full of praise for Snowden, and the necessity of the cuts to balance the budget and save the gold standard. Then, blithely pivoting on a sixpence, he continued: 'Our abandonment of the gold standard ... made a radical difference to our economy and left us with a greater freedom to deal with our internal problems.'[44] With the pound floating, exports began to revive and interest rates fell. Unemployment did not hit four or five or ten million; not long afterwards, at least for a while, it fell. One of Labour's ousted Cabinet Ministers reportedly lamented: 'No one ever told *us* we could do that.'[45]

Snowden claimed that the reason the departure from gold had not been a disaster was because the coalition's Budget, unlike Labour's August one, was balanced—meaning there was no danger of having to print money and trigger 'uncontrolled inflation'.[46] But the *New Statesman* mocked him as 'the high priest of ancient orthodoxies'.[47]

What had finally chased sterling off gold was the spectre of mutiny. This too was overblown—the incident may have raised fearful echoes of the German and Russian revolutions, but in reality the protests remained respectful. When the sailors' complaint was dealt with, they went quietly back to work. The public-sector pay cuts went ahead. Bank and Treasury veterans were aggrieved that the 'unrest' in the Navy had been blown out of proportion abroad.[48] But they had had no qualms about defending the gold standard with their own overblown nightmares of inflation. They could scarcely object to it being broken by overblown nightmares of insurrection.

In the Commons, Aneurin Bevan asked Prime Minister MacDonald if the same concessions given to the sailors would be forthcoming 'if the unemployed showed the same rebellious tendencies?'[49] In time, the means test would indeed provoke demonstrations in Parliament Square, which were charged by the police. In Birkenhead, bottles and railing spikes were thrown at officers, as fighting ran on for three days. In retaliation, there were police raids. Nevertheless, with the end of the gold standard, one of the pillars of the consensus had been shattered, and a new nightmare—the sufferings of the unemployed and underpaid, and behind them, the threat of unrest—had become a little more prominent.

* * *

On Sunday 4 October 1931, a young woman from radical Bradford, birthplace of the Independent Labour Party, took a train to Scarborough for the Labour Party's annual conference. Like a lot of people from 'modest' origins who win a place at Oxford, Barbara Betts was driven onward by ambition, dragged back by self-doubt, driven on again by guilt. She was travelling with the young ILP politician Jennie Lee, and Lee's parliamentary colleague—and lover—Frank Wise, fresh from lambasting Snowden in the Commons. Lee had gone even further, telling fellow MPs that capitalism was finished and it was time to nationalise the banks. A Treasury minister had accused her of wanting to pull down the pillars of the temple, but the pillars seemed riddled with cracks already. Now a general election was expected any day. Could Labour regroup in Scarborough for the new, post–gold standard era, and win back power on a radical platform?

Barbara was going to the conference to report for the *Bradford Pioneer*, her father Frank's outspoken, home-produced newspaper. (Back in Bradford there was a boy called Vic Feather who also worked on the paper and had wanted to go to the conference, but had lost out to the editor's daughter.) Frank Betts had joined the ILP early, and was 'a one-man challenge to orthodoxy'.[50] Growing up into a socialist household, which had played host to the children of striking miners, Barbara had joined the ILP League of Youth at sixteen. And she had worshipped Ramsay MacDonald.

On the first day of Labour's post-split conference, the turncoat MacDonald was expelled. Barbara approved. By now, 2.88 million people were out of work, and she thought the break with MacDonald and Snowden had given the party an overwhelming new sense of mission: 'If the unemployed are not to suffer, something drastic must be done immediately, therefore for the first time the Labour Party is ready to contemplate the prospect of Socialism in our time.'[51]

For an amateur journalist, this was far-sighted: the nightmare of mass unemployment would eventually go on to form the basis of a whole new political consensus, in which Barbara would be a pivotal figure. But in October 1931, six weeks after being thrown out of power, the only way Labour could see to cure the evil of unemployment was to get rid of capitalism, root and rotten branch. The conference chairman opened proceedings with a denunciation of the bankers, for using their power to force workers to pay for financiers' mistakes. The next day, the conference voted unanimously in favour of nationalising the banking system. The party, Barbara reported, was in febrile mood:

> Its great source of strength at present lies in its *united determination to stand by the unemployed* whatever financial calamity may threaten, for in this crisis those who stand by the unemployed must stand for revolutionary Socialism ... The Labour Party's instincts are sound—it's [sic] spontaneous rally on behalf of the unemployed has carried it a long way on the path to constructive revolution.[52]

Confronted by the power of banks apparently ready to break left-wing governments, many on the left were unable to see a democratic way to end mass unemployment. If democracy was a sham, as August's rupture seemed to show, then the movement might have to fight back in kind. Barbara reported a trade unionist saying that extra-Parliamentary force had better be ready for revolution, and to seize power. There was talk of the risk, if Labour were smashed in the coming election, of a National Government masquerading as a democratic government, but becoming a dictatorship.

Barbara Betts' response to this revolutionary mood was revealingly ambivalent. She seemed to see through the 'noisy rhetoric' of speakers and their 'comforting assurance that the Capitalist system is collapsing speedily about our ears.' But she clearly had plenty of sympathy for the left's ardour 'to press home the urgency of the problem, the necessity for drastic and immediate measures, and to urge the party to grasp the fact that this is a new situation which can only be dealt with in a revolutionary manner.'[53] It was not simply a concentration of power that had to be overcome, but the widely held beliefs that underpinned it.

* * *

British politics had become a battle over the credibility of each side's nightmares. Labour warned of the perpetuation of mass unemployment, and raised the spectres of dictatorial bankers and fascism. The National Government warned of inflation and ruin, and raised the spectres of dictatorial trade unionists and bolshevism. What better time for a general election?

All elections involve dire warnings of the consequences of voting for the other side, but normally these wash over most voters. In crisis, that can change, because the normal political limits seem less secure. In a year that had already brought financial panic, a run on the pound, emergency weekend Cabinet meetings, prime ministerial dashes back and forth to the Palace, a split in the Labour Party, the formation of an emergency national government, an apparent naval mutiny and the end of the gold standard, doomsday scenarios seemed a little more plausible than usual. But the question was whether Labour's warnings were compelling enough to dislodge the fear that underpinned the National Government. It was a difficult target: in the wake of falling off gold, ministers had coolly smoothed over this huge breach of orthodoxy, but they were still running for re-election on the basis that only they could protect Britain from the horrors of inflation, and pull off a sound economic recovery.

Ramsay MacDonald headed to Seaham, south of Sunderland in County Durham. He had represented this coastal mining constituency only since 1929, and his old party thought they could take it back, ousting the treacherous Prime Minister from Parliament. Across the county, fully 38.7 per cent of the population were now reportedly unemployed, a total of 412,880 people. But, as bad as that was, MacDonald was ready to fight back, with the government's overriding nightmare: the raging inflation that would follow a Labour win and the loss of foreign confidence. He told an audience of over a thousand at the Hippodrome at Easington Colliery, about how, in 1923, he had witnessed workers at a German factory being paid with banknotes that had to come in heaps. At nearby Shotton, he showed the crowd a German banknote for 50,000,000,000 marks, which, he said, had been worth tuppence.

Snowden stayed in Downing Street and turned his artillery on his old party from there. The choice, he insisted, was between a 'strong and stable Government'[54] or his irresponsible former colleagues who had run away from the crisis. Labour was now promising to commit a new, mortal sin against orthodoxy: nationalising the banks. The Prime Minister had drawn on the German hyperinflation to enliven his nightmare of Labour government; in a radio broadcast on 17 October, the chancellor now summoned the ghosts of the Russian Revolution:

> The banks and financial houses are to be placed under national ownership and control, which means, I suppose, that they are to be run by a joint committee of the Labour Party and the Trades Union Congress. Your investments are to be ordered by some board, and your foreign investments are to be mobilised to finance this madcap policy. This is not Socialism. It is Bolshevism run mad.[55]

The effect was electric. The *New Statesman* fired back with a piece titled 'Snowdenism run mad'.[56] Three days later, Snowden wrote an incandescent *Daily Mail* article headlined 'Labour's Little Lenins', contending that the dictatorial trade unions would replace the City of London.[57]

Labour made the equal and opposite allegation: that the National Government was a financiers' dictatorship in waiting. At its Scarborough conference, the party had cast the coming election as a struggle for power between the bankers and the people. Now some Labour candidates claimed that the Tories would starve the people under the diktat of foreign financiers. This was ineffective, but meanwhile, there was that more tangible nightmare: mass unemployment. Yet, for all that they had sacrificed their place in government to try to defend the unemployed against the benefit cuts, Labour just could not make this work as an election issue either. They promised to solve the problem with nationalisation, planning and emergency powers to force through change, but they had all the disadvantages of both having just been in government and now being in opposition: they could be painted simultaneously as a failed administration and as dangerous outsiders. Worse for Labour, the unemployment total actually dipped during the campaign. The National Government campaign produced a poster showing a worker reaching out imploringly, with the slogan 'Mates—Help Me Get a Job. Vote National.' A hostile press, meanwhile, threatened those considering voting Labour with misery, chaos, catastrophe and starvation. And, for many voters, unemployment remained an issue affecting people somewhere in the distance.

Labour knew they had a poor hand to play, but did not expect an outright massacre. On the last Sunday of the campaign, Barbara Betts wrote jauntily to her parents to say that she had been engaged in 'hectic electioneering' in Reading.[58] The letter shows no inkling of how voters were responding.

Labour's vote share fell 7 per cent, to 30 per cent. Faced with the other parties in a united front, this national swing was enough to lose the party Reading, and another 232 seats besides. In Colne Valley, the Wilsons watched their seat go Liberal, for the first time since Philip Snowden had won it for Labour in 1922. Snowden himself, ill as he was, listened to the results on the radio in his room at Number 11 until three o'clock in the morning. 'It seemed almost incredible,' he would write later, 'that Labour seats which had been held at previous Elections by enormous majorities should have fallen to the assault of the National candidates.'[59] In the Durham coalfield, with almost half a million people unemployed, Ramsay MacDonald won Seaham against his old party; overall, Labour lost nine of Durham's eleven county seats.

On 23 August, Labour had been in government, with 285 MPs. Now, barely two months later, all but eight of its ministers were out of Parliament; Labour now had just fifty-two MPs, even including the remnant of the ILP. The National Government had more than ten times that number. 470 of the 532 'National' MPs were Conservatives, many for depressed northern seats captured straight from Labour. According to the New Statesman, 150 lived on inherited wealth rather than working, 111 were lawyers, seventy-three were businessmen, and forty-four were either bankers or financiers. So much for 'the bankers versus the people'.

By the winter of 1931, the banks' concentration of power had become much more visible. The gold standard had gone, and free trade was on its way out—but the commandment to balance the budget remained all the more sacred, protected by fearful tales about what would happen if that were abandoned too. This imposed strict limits on what government could do to help get people back to work. Mass unemployment had not overridden those worries.

And so, as the National Government settled in with what is still the biggest majority in British history, here they were: the dole queues and the dulled eyes, the hungry children with dirty feet, the hungry, worn-out mothers letting in the means test man, the hungry, desperate Germans beginning to think about giving Hitler a try—and Herbert Wilson, coming home at evening to his waiting wife and son, still without a job.

2

WE HAVE BEEN WARNED

1932–5

To save the unemployed, Labour had vowed to become a plucky David, psyching itself up to bring down the Goliath of high finance. But it seemed clear—at least to leading left-wingers—that this would provoke ferocious retaliation. A future socialist government would have to race to stop the 'capitalist class' withdrawing their money from the country, and to block the banks from deliberately engineering a crisis to destroy the Labour administration—as they supposedly had in the summer of 1931. In 1933, the left-wing novelist Naomi Mitchison was hard at work sketching out the reaction she and her comrades feared a new socialist government might encounter.

In *We Have Been Warned*, Labour is swept to power in a general election in 1935, winning its first proper majority. A freshly elected Labour MP tells his euphoric aides that the new government has just 48 hours to take control of the banks (and the big industries, the press and the BBC), 'before they can get England's money away from us'. But within days, a brutal counter-revolution forces Labour from office, entrenching its control with a vicious new armed police force. The 'Specials' hunt down the left-wing supporters of the deposed administration, committing atrocities as they go. In Oxford, they launch a gas attack, and carry out summary executions and gang-rapes. Terrified socialists scramble to burn their election posters. Refugees set out for Scotland on foot, as left-wing fighters struggle to hold on to the Midlands and the north. Finally, news reaches the MP's wife that he has been caught and is to face a firing-squad, along with several of his Labour colleagues.

33

This chapter follows the story of how the Labour left resolved to stop this nightmare, by trying to wage a struggle for power against the banks and their allies. We will discover what, if anything, this did to change the boundaries of the politically possible, in a way that might relieve the real and present nightmare of the unemployed. This is also the story of how, at the same time, the National Government sacrificed elements of the prevailing economic orthodoxy, in an attempt to preserve Baldwin's consensus and save capitalism. This was the strange, febrile milieu that shaped the early political career of Barbara Castle, and of another leading politician of the 1970s, Michael Foot.

* * *

In January 1932, unemployment was approaching 3 million. There was particular concern that the young unemployed might be drawn to the political extremes. Barbara Betts had written about the need for revolutionary socialism to help the millions out of work; now she went home and joined their number. She had nothing to show for her time at Oxford but a third-class degree and a large debt to Bradford Council. Her father's job had uprooted the family from their beloved home city and transplanted them to Hyde, a Lancashire mill town in one of the many run-down northern seats the Conservatives had just won from Labour. She landed a job on a local paper, but it folded before she could start. In Bradford, there would at least have been some fun to be had. Hyde could boast only a shabby cinema and the white tiles of the United Cattle Products café, offering tea, and tripe and onions. Sixty years later, she would write that 'few people today can grasp the bitterness and frustration of that period,' as 'unemployment hung like a black pall over the old industrial areas, destroying whole communities.'[1] What was to be done?

All around her were earnest leftist men, coming to the wrong conclusions. At Oxford she had admired the work of Professor GDH Cole, who had set up a Society for Socialist Inquiry and Propaganda to try to find a workable answer to the unemployment emergency. But then, in a grotty basement in Manchester, Barbara went to see a speaker from the Society, only to marvel at how out of touch he was with the realities of life in north-west England. In July, her father's treasured Independent Labour Party decided to split from Labour, to offer the working-class a revolutionary lead as capitalism collapsed. After Oswald Mosley's stillborn New Party and MacDonald's 'National Labour', this was the third ill-thought-out breakaway from Labour in three years. Along with a large minority of the ILP, Barbara and her father refused to leave Labour, arguing that the split was a terrible idea. They were soon proved right, as the ex-Labour independents crumbled to nothing. In the Hyde Labour Club, she found herself arguing with Marxists whose ideas she found fantastical. She started studying economics with more application than she ever had at Oxford, the better to make her case.

Meanwhile, Germany had yet another election. A lot more people drew the wrong conclusion about how to respond to the country's desperate unemployment situation. The Nazis became the largest party in the Reichstag.

* * *

Another of GDH Cole's many student fans was an angular young Liberal called Michael Foot. Peppered in eczema, fizzing with satirical zeal, Michael was from a West Country family, fanatically committed to Liberalism, religious Dissent and the memory of Oliver Cromwell. He was the fourth son of Isaac Foot MP, a diehard free trader who resigned from the new National Government. As Michael came of age, the Depression was putting the Foots' political assumptions under pressure. In the 1931 election, Michael's elder brother Dingle was elected in Dundee. Opposite his constituency party office he came across a graveyard, in which the unemployed sat out their empty days.

At Oxford, Michael had made friends with former Labour minister Sir Stafford Cripps' son John. Students would stay up late, drinking too much coffee and worrying about the unemployment crisis, but Michael remained committed to Liberalism. When John invited him to come and stay at his father's country home, 'Goodfellows', this offered a chance to meet people who thought very differently: senior Labour politicians who planned to take over the banks and force through a social revolution.

One of Cripps' distinguished guests was George Lansbury, the mutton-chop-whiskered Cockney pacifist, who had long served as the Labour Party's righteous grandpa. With almost every minister from the last Labour government now out of Parliament, Lansbury, though past 70, would in 1932 become Leader of the Opposition. For the party's right wing, this was maddening. But for old believers, after the tawdry compromises of government, the party was back to its socialist principles. Then there was Lansbury's dull, clipped deputy, Major Clement Attlee—one of the very few ex-ministers to have held on to his seat in the election wipeout. He looked to Cripps for his political direction. Michael was a great deal more taken with Aneurin Bevan, another occasional visitor to Goodfellows whom he had first met in London; and a comrade, at this point, of men who had given up on parliamentary democracy and embraced real extremism.

But the person most seized by that vision was Sir Stafford himself. Michael was very impressed by his friend's famous father. 'A Rolls Royce mind,' as he put it almost seventy years later; 'you knew as soon as you met him.'[2] Cripps was qualified as both a chemist and a barrister. During the First World War he had run an arms factory; now he was a dazzling patent lawyer. To Michael, Cripps 'combined a deep religious conviction with a brilliant mastery of any brief set before him'.[3] But crisis had now recast a moderate, high-born politician as a hardline tribune of the people. After 1931, Cripps decided that to save the unemployed, Labour had to break with genteel convention and confront the power of capital head-on.

During Michael's visits, he and Cripps began to bond. They played tennis, and Michael made sure not to beat his autocratic new mentor. He was moving towards socialism—but it would take more than Cripps' charismatic zeal to prise him entirely away from his family's Liberal creed.

* * *

On Monday 3 October 1932, as unemployed hunger marchers trudged towards London, delegates to the Labour Party's annual conference gathered in Leicester, under the elegant, self-consciously modern white curves of De Montfort Hall. From the first session, the conference heard aggrieved attacks on the power of finance, and its new weapons: the dole cut and the family means test. One union leader alleged that these were deliberately designed to break the spirit of the working class. Another delegate claimed the conditions were forcing working-class women into prostitution.

The following morning, a new movement within the party, the Socialist League, set out to convince the delegates that the party must be ready to overturn capitalism, whatever it took. Cripps had set up its leadership council, which included Frank Wise and GDH Cole; Aneurin Bevan and Clement Attlee were also involved.

In the debate on banking, the National Executive Committee's approach was presented by Hugh Dalton: economist, influential ex-Foreign Office minister, and Eton-educated son of the former tutor to King George V. When Dalton announced the NEC's proposal to nationalise only the Bank of England, the League's Frank Wise attacked. To make socialist control of finance effective, and to carry out the party's plans to nationalise and direct the economy, he insisted that Labour would have to take control of 'the very centre of capitalist power'. That meant ensuring there was 'no possible danger of sabotage or obstruction' by the joint-stock banks, which currently decided where credit went. When Ernest Bevin argued that a Labour government could simply circumvent the joint-stock banks, he was yelled at, and accused of being 'steeped in financial orthodoxy'. Seconding the League's amendment, Cripps insisted the party should make clear that they intended 'to take the whole of the financial power out of the hands of the capitalists at once.'[4]

The amendment passed. Within 48 hours of its formation, the Socialist League had scored a major victory, despite lacking trade union support. Three weeks later, the 2,500 hunger marchers arrived in London, with their petition signed by a million people—but its message was lost amid fighting in Hyde Park. The *Daily Mirror*, not yet a left-wing paper, dismissed the marchers' efforts as uselessly putting confidence at risk. The unemployment problem, it lamented, 'has cost the nation millions. It has threatened to overbalance our Budgets.' It was 'the nightmare of Ministers.'[5] In the New Year, unemployment in Britain hit a new peak: 23 per cent. In Germany it had hit 33 per cent, and on Monday 30 January 1933, President Hindenburg appointed a new

Chancellor. Hitler promised to set democracy aside and help 6 million suffering people back to work.

* * *

That morning, before the news had arrived from Berlin, British newspapers revealed another plan to suspend democracy in order to help the unemployed. The previous day, Stafford Cripps—Labour's one real parliamentary star, a plausible future Prime Minister—had delivered a lecture organised by the Socialist League. It was called 'Can Socialism Come by Constitutional Methods?'

Sir Stafford began by claiming that the 'ruling class'—to which he himself so audibly belonged—would 'go to almost any length to defeat Parliamentary action' over 'the continuance of their financial and political control.' On its first day, the new socialist government would have to push an Emergency Powers Bill through Parliament, to allow rule by ministerial order, and stop the capitalists weaponising the finance and credit systems. But the Bill would need to be passed by 'the stronghold of capitalism'—the House of Lords, which might reject or delay it. Either way, the Labour government would have to overpower the Lords, with the help of the King in creating new, pro-socialist peers. And if the King refused? Then the government would either have to resign... or ignore the constitution and plough on, even though this 'would almost certainly result in an uprising of the capitalists which would have to be quelled by force'.

If, instead, the government resigned to trigger an election, and settle the fate of the Lords that way, Cripps thought Labour would win. If the capitalists *still* did not give in, 'the Socialist Government, reassured of the country's support, would be justified in overriding any obstruction it found placed in its way.' Or, if none of the party leaders were prepared to form a government, the stalemate might lead to a capitalist military dictatorship. To stop this, Labour should 'make itself temporarily into a dictatorship until the matter could again be put to the test at the polls.'[6]

The *Daily Sketch* noted that he 'spoke of a possible dictatorship'. Not long afterwards, an MI5 officer typed up a transcript of the *Sketch* report, putting that line about dictatorship in red ink. The security service had decided to open a file on Cripps.[7]

A few weeks later, the new US President, Franklin D. Roosevelt, took extraordinary measures to tackle the Depression. The economic storm had hit the United States far harder than Britain; nonetheless, Roosevelt's 'New Deal' struck some in Britain as a precedent, more respectable than Germany's, for overriding British democracy, at least for a time.[8] Neville Chamberlain, the new Chancellor of the Exchequer, told the Commons that the unemployment problem might well take another decade to fix, drawing gasps from MPs.[9]

Through 1933 and 1934, the Socialist League would build up its image of the forces the left had to be ready to fight. The standard face of 1930s fascism is the former Labour MP Oswald Mosley, leading his new Mussolini-inspired British Union of Fascists—a target of Britain's small but thriving Communist Party. But for Cripps and the League, fascism was an invisible force 'growing rapidly in our midst, not in the number of people wearing Black Shirts, but in the minds and actions of the ruling classes and of the Government itself'; in the press, the police and the air force.[10] Cripps argued that the National Government was preparing a fascist turn by stealth, through its appointment of the RAF's founder, Hugh Trenchard, as a militaristic head of the Metropolitan Police. Trenchard wanted to restrict who could join the force. This, Cripps warned demonstrators in Bristol on 7 May 1933, was part of preparations 'for the moment when the police will be required to be used against the workers'. The same day, Labour's leader George Lansbury told a protest in Hyde Park that the TUC should plan a general strike, to protect a Labour government from being crushed with the help of Trenchard's new anti-working-class police force.[11]

Cripps next identified a potential fascist leader: Winston Churchill. This was not quite as absurd as it now sounds. The former chancellor had a record of aggression against the trade unions, and as an open admirer of Mussolini. In the 1920s, HG Wells had portrayed Churchill as a militaristic leader of men in two different novels.[12] In a third, *Public Faces*, Harold Nicolson had imagined Churchill in government with Mosley. In 1933 Churchill was languishing out of office, leading a rebellion of hard-right Conservative backbench 'Diehards', some with extreme views, against ministerial moves to grant limited independence to India. Cripps told Hugh Dalton that if Churchill won on India, he would form a government, 'introduce Fascist measures', and suspend elections; the King would accept this as better than a socialist government.[13] All these signs of coming fascism justified the Socialist League's plans to secure Labour in power. It was vital, Cripps insisted, to avoid the fate of the German left after Hitler took over.[14] There seemed no democratic way to overcome the entrenched forces of orthodoxy and end the suffering of the unemployed. Instead, the impasse was beginning to trap Cripps in a nightmare.

* * *

On 2 October 1933, the Labour Party gathered on the south coast under an overcast sky, for a conference spooked by political killing. Since Hitler had seized power in January, a hurricane of violence had torn through German politics, as communists, socialists and trade unionists were arrested, tortured, sent to new concentration camps, or worse. Inside Hastings' White Rock Pavilion, Chairman Joseph Compton opened a debate titled 'Democracy v. Dictatorship' by asking delegates to rise in silent tribute for their 'many old friends' murdered by the Nazis. The former MP Ellen Wilkinson had been in Germany and reported on the persecution for the *Daily Herald*; now she warned delegates that they should not assume such things could never happen to them.

The delegates may have been united in horror, but the fate of the German left still exposed a sharp division. Was the Socialist League's emergency plan vital to stop a fascist takeover in Britain? Or was their flirtation with dictatorship the reckless breaking of a taboo— not locking the door against fascism, but flinging it open?

The League's chair, Frank Wise, contended that thinking 'we are going to carry through a Socialist programme by the kind permission of the House of Lords is nursing a dangerous delusion'. Believing that you could improve living standards under capitalism ignored British Labour's fate in 1931 and the German left's fate two years later: 'We are at the parting of the ways. We have either to go forward to Socialism or acquiesce in Fascism.' This was predicated on the idea that, as the chair of the conference himself put it, 'Fascism stands for Capitalism'.[15] An electricians' delegate, meanwhile, implied that the power stations should be shut to thwart any fascist takeover.

To Labour moderates, this was all crazy. In April, Hugh Dalton had visited Berlin, where he was told of the screams of the Nazis' victims. This did not appear to be merely the free market with the gloves off. But, no matter what Dalton said, Cripps held on to his nightmare of a fascistic capitalism crushing the working class. The party's most prominent frontbench MP was becoming, Dalton lamented, 'a dangerous political lunatic'.[16] Cripps apparently could not see how he was opening Labour to charges of wanting a dictatorship. When the head of the TUC, Walter Citrine, accused the Socialist League of arguing that socialism would require dictatorial control and probably revolutionary violence, MI5 noted Cripps' riposte: 'Democracy is not synonymous with 19th century parliamentarianism. No party faced with a revolutionary situation can merely sit down and wait for what comes to it.'[17]

All this, of course, was a propaganda gift for the studiously consensual National Government. Back at the Hastings conference, meanwhile, Dalton's ally Herbert Morrison told delegates that capitalism was not in fact 'perpetuating itself on the basis of Fascism', and that the premise underneath this whole scenario was disastrous. Labour could not condone left-wing dictatorial methods to try to forestall a future right-wing dictatorship: 'We are preparing a political psychology which, if we justify one form of dictatorship, gives an equally moral justification for a dictatorship in another direction.'[18] Hitler had, after all, cemented his power with an Enabling Act, which allowed ministers to bypass Parliament and rule with sweeping powers, supposedly to help alleviate economic misery.

While Morrison challenged the League's logic, Ernest Bevin attacked its strategy. Trying to abolish the House of Lords was picking a fight, and the British public might side with the embattled peers. Labour should just get on with putting forward their proposals to deal with unemployment, and only then, 'if we find resistance, call for support to overcome the resistance'.[19]

Should Labour members trust Ernest Bevin, the 'dockers' King's Counsel', and be optimistic about democracy? Or should they side with Stafford Cripps, a real King's Counsel, and prepare to face down the capitalist backlash? That winter, two plays about the problem of the unemployed had their premieres, one in

London and one in Manchester, and each reflecting one side of Labour's dilemma. The reception of these new dramas gave a hint of which strategy might be more effective in breaking the economic orthodoxy, and so making radical measures on unemployment politically possible.

The first play was by George Bernard Shaw, world-famous friend of Prime Ministers, and apologist for revolutionary violence. *On the Rocks*, which premiered at the Winter Garden Theatre in Drury Lane on 25 November 1933, opens in the Cabinet Room at 10 Downing Street, as vast crowds of 'the Unemployed' are gathering outside. The Prime Minister, at the head of a national government, is Sir Arthur Chavender—a posher version of the real Prime Minister. Like Ramsay MacDonald, Chavender is sympathetic to the plight of the unemployed, but laments that he is powerless to help them. So when a mysterious Lady tells him that he is dragging Britain back into the past and offers to cure him, he accepts—and returns, radicalised, to nationalise the banks. To the objection that he won't get his programme through Parliament, he threatens to prorogue it. But, almost immediately, he gives up, saying the only way to force change in less than fifty years is through a dictator—which, he suggests, is exactly what the working class wants. The *New York Times* reviewer drew the obvious link to Cripps and the Socialist League, and their threat to 'establish a dictatorship of the Left'.[20] Shaw was more extreme even than Cripps, but in both their worldviews, there's a similar absence: the voices of the unemployed themselves.

In some ways, the stage version of *Love on the Dole*, which opened at the Manchester Repertory Company's Rusholme Theatre on 24 February 1934, is rather like *On the Rocks*. Both plays sympathise with the unemployed, especially when they protest and are beaten up by the police. Both bemoan the unfairness of the 1931 benefit cut and the meanness of the means test. But *Love on the Dole* was by Walter Greenwood, a nobody with no job who had written a bestselling novel, before co-adapting it for the theatre. The stage version showed audiences what it felt like to be poor, then to lose your job. There is Harry, the teenager who has to stay at home on his Sundays off from the factory because he can't afford long trousers. There is the way his father Mr Hardcastle assumes, when he sees Harry moving a table, that he is taking it to the pawn shop. We glimpse what it feels like to walk round twenty firms in a morning, only to hear: 'No hands wanted, though they don't usually say it so polite'. We hear the story of a man driven by the strictures of the means test to the point where he 'cut his froat an' jumped through bedroom winder'.

The play presented its audience with a choice of unthinkables. Either Harry's older sister Sally, having seen her fiancé die, must go on drudging forever to support her workless family, or she can become a lecherous bookie's kept mistress. Justifying her decision to abandon 'respectability' for access, at last, to some money, she says:

> It's sick Ah am of codging owld clothes to make 'em look summat-like. An' sick I am of working week after week and seeing nowt for it. I'm sick of never having nowt but what's been in pawnshops and crawling with vermin...

Shaw's *On the Rocks* closed after forty-one performances; *Love on the Dole* ran and ran. The *Daily Express* critic confessed that 'I cannot write adequately of this play; my heart is too violently in sympathy with it'. There were 'repeated curtain calls ... amidst enthusiastic applause'.[21] The company spent much of the rest of 1934 playing the Palaces and Hippodromes of Lancashire, Cheshire and Yorkshire, performing in cinemas where the town had no theatre. In Morecambe, they performed at a venue which also offered dancing, and boxing.

Cripps praised how the novel and play alike had brought alive 'the stark tragedy of life to the younger generation to-day'.[22] Later that year, Walter Greenwood became a Labour councillor. His politics were not all that far from the Socialist League's, but he had found a way to use fiction to advance the cause more powerfully than any of them had. Economic orthodoxy said that means tests and balanced budgets were necessary; *Love on the Dole* put a human face on what that meant. The expected destination for hit productions was a run in London, where the play might conceivably have an effect on politics. West End theatre managements, however, decided that their sophisticated audiences would find an evening with the Hardcastles too depressing.

* * *

As *Love on the Dole* premiered in early 1934, elsewhere in Manchester Barbara Betts was spending her days standing in shop doorways, trying to sell sweets, and failing to recruit her timid fellow sales assistants into her trade union. One Saturday, at a Socialist League weekend school in a dingy hall in Hyde, she met a revolutionary.

William Mellor of the *Daily Herald* was one of those intense men of the 1930s who knew that capitalism was finished and the only possible futures were socialism or fascism. He was a former conscientious objector, an ex-communist and now, in his mid-40s, one of the leaders of the League: a militant Labour intellectual, steering Cripps to the left. Now he stood in his Savile Row suit, surveying Betts, her mother and the rest of his down-at-heel audience, and informed them that he had just spent as much on his lunch as they earned in a week. 'How much longer,' he enquired, 'are you going to put up with it?'[23]

Barbara's life was never as bad as Sally Hardcastle's, but she might have recognised Sally's desperation to escape the drabness of Depression Lancashire. When she and Mellor began an affair, he transported her, she wrote, 'to a new world': stylish restaurants, hanging out with actors in the Midland Hotel grill, disappearing at weekends into the Derbyshire countryside or the Lake District. She credited him with becoming her 'intellectual mentor', restoring her self-confidence by asking her advice, and taking up her suggestions for party policy statements.[24]

Mellor's torrent of letters to his young lover are full of his fear of imminent fascist takeover, and of a true believer's struggles to find a democratic path to revolutionary change. On his way to make a speech one Wednesday evening in March 1934, Mellor found himself walking through the Lambeth slums. He had been a left-wing activist for decades, but what he saw there left him unable him to sleep. In a letter to Barbara the next day, he described the 'faces that spoke of privation and lack of air and sun, children in rags—and with it all an air of fatalistic resignation ... Even hell couldn't be worse.' In line with the thinking he had helped inspire in Cripps, Mellor was convinced that the only solution was the destruction of capitalist power. A month later, as Mellor was addressing a political meeting in Enfield, a young unemployed man at the back of the hall fainted from hunger. It left Mellor full of rage, he told Barbara, 'against the whole damned system. I wanted to break it unmercifully.'[25]

For Barbara, stuck selling sweets in Lewis' on Market Street, the relationship suddenly gave her access to the heart of the left's would-be battle for power; and, before long, a shortcut to joining it herself—just at the moment when the political situation seemed, to her new comrades, to be growing more dangerous than ever.

* * *

In much of Britain, Mellor's fevered talk about breaking the whole damned system would have seemed delusional. Not for the last time, crisis was inspiring not radical change, but a renewal of the existing consensus, leaving heretical voices stuck shouting inaudibly on the fringes. For many people by 1934, the Depression was lifting, and life was looking up. Prices were rising, but wages were rising faster. The National Government continued the Conservatives' 1920s reforms of housing provision and public health. For those in a job, the government's consensual approach—keeping a firm hold on some aspects of the orthodoxy, relaxing its grip on others—was working out nicely.

In 1932, after eighteen months of workless purgatory, Herbert Wilson had finally found a job. The Wilsons had bid goodbye to their black valley, and moved south to the gentler landscapes of the Wirral peninsula. The agent of Herbert's deliverance was a dyestuffs company called Brotherton's; the family had settled near the company's plant, in the small, expanding town of Bromborough. Harold landed on his feet at the new Wirral Grammar School, where being the first and only sixth former finally helped him onto the path towards Oxford. On the Brotherton's company tennis court, he even fell in love: with a girl called Gladys, dressed all in white, who worked for the detergent company Lever Brothers in nearby Port Sunlight.

Many people left places like Colne Valley in the mid-1930s. In the Midlands and southeast England in particular, young, light industries—like electronics, radio, aerospace, consumer durables and Herbert's sector, chemicals—were thriving. Rail and motor transport snaked distribution networks across the country. In place of endless small suppliers, one or two big firms, assisted by middlemen, came to dominate particular household goods. Harold's future wife's employer, Lever Brothers, and its parent company Unilever, cornered the market in soap. All these goods, and much else besides, poured into the hundreds of thousands of new houses being built and bought at low interest rates made possible by the end of the gold standard. For an additional cost, the purchaser of a new semi in Bromborough could acquire a garage for one of the new motor cars chugging out of the booming factories of the West Midlands, whose workers were too well-paid to feel much need to join trade unions, or to listen to the gripes of their jobless members in the north.[26] A new, modern workforce was taking shape, neither traditionally urban nor rural, neither aggressively proletarian nor stiffly bourgeois: technicians and laboratory staff, ad men and middle managers. While Herbert Wilson remained a socialist, it is not difficult to see how all this made the case for the bright, whitewashed, 'property-owning democracy' that progressive Conservatives like Baldwin and Neville Chamberlain had wanted to build since the 1920s.

The National Government seemed to be renewing the consensus with no need for a dramatic struggle for power. In March 1932, Chancellor of the Exchequer Neville Chamberlain had introduced an array of import duties, so consigning the great Victorian shibboleth of free trade to the grave. 'For thirty years,' observes the historian Peter Clarke, the tariff issue 'had caused one political crisis after another; yet as soon as tariffs were implemented they appeared less important, either for good or ill.'[27]

This was the second great break from economic orthodoxy in five months. It was supposed to bring salvation, but did little for trade or Britain's creaking staple industries; while toppling off gold, which was supposed to bring destruction, had proved actively useful. A cheap currency helped exports, held off imports, and made it possible to cut interest rates, making it easier for industry to borrow and invest. The 'Bank Rate' was held at 2 per cent right through to 1939. The Treasury kept the pound's value stable, but helpfully low; there was a modest rise in prices, boosting productivity, investment and employment. Chamberlain oversaw other careful departures from strict orthodoxy, gingerly embracing the good that government could do: quotas and price-setting schemes, restrictive agreements and marketing boards. Government cajoled small firms in failing industries such as cotton and coal to amalgamate and rationalise, to reduce excess capacity, like the big 'public corporations' which had already been set up to run London transport, broadcasting and electricity generation.

All this did some good—but it also led to the closure of some local areas' main source of employment, such as Palmer's shipyard in Jarrow, Tyneside. Labour charged that the government was readier to intervene to help capitalists than their workers. Unemployment still stood at well over 2 million: the wave of short-term, cyclical joblessness had receded, exposing the structural unemployment in older industries, in south Wales, Scotland, Cumberland and northeast England. In November 1934, Chamberlain's Cabinet colleague Sir John Simon wrote in his diary that 'the plight of the utterly depressed areas throws into shadow the enormous improvement elsewhere.'[28] But perhaps that improvement was enough. The poor are always with us—and anyway, could they not find work if they really wanted to? In his 1963 account of the inter-war years, *The Age of Illusion*, Ronald Blythe wrote that unemployment was the constant, boring backcloth which, by 1935, 'had existed for so long and had proved to be so irremediable that it came to be regarded as a normality.'[29]

Chamberlain made changes, but dared do nothing transformative. In his 1934 Budget, he used surplus funds to restore the 1931 cut in unemployment benefit... but spent the rest of the money to clear debt and tax. His new Unemployment Assistance Board at first set rates so tightly that many unemployed people actually took a cut in their benefits. In Sheffield, 12,000 unemployed workers protested, some attacking the police with rocks and poles.[30] Unemployment blackspots, which had become known as the Distressed Areas, were now euphemistically declared 'Special Areas', with commissioners to help revive their economies. The new Commissioner for England and Wales bubbled with plans for clearing Bishop Auckland slagheaps to make recreation grounds, building a new fish quay for Sunderland, launching new industries in the riverside district of South Shields. But the Commissioners' budgets—£1 million each—provoked groans of disappointment.

They were not allowed to finance any project conceived purely to create jobs or make a profit.[31]

Long-held fears still shaped Chamberlain's views. The budget had to be balanced; any drop in sterling's value below $3.65, said a Treasury official, would trigger a 'vicious spiral' of inflation.[32] For the historian Daniel Todman, the government's very claim to power was based on its determination 'not to allow the plight of the jobless to endanger the interests of the nation.'[33] When an MP complained about Chamberlain's 1934 Budget, the chancellor said he was simply unconvinced that 'by spending enormous sums of money [one] can bring back prosperity to the country.'[34] In 1935, Baldwin's dynamic old high-spending enemy David Lloyd George, still a Liberal MP, presented his Keynesian plans for a British version of the New Deal to the Cabinet. They were politely declined.

* * *

For Mellor, Cripps and the Socialist League, the only way to save the unemployed was to throw capitalism out altogether and introduce socialism. In that light, Chamberlain's patching seemed deeply sinister. The government was rescuing a sinking system by taking control of the economy: fusing with business and even compliant unions in a Mussolini-style fascist 'corporate state'. Mellor wrote urgently to Barbara that the labour movement must turn itself into an 'instrument of struggle', and organise demonstrations with the unemployed 'to fight actively against capitalist reorganisation!'[35]

In February 1934, Mellor's paper, the *Daily Herald*, was packed with dispatches from Austria, where the Mussolini-backed dictator Engelbert Dollfuss was crushing his socialist rivals. In their drive to root out the left-wing Schutzbund militia, Dollfuss' troops opened fire on one of Vienna's working-class housing estates with a howitzer, slaughtering women and children. The lesson from Vienna, Mellor told Barbara, was 'Be Not Too Late!' British capitalists might well be clever enough to find constitutional means to create their corporate state, but it would be a British version of fascism nonetheless. Already, there was a drive 'towards control and regulation' to protect profits. If the labour movement acquiesced to a corporate state, there would be only 'moderate suppressions' and no violence. But this would mean accepting class domination, 'wage-slavery and private profit', and all hope of socialism would be lost.[36]

On 1 May, Dollfuss entrenched his dictatorship in Austria with a corporate state. The League's apocalyptic new policy statement, *Forward to Socialism*, warned that a similar fate was imminent in Britain, once fascism threw off 'the democratic mask'. The League had to act to stop the workers' 'enslavement by a Fascist Capitalist dictatorship'[37] before it was too late. Mellor thought they only had eighteen months to save democracy.[38]

In January 1933, a pro-League journal had called for the urgent creation of 'advance guards of the revolution'.[39] In January 1934, Cripps said: 'I do not believe in private armies, but if the Fascists started a private army it might be for the Socialist and Communist Parties to do the same.'[40] The League's Raymond Postgate argued in his book *How to Make a Revolution* that the next Labour government should 'hold on to office as firmly as Stalin's or Mussolini's' regimes were doing, and that there was no hope of social revolution in Britain 'without the creation of such an organisation of storm troopers or ironsides'.[41] In south Wales, Aneurin Bevan actually organised a Workers' Freedom Group, taking inspiration from the Austrian Social Democrats' doomed militia. He led groups of young recruits tramping across the Welsh mountains, instilling his ideological message as they marched. Michael Foot would later affirm that 'socialists in South Wales really did believe that they might see Fascist jackboots in operation within a few years'—though he reassured his readers that Bevan's proto-militia 'acquired no weapons'.[42]

That October, the League took seventy-five amendments to the Labour conference at Southport. Mellor led the way in introducing them, and Barbara Betts wrote that she 'had never admired him more than when he went to the rostrum time and again to confront the open hostility of conference.'[43] But a spiky young party candidate, AL Rowse, told delegates that the League's mistake was that it was stuck in the crisis of 1931. Every single League amendment debated was rejected.

In the wake of the conference, the cover of *Socialist Leaguer* magazine offered readers pieces by Stafford Cripps, William Mellor—and Barbara Betts, who had succeeded in cajoling her employers to move her to London. She could now throw herself into political activity, but that post-conference edition of the League's magazine struck a bleak, militant note. Cripps seemed impatient for a decisive crisis, and even to envy foreign socialists' oppression. He complained that with 'an "underground" or "persecuted" party it is perhaps easier to accomplish the spirit that we must create'.[44]

He and his remaining followers were wandering into the wilderness. Moderate Labour and trade union leaders were simply not convinced that a desperate capitalism was souring into fascism. Bevin had been arguing since at least 1932 that capitalism was not collapsing, but adapting. Even Attlee was turning in this direction, noting in the summer of 1934 that people had 'an idea that the thing will not be pressed to extremes.'[45] Dalton agreed with the League that the next Labour government would meet 'obstinate resistance from powerful and selfish vested interests', but was confident that, with public support, this could be overcome. He dismissed 'all panic talk, whether from Right or Left, of an "inevitable crisis," and all theatrical nightmares of violent head-on collisions, wrecking the train of democracy.'[46] But at least Cripps et al had shown some sense of urgency. If the economic orthodoxy were not to be changed through emergency powers and private armies, how long would the long-term unemployed have to wait?

* * *

At Labour's conference, as the League hit the buffers, a representative from the Distressed Areas tried to shake the party out of its complacency. Ellen Wilkinson had lost her Middlesbrough seat in the 1931 wipeout; now she was the candidate for Jarrow, the shipbuilding town on Tyneside whose shipyard had been shut down as a result of the National Government's moves to reduce excess production capacity. Economic critiques and policy resolutions were all very well, but Wilkinson insisted something was missing. She appealed to the party's national executive to 'get into closer touch with the human problem of the mass of the unemployed themselves', the families that 'are starving now ... and have been for ten years'. Abstract resolutions seemed 'so far away from the men who are actually suffering in the devastated areas'.[47] She suggested that, however sympathetic they were, the executive's 'lack of imagination' was holding them back from effective action: they had missed the chance, earlier that year, to swing Labour behind both the hunger march, and the mass protests against Chamberlain's Unemployment Bill.

There is a broader implication in Wilkinson's argument: that if only people could be induced to empathise with starving fellow citizens, apparently impossible political change might be opened up—without Cripps-style bids to smash the power of finance. But pamphlets, sermons, marches and deputations aimed at stirring the necessary action had got nowhere. It seemed remarkably difficult to push the nightmare being suffered by millions of people up the list of political priorities. Coaxing people 'into closer touch with the human problem' of the unemployed evidently required something bigger and more moving. In 1935–6, two different spectacles would try to make this breakthrough.

From London out to the Distressed Areas went famous men— journalists and authors, the new Commissioners, and even King Edward VIII—to declare that something ought to be done. From the Distressed Areas to London came hunger marches, and thousands of young women to work as domestic servants, bringing a tremor of distant distress into wealthy southern homes. And now *Love on the Dole* made it, at last, to the capital. It opened at the Garrick Theatre on 30 January 1935, just as the Unemployment Assistance Board was provoking demonstrations across the country. After the capital's theatre managers had turned down the chance to stage the play, the theatre company itself had risked all the money made on tour to buy its way into the West End.

The programme for *Love on the Dole*'s run at the Garrick suggests the imaginative chasm the actors had to reach across to touch their audience. Opposite a list of the play's settings—'The Hardcastles' kitchen', 'An Alley'—is a full-page ad boasting that the Triumph Gloria has won the Monte Carlo Rally (Light Car Class). Between the programme's advertisements for Huntley and Palmer's cake and Piccadilly banqueting rooms, a Grosvenor Place charity implores theatre-goers to send a garment each to help clothe the people in the Distressed Areas, on top of the 300,000 items dispatched in the

51

previous three months. As the house lights dimmed, as programmes closed and eyes were raised to the stage, the question was whether the play could transfigure the residents of Hanky Park from a mass of charity cases into these affluent Londoners' fellow citizens.

The producers need not have worried: most of the critics applauded the play as a deeply felt work, presenting the unvarnished truth—an effect assisted by the actors' real-life northern accents. Some academics have criticised *Love on the Dole* for letting its middle-class audiences off the hook, rather than blaming them. But a theatre is not a lecture theatre: you show, not tell. *Tatler* suggested that if the play had been 'written in bitterness, or as a tract for the times, it would have a lesser effect on the heart and the mind'. Instead, it left 'the audience to search for cause and effect'.[48]

Love on the Dole became a defining play of the decade. By 1940 it had reportedly been seen by 3 million people, including the King and Queen. On 4 March 1935, the Liberal leader Sir Herbert Samuel invoked it in the Commons; when the beleaguered Minister of Labour, Oliver Stanley, tried to claim that the unemployment figures were not as bad as they looked, because 'only' 400,000 people had been out of work for more than a year, Samuel turned on him:

> That is a dreadful figure. Imagine 400,000 families with the breadwinner sitting in his home, day after day, week after week, month after month, yes, year after year, without hope of getting back into industrial employment and seeing his family reduced to penury. I wonder whether hon. Members have seen a play which is now being performed in London, called 'Love on the Dole.' If not, I would urge them to see it. That play paints in very poignant fashion the position of those 400,000 families who are in the state which I have just described.[49]

Sir Herbert pointed out that the government could have been taking 'far more vigorous action' to find work for those 400,000, had they not rejected Lloyd George's proposal for the government to take out a 'great prosperity loan', to create a million new jobs through public works.[50]

The following year, back in Parliament as the new Labour MP for Jarrow, Wilkinson herself was instrumental in another piece of political theatre that forced people to pay attention. In July 1936, a plea for help for her constituency's devastated economy drew a cool rebuke from the President of the Board of Trade, Walter Runciman: 'Jarrow must work out its own salvation'. In response, local officials suggested marching to London to petition Parliament in person. Wilkinson, who was tiny, joined the 200 well-built shipbuilders for much of their 300-mile trek. They tramped the last few miles through London, wearing groundsheets as capes against the weather, flanked by policemen, self-conscious before the press photographers. The government offered no help, despite Wilkinson weeping at the Despatch Box when she presented Jarrow's petition, and the marchers went miserably home by train. The 'Jarrow Crusade' is remembered for its poignancy, but is also often seen as disappointingly mild and non-political, erasing from popular memory the righteous radical anger of the hunger marches.

But that reflected a publicity strategy. Wilkinson was using the march to try to get the public 'into closer touch with the human problem'. As with *Love on the Dole*, this was a disciplined piece of theatre: it knew what to leave out. The march leaders were militant leftists, and Wilkinson herself a former communist, so she carefully avoided handing their enemies any ammunition: by maintaining a clear distance from a simultaneous, communist-led march, and by keeping the text of the petition apolitical. The march presented the unemployed of Jarrow in their caps and capes without any angry, alienating slogans, leaving those who saw them to 'search for cause and effect', just like *Love on the Dole*. Wilkinson knew what she was doing: 'what propaganda speech in your life,' she asked Labour's conference, could compete with the 'vast object lesson' symbolised by the march?[51]

Not everyone responded as she thought they ought to. The march provoked plenty of apathy, as captured by the artist Thomas Cantrell Dugdale. In his painting *The Arrival of the Jarrow Marchers in London, Viewed from an Interior* (1936), a young lady in evening dress peers out from a high window at the marchers far below, while a gentleman lounges beside her, blowing smoke rings, not bothered. Nonetheless, the Crusade aroused public sympathy far more effectively than the overtly militant hunger marches. While it failed in its primary objective, it succeeded in creating an unforgettable image. If such political theatre, on street or stage, could engage people's imagination sufficiently to make mass unemployment intolerable, perhaps there might one day be democratic consent to set aside old financial nightmares, and prioritise full employment. Perhaps.

* * *

In 1935, sights like this finally drove another future politician to join the Labour Party, and to sign up for the struggling Socialist League. That January, as *Love on the Dole* arrived in London, Michael Foot went to work in Liverpool, for the Blue Funnel Line. His office was in the shipping company's palatial new American Beaux Arts headquarters near the dockside. Each day he caught the tram from his lodgings, entered under the Florentine arches and bronze lamps, passed fluted marble columns and took the lift up to the offices. Here he could watch his bosses, including Sir Stafford's Tory brother, Major Leonard Cripps, trying to stitch up the sort of company amalgamation that would have gladdened Neville Chamberlain's heart. Michael wrote to his mother Eva that the head of the company, Sir Richard Holt, was 'just the last word in malignant density', whose 'sordid and unrelieved money-making has received a fitting recognition in a knighthood at the hands of the National Government.'[52] The young Foot was already sharpening his rhetorical skewers for a life in the political fray.

He had drawn close to socialism through all those talks with John Cripps in their Oxford rooms, and with Sir Stafford by the yew trees at Goodfellows. His conversion was further coaxed along by reading HG Wells on the tram to work. But he also spent time wandering among the run-down dockside backstreets, where the city's heavy unemployment was visible on the street corners. In 1933, JB Priestley—whom Michael would later call 'the conscience of the country'[53]—had visited these same slums and found the buildings 'were rotting away, and some of the people were rotting with them.'[54] Within his first month in Liverpool, Michael had broken from the Liberal family creed, and joined the Labour Party.

It is perhaps a measure of the impact of what he saw that, only a few months earlier, Michael had been publicly scathing of the Socialist League's line on what needed to be done. In an article called

'Why I Am a Liberal'—which would later prompt much teasing—he criticised some of the left's ideas about suspending democracy. Once he joined Labour, this scepticism apparently evaporated. Much later, he would even defend the fevered early 1930s talk of using emergency powers, and claim that no one did more to revive Labour's fortunes than Stafford Cripps. Having cut his teeth as a Liberal debater at the Oxford Union, he was now giving socialist speeches, standing on a soap box on Liverpool street corners: a better training, he suggested, than anything Oxford had had to offer.

A talent for invective, a knack for stump oratory, a righteous anger at the nightmare of the slums: within five years, all this would make Michael Foot one of those figures who would turn the 'Thirties' into a dirty word, and help to break the old consensus. But not before he had to face up to a choice between two even more threatening new nightmares.

* * *

Guests making their way to Hammersmith to visit River Court House would come upon it tucked away on Upper Mall—a short, quiet street right next to the Thames, closed to vehicles at both ends. Here, for much of the 1930s, the novelist Naomi Mitchison hosted parties with her husband for the leading lights of the left, among them Aneurin Bevan and Jennie Lee, Ellen Wilkinson, and Douglas and Margaret Cole. William Mellor would arrive with his wary, awkward young girlfriend Barbara in tow. Other future Labour Cabinet ministers, including Michael Foot, were invited too. Sometimes the retired novelist EM Forster or the radical poet WH Auden would come to watch the Boat Race. The Socialist League had failed—but in 1935, this swathe of the London left was as confident in their worldview as you might expect in a setting like this. No ideological cul-de-sac was ever so elegant.

They knew what they feared: fascism in England. As Bevan had told the 1934 Labour conference: 'Hitlerism is the defence of capitalism by violence when democracy threatens capitalism'. On 7 June 1934, Naomi Mitchison had gone along to the vast Olympia exhibition hall, a mile and a half up Hammersmith Road, to watch Oswald Mosley speak. Mitchison's friend and fellow novelist Storm

Jameson went too, and both saw hecklers beaten up and bundled out. Jameson saw five Blackshirts carrying a young woman past her, 'her clothes half torn off, and her mouth and nose closed by the large hand of one; her head was forced back by the pressure'.[55] In June 1935, Naomi's novel *We Have Been Warned* was finally published, with its horrifying images of a Labour government crushed by firing squad and gas attack.

That summer, Storm Jameson set to work on her own version of the nightmare her friend had already brought to life. Jameson's novel *In the Second Year* imagines a Labour government broken by a financial crisis, orchestrated partly by its enemies in the City. The party splits, and moderate Labour figures go into government with Conservatives and fascists, while left-wing opponents of the new 'National State' are sent to 'training' camps. Strikingly, this includes a character called Mellor and his 'young wife': Barbara Castle in an English concentration camp. One reviewer praised the novel's 'nightmare plausibility'.[56] 'Hitlerism in those days,' Michael Foot wrote later, was seen by most militant socialists 'not as a military menace from abroad, but as a warning of what might happen here if British democrats showed the same meekness as the German democrats.'[57] At the general election in November 1935, Michael Foot stood for Labour in a no-chance seat, insisting that 'Fascism represents the last attempt of those who control economic power to maintain their supremacy'.[58] But this was a long way from most voters' priorities.

On 4 March 1935, with Hitler rearming at speed, the government had issued a Defence White Paper, calling for a bigger, stronger Navy, more spending on the Army and Royal Air Force, and a significant expansion of coastal and anti-aircraft defences. Stanley Baldwin, who returned to Number 10 that summer to replace an ailing MacDonald, was no hawk; but he warned that German re-armament put peace under threat. Britain was facing a huge new external danger, which threatened untold numbers of deaths. This could only be tackled at terrible economic cost. After the National Government's decisive re-election that November, Baldwin continued to wrestle with the implications. It would put the worldview of everyone in British politics under ever more pressure, forcing more choices between unthinkables.

Throughout the early 1930s, the Socialist League had been trying to find a way to win a struggle for power with the massed forces of finance, and had, unsurprisingly, got nowhere. Its impotence in the face of the impregnable Baldwin consensus left it seeing fascists everywhere. But now they felt that the gathering threat from Germany was giving their nightmare of a fascist Britain new credence.

On 7 March 1936, in defiance of the Treaties of Versailles and Locarno, Hitler sent his troops into the Rhineland. Afterwards, Storm Jameson remembered, 'I seemed always to be listening to the sound of approaching footsteps and counting stairs.'[59] But were the jackboots she was afraid of German, or British? In the last years of the 1930s, she, Cripps and Mellor, young Michael and Barbara, the rest of the League, the left and everyone in British politics all had to decide which was the more pressing nightmare: a Britain turned totalitarian by preparations for war, or defeat at the hands of the Nazis.

3

GAS PARALYSES

1936–40

The Socialist League had spent years obsessed with mass unemployment, bashing its collective head against the Baldwin consensus,
with little result bar some fantasies about fascism. There was a
reason why the National Government had won another convincing
victory at the ballot box in late 1935, rather than Cripps sweeping
to power and seizing control of the banking system. In the many
parts of Britain that were now thriving, there was broad support for
the government's mix of budget orthodoxy, careful social reforms
and encouragement of new industries and housebuilding.

In this context, mass unemployment, however tragic, was too
small a problem to justify throwing orthodox caution to the winds.
Running up deficits could bring national bankruptcy; government
direction of industry risked creating a bloated, overbearing state.
This chapter is about how these longstanding fears combined with
the stormclouds gathering over Europe in the late 1930s to induce
the oppressive feeling that there was no way out—until, finally,
something had to give. Let's begin with what Chancellor Neville
Chamberlain was offering as a solution to the miseries of the
unemployed, a solution with no danger of triggering a deficit or a
dictatorship: the great British spirit of volunteering.

The Depression had already spurred existing voluntary traditions
into action. With the help of such groups as the Quakers, students
hurried to help in the Distressed Areas, teaching, digging allotments,
and running holiday camps for the unemployed. Cambridge
undergraduates fed hunger marchers, and bathed and bandaged their

feet. In Oxford, worries about unemployment skittered through the features, book reviews and debate reports of the students' weekly magazine, *Isis*. Inwardly, the future Labour minister Christopher Mayhew remembered, he was 'perpetually apologising for my enjoyment of life to a vast, ghostly audience of hungry and resentful working class families.'[1] The university Labour Club promoted its camps for the unemployed as a chance for Oxford students to work alongside the workers, 'so that social barriers can be broken down'.[2] A schoolfriend of Michael Foot's, digging allotments in Oldham, found that it was 'a good way to learn how it felt to be unemployed and have barely enough to eat.'[3] This now reads like tin-eared poverty tourism, but it seems to have had a real effect. One student concluded that, for he and his fellows, volunteering had meant that 'the unemployment problem became understandable in terms of human suffering'.[4] Music to Ellen Wilkinson's ears.

Many of these students were on the left, but volunteering to help the unemployed was 'a "popular front" effort',[5] also drawing in Liberals and Tories. Here was a hint of a new consensus among the politically minded young: an indication of what their priorities might be once they rose to power. One such young Conservative was the son of a Jewish businessman in London called Sir Samuel Joseph. As a child in the 1920s, Keith Joseph's social conscience had already begun to tug at his coat-tails. He took to pinching food from the family breakfast table to give to a beggar in Sloane Square, on his way to his Chelsea primary school. As a student at Magdalen College, Oxford from 1936 to 1939, he volunteered to be sent by a Quaker group to work with the unemployed in Maltby, near Rotherham and Orgreave.[6] A miner's family in the South Yorkshire coalfield, still mired in the miseries of the Depression, found themselves playing host to the future intellectual architect of Thatcherism.

One of the decade's signature rituals of class mixing was going down a coal mine: literally descending into the lower depths. As Joseph would reveal in the Commons two decades later, 'I worked for a week down a pit'.[7] It is not clear from this, or from his biographies, exactly what was going on here, given that he was there to help the unemployed. Perhaps, like some of the other young volunteers, he was helping out-of-work miners who were running pits on a co-operative basis. One account reports that he was there to help disabled mineworkers.[8] Whatever the precise circumstances, the experience of this 'dangerous and unpleasant industry' gave young Keith 'the greatest respect' for the men for whom, even when they were in work, this was a daily routine. As he readily admitted to fellow MPs of his stint underground, 'One week was quite enough for me.'[9] Looking back to this 1930s adventure after his retirement from Thatcher's Cabinet, he would judge it a significant part of his growing up.

* * *

None of this was enough. On 8 October 1936, as the Jarrow marchers reached Yorkshire, the Special Areas Commissioner for England and Wales, charged with helping towns like theirs, resigned in frustration. In his earlier reports, Malcolm Stewart had complained that he could not do anything useful, like fund public works, or attract firms to set up new works in areas like Tyneside.[10] He had written to a litany of companies urging them to consider establishing new works in the Distressed Areas; most did not even bother to reply. He had had enough of chafing against the restrictions on his powers.

After years of fruitless debate, two years of Special Area status, Stewart's resignation, the Jarrow Crusade, and the arrival in London of a separate hunger march a few days later, there was a rising feeling that the government's efforts to bring work to the workless were proving not remotely adequate. Forty Conservative backbenchers threatened to vote against their government: a serious enough threat, in the 1930s, to force Chamberlain to do more.

The chancellor offered a new amended Special Areas Bill, giving the commissioners greater powers, and buttered this dry offering with promising talk about the need to go beyond old orthodoxies. But after years of government foot-dragging, the dissident MPs were not inclined to trust him. During the bill's Commons debate, the threatened revolt was led by a right-wing diehard, Viscount 'Top' Wolmer. Even Sir Robert Horne, once a budget-cutting chancellor, joined in. This collection of Conservatives denounced the National Government for drift, indecision, failure to act on Stewart's ideas, failure to have any of their own, hopeless lack of foresight and generally trying everyone's patience.

The dominant theme of the 1930s was increasing prosperity, but for these MPs, that contrast only made it worse. Days earlier in the Commons, Duncan Sandys had expressed hope that 'the social conscience of the people in places where prosperity has returned' might be awakened by the sight of Tyneside's luckless men marching down their high streets.[11] Now, one diehard promised support from the Tory backbenches 'for direct action, however unorthodox' to tackle this 'crying social evil.' He wanted wages in south Wales factories subsidised up to 100 per cent. There were demands for more government spending; for the appointment of a Cabinet Minister to take charge; even for state direction of industry, one of the old consensus' last taboos.

Chamberlain appeared to entertain the idea…but then made very clear that it was not going to happen. His one solid concession led to the establishment of some trading estates, but even historians who strongly defend Chamberlain's approach do not claim the move made a substantial difference. One of the traits that antagonised his critics was a willingness to sound bold and iconoclastic, without actually doing very much. From the backbenches, Harold Macmillan, maverick Conservative MP for Stockton-on-Tees, jeered: 'I have never known unorthodoxy bought at so cheap a rate.'[12] A few days after this debate, even that modest reform was delayed.[13]

Macmillan was first elected for Stockton in 1924. This was not a traditional Tory seat, and its young MP felt he had to show his unemployment-hit voters what he could do for them. Driven by the sight of working men 'walking up and down vaguely, through the area, looking for a job everybody knew wasn't there',[14] and the contrast with his life in Sussex, he began to think the unthinkable. By 1931, he was denouncing the City and the Treasury as 'banksters'.[15] The financial crisis had acted to 'liberate men's minds,' he wrote, 'from a continued subservience to the economic orthodoxy of the pre-war world.'[16] The barrage of ideas that Macmillan's fellow Conservative dissidents aimed at the government during the November 1936 debates suggests that, by this point, the case for breaking from orthodoxy was gaining some traction. In 1938, Macmillan set out an alternative: *The Middle Way*. This was an astonishing book for a Conservative MP to have written, let alone a future Prime Minister. But it is precisely because he was so at odds with the old orthodoxy before the Second World War that, afterwards, he could preside over the new one. That old orthodoxy, in its reduced form, still ruled in the Treasury and the Cabinet; but the reach of consensus support for it beyond that was shrinking.

To Macmillan, Chamberlain's half-hearted interventions had left Britain stuck with the worst of both worlds. British politics remained focused on the wrong nightmare. *The Middle Way* asserted that the priorities of the City, and bankers' worries about investor confidence, were simply less of a priority than liberating the unemployed from 'the humiliation and restraints of unnecessary poverty' and 'the haunting fear of insecurity'. With the downgrading of exaggerated fears, power could be better distributed. Finance was a mere service, and had no business dictating to the rest of the economy. A National Investment Board should take over some of the work of the Stock Exchange to eliminate the 'speculative evils' which turn it into a 'casino'. The Bank of England should have its Governors appointed by the state. Freed from the City's tyrannical whims, industry could be organised, and booms and slumps smoothed out. A National Economic Council, including representatives of the TUC General Council, should oversee a concerted industrial policy. The coal mines should be nationalised, and transport policy unified across all its forms. The state might have to compel the obedience of 'anti-social' private monopolies. If need be, the government would take them over.

For Macmillan, it was worth taking the risk of breaking the old economic taboos for another reason too. Not only to rescue the unemployed, but to avoid that other political nightmare that pulsed through the 1930s: the death of democracy. 'Muddling along from one disaster to another' would lead to 'internal social conflict culminating in dictatorship and tyranny of one variety or another'. The status quo, Macmillan insisted, was now more dangerous than his heterodox ideas.[17]

* * *

The Tory rebellion against Chamberlain spread beyond the Commons. Similarly radical thinking began to flower among the Conservative party's next generation of leaders, already in training at Oxford.

Not least one who had family experience of the problem. In the autumn of 1936, a gawky, intensely ambitious young Kentishman called Teddy Heath, the son of a builder from Broadstairs, was starting his second year at Balliol College. He would go on to write that his later childhood had been 'haunted by the daily spectacle of witnessing so many people enduring hardships, hopelessness and loss of dignity'.[18] In 1930, his father William had lost his job, and built a construction company from scratch, at heavy personal and financial cost. William had a horror of debt typical of the time, and refused to borrow money. Amid the post-Depression construction boom, his business made good, but even then, he could not really afford for his boy to go away to university, let alone to Oxford. He only agreed, after much cajoling, when he realised that to refuse would have broken his son's heart. When Teddy won Balliol's organ scholarship, it meant that, for the first time in his life, he could afford to buy records and books.

Still, this increasingly political young man was coming to realise that, compared to some parts of the country, Kent had got off lightly. The day after the Special Areas debate in the Commons, King Edward VIII visited an abandoned steelworks at Dowlais in south Wales, and told the crowd that 'Something should be done'.[19] But what?

Heath plunged into student politics, as a Conservative. The confidence factory of the Oxford Union, modelled on the House of Commons, transformed the awkward schoolboy into an aspiring statesman. In November 1937, the first motion was 'That this House approves Labour's Immediate Programme'. This was the Opposition's newly minted vision of a planned Britain. It envisaged state control of credit, the Bank of England, coal, electricity and gas, the land, and transport. There would be an end to 'the ruin of industry by unscrupulous financiers', higher taxes to fund better social services, a 'financial plan for the full employment of our people', public works schemes, and 'drastic and immediate action' to rescue the Distressed Areas, including state location of industry. The Union's star guest for the debate was the Programme's author, the Shadow Foreign Secretary, Hugh Dalton. Here was Teddy's chance to take on one of the most forceful politicians of the day.

He began by needling the high-born Dalton that his 'intimate knowledge of the working classes was no doubt gained on the playing fields of Eton.'[20] Labour's *Programme* had little, Teddy suggested, to offer the working class or the Distressed Areas. 'I concluded,' he would later recall, 'by listing the achievements of the National Government in reducing unemployment, supporting new factories and new industries, together with trading estates...'[21] Dalton boomed back that the government 'had not taken strong action to secure the location of new industries' in the unemployment blackspots. Labour would launch Britain on the way to 'a full policy of economic and financial planning'. This would 'eliminate the curse of mass unemployment by planning [state] resources and putting order into the economic system,' as it had in social-democratic Sweden, and Soviet Russia.[22]

Teddy's side won and, to his delight, Dalton 'stalked out'. Yet privately, his thinking was closer to Dalton's than he let on. Teddy thought that 'the National Government lacked imagination and compassion when it came to dealing with poverty'. He accepted the priority Labour was putting on the Distressed Areas and, though he defended the National Government's record, he supplemented it with at least four policies of his own. He and Dalton were focused on the same problem, and some of their solutions were similar. In 1938, Teddy read *The Middle Way*, and thought he had found the 'something' that 'should be done': planning. He seems to have accepted Macmillan's warning that, without it, democracy was in danger. A 'degree of economic planning,' Heath considered, 'could make commerce and industry more efficient and generate the resources which would help protect the needy in society, without any threat to individual liberty.'[23]

For much of Teddy's time at Balliol, 100 yards away in Jesus College, there sat another hard-up, driven young man whose father had been unemployed, and who was thinking hard about what had to change. But where Teddy poured his energy and determination into student politics, Harold Wilson invested his in study. This culminated in a Herculean bout of scholarship that transformed Harold from a northern nobody into one of Oxford's coming men. Over ninety-one pages, his 1936 Gladstone Memorial Prize–winning essay, 'The State and the Railways in Great Britain 1823–63', portrays a government, in the person of William Gladstone, untangling a coagulated spaghetti bowl of privately owned railways to assemble a single, orderly network, overseen by the state. The essay was a manifesto for planning: using the leverage of the central state to take on vested interests and force a transition away from laissez faire economics for the public good. It was a meditation on the logic, wit, iconoclasm and blunt force of personality it took to break and remake a consensus.

A year later, Harold won a top first. The day after his last exam, his family wrote to tell him that his father had once again lost his job. Could planning the economy have prevented this?

Over the eighteen months it took Herbert to find work again, Harold's academic career took off. Unlike Herbert's last stint on the scrapheap, his son was now able to support him financially. He re-joined the Labour Party and became an advocate of socialist planning. Unemployment played a significant part in this; he appears to have decided it was evil. The new head of University College, Sir William Beveridge, hired Harold as his researcher on a huge investigation into unemployment and the trade cycle. It sent him touring the country's labour exchanges to gather data, and these encounters, alongside his father's first-hand experience, very likely reinforced his political turn left.

Harold was one of many such converts to the idea of planning; as yet, however, there was no agreement on the plan to be followed. Macmillan offered one way, Dalton's *Immediate Programme* another. There were many more. How could the unemployed be rescued from the misery that capitalism had been powerless to quell, without handing power to anti-democratic planners, as in Europe? Many young economists hunting for a solution felt as though they were stuck at a dismal crossroads: trudge onward under the burden of mass unemployment, or turn left, or right, to totalitarianism.

In February 1936, John Maynard Keynes published his alternative: *The General Theory of Employment, Interest and Money*. The problem was not that the unemployed were unwilling to accept lower wages: it was a lack of 'effective demand'. The state should boost that demand by cutting tax and raising spending. Beneath this was a more fundamental insight: that fear of the future had held investors back, causing unemployment and even the Depression. This proclamation of a new approach struck those young economists in particular with the force of religious conversion. Keynes had found not only the flaw in capitalism, but the cure. One devotee embraced the new faith because it offered a 'hope that prosperity could be restored and maintained without the support of prison camps, executions and bestial interrogations'.[24] There was a democratic way through after all!

Edward Heath would later reflect that Keynes' 'wholly new' strategy of counter-cyclical intervention to maintain full employment was—along with Macmillan's *Middle Way*—what 'convinced me, once and for all, that neither socialism nor the pure free market could provide the answer to the problems which beset us.'[25] Though he remained more of a planner, Harold Wilson read *The General Theory* too. As a child, he could never understand 'why an unemployed Colne Valley weaver was without coal when ten miles away a miner was out of work because nobody wanted his coal.'[26] Here was an answer.

If sections of the political class were now coming around to these ideas, the Baldwin government's gaze was still fixed on the nightmares that deficit spending could trigger: uncontrollable inflation, a run on the pound, national bankruptcy. The remaining champions of the free market, meanwhile, warned that even a partially planned economy would collapse into the tyranny of collectivism. But by 1936, the fear of bankruptcy and of dictatorship was being exacerbated by a new nightmare. This would put British politics under excruciating pressure, pushing it, at last, to breaking point.

* * *

In the long shadow of 1918, the prospect of facing a *second* world war, with far more fearsome arsenals on all sides, was unthinkable. Britain's great strategic birthright, the protection of the sea, had been cancelled: even the Royal Navy could not stop air attacks. The axiomatic expression of Britain's sudden helplessness, 'the bomber will always get through', was coined by Stanley Baldwin in the Commons in 1932. The fear that another world war would mean the death of civilisation was very widely held. In *People of Britain*, a 1936 propaganda short bankrolled by Stafford Cripps, which was seen by over 2 million cinemagoers, a terrified old woman scrambles gas masks on to a child, then herself, as voices

67

tell us, 'Gas burns! Gas blinds! Gas chokes! Gas paralyses!'[27] Neil Bell, author of a 1931 near-future dystopia titled *The Gas War of 1940*—one of many such novels—wrote that 'man has created a peril he must at all costs avoid'.[28]

At *all* costs? For those who thought another war meant the end of the world, clear thinking began to prove difficult. Some did follow this sentiment to its logical conclusion, and became pacifists. More people put their faith in 'collective security' through the League of Nations—the toothless UN precursor founded in 1920, after the Paris Peace Conference. The cost of collective security was re-armament, so that the League could credibly threaten military intervention as a deterrent, but not all League supporters accepted that. Many people feared that, far from preventing a war, re-armament would actually provoke one—wrecking the economy along the way. Every road led straight to nightmares. The historian Richard Overy suggests that, in the late 1930s, 'important sections of the British public were gripped … by a war psychosis':[29] a desperate sense that there was no way out. Before it ever arrived, the very thought of war was paralysing.[30]

For the left, war was not just a threat in itself. It also intensified their existing fear that, in desperation, capitalism would set up a fascist total state. In his 1936 book *The Struggle for Peace*, Cripps argued that capitalist democracy was 'planning for barbarism', as the militarist hardliners in the Cabinet came to dominate: 'It is quite usual to-day to hear eminent Conservative politicians envying the efficiency of Hitler's methods, which is, of course, the first step towards their adoption.'[31]

On New Year's Day 1937, Cripps launched *The Tribune*: a new weekly newspaper whose mission was to halt the advance of war, and the fascistic British state banging the drum. It was the flagship of Cripps' 'Unity Campaign' to forge a Labour–ILP–Communist front, which would help lead the international working class to resist capitalism, fascism and war, before workers could be sent to slaughter each other, as they had been twenty years before. Through 1937 and early 1938, *The Tribune* dedicated a lot of column space to the horrors of bombing, from Abyssinia, China and Spain to the prospect of London on fire. Putting all that together, we can reconstruct the nightmare the magazine saw coming. It went something like this…

Even if the enemy bombers are spotted in time, we will not be able to stop them. They are too fast, and there are not enough anti-aircraft guns to shoot them all down. In the whole of the Great War, 300 tons of bombs were dropped on Britain. If there is a second world war, more than that will be dropped every 24 hours, for many days at a time. For all their promises, the government has failed to protect people from external attack. There are barely any air raid shelters. Only adults have gas masks, and anyway they will prove useless. Fire bombs will smash through roofs and ceilings and land on beds, burning white hot. Government advice is to try to get rid of them using sand, and a shovel... 500-pound high explosive bombs will crash through even ferro-concrete buildings, and explode in the basements. Any houses hit will be obliterated. Skeleton schemes for fire-fighting, gas decontamination and evacuation are futile. Everything will burn. Our children will die in gas-choked cellars.[32]

As editor, Cripps hired William Mellor, who brought in Barbara Betts as a freelance contributor. Her friend Michael Foot, whom she knew through the Socialist League, joined the staff. Foot had moved to London to scratch a living as a journalist, and had helped Cripps write his peace book. *The Tribune* was militantly against the National Government's re-armament programme, because they feared what it would do with its new weapons. Only the workers and a workers' government could be trusted to bear arms against fascism, in Britain or abroad. In a speech for the Unity Campaign in 1937, Betts denounced the government—now led by Chamberlain, Baldwin having retired. She charged that it was a regime that 'uses armaments only in support of Fascism, of imperialist War, of Reaction and of Colonial suppression.'[33] Each Monday or Tuesday night, at Betts' little flat near St Pancras Station, she and Foot would write their 'In Industry Today' column, then read books—Dickens, Marx—and talk politics. Their pieces echoed their editor's and publisher's intertwined nightmares of fascism and war.

This worldview produced an astonishing conclusion. In Stockport on 15 November 1936, Cripps had reportedly said that 'he did not believe it would be a bad thing for the British working class if Germany defeated us.'[34] A few months later, he was arguing that workers should refuse to make arms, and calling for a general strike if war broke out. Likewise, at Labour's 1936 Conference, the leader Clement Attlee had told delegates that supporting government re-armament unconditionally would 'lead you to demand after demand being made on your liberties', and from there to 'a demand that you shall accept Fascism practically, in order to conquer Fascism.'[35]

This dark scenario was fleshed out by a young left-wing writer, George Orwell, who had at least one comrade in common with Foot and Betts,[36] and whose political fears were practically identical to theirs. He regarded the idea of Britain fighting for 'democracy' against foreign 'fascism' as a ruse, which would 'allow Fascism, British variety, to be slipped over our necks during the first week.'[37] In Orwell's 1939 novel *Coming Up for Air*, a middle-aged insurance salesman tries hopelessly to shake off his dread of imminent war by escaping to his old Thames Valley hometown. The title is an ironic play on that suffocating certainty that there *was* no escape. Throughout the novel, Orwell's salesman obsessively recites his vision of the militarised total state's overwhelming power, from huge posters of a leader to concentration camps:

> All the things you've got at the back of your mind, the things you're terrified of, the things that you tell yourself are just a nightmare or only happen in foreign countries. The bombs, the food-queues, the rubber truncheons, the barbed wire, the coloured shirts, the slogans, the enormous faces, the machine-guns squirting out of bedroom windows. It's all going to happen.[38]

* * *

The threat of what war would do to Britain put both main political parties under more and more pressure. The tribes of the British party system began to break apart, as politicians were pushed ever closer to a choice between unthinkables. For the doves in both parties, the overriding nightmare was the intolerable cost of war—in both blood and borrowing—and the creation of an authoritarian state. If that scared Orwell, the *Tribune* staff and the leader of the Labour Party, to a surprising extent, the Tory leaders agreed. Like Foot and Cripps, Neville Chamberlain would publish a book called *The Struggle for Peace*, bewailing the waste of 'vast expenditure upon means of destruction'—which, he said, 'drives the Government always to search for a way out'.[39]

So the government endeavoured to re-arm, while staying clear of its nightmares. It wanted to prepare not for total war, but a 'war of limited liability.'[40] It focused spending on air and sea capability, but did not conscript a large, costly land army. It could not allow the growth of a militarised state, which would suffocate freedom and hamper commerce. Reluctantly the Treasury suspended orthodox rules on balancing the budget. In February 1937, the government announced that, over five years, £1.5 billion would be spent on defence, including a loan of £400 million. But very soon it looked as though that would not be enough, and there were already signs of rising inflation. One businessman insisted that 'there is some other way than the settling down to make ourselves a country of armament makers.'[41] As Stanley Baldwin's premiership drew to a close, he was haunted by the graves of the last war, and yearned to turn away from the horrors of the next one. But, as for Orwell's salesman, there was no such solace.

The Admiralty, the War Office, the Air Ministry, the Foreign Office and the military planners were demanding faster, more expensive re-armament as a matter of dire urgency. Old orthodox fears about spending and the expansion of the state must be swept away. In October 1936, the Joint Planning Subcommittee of the Chiefs of Staff prepared what the historian Joe Maiolo argues was a deliberately crafted nightmare scenario, intended to 'shock the politicians' into accepting that Germany's war production was dangerously outstripping Britain's.[42] The Nazis had 'an organisation for industrial mobilization under which the whole industrial machinery of the country comes under the control of the State.' Britain's problem, the committee warned, was how to compete while labouring under 'democratic conditions.'[43] Its report left Baldwin infuriated.

Likewise, the planners' ally Winston Churchill was calling for sweeping new ministerial powers to take over industry. In July 1936, he suggested that 20–30 per cent of Britain's industrial production capacity should be turned over to making munitions, and called for the proclamation of 'state of emergency preparations' to intensify re-armament—even if that meant giving up 'a good deal of the comfort and smoothness of our ordinary life'.[44] In the Commons on 12 November, the rival nightmares clashed. Churchill told Baldwin that his government was 'decided only to be undecided'. He demanded a Ministry of Supply to get a grip on the re-armament issue before it was too late. Britain faced an 'emergency', a 'terrible reckoning'. Baldwin shot back that 'dictatorial methods' were not superior to 'the co-ordination of free effort'. He warned that re-armament was already making heavy demands on industry and on the state's resources; Churchill's call for a Ministry of Supply with compulsory powers, which would have to cover the whole of British industry, involved 'grave risks'. Such a move would 'dislocate the ordinary free working of industry'; Baldwin warned that he 'hardly dare[d] to reckon how it might react on finance', which the National Government had, after all, been created to defend.[45]

The trade unions harboured strikingly similar suspicions of onerous state controls, which would threaten their freedom to agree pay deals. For those who took Baldwin's and Chamberlain's view, the nightmares that had, somehow, to be evaded were clear: war, economic calamity, and an authoritarian state. They could not imagine that embracing one of those nightmares might actually become the way through to a new consensus. But that is exactly how it turned out.

* * *

For others on the right, the spectre of war was making a bigger, more deficit-dependent state seem more acceptable. These were the solutions some on the left had long been suggesting to the unemployment problem. Now a link was made between the alleged failures to act on re-armament, and on the plight of the unemployed. This was quite a powerful connection: it would help to change British politics for decades.

In the 1935 general election, the National Government's manifesto had tentatively suggested that re-armament could be used to bring work to the Distressed Areas. In time, allocating defence contracts did generate much-needed jobs. But five days after Churchill excoriated Baldwin over the 'locust' years of drift on re-arming, Viscount Wolmer had made the same criticisms of the government over unemployment:

If those years had been spent as they ought to have been spent, we should have been building our new munitions factories at our leisure, with proper consideration and proper planning; we could have built them where they are needed, both from a strategical point of view and from the point of view of unemployment. It is an added tragedy that the years that the locusts have eaten in regard to national defence should have their repercussions on the unemployment situation in the Special Areas.[46]

Not only was the criticism on both crises the same—indecision, drift—the solutions demanded were remarkably similar too: more money, and a new government ministry. Chamberlain's reluctance to re-arm 'at all costs', and his reluctance to break decisively from orthodoxy to help the unemployed, seemed to spring from the same fear of an over-powering, over-spending state. But now, for some on the right, the power of the state seemed doubly necessary, to fight the nightmares of unemployment and Nazi aggression. The dissidents' perspective was still very much a minority view among Conservatives, but to the next generation, this thinking offered a solution. At Oxford, Teddy Heath espied an 'emerging new Conservatism' which he associated with Macmillan, and the young Foreign Secretary Anthony Eden, but also Churchill.[47] To him, it meant fighting Nazis and unemployment alike.

Having briefly sat at Churchill's feet in Oxford, Teddy now brushed shoulders with Hitler. In the long 1937 summer vacation, he travelled to Germany alone, and was invited to attend the Nazi party congress in Nuremberg. At a reception Teddy would shake the flaccid hand of Heinrich Himmler. But it was the rally held on 6 September that seared itself onto his retinas. In a white stone stadium, painfully bright in the sunshine, he witnessed the Führer standing in a black Mercedes, being driven through to watch the parades. Surrounded by *Sieg heil*-ing Nazis, Teddy watched the squads of Brownshirts and Hitler Youth under the endless flags, and felt the 'numerical strength and internal power of the regime burst upon me for the first time'.[48] When war came, as now he knew it would, he and his friends would have to fight. But war was no longer the nightmare to be avoided at all costs. The overwhelming nightmare was Nazism.

Teddy barely spoke German and so may not have grasped this, but in the speech he witnessed, Hitler was boasting that 'Germany has solved its most pressing social problem, and solved it absolutely:

there are no longer any real unemployed in our country.'[49] Here, still, was the conundrum: how could you organise a country to tackle unemployment, and to re-arm as required, without sliding into the inhuman regimentation of Nuremberg? It was not long after this that Teddy first read Harold Macmillan's *The Middle Way*.

* * *

If the threat of Nazi Germany was driving some on the right to accept a bigger, more powerful state, it was driving some on the left to accept war.

This jarred against the party's instincts: in the 1935 general election, Labour had put up posters instructing voters that the choice was 'Labour Plans or Tory "Planes"', and contrasting the paltry grants to the Distressed Areas with the vast sums being spent on re-armament.[50] In *The Tribune*, as late as March 1938, Betts and Foot were denouncing the National Government for bringing war nearer. But, once again, Hugh Dalton pushed back. At its 1936 conference, he had confronted the party with 'the central brutal fact in Europe': the re-armament of Nazi Germany. The 'magnitude and speed' of this was 'quite unprecedented', and there was now 'the possibility of a direct attack upon this country'. If this came, Dalton had suggested, there would be no warning. He acknowledged that raising this touched 'deep nerves' in the party, given its fear and loathing of war. But with the threat of Nazi attack, Labour now had to break with its traditions, and its gut, and its hatred of the allegedly pro-fascist National Government. It had to support re-armament. Dalton insisted this did not mean supporting Chamberlain's foreign policy, nor did it mean abandoning plans to nationalise arms manufacture, or dismissing the hope of peace. Nevertheless, Dalton told them, he found it 'difficult in logic to believe that the Labour Party Conference can support unilateral non-rearmament in a world where all are increasing their armaments.'[51]

This was a direct attack on the left-wing view that war and fascism were capitalism's demon twins. Attlee thought his Shadow Foreign Secretary's speech was stupid. He acknowledged the threat from Europe's 'Fascist dictatorships' but was wary of 'a line-up for a war', still concerned about fascism at home.[52] But more and more people were re-thinking. Even *The Tribune*'s two young tyros, Michael Foot and Barbara Betts, began to turn away from their elders' line that what was needed, in the event of an 'imperialist' war, was a general strike. In late 1937, travelling through Nazi Germany, Betts saw air raid precautions being practised, and decided that that would be more useful. Given the supposed incipient fascism of the National Government, there was suspicion on the left that air raid precautions were a form of war-mongering. Barnsley's Labour council refused to have anything to do with them. By this time, Betts herself was a borough councillor in St Pancras, and faced this stern dilemma first-hand. In *The Tribune*, an article appeared by a 'Woman Councillor', which argued that finding out how to help if your borough was bombed did not amount to handing the Chamberlain regime *carte blanche*. This triggered outrage in the paper's correspondence columns.

Michael Foot confronted this same dilemma via the plight of the Spanish Republic. Here was a war being fought—apparently—by a democratic government against a fascist military insurgency. The National Government refused to support the legitimate republic. Events in Spain finally persuaded Foot that war had its uses. Cripps continued to advocate a general strike in response to any 'imperialist' war, but his protégés were moving on. The next time Foot went to stay with Cripps at Goodfellows, Betts was invited too, and when the two of them played tennis with Cripps and his son, they did not let the great man win.[53] Soon enough, Cripps would join them in the pro-war camp.

After another year of cajoling by Dalton, the 1937 Labour conference voted to support re-armament. The party was now committed, as *Labour's Immediate Programme* had it, to stand firmly for democracy and 'strenuously resist all attacks on British liberties'.

As Labour's thinkers came to terms with the idea that war was coming, and re-armament was necessary, they realised that one nightmare might cancel out another. Instead of offering the electorate a choice of Labour Plans or Tory Planes, a British government could plan *for* planes—and then for jobs and social services. Preparation for war was not just a matter of confronting the unthinkable. It was also a way to make the left's once-unthinkable policy ideas practical reality. As the historian Richard

Toye has noted: 'as war came nearer, Labour's calls for ... planning became not only more urgent, but increasingly plausible.'[54]

Under external pressure, the re-alignment of British politics accelerated. Churchill and the military establishment were pushing in the same direction as Labour leaders: towards a more dominant, planner-led state, which would take over parts of industry and up the pace of re-arming. For Churchill et al, the nightmare of defeat overrode the nightmare of the total state. For Dalton et al, the nightmare of defeat overrode the nightmare of war.

* * *

As Prime Minister, Neville Chamberlain sustained the effort to keep arms spending under control through the winter of 1937–8. But the upward pressure could only be held down for so long. It had already forced the Treasury to run a deficit. It was now clear that the government was 'in grave danger of building up the Defence Forces out of borrowed money to a level which is beyond our power to maintain'.[55] The defence co-ordination minister insisted that the £1.5 billion budget should not be breached, and that if the international situation grew so bad that even more had to be spent, this could 'only be met by heavy increases in taxation'. Since 1931, cuts to social spending had become virtually unthinkable. Raising taxes was more orthodox than more borrowing, but the standard rate of income tax was already 25 per cent, which was thought very high. Yet the Cabinet approved the proposal; in his April 1938 Budget, Chamberlain's chancellor, Sir John Simon, duly set the standard rate 2.5 per cent above the acceptable limit of 25 per cent. MPs gasped. But would even this be enough? Simon warned that raising defence spending was impossible 'unless we turned ourselves into a different kind of nation.'[56]

On 12 March 1938, the German army invaded and annexed Austria, with Nazi death squads following behind. Among all the nightmares crowding in on the British imagination, Nazism began to elbow its way to the front. Stories reached Britain of the public persecution of Austrian Jews, and of the desperate measures taken by some of those who really did have no way out. A former Cabinet secretary recorded how 'the daily tale of persecution, repression and suicide arriving from Austria is having the effect of making this people determine that [Hitler] shall never apply that regime here.'[57]

When Hitler demanded the German-speaking region of Czechoslovakia, Chamberlain launched his famous personal mission to stop war—which, he told radio listeners across the Empire, 'is a nightmare to me.' He meant both the destruction of precious lives and of 'precious savings'.[58] On his flight home after a fruitless encounter with Hitler, he had imagined his plane was a German bomber. Looking down at the vast swathe of houses stretched below, he had asked himself what protection the government could offer them.[59] At last, Chamberlain did discover 'a way out', without bankrupting the economy by turning the state into a Churchillian war machine.[60] The cost was Czech sovereignty.

The Dean of St Paul's Cathedral declared that the 'general opinion is that the PM has saved civilization',[61] but for those on left and right who had concluded that trying to avoid war would lead to something worse, Munich was the breaking point. The Foreign Secretary Lord Halifax may have thought the government faced 'a hideous choice of evils'[62]—horror or humiliation—but they believed that Chamberlain had humiliated himself, and that the horror would be along soon enough. 'If at first you don't concede, fly, fly and fly again', mocked Teddy Heath at the Oxford Union.[63] Despite the threat of deselection, around thirty Conservative dissidents abstained in the vote on Munich. Among them were some who had also protested, two years earlier, against Chamberlain's failure to do more for the unemployed.[64] In 1925, Baldwin's plea for an end to industrial strife—for 'peace in our time'—had looked forward to a renewed consensus. Chamberlain's declaration of 'peace for our time' thirteen years later would become that settlement's epitaph.

* * *

Against expectations, there was no snap election; but, as Teddy Heath's luck would have it, there was a by-election due in Oxford that October. The Conservative candidate was to be a young pro-Munich lawyer called Quintin Hogg. His father, Lord Hailsham, was a Conservative Cabinet minister, so deeply orthodox that even

Ramsay MacDonald had refused to admit him to the National Government, in retribution for his anti-union legislation. One of Oxford's young Keynesian dons, Roy Harrod, proposed that a single 'popular front' candidate should stand against Hogg, on an anti-Munich platform. The Master of Balliol, AD Lindsay, consented to stand as an 'Independent Progressive'. Those from left, right and centre for whom Nazi attack now overrode all older nightmares could now unite publicly to campaign against Chamberlain.

Lindsay was perfect casting: a former vice-chancellor of Oxford, but also a socialist democrat, who had supported the General Strike, and frequently went to south Wales to teach out-of-work miners through the Workers' Education Association. At Balliol, his mission was to open the college up to a wider social range of students—people like the teenage Teddy Heath, who used to cycle 10 miles each way to economics lectures run by the Association. He would later remember how Lindsay preached the virtue of discussion as the 'best possible buttress of a free society',[65] and he admired his faith in democracy as an achievable ideal.

It cost nothing for Liberal and Labour students to back Lindsay, but Teddy had built a serious reputation in the Conservative Party, becoming president of its national student federation. Now his mentor was running against his party's candidate. Rubbishing his good name with the party to land a feather-punch on Chamberlain would be a brave move, especially for someone without a rich, powerful father to run to afterwards. But Teddy threw himself into the campaign, drawing other student Conservatives after him.

Regardless of whether he won or lost, Lindsay's candidacy was a political event in itself. He strove to demonstrate that, despite Munich, democracy was not wilting under the fascist threat. But this campaign was also about preparing to fight for democracy by expanding the power of the state. It was about planning, and the good that government could do. In his opening election address at Oxford's town hall, Lindsay set out an ad hoc manifesto which was strikingly far-reaching for a single-issue, non-affiliated campaign. This was a stride towards something new: a public declaration, from an independent candidate, of the coalescing plans to fight Hitler and unemployment alike, framed with confidence that this could be done democratically.

He insisted that re-armament must be 'a truly national effort', not 'scamped for private profit or thwarted through private control'. This meant 'a profound change in the industrial structure of the country'. He recognised that, even now, this raised the nightmare of the total state, but insisted that 'the English people' could 'rearm on the scale required of us and remain a democracy', because of their 'wonderful power of voluntary organisation'. This meant the trade unions had to be 'taken into co-operation and into the full confidence of the Government.' Chamberlain had begun this process, as tentatively as ever, but it would need to go much further. This alchemical mix—a domineering, yet democratic state—could ward off the threat of both military defeat and domestic dictatorship. Better yet, it could tackle unemployment, which was heading back towards 2 million. Re-armament, Lindsay told his audience, 'must be used to abolish unemployment.' It was 'madness', he contended,'to have a shortage of skilled labour in the Midlands and an enormous reservoir of capable unemployed men with nothing to do in just those special areas which are farther removed from danger by air: Wales, West Cumberland, and parts of Scotland.'[66]

Galvanising the desire to unite to fight fascism was the disaster still unfolding in Spain. Lindsay's supporters even adopted the Spanish Republic's red and yellow. Teddy had seen what the Republic was up against that summer: on a visit to Spain, his hotel had been hit by a fascist bomb, and the car he was travelling in strafed. Now he fought back by slogging round Oxford on his bicycle, trying to use the organisational skills learnt as a student administrator to pull Lindsay's campaign into shape. Meanwhile, the Conservatives' Hogg was banging the drum for national unity, rallying behind Chamberlain the peace-maker and acclaiming Munich as 'the greatest miracle of modern times performed by a single man'.[67]

Reporters were surprised by the lack of excitement all this generated among Oxford's residents, but it was a tussle for the soul of the establishment. Manifestos and letters of support proliferated, as public figures queued up to speak, usually for Lindsay—among them were Ellen Wilkinson and Stafford Cripps, both growing more exercised by the Nazi threat than their old nightmares of war. Harold Wilson's boss Beveridge wrote congratulating Lindsay on his radical opening speech. Heath later recalled Churchill phoning in his support, bellowing, 'Lindsay must get in!'[68] Harold Macmillan came to deliver the same message, ignoring threats of deselection. Underneath all the high-flown rhetoric was the sound of people willing themselves to break from allegiances and habits of mind, before they brought disaster.

Lindsay gave his final speech in a packed town hall. Edward Heath claimed later that his mentor, quietly making the case to stand against Nazism, moved people to tears. The candidate returned to his theme that the war could bring radical reconstruction: 'a nation rearmed in spirit, with courage in its heart, can still build a new world'.[69] The next night, a huge crowd waited outside the town hall to hear the results. Hogg won, with a reduced majority for the Conservatives.

Three weeks after the election, Teddy told the Oxford Union: 'What this country needs is a government which will call on the people of every type and class'; this would 'show to the world that it still believes in individual liberty', and would be an administration 'in which the people can have confidence.'[70] The following day, he acted this out in miniature: with the help of non-Conservative, anti-Chamberlain votes, he was elected President of the Oxford Union. As for Westminster, the by-election may have served a useful purpose in generating momentum, but any breakthrough would require not a coalition of the commentariat, but the involvement of Labour and its massed support. Only then could a new, truly national government emerge and break from the old orthodoxy. For the moment, Attlee was watching and waiting.

* * *

The Munich Agreement was supposed to ease the inflationary pressure of re-armament, but it did not calm City nerves for long. Barely three months later, the chancellor warned that the country's financial situation was slipping back towards the kind of catastrophe that the National Government had been formed to prevent in the first place. Recent conditions, Simon told Cabinet, had been 'painfully reminiscent' of those 'immediately prior to the financial crisis of 1931'.[71] Once again, the Bank of England was having to spend more and more gold to shore up the pound.

This time, the problem was not the rocketing cost of unemployment benefit, but of tanks, guns, planes, ships and shells. Cutting spending might mean not the bearable nightmare of the hungry unemployed, but the unbearable nightmare of successful Nazi attack. On the other hand, if the government overspent, it risked withstanding the Luftwaffe's opening onslaught—only for the economy to crash. That would leave the state unable to afford to keep fighting. Treasury officials struggled over how to raise sufficient spending power: the markets were more frightened of higher tax than higher borrowing; the newspapers broadly took the same line. The government would hold off raising the standard rate of income tax again until after the war began.

On 15 March 1939, the Wehrmacht marched into Prague, extinguishing Chamberlain's hopes for peace. War per se was no longer the worst nightmare facing Britain. Media and political pressure had already built for a compulsory national register of workers who could staff the war effort. Chamberlain had agreed only to a voluntary register: for three years, he had resisted creating a land army big enough to fight in Europe, and the hugely expanded state it would require. A land army would need a Ministry of Supply—the longstanding demand of the Tory dissidents around Churchill, more recently of the hawkish Labour planners like Hugh Dalton, and now even of Cabinet ministers. With the Nazi takeover of Czechoslovakia, Chamberlain could hold the line no longer. On 20 April, he announced the creation of the new ministry, with powers to intervene, impose, direct, divert and compel.

This marked the advent of the planners' warfare state…even if the announcement of Chamberlain's chosen minister, the well-meaning Leslie Burgin, induced 'a groan of pain' from MPs.[72] Then, on 26 April, the Prime Minister announced conscription. This triggered fury among the more doveish Labour MPs, for whom forcing workers into the service of a Conservative-run big state remained unthinkable.[73] But, on right and left alike, the old spectre of British totalitarianism was being overwhelmed by the threat of the flesh-and-blood version in Germany.

Many on the left were managing to shake off their suspicions of Churchill as a potential ally against fascism. On 1 May, Hugh Dalton denounced the Budget for failing to organise a 'near-war economy'.

He proposed effective defence against both bombs and poverty: 'a deliberate and efficient scheme to mobilise men, money and materials for the common good and for the security of all.'[74] As the historian Richard Toye notes, 'By thus linking social justice, full employment and sound defence, Dalton built up a powerful indictment against a government which, in Labour eyes, had failed in its duties on all these points.'[75]

A few weeks later, Dalton made an audacious grab for the flag. Labour had only recently come round to re-armament, and had just voted against conscription, and yet the Shadow Foreign Secretary felt able to proclaim:

> No supporter of this Government should ever again without shame lift up the Union Jack at a public meeting or on an election platform. The Labour Party alone is entitled to lift not only the Union Jack which stands for Britain, but the Red Flag, which stands for Socialism and democracy. The 'old man of Munich' and the rest could only raise the white flag of the coward on the one hand and the black flag of the traitor and the robber on the other.[76]

Aneurin Bevan, who had once argued that re-armament forced the unemployed 'to dig their own graves',[77] was one of the leading leftists who now switched, arguing that the coming war could be the death rites of capitalism—a radicalising people's war.

The pressure to expand the state intensified. Scrambling together a continental land army had doubled defence borrowing. By 18 May, the chancellor was worried that Britain's shift to a quasi–war economy could only run for another nine months before it was financially exhausted. As Joe Maiolo writes, 'In private, Treasury officials now thought the previously unthinkable: introducing price controls to keep inflation in check'.[78] By the summer, the Treasury was advising the government that 'quasi-wartime controls over the economy would be required to maintain current defence expenditure after the autumn',[79] and 'that the moment was already in sight when financial weakness would make victory in war impossible'.[80] The government was trapped: the more prepared the armed forces, the less 'able the country would be to support them'.[81]

Yet even then, in the summer of 1939, Chamberlain was still desperately hoping that the old ways would survive–that Berlin would think rationally, and realise that, given Britain's defences, it could not achieve what it wanted by force. If only Hitler and his fellows would act in their own best interests. But, as Keynes had pointed out, the Victorian model of human behaviour, *homo economicus*—the rational Economic Man on whom the orthodoxy was founded—failed to factor in fear, or hubris. If anyone embodied those 'animal spirits', it was the increasingly bestial Nazis. Chamberlain could not compute a regime that *wanted* war. No wonder his radio broadcasts sounded funereal. Like Baldwin before him, he was an old man, a Victorian, mourning the death of his world.

* * *

As the summer waned, Harold Wilson travelled to the annual conference of the British Association in Dundee; he was to give a lecture on exports and the trade cycle, based on his work on unemployment with Sir William Beveridge, who was in the audience. Teddy Heath, meanwhile, had been on a last student vacation, with a half-Jewish friend called Madron Seligman—to Poland, in August 1939. They had travelled via Berlin, where they gaped at the Nazis' architectural elephantiasis, and caught a train full of drunken Austrian labour conscripts to Danzig. This was the free city on the Baltic run by the League of Nations, and Hitler's next territorial claim, which was filling with German troops. The boys were repeatedly told they should leave as soon as possible. They went to Warsaw, where a gap in high walls led them into 'another world': the Jewish quarter.[82] Back in Germany, after hassle at the border, they saw huge columns of German tanks and troop trucks coming the other way, rolling eastward. At Leipzig station, they saw the headlines announcing the Nazi-Soviet pact, and fled for the French border. In a blacked-out Paris, a British Embassy official told them that if they did not leave now, 'you will never get out at all'.[83]

On 1 September 1939, while Wilson was in Dundee, Heath was racing back from Calais. The boat was packed, and awash with rumours. As Harold was delivering his paper, someone brought a note in and handed it to the chairman. Germany had invaded Poland. At this point in his lecture, he would later remember, 'the distinguished academics rather lost interest'.[84]

The same day, Chamberlain offered Labour a junior role in an expanded coalition; Labour, still awaiting the right moment, declined. By the following afternoon, despite his guarantee to Poland, Chamberlain had not yet declared war. Were the Poles in for the same sort of support that the British had given the Czechs?

Chamberlain was waiting to declare war jointly once France was ready, but in the Commons, as he appeared to vacillate, Conservative rebels like Duff Cooper and Leo Amery boiled with frustration. Labour's deputy leader Arthur Greenwood, standing in for Attlee, insisted on the need to share sacrifice, and to build a better world after the war. Delay, he told Chamberlain, was dangerous.

This may have been unfair. Political narratives often are. But Greenwood's bayonet thrust would not have done the Prime Minister such injury had it not skewered a widely held perception: that Chamberlain was so hemmed in by other fears that, when the nation was under severe external threat and he had to think and act quickly to save it, he could not face down his nightmares and make the necessary decision in time. Trapped in the old orthodoxy, he had been convinced that the only way to ward off the nightmares of bankruptcy and a total state was to avoid war.

Next morning, Chamberlain finally declared war—and told the House of Commons that 'everything I have worked for, everything that I have hoped for, everything that I have believed in during my public life, has crashed into ruins.'[85]

Edward Heath, Keith Joseph and Quintin Hogg went off to fight. Harold Wilson went to work for Potato Control, but would clamber closest, before the war was over, to the heart of power. Barbara Betts was stuck in the Air Raid Precautions service, looking for a job. And Michael Foot was up on the roof of the *Evening Standard*, plotting the fall of a political world.

4

IF HITLER COMES

1940–1

When a nation comes under attack from a deadly enemy, it swings an unforgiving searchlight on to the competence of the state. Amid disruption, death and the fear of death, people ask why we are not adequately prepared. Why the government seems incapable of making the right decisions at sufficient speed. Why frontline equipment is sorely lacking. As this new external threat sweeps all before it, long-established limits start to look dangerously irrelevant, blocking the urgent action needed.

In 1940, the pressure this brought to bear on Neville Chamberlain's struggling government was enough to override the fear of creating a total state, and the fear of bankrupting the Treasury. These nightmares had kept certain grave measures unthinkable. Now, the threat of invasion overwhelmed all that.

The state suddenly looked woefully inadequate, well beyond the Distressed Areas. A hundred and forty thousand patients were sent home to make space for the victims of the coming onslaught. The Ministry of Health hired tents to 'provide cover for ten thousand beds for air raid casualties who could not be accommodated inside the emptied hospitals'. Before long, the tents blew down. Government posters appeared, issuing sloganised instructions to carry your gas mask at all times; but official messaging in leaflets and adverts was 'often vague and sometimes self-contradictory'.[1] It could also be gratingly top-down: 'Your Courage, Your Cheerfulness, Your Resolution—Will Bring Us Victory'. The Ministry of Information reported that the people of Manchester, for example, 'continue to ask what they are expected to do in the present crisis.'[2]

The government and elements in the right-wing press had worried that people would chafe against a more domineering state, but the public embraced onerous new emergency powers, including restrictions on freedom of movement. (It is easy to dismiss the difficulty of the government's decisions, but judging the right moment to impose draconian curbs on liberty is never straightforward.) There was much more objection to people trying to get around these rules. A government minister who apparently broke regulations by leaving his shelter before the 'All Clear' sounded found himself on the sharp end of public ire.

But Chamberlain and his most senior allies could not just shake off old nightmares in a blink. Nor could they instantly transform the government machine, not even to make the existing system more efficient, let alone to plan the future. The government continued its habit of overselling its policies, more concerned that the air force was impressing the electorate (and the Germans) than that it was effective. At the start of the crisis, Chamberlain's popularity had surged to new heights, but as the threat of attack increased at the start of May 1940, it suddenly plummeted. The government seemed to drift.[3] Both parties' records could be criticised, but Labour had been out of power for almost a decade. The Ministry of Information reported 'an increased tendency to say that there has been disgraceful neglect in the past, that something must have been badly wrong at the top.'[4]

Volunteers surged in to help the struggle against the enemy: within a week of a government appeal, 250,000 men volunteered for what became the Home Guard. By July, this had risen, at least nominally, to 1.5 million. Instead of volunteering being a way to avoid expanding the state, it now helped to build the moral case for it. Here were ordinary people making up for the inadequacies of government provision. If the public could act so unselfishly, in mutual aid, should the state not ease their burdens?

Ordinary workers, easily taken for granted, were suddenly on the front lines of the home front, while middle-class people found themselves having to use the benefits system. By late 1940, under the Blitz, the Treasury was doling out huge sums to help local authorities cope with the impact of bombing raids. But external attack brutally exposed inequality. The education system came under huge pressure. Schools were bombed out; over a million were 'left to run wild'.[5] Some poor children reportedly forgot how to read. If you were rich, your house was a refuge. If you were middle-class, you at least had a garden and could build an Anderson shelter. If you lived in a slum, you were much more exposed to attack.

Life was wrenched out of shape. As the war began, JB Priestley found himself walking north London streets 'as empty of life as old cities of the plague'.[6] Later, he would compare the Nazis to typhoid. The prospect of going on holiday, even on day trips, fell away as beaches were cordoned off. New rules, fines and snoopers appeared. Rumour swirled. Local elections were suspended. Leaving your home took on dramatic significance. Everyday habits needed to be reinvented for a more treacherous and monitored world; everyday products vanished from the shops. And yet, on a grander scale, new possibilities seemed to open up.

* * *

On the afternoon of Tuesday 7 May 1940, Michael Foot, now working for the *Evening Standard*, was squeezed into a seat up in the packed Press Gallery of the House of Commons. He had been turned down for military service because of his asthma; nevertheless, he was spoiling for a fight. Peering down from above the Speaker's Chair, Foot could watch MPs gather their nerve for Parliament's highest-stakes confrontation in decades: between the guardians of the embattled orthodoxy, and their opponents, who thought the old ways were opening the country to destruction.

MPs were gathering in the wake of Britain's sorry failure to cut Germany's iron ore supply route where it ran down the Norwegian coast. After months of 'phony war', the British military had finally engaged Nazi Germany, and had been humiliated. The campaign had only begun after Germany pre-emptively invaded Norway to protect its supply lines. The Germans' decisiveness had won them the advantage. Foot had written in the previous evening's *Standard* that 'Britain in Norway chose to defy the Nazi air power without preparing the means for combating that air power.' This was the 'blunder' he told readers to remember when Chamberlain spoke: the government had failed to plan.

The British party system can stay unchanged for decades, but under sufficient external pressure—over Ireland, or Europe, or war—party loyalties crack. Behind the scenes, Westminster was alive with plotting, as MPs, back from a weekend facing discontent in their constituencies at the state of the war, coalesced in cross-party shoals: the Watching Committee, the All-Party Parliamentary Action Group. But below Foot on the right of the Chamber, there was still a huge bloc of Conservative 'yes-men' lined up behind Chamberlain. And on the other side, Attlee was waiting for the anti-Munich Tories to move first. Would enough Conservative MPs defy the whips to force some kind of change, before it was all too late?

The Prime Minister opened with an account of how Britain was racing to catch up with German arms production. His speech flopped; even one of his supporters recognised that the House was 'restive and bored'.[7] The people, Attlee told him, 'see everywhere a failure of grip, a failure of drive, not only in the field of defence and foreign policy but in industry. The Government are not organising the resources of the country.'[8] Liberal leader Archibald Sinclair told stories of troops sent to fight in Norway without white coats or snow-shoes, and echoed what was becoming an insistent point: that there were still a million men unemployed. Two weeks earlier, *The Times*, long established as the appeasers' gazette, had attacked Sir John Simon's Budget as inadequate, and denounced the failure to find war work for the unemployed as 'a standing reproach to our capacity for economic organization'.[9]

The famous climax of the first day was delivered by one of Chamberlain's fellow Birmingham Conservative MPs. When Chamberlain had seemed to dither over declaring war, Leo Amery had urged Labour's Arthur Greenwood to 'speak for England'. Amery's speech is remembered for his shattering quotation from Oliver Cromwell: 'in the name of God, go!' It was all the more effective because Amery was a man of the right, a stalwart imperialist. Ever since the Edwardian movement for 'National Efficiency', however, he had also been an advocate of planning. Amery's argument, building to his Cromwellian punchline, was about the need for foresight and 'swift, decisive action'; an attack on hesitation and slowness in the reorganisation of industry and the retraining of workers; and a demand that the trade unions be brought closer into government. Tellingly, he connected the National Government's timorous fumbling of the war effort back to its foundation on a 'false alarm': the groundless fear, in 1931, of coming off the gold standard.[10] Nine years on, the government was still stymied by phantom nightmares, even as the Nazis advanced.

Second Lieutenant Quintin Hogg, the pro-Munich victor of the Oxford by-election, was one of many MPs back on leave from military service who were pointedly wearing their uniforms. He was angry about his unit's inadequate equipment and determined to say so. But over the two days of debate, the Speaker seemed reluctant to call members in uniform. On the second day, when one of his senior colleagues on the Tory benches insisted that most people hoped Chamberlain would stay in office, Quintin jumped up to yelp, 'No; a thousand times, no. And not one serving Member holds that view either.'[11]

When David Lloyd George, Britain's previous wartime Prime Minister, prepared to speak, the *Times* reporter, up in the press gallery with Foot, thought 'the temperature of the debate rose as quickly as the House began to fill'.[12] The man from the *Manchester Guardian* reported that the debate 'took a furious turn. Mr Lloyd George in all his fighting career has never so "savaged" a Government as he did the present one to-day.'[13]

Michael Foot had long left the Liberal Party, but he still counted the old rogue, 77, bronze-faced and white-haired, as one of his heroes. This was the corrupt, mischief-making, combat-addicted political activist of a Prime Minister whom Stanley Baldwin had forced from office in 1922, ushering in what could now be cast as eighteen years of soft consensus. Lloyd George had been a classic casualty of the process needed to form a new settlement, a man out of time, who had not been able to gain traction for his Keynesian schemes.[14] Through Lloyd George's old champion Lord Beaverbrook, owner of the *Evening Standard*, Foot had been in touch with 'LG'. He and his editor had been tasked with encouraging the old man to help topple the government. One reason Foot liked Lloyd George was his 'healthy contempt for financiers'.[15] Now, as the long reign of cautious, financier-friendly consensus seemed badly wounded, Lloyd George made his way to the Despatch Box to administer its death blow.

He 'contemptuously denied the Government the right to praise the gallantry of men whom it had fooled.'[16] The 'whole House', wrote Foot, was 'gasping at the menace of his tone and features'.[17] Looking his old enemy Chamberlain in the eye, Lloyd George demanded 'real action and not sham action'.[18] Had an unemployed man been watching from the Strangers' Gallery, he might have smiled. The war was giving the whole country a flavour of the years of frustration. Throughout the Norway debate, MPs' speeches seethed at the complacent tone of Chamberlain and his ministers. Months of vexation had exploded. Lloyd George closed by demanding that Chamberlain join the rest of the country in making a sacrifice, and resign. Years later, Foot was still acclaiming the way Lloyd George's 'invective pierced the armour of Chamberlain's conceit and then was mercilessly twisted to inflame the wound'.[19] Others thought he was just getting his own back.

Finally, as MPs trooped out to vote on Labour's motion to adjourn—in effect a confidence vote—Tory loyalists spat that those of their colleagues turning on the government were 'rats'. The rebels called the loyalists 'yes-men'. In an agony of indecision, Quintin Hogg finally let gut override brain, and raced to squeeze into the dissidents' lobby, the last MP through the door before it was locked. Two hundred and eighty-one MPs had backed the government, 200 had voted to censure it—including what Foot called 'the for-ever-to-be-honoured handful of Tory rebels'.[20] It was a Pyrrhic victory; Chamberlain's credibility was gone. Foot would cherish the memory of the shouts of 'Resign!'

* * *

Two days later, the Germans invaded Belgium and Holland; some expected an attack on Britain at any time. Hogg had caught the train back to his unit in Lincolnshire, miserable and stuck in a carriage with a fellow MP who kept telling him he would regret how he had voted for the rest of his life. But at five o'clock that afternoon, Attlee called 10 Downing Street to say that Labour was willing to join a coalition under a new Prime Minister. Within an hour, Chamberlain had gone.

And so Winston Churchill entered Number 10. Many Conservative MPs did not trust this half-American serial rebel who had spent two decades as a Liberal, and they did not take kindly to him bringing socialists into government. The left, meanwhile, had loathed him for decades. He had supposedly sent troops to crush striking Welsh miners, and the infant Soviet Union. He had been the chancellor who had forced the pound back on to the gold standard in 1925, then treated the General Strike like a schoolboy war game. He had backed Mussolini and Franco as they killed socialists and trade unionists.[21] Yet here he was, leading a government alongside Stafford Cripps' old ally Clement Attlee, and it was Attlee, as much as anyone, who had put him there.

As Churchill began his ascent to greatness, Cripps' old apprentice Michael Foot was delighted. This was the moment, he would later claim, 'when the British people much more surely than their leaders (on Churchill's own testimony) decided to expiate all the crimes and follies of those who had fed the fascist monster.' The source of Churchill's strength, Foot wrote later, was that he grasped this.[22] In the face of the fascist monster, a militaristic, bloody-minded old Tory who relished the idea of commanding a big state was just what was needed.

Less than nine years after its near-destruction, Labour was back in office, with policies—even if they could not yet introduce them—markedly more radical than MacDonald's. Those men who had lost their seats in 1931, like Hugh Dalton and Herbert Morrison, were now near the heart of power.[23] Labour now held sixteen government posts; the Conservatives kept fifty-two, but they were not entirely the same Conservatives. Some of the most senior Chamberlainites were out; Macmillan, Eden and Amery were in.

In the crisis of 1931, the National Government had been founded on a nightmare that evaporated on contact with daylight. Nevertheless, it had remained entrenched in power, protecting what it could of the old orthodoxy. In the crisis of 1940, the dynamics of 1931 were reversed. This time, all the pressure came to bear on the Conservatives; it was Labour that entered government to rescue the situation. Now the confidence that mattered was less that of foreign financiers, more that of the people. The new coalition asked Home Intelligence, a Ministry of Information unit, to monitor the confidence of the public in the war effort, with all the attention usually given to the Stock Exchange.

The Chamberlain government had established new ministries to prosecute the war effort and, from October 1938, had begun to bring in expert non-party ministers from the civil service, the Navy and business. For all that, and despite the interwar governments' interventionist moves, it was Churchill's war administration, filling up with young technocrats, that would bring Britain far closer to the long-imagined reign of the planners. Shortly after leading Labour into the new coalition, Attlee, now a key member of the War Cabinet, went on the radio and announced:

> Today on your behalf Parliament has given to the government full power to control persons and property. There is no distinction between rich and poor, between worker and employer, between man and woman. The services and property of all must be at the disposal of the government for the common task.[24]

Two of the new ministries that symbolised the state's deep incursion on freedom—of speech, of the market—were also physically imposing. The Ministry of Information was based in the University of London's Senate House; the Ministry of Supply was in Shell Mex House on the Strand. These likely inspired the huge white concrete pyramids that house the totalitarian Ministries of Truth and Plenty in George Orwell's *Nineteen Eighty-Four*, which drew heavily on life in wartime London.

Within days of taking office, Churchill did something that, without the war, would have been unthinkable. The war effort needed the goodwill of the trade unions, which the Chamberlain government had struggled to win, given memories of promises broken after the last world war. On 13 May, Churchill brought the union boss Ernest Bevin into the Cabinet, as Minister of Labour. A Joint Consultative Committee was set up, bringing together the TUC and the British Employers' Federation, along with 6,000 Joint Production Committees. All this fulfilled Leo Amery's wish to see the unions in government; it suggested the kind of corporate state cabal of business, unions and technocrats that Stafford Cripps and

William Mellor had once damned as fascism. But who cared about that now? The Ministry of Information snoops reported that, among Londoners, 'All are glad Bevin is in the Government'.[25] JB Priestley, sitting in the Commons gallery, saw Churchill and Bevin squeezed in next to each other on the front bench, and thought they represented the two halves of England.

A few months earlier, Bevin had written that 'The working classes are faced with two offensives, one by Hitler which we must defeat, and one by the bankers which, if the Government does not stop, will lead to the defeat of our nation.'[26] Now, in his first speech in office, he affirmed that

> the War Cabinet will not allow vested interests, profits or anything else, to stand in the way of maximum production. If this is the policy of the Government, I will ask my people to work like hell to save the lives of our lads ... There must be in the workshops, among shop stewards and others a feeling that they are part of the Government. Then they will stick it through to the end.[27]

Power was shifting. Of the significance of his new job, Bevin liked to observe: 'They say Gladstone was at the Treasury from 1860 to 1930. I'm going to be Minister of Labour from 1940 to 1990.'[28]

* * *

Chamberlain and several of his allies were still serving at the most senior levels of government. On the afternoon of Friday 31 May, terrible news was reaching Fleet Street, for which these men seemed to be to blame. In the *Evening Standard*'s building on Shoe Lane, Michael Foot and his editor, Frank Owen, put the paper to bed and went up onto the roof with Peter Howard, a columnist for the *Sunday Express*. It was a place to remind themselves, Foot remembered, of 'what might happen to our city and our country.'[29] Over to the east was St Paul's Cathedral, where air raid preparations were in hand in the heart of the City; below, the capital stretched out for miles around them, full of millions of people, waiting for the bombers. The three journalists were trying to take in the news from the south coast, with which Foot and Owen had just filled their paper: of British troops returning, newly rescued, from across the

Channel. In the news stories, they played up the soldiers' bravery, but the leader column suggested the darker side of the story: that British forces had been let down by years of government miscalculation and outdated thinking.[30] Soldiers reported having fought the Battle of France with too few anti-tank guns and inadequate equipment, and after retreating to the sea, the desperate, days-long wait for rescue from the beaches of Dunkirk under Nazi bombardment, with no sign of air cover from the RAF.

There were already demands in the press, public and Parliament that the Chamberlainites resign. The three journalists on the roof resolved to force them out, by detailing the charges against them. Only then, Foot considered, could the Churchill government truly represent the new mood among ordinary people: that things could be done in a radically different way. He and his colleagues could not wage this campaign through their newspapers, not least because their boss, Lord Beaverbrook, had been an arch-appeaser, and was now Minister of Aircraft Production. Instead, they decided to hammer out a book, which they would publish anonymously. They got it done in four days: at Peter Howard's country home, in the Café Royal, at the Two Brewers pub, and up on the roof of the *Standard*. In great secrecy, the left-wing publisher Victor Gollancz rushed it into print. Foot picked the title: *Guilty Men*. On 22 June, France fell to the Nazis.

When the book came out on 5 July, under the pseudonym 'Cato', *Guilty Men* caused uproar. WH Smiths, Wymans, Simpkin Marshall and Boots Libraries refused to handle it. Regardless, it sold out twelve impressions in its first four weeks. By November, it had been reprinted 26 times. Sales reached 217, 432—a remarkable figure for a political tract, even in the book-hungry 1940s.

Guilty Men begins with Foot's ferocious account of the contest of British flesh against German steel on the beaches of Dunkirk, culminating in quotations from newly returned soldiers. One says: 'We never had a fair chance, but our time will come.' Much of the book attacks the ministers of the late Chamberlain administration for failing to re-arm sufficiently—to plan and spend. And it casts this as the disastrous climax of a decade of failure that left soldiers ill-equipped while a million men still languished on the dole, denied a fair chance by the National Government's timidity, complacency and indecision.

The authors take their search for the origins of the calamity back to the general election campaign of 1929. This is cast as a battle between boldness and lethargy. The hero is David Lloyd George. Ranged against him are Stanley Baldwin, campaigning on the slogan 'Safety First', and Ramsay MacDonald, making hollow promises to the unemployed. We learn that they met during the campaign and agreed that Lloyd George must be kept out of office, or he might instigate 'an energetic and grandiose programme of public works to "conquer unemployment".' Labour won that election, and two years later the National Government was formed.

Likewise, the failure to re-arm properly is blamed in part on the fact that the chancellor, Sir John Simon, was an adherent of Treasury orthodoxy on tight spending controls, with his views 'reinforced by the Banks, representing Big Business'. These people did not want a total warfare state, but rather wanted 'to manufacture pins and bicycles and films and vacuum cleaners so that we can make profits, contribute to taxation and pay for the war'. While Germany forced its population 'by lash and boot' into an all-out drive to re-arm, the British employment minister was fussing about the weather. With almost a million still unemployed in May 1940, 'citizens, disenfranchised in the most heartbreaking way', could 'contribute nothing to the nation' and were 'compelled to be a burden on it'.[31]

Guilty Men is in many respects wildly unfair. Historians have been disputing its claims about re-armament ever since. The book makes a strong case on the lack of equipment, and represents fairly the widespread complaint among soldiers about the lack of air cover at Dunkirk. But that was partly because planes had to be preserved to protect the home islands. 'Cato' does not engage with the choice of nightmares ministers had had to confront. The book makes a hero of Churchill, who some historians doubt could have done things all that differently, other than prioritising bombers, which would not have helped in the Battle of Britain. It also lets him off the hook for his part in the gold standard, among much else, and whitewashes the record of the Labour Party, particularly that of its anti-militarist left-wingers—like Michael Foot.

All this only matters, however, if *Guilty Men* is considered as a work of history. Much as Foot always stood by it, it was hardly a scholarly weighing of the evidence. It was a political bomb. Its impact was not in driving the Guilty Men from office—in Chamberlain's case, cancer intervened—but in exploding the whole basis on which they had governed. It used Dunkirk to entrench the narrative that the 1930s was a time of government failure and timidity, constrained by financial austerity, which had brought the country to the brink of disaster, with ordinary people paying the price.

Chamberlain and his colleagues had few grounds to complain. In 1931, the Conservative-dominated National Government had been quite happy to blame Labour for unemployment racing upward on their watch, after Labour was luckless enough to be in office as a global financial crisis struck. Now the same effect was at work, in reverse. However dubious Labour's record on re-armament, it was the National Government that had been in power, and had to take the blame. Baldwin and Chamberlain had had good cause to re-arm only as far as their fears of bankruptcy and a total state permitted; but now that those nightmares looked obsolete, their decisions read as fatal errors. *Guilty Men* ends with a demand, in strident capitals, for total war, and an appeal to win the confidence of the people by getting rid of the men who had let the walls fall into ruin.

In the wake of this barrage, a whole battery of such publications was trained on the old gang. The populist left widened its target— from the appeasers in Parliament to their cronies in the City, and allied 'vested interests'. In the shadow of Dunkirk, a full-scale onslaught began, to smash what remained of the old consensus, left hopelessly unprotected by its crumbling, irrelevant taboos.

* * *

Four weeks after *Guilty Men* came out, the London correspondent of the *Birmingham Daily Gazette* awoke from a 'terrifying nightmare'. The cause, he told his readers, was a new novel, which he had settled down to read at midnight, and finished in a breathless ninety minutes. *Loss of Eden* was another short, angry, rapidly produced book, co-written by progressive journalists and hurried into print to warn against the treachery of the establishment. In the wake of Dunkirk and the French surrender, the rising threat of defeat and humiliation had sharpened into fears of imminent Nazi occupation, through either invasion or capitulation. (In May, there were still MPs who wanted a peace settlement; Churchill feared that Lloyd George might take up this cause. Even inside the War Cabinet, Halifax insisted the idea be kept in play.) Naturally enough, the prospect of Nazis on British soil began spawning vivid scenarios.

In *Loss of Eden*, later re-titled *If Hitler Comes*, Christopher Serpell and Douglas Brown imagine the British losing enthusiasm for the war, and sinking back into the mentality of the 1930s. A new government makes peace with Hitler and signs first a trade deal, then a military alliance, with Berlin. Before long, German officials in London are insidiously gathering influence, until, step by step, Britain, frozen in 'moral paralysis', becomes a Nazi slave colony under the totalitarian rule of Joachim von Ribbentrop, the former Nazi ambassador to London. The novel depicts a Britain sinking into a 'nightmare world' of 'horror and humiliation', made all the more vivid by incorporating real public figures. While the Nazi traitor William Joyce, 'Lord Haw-Haw', starts work at Broadcasting House, Churchill and Eden are subjected to a show trial in Westminster Hall, then consigned to the Godalming concentration camp.

The reviewers found this 'cautionary tale' a 'terrifying picture', 'uncannily vivid' and 'relentless in its logic'.[32] Serpell and Brown dedicated their book, in *Guilty Men*–style capitals, to 'THOSE WHO WILL NOT LET THIS HAPPEN'. It sold well enough to be reissued three times in nine months.

Aside from the fact that the novel appeared while its vision was a live fear, the most striking thing about it is its target. Alongside the politicians who sell out their country, Serpell and Brown point the finger at business, and particularly at the City, which welcomes the return of anti-war feeling, and the flow of profits, dividends and tax cuts it promises. Representatives of the Stock Exchange happily trot down a swastika-bedecked Strand to a party at the huge new German embassy in Bush House. But soon the City is 'a minor Nazi counting-house', profit is abolished, the pound is no longer legal tender, and the middle classes are scratching a miserable existence in the fields.

The other constant fear in the summer of 1940, Nazi invasion, prompted similar accusations against high finance. One of those determined not to let a successful Nazi occupation happen was an

THE DEATH OF CONSENSUS

ex-communist called Tom Wintringham, who had been an officer in the International Brigades in the Spanish Civil War. In photo spreads for *Picture Post*, in columns in the *Daily Mirror*—for which he was Military Correspondent—and in bestselling Penguin Specials rattled out in weeks, Wintringham went all out to proselytise the guerrilla techniques he had developed in Spain.

Like 'Cato', like Serpell and Brown, Wintringham took aim at Guilty Men. In August, his Penguin Special *New Ways of War* came out, with illustrations explaining how to fire a rifle, build cover, deploy crossfire, dig anti-tank trenches and make a sponge bag into a grenade. Within months, it had sold 75,000 copies. Wintringham finished the book with a blast against capitalism and the vested interests hampering the people's war against fascism. The million left unemployed 'have been made less fit for work and less fit for fighting than they would have been'. Their children, 'many of whom are now of military age, have had too much to worry about and too little to eat.' Capitalism was too inefficient to distribute work: some miners were unemployed, others over-worked. Re-armament had fallen short because Chamberlain was too close to industrial interests who wanted to make money. Men and materials that could have been producing fortifications were tied up building cinemas and office furniture. Anti-tank grenades, spat Wintringham, his mind fixed on imminent invasion, were not 'profitable'.[33]

* * *

The *Mirror*'s star columnist William Connor, who wrote as 'Cassandra', likewise bombarded the 'vested interests' that risked thwarting the war effort. His 1941 book, *The English at War*, blasted the City for wanting to return to the world before the war, and lambasted industrialists still focused on profits, pointing out that 180 Conservative MPs between them held more than 700 company directorships. 'Do we fight,' he demanded to know, 'to secure the wealth and prosperity of the nation in the hands of a few bankers who control credit for their own ends?'[34]

In the 1930s, Labour had looked like they were concerned largely with the pains of heavy industry's sad decline, while the National Government championed the new. The demands of war-time planning upended all that. Now modernity meant the smart young men like Harold Wilson flooding into Whitehall, planning for victory with pencil-sharp efficiency, or innovative young journalists like Michael Foot. The push to cast an entrenched elite as old-fashioned is a good weapon for breaking an old consensus, regardless of the competing ideologies involved—like the push to define that elite as traitorous.

Cassandra's *The English at War* was one of a series called Searchlight Books, set up by George Orwell. Orwell's own contribution to the Searchlight project was *The Lion and the Unicorn: Socialism and the English Genius*, much admired by Foot. Just before the war began, Orwell had followed many of his fellow leftists in abandoning the nightmare that a militarised Britain would become fascistic in the face of the threat of Nazi attack. Now, Orwell saw the war effort as a spur to scrap 'the rule of the old'. Revolutionary socialism and English patriotism could and must come together to break the old concentration of power, win the war, and transform the nation:

> The bankers and the larger businessmen, the landowners and dividend-drawers, the officials with their prehensile bottoms, will obstruct for all they are worth. Even the middle classes will writhe when their accustomed way of life is menaced. But just because the English sense of national unity has never disintegrated, because patriotism is finally stronger than class-hatred, the chances are that the will of the majority will prevail.
>
> . . .
>
> The swing of opinion is visibly happening, but it cannot be counted on to happen fast enough of its own accord.[35]

The left would keep battering away at this message right through the war. Foot himself—named Editor of the *Evening Standard* in 1942, at just 29—would return to the attack under a new pseudonym. In 1943, *The Trial of Mussolini* by 'Cassius' was published by Victor Gollancz, in the same Victory Books series as *Guilty Men*. As the cover of one impression proudly announced, 'The first 4 editions—total 100,000 copies'. The book is a mock transcript of the Italian dictator's trial for war crimes, but largely consists of the testimony of various British Conservatives—living and dead, Churchill included—who are summoned to court to repeat their inter-war paeans to Italian fascism. Foot has an Italian victim of the Mussolini regime warn British socialists that 'The blunder of the Left was that they did not drive home their advantage when they had it.'[36] The row triggered by the book would cost Foot his job. Unabashed, he would later produce yet another short polemic, defending these books as having been written 'to force on the public memory a recollection of the most shameful period of our history and to prevent from returning to power the people who brought it about.'[37]

A crucial part of this populist onslaught on power was what the historian David Edgerton calls a '*critical* left nationalism'.[38] At the time of the 1931 crisis, the interests of finance were held to be identical with the interests of the nation, on the principle that the national currency had to be protected from too much spending on the unemployed. The Bank of 'England' was central to this. It led to the formation of the 'National' Government. No matter that the confidence of foreign investors was also a key part of this. These books of the early 1940s took back the flag, redefining the nation as the mass of ordinary people, condemning the elite as anti-patriotic. The appeasers and their allies in the City were now enemies of the people; the enemy within. At times, the onslaught against the old gang came close to conspiracy theory. Foot, Serpell and Brown, Orwell, Wintringham and Cassandra were a revolutionary vanguard, seizing the moment to break the hold of old ideas, and the concentration of power protected by those ideas. Only then could a new consensus start to take shape.

* * *

Taboos against borrowing, taxing and spending had cast mass unemployment as a sad business that couldn't be helped. With the old nightmares of bankruptcy and total states destroyed by the pressures of war, and their guardians discredited, that other nightmare that had languished in the backs of politicians' minds now came to the fore— helped by that striking analogy we explored in Chapter 3.

In *English Journey*, published in 1934, JB Priestley had visited County Durham, where he had glimpsed a miserable workers' shanty-town: 'a nightmare place ... all sprawling in the muck outside some gigantic works'. Amid the rusting cranes of Tyneside, he had seen men with no work at all, hanging about the streets— 'hundreds and thousands of them' in Jarrow, and in Hebburn 'skilled men ... waiting for Doomsday'. In Stockton-on-Tees, as in North Shields, they stood around 'in caps and mufflers' against the cold, shuffling up from the Labour Exchange. In 1940, these images had returned. Now they could no longer be dismissed as sad but unavoidable.

Beyond the shift in hard economic logic, there seems to have been something more psychological at work here, too. During the slump, unemployment had got so bad that people were comparing it to a war long before Hitler ever crossed a border. In 1933, Priestley had insistently described the impact of the Depression this way, writing first in Lancashire and then Durham, that 'there is a war on'; that in East Durham 'the allied enemies are poverty, idleness, ignorance, hopelessness and misery'; that men in Jarrow 'wore the drawn masks of prisoners of war'.[39] Some who wanted action against unemployment cast it as an enemy on the attack. In 1936, the Conservative MP Viscount Wolmer had argued that if the devastation of the Distressed Areas were seen as the impact of an 'economic air raid', then, perhaps, the government would help.[40]

The advent of an actual war brought all that to fruition. This constant entwining of war and unemployment seems to have provided an intuitive logic to the idea that, once the Nazi nightmare had been destroyed, the old unemployment nightmare must be dispelled too. In April 1940, Priestley recorded a *New English Journey* for the BBC, which ended with his insistence that, after the war, 'the heartbreak of long unemployment must vanish, as Hitler and his crooked cross must vanish, like an evil dream.'[41] Alongside this lurked the knowledge that it was mass unemployment in Germany that had given Hitler his chance. In his hugely popular 'Postscripts to the News' on BBC Radio, Priestley talked of the Nazis as 'these evil apparitions from the night of men's bewilderment and despair'.

The Ministry of Information itself made these images part of its propaganda repertoire. In its 1941 short film *The Dawn Guard*, a young Home Guard volunteer tells his older comrade that there were no unemployed at Dunkirk, adding that 'There mustn't be no more chaps hanging around for work that don't come ...We can't go back to the old ways of living…'[42] In another Ministry of Information short, *Wales: Green Mountain, Black Mountain*, the poet Dylan Thomas brought together some of the standard images, over footage that rhymed with his exhortation:

> Remember the procession of the old young men
> It shall never happen again.

Back when unemployment was a live issue, the stage version of *Love on the Dole* had failed—despite all those ticket sales—to make a decisive political impact. But now Walter Greenwood's story was revived. After years of resistance to its supposedly radicalising content, a feature film version was finally greenlit in early 1940, backed by the Ministry of Information. Its tale of despair was re-cast: Sally's nihilistic self-prostitution becomes saintly self-sacrifice; the film ends with her mother, dewy-eyed, telling the camera that 'people'll begin to see what's been happening, and once they do there'll not be no Hanky Park no more'. There is even a postscript from a Labour minister, AV Alexander, vowing that 'Never again must the unemployed become the forgotten men of the peace'. Commercially, the film flopped. In the small Lincolnshire town of Grantham, a teenage grocer's daughter called Margaret Roberts did not much take to it, despite having seen dole queues, and having unemployed American relatives. But the movie was a critical success.

These images had all been ready and waiting. What had changed was that the nightmares that had held them at bay in the 1930s were in retreat. If the apparent solutions to unemployment were no longer intolerable, there was no barrier to facing the problem. In 1944, George Orwell considered that, to most of the nation, of all political issues, economic security was 'by far the most important, unemployment being an even greater nightmare than war.'[43] But if there was to be no going back to the nightmare, what was to be done?

* * *

Destruction was creating possibilities. Councillor Barbara Betts began to see the Blitz's political potential. At first, lonely in her little flat in Coram Street, her imagination churned up by the traumatic memories of Spanish refugees staying with her parents, she had dreaded a Guernica in St Pancras. Before the Blitz began, she thought she would not be able to stand it. She threw herself into her duties as a voluntary air raid warden, cocking her tin helmet and playing her part in the battle with blazing gas mains, flooding basements, drenched electrical cables.

Barbara was one of many people whose precarious finances came under severe pressure amid the onslaught of danger and restriction. The magazine she wrote for was close to folding as advertising dried up. She tried to write a book about the Blitz, but it was impossible to concentrate. However, fragments of what she wrote about it survive in her papers. Among the references to trapped casualties and 'Jerry' dropping 'eggs', she was clearly thinking through how the crisis forced Londoners into collectivist solidarity. Betts was well aware that she and her fellow wardens depended on others. She suggested that this was 'a great opportunity for proving to the better-off ratepayer that social services are nt [sic] just a sop thrown to the poor'. She vowed that 'We have got to learn to live communally this winter. We shall sleep together, eat together, possibly be entertained together.' In time, she hoped, 'old mistakes' would give way 'to great social advance'.[44] Three years later, she would remember the promise of 1940 that 'property was to be no more sacred than persons', and that 'We were all to become "equal before the War."'[45]

Amid all the mud, blood and misery—and theft too—the Blitz was blasting away the old, exposing inequality, and forcing some solidarity in the ruins. Barbara was unimpressed by the government's provision of shelters. She had seen people taking refuge in the Tube, and spent one night in an Anderson shelter, stuck under a thin metal sheet, listening to a bomb 'come with a rushing sound from a dreadful height' and land horribly near.[46] She wrote sardonically about the need for shelter facilities to be provided 'presumably without means test'.[47]

She saw much less of Michael Foot, but he too was hammering away at the idea that the Blitz had torn the façade off British society, exposing the depths of inequality behind. In his leader column on 13 September 1940, he was almost overcome by the fortitude of an East End mother sitting in the street by 'the pile of ruin that was once her own home'. He insisted that the community must immediately provide deep shelters with proper amenities, and homes for heroes like this woman. Local authorities 'must be given all possible aid' to help alleviate the devastation of their local population, especially as it had hit the poor hardest.[48] For a piece published on Christmas Eve 1940, he visited a London school and found that most of the pupils had only just returned, after months of absence. The government, he wrote, should declare a charter of the Rights of Children, and protect their health and education, to ensure that freedom of thought survived.

For the first time in their political lives, Betts and Foot were not swimming against the tide. The demands of war had sent the Budget through the roof, and that money was being spent by a protective, interventionist state, wielding centralised, near-dictatorial power. And plans were afoot to use this state to build a different country when the war was over. At the end of a week that began with the fire-bombing of the City, *Picture Post* turned over the whole of its first issue of 1941 to 'A Plan for Britain'. This was a response to the way that, as Betts found in the Blitz, 'we have been forced into a knowledge of our dependence on each other.' There was a plan for social security, a plan for the land, for health, for retirement; a plan for town planning, for education and for full employment. Thomas Balogh, one of Harold Wilson's Oxford colleagues, contributed a plan for 'The First Necessity in the New Britain—Work For All', which would involve taking control of the labour supply and the banks. Underpinning all this were the familiar images of the nightmare to which Britain must never return.

This radicalism was presented with reassuring notes of patriotism and tradition. Priestley had set the tone, and it was there in Orwell too. This was the other side of the process to the onslaught of Foot and his friends. Baldwin was a Guilty Man, but once the lineaments of a new consensus, leaning decisively to the left, started to emerge, rather Baldwinesque imagery of unity and gentle English landscapes was revived to help sell it to the nation.

But how could 'Work for All' actually be achieved? To overcome the fear that peace-time 'planning' would mean a total state—or simply would not work—would require something more official, detailed and convincing. Away from the media's image-making, this was beginning to come together.

5

NEVER AGAIN

1942–5

In July 1940, as the old guard was coming under fire from *Guilty Men*, Harold Wilson was transferred to the Economic Section of the War Cabinet Secretariat. Here, economists and statisticians assembled progress reports and statistical digests for ministerial committees. All this was of a piece with the 'expansion of expert departments, and of the number of specialists', which, David Edgerton argues, 'went hand in hand with Treasury loss of power'.[1] If Foot was in the ostentatious vanguard, smashing the old consensus, Wilson had joined the quieter cadres who were planning its replacement.

The Section was headed by Professor John Jewkes, the son of a sheet-metal worker from Barrow, who had been drafted into the Cabinet Office from the University of Manchester. Among the other recruits were James Meade, a 33-year-old Oxford don, friend of Labour and disciple of Keynes; and Professor Lionel Robbins of the LSE. Robbins had been a prominent free-marketeer, but even he was now embracing Keynes' ideas. Later, he would cast this period in heroic terms: 'After the nightmare frustration of the Chamberlain period, the actual outbreak of war came as something of a relief.'[2] For some of Wilson's new colleagues, the 'nightmare frustration of the Chamberlain period' included the drawn-out agony of unemployment. Meade in particular considered it a social evil. Wilson's biographer Ben Pimlott calls the Economic Section a 'Keynesian fifth column', spreading heretical ideas through the ministerial committee system.[3]

Keynes himself had been drafted into the Treasury. With the help of Meade and others from the Economic Section, his influence was soon visible, in the April 1941 Budget. The demands of what one MP called 'totalitarian war' included ballooning debt, and state control of food, prices, wages and industry.[4] The chancellor Sir Kingsley Wood's speech marked the transformation of the whole point of a Budget, along lines that would long outlast the war-time state: it was now to be the primary mechanism for managing the economy. Meade, Robbins and Jewkes, meanwhile, would figure out how Keynes' ideas could be used to underwrite full employment.

* * *

Deficit spending was no longer taboo; nor was a planned, interventionist state. By the time of the 1941 Budget, Harold Wilson had left the Economic Section behind, and been drawn back to work for the champion of the planners: the insufferably demanding Sir William Beveridge. His old boss had not changed. Wilson was 'shocked sometimes to see men of great reputation treated by him like stupid office boys'.[5] But this intolerable man was on his way to changing how British politics thought.

First, though, Beveridge had had to change his own thinking. In the face of the Depression, this former planner in the Lloyd George warfare state had careened across the political spectrum to become a champion of the free market, backing Philip Snowden's 1931 cuts to the dole and, as head of the LSE, bringing the liberal economist Friedrich Hayek to Britain. Then, as his biographer Jose Harris has written, Beveridge 'began to wonder whether a short sharp conversion to a totally planned economy might not be preferable to the long drawn out agony of capitalism in decline.' He thought British governments were too scared of damaging private enterprise to tackle the Depression effectively. He even admired the way the Soviet planning system had eliminated unemployment, though not how it eliminated dissidents. Like so many others in the 1930s, he found that all roads led to nightmares: 'I see the dangers and difficulties alike of complete socialism and complete laissez-faire,' he wrote despairingly to a friend in 1933, 'and at the same time I am not sure that there is any practicable half-way house between the two.'[6]

Now, the threat of Nazi attack shocked Beveridge out of his frantic ideological paralysis, and turned him right back into a planner. The British public's response to the demands of the war-time state had soothed his 1930s fears, convincing him that planning could work without destroying freedom. He had reached the conclusion that ordinary people had to be offered a better future to come after the war.[7] When he won a post in Bevin's Ministry of Labour, he made a thorough nuisance of himself, and pushed for a total system of planning. He wanted new factories to be located in areas with ongoing unemployment, a wages policy, and greater deployment of emergency powers. In the end, Bevin gave him the boot. Beveridge was side-lined, set to work on harmlessly obscure studies, including one on social insurance.

Or so Bevin thought. Beveridge would soon turn his report into one of the founding documents of the post-war British state. Beveridge invited Harold Wilson to work with him, but his former protégé had already found another job, at the Mines Department. Wilson thus missed the chance to claim a role in the creation of the Beveridge Report: a document that would help to shape the settlement within which he would spend his political career. Nonetheless, Wilson had already acquired a vital understanding of Beveridge and his thinking, which would frame his approach right through to the 1970s.

Once complete, Beveridge's plan became the symbol of a mythic struggle between a bright new future and the dystopia of the past. As Harris notes, many of those who had given testimony to Beveridge's inquiry were expecting 'utopian change'.[8] From July 1942 onwards, he had cast the aim of his proposals in eye-catchingly nightmarish terms, turning the imagery of the Depression into a puritan-style allegory: the need to overcome 'five giants on the road to post-war reconstruction': Want, Disease, Ignorance, Squalor and Idleness. Beveridge now had a clear sense of which road he wanted to take, and that the obstacles in his way could be overcome. His apocalypticism helped to break old rules and force through a new settlement. It became a kind of national asset.

* * *

If one image embodied the waste of unemployment, it was men standing in the street, waiting. On the evening of 1 December 1942, a queue began to form outside York House at 23 Kingsway in central London, home to Her Majesty's Stationery Office. All those people huddled against a London winter's night under the bare branches of the plane trees were waiting to buy a two-shilling copy of Beveridge's report—and with it, the promise that malnutrition and the means test would not be coming back. The story goes that at one point the queue was a mile long.

That morning, the Labour minister Arthur Greenwood, who had commissioned the report, had opened a Commons debate on post-war reconstruction by claiming that 'There are two words graven on the hearts of the overwhelming mass of men and women: "Never again."'[9] Next morning, within hours, 60,000 copies were sold. A fortnight later, the British Institute of Public Opinion reported 'that 95% of the public had heard of the Report, with 88% in favour'.[10] Including a shortened version, priced 3d, sales of this dense social policy document soon reached 635,000.

The report is famous for setting out a plausible plan for a 'cradle to grave' welfare state for all: 'the generalisation through the State', as Beveridge put it, 'of what has been begun by voluntary agencies.'[11] What is less well-remembered is that Beveridge's shift towards a more dominant state was not just about welfare per se. It was underpinned by a more radical reversal of 1930s orthodoxy. Amid its pages of celebratory coverage on the day the report was finally published, the *Mirror* warned its readers that:

> Mass unemployment could defeat the whole scheme. Sir William therefore asserts the need for the state to concern itself with maintaining the demand for labour and to 'ensure for all not indeed absolute continuity of work but a reasonable chance of productive employment.'[12]

Beveridge made clear that his plan rested on three assumptions. The first two were family allowances, and comprehensive medical provision. The third, 'Assumption C', was that there would be 'full' employment.[13] According to Jose Harris, Beveridge allowed for post-war unemployment averaging 8.5 per cent, but his Assumption C effectively defined full employment as 3 per cent of working people being out of a job at any one time. Apart from the human cost, running his system amid 1930s levels of unemployment would be far too expensive. His social security plan, he thought, would only work as part of a much more fundamental approach to planning how Britain worked. It was the cherry, not the cake.

Once the report had been published, the ministerial Committee on Reconstruction Priorities had to work out how producing full employment could be paid for. They asked Wilson's old colleagues in the Economic Section to help. James Meade had already done preliminary work on this, along Keynesian demand management lines. Keynes himself, who had greeted Beveridge's plans with 'wild enthusiasm', made himself Beveridge's advocate inside the Treasury.[14] While the plans suggested by Beveridge and by the Keynesians were by no means the same, they shared the essential goal of maintaining full employment. But to be realised, Beveridge's proposals would need support from both main parties, inside as well as outside the coalition government. The question was whether they could overcome the rear-guard resistance already being put up by those who still cleaved to old orthodox thinking.

* * *

Captain Quintin Hogg MP had been away. Ten days after the publication of the Beveridge Report, he landed at RAF Lyneham late at night, and headed home to his quiet, lightless square off Victoria Street, hoping to give his wife Natalie a nice surprise. Having voted for war, Hogg had wanted to be on the front line. When he was finally posted to Egypt, he had tried to take on three Messerschmidts with a jammed Bren gun, and had been shot in the knee. He was given a staff job behind the lines, but after he caught hepatitis on a walking tour of Lebanon, he was declared no longer fit to fight. He had not entirely recovered when he arrived home to find that a Free French officer was living with Natalie, and had been for over a year.

His life, he wrote later, was 'in ruins'.[15] But while travelling among Lebanon's ancient stones, then while stuck in hospital, Hogg had had time to think about the world after the war, and had begun to re-examine his own ideological foundations. Like Edward Heath, he was drawn to Harold Macmillan's ideas on public ownership in

The Middle Way. He had had little room to say so in the Oxford by-election, but in the early 1930s he had served as a 'poor man's lawyer', dispensing free fortnightly advice in Deptford to people who could not afford their rent. His time away in the army had intensified his views. As he prepared to fly home, he had written that the 'basic cause of our feeling of social insecurity before the War was the problem of unemployment'.[16]

He had heard that the Beveridge Report was to be debated in the spring, and had come back determined to speak up about the near-universal support for it that he had found in the armed forces. The report was 'a flag to nail to the mast' and 'an opportunity to re-establish a social conscience in the Tory Party.'[17] He threw himself into the drive to rebuild the country.[18]

Over the next few months, Hogg worked out his thinking in a stream of speeches and articles. He explicitly rejected the economic faith of the pre-war years, of which his father had been an apostle. He rejected 'the orthodox view of the place of finance in national policy', and wrote: 'We have to admit the old economics was plain wrong. A new economics based on social advantage has to be developed to take its place.' As radical, communitarian young Tories tend to, he invoked Benjamin Disraeli, cleverly arguing that Gladstone's laissez-faire economics had been an 'abandonment of the true Conservative and Tory doctrines of finance'. He blamed the inter-war faith in narrow-minded free-market doctrines for 'our failure in the matter of armaments and of social reform alike'[19]— just like Michael Foot in *Guilty Men.*

Towards the end of January 1943, this old Etonian heir to a peerage put the case, in *The Spectator*, that it was time to scrap privilege based on birth and wealth in favour of a meritocratic 'classless democracy'. He likened his party's fear of radical social change to its historical hostility to the coming of the railways, dismissing the idea that trade unionism had anything to do with Bolshevism, and telling his more timid colleagues that nationalisation had 'lost its terrors'.[20] Social security, he preached, would not destroy recovery and enterprise: it would underpin it.

Hogg had an apocalyptic turn of mind, keenly attuned to his 'revolutionary times'.[21] He was sure that a new generation, possessed of fresh insights, who knew what the emerging Britain needed, was poised to sweep away the old.[22] He soon fell in with a group of around forty younger Conservative MPs, most of whom had served in the armed forces, who were meeting frequently over dinner to plot a progressive turn: the Tory Reform Committee. The crunch debate on Beveridge was due to start on 16 February. As it approached, with no guarantee the report would win Commons backing, they resolved to make their objections felt. They tabled an amendment, calling, as Beveridge recommended, for the creation of a new Ministry of Social Security. In the 1930s, Churchill and his followers had pushed for a supply ministry to take control of the warfare state. Now this fresh group of Tory dissidents pushed for a new ministry to take control of the welfare state.

* * *

The debate on Beveridge's plan was all set to pit old nightmares against new ones. On one side were those still animated by the fears that had dominated the 1930s: government bankruptcy, and the total state. Against the threat of Nazism, these nightmares had been put aside as lesser evils; but to let go of them permanently in peace-time was another matter. At one point, Beveridge's critics had seized on his use of an ominous phrase, 'halfway to Moscow', to describe his plan. In the run-up to the debate, a Conservative committee told party leaders that Beveridge's proposals could 'only be achieved at the expense of personal freedom and by sacrificing the right of an individual to choose what life he wishes to lead and what occupation he should follow.'[23] This committee could claim to represent close to 90 per cent of Conservative MPs.

These naysayers were up against those articulating a newer fear: that the Beveridge plan would be blocked by 'vested interests', and the population left to the mercies of a new post-war slump. The British Institute of Public Opinion reported concerns across most regions about obstruction by 'big business', and particularly the insurance companies, who stood to lose heavily if Beveridge's proposals to replace their schemes with 'national' insurance were made law.

On the first day, the chair of the government's reconstruction priorities committee, John Anderson, acknowledged that eliminating mass unemployment was the 'bedrock' that Beveridge's plans were based on. He promised that, even though the government could not be sure it could achieve that, it would 'strain every nerve' to try.[24] To Opposition MPs, who wanted immediate action, this was not good enough.

Strikingly, Beveridge's opponents did not try the 'halfway to Moscow' line of attack. They leant instead on the argument that a post-war slump would make the plan unaffordable. Kingsley Wood, the chancellor, raised the risk of financial collapse. But Labour's Robert Morrison reported that members of the public were just smiling at that argument, and asking him, 'How much per day is the war costing?'[25] He said people were telling him 'that if we are asked to do all we know to defeat Hitler, the same attitude should be adopted to defeat the spectre of unemployment.'

When Hogg finally had his chance to speak, late on the second day, he was determined to face down his Conservative colleagues' resistance and the ministerial foot-dragging. Anxious as he was, making his first proper speech to the House since 1940, and still strained by the death of his marriage, he resolved 'to take a smack at the Government and to fly again Disraeli's banner of Young England.'[26]

He insisted that the government should place the morality of social security over the economics, and that the 'grim world' awaiting the British economy after the war was actually an argument in favour of sustaining the war-time community spirit and building a system of social security. He took aim at one of the slogans of 1931: 'there can be no equality of sacrifice between those who have plenty to eat and those who have not plenty to eat'. Turning on his colleagues, Hogg told them that 'so long as there remain people who cannot have enough to eat, the possession of private property is a humiliation and not an opportunity.' He exclaimed that, 'if you do not give the people social reform, they are going to give you social revolution.'[27]

Hogg's speech was cheered, said *The Times*, 'with almost embarrassing fervour from the other side'. By his fellow Conservatives, not so much. *The Times* judged it 'the most remarkable speech' of the day's debate, 'forceful and eloquent', and backed Hogg's call for a Ministry of Social Security as making it 'possible to start seriously upon the planning of full employment'.[28] In the largest Commons revolt of the war so far, almost every Labour back-bencher voted for the Opposition motion, determined that the government commit to implementing Beveridge. Hogg and his allies encouraged the rebellion, even if they would not themselves dare to rebel for another year. But the coalition resisted the clamour for 'Beveridge Now' and stuck to its maddening promise to do its best, without a firm commitment.

In its monthly report, the Ministry of Information's Home Intelligence division reported cynicism, disappointment and anger, some of it among middle-class people and Conservatives. Nine regions reported that the debate had 'crystallised people's worst fears of the post-war period'; six that 'vested interests have won again'.[29] Mass Observation investigated this further, probing soldiers' and civilians' 'twin fantasies of peace-dream and nightmare'.[30] Much as Mass Observation had a tendency to let the vicar interview the choir, the answer their researchers received, again and again, was that people expected another slump, and a return to mass unemployment. The report, *The Journey Home*, showed that the roots of this fear reached back to the aftermath of the First World War, when unemployed veterans had been left singing for pennies in the street.

The problem for the politicians was that hostility to bankers and vested interests was not fuelling idealistic support for either Labour or Hogg's Young Tories and their democratic solutions. Mass Observation identified a 'soldier's nightmare': a cynical instinct that there was no hope of better things, that 'The Government won't even give us Beveridge', that things could be improved, but that ordinary people were being 'diddled' by 'them'.[31] There were even fears that, if a post-war slump did bring a fresh wave of unemployment, ex-servicemen might react angrily against democratic politics. The fate of the Beveridge plan in the hands of Churchill's coalition was coming to symbolise whether the old consensus was really dead, and whether there was really any hope of a new one.

* * *

When years of financial angst and strain finally corroded an ulcer in the wall of William Mellor's intestines, his doctor told him he had to choose between resting for six months, and risking an operation. He was finally back at the paper he had once edited, the *Herald*, which at least meant a steady income; as Barbara Betts remembered it, he was scared of unemployment. He chose surgery. She saw him in hospital afterwards, 'weak & bewildered & powerless while his life's energy drained away', and resolved to leave him be until he rallied.[32] At the funeral, Michael Foot and another friend stayed at her sides 'like a protective bodyguard'.[33]

Six months after Mellor died—around the time he might have surfaced from his rest-cure, had he not been so frightened for his job—the Beveridge Report appeared, and Betts threw herself into activism promoting it. Her autobiography implies that this was a way through her grief. Her amorphous musings under the bombs in 1940, about the war producing a more communal society, now became a personal battle for change.

On 21 March 1943, Churchill was cajoled into saying something to soothe public frustration at the debate and the news that the government was declining to make Beveridge's plan law straight away. The Prime Minister considered Beveridge 'an awful wind-bag and a dreamer';[34] but, reluctantly, he broadcast a speech called 'A Four Years' Plan'. It was freighted with warnings about cost, inflation, tax and bureaucratic infringements on freedom, but Churchill, the old scourge of trade unionists and Bolsheviks, spoke the language of public ownership and 'cradle to grave' welfare. Crucially, he echoed Beveridge's Assumption C, saying: 'the best way to insure against unemployment is to have no unemployment'.[35]

But by the summer, the government—its Labour ministers included—was still refusing to commit to implementing the Beveridge plans. This set the stage for another confrontation, during Labour's conference at Westminster Central Hall. After years of pushing, Barbara Betts had been picked as her constituency party's delegate. Labour back-benchers were increasingly frustrated with the way Churchill's national unity coalition was constraining Labour's leaders. From the stage, they worried aloud that their leaders in the War Cabinet would fail to stand up to 'big finance', repeating Ramsay MacDonald's claims that helping the working class was too expensive. But then, to cries of 'Shame!', the acting leader of the TGWU attacked the Labour MPs' vote against the government. He backed the Beveridge plan, but insisted the party must be patient and support their colleagues in the coalition, not undermine them.[36] Betts was already running a campaign to end the union leaders' block vote, and when her turn came to speak, she attacked them from the left. Denouncing the government for offering 'Jam tomorrow', she cried: 'WE WANT JAM TODAY.'[37]

The speech made her name. She kept on campaigning for Beveridge, turning up to speak at endless small meetings of constituency parties, trade unions and co-operative societies, not least across the north of England, heralding Beveridge himself as 'one of the new scientific planners the post-war world needs', and championing his plan as 'another positive step forward out of fear.'[38] She attacked those she saw as trying to stop the building of the new Britain. Alongside 'hard-headed business men', there was a more insidious enemy: the 'brilliant young politicians who want to put Toryism in to more attractive trim.' Namely, the Tory Reform Committee. Quintin Hogg, she said, might want reform for fear of revolution—but only 'revolutionary change' would bring 'real reform'.[39]

Why this hostility towards Hogg and his fellow Tory reformers, given that they and Betts wanted many of the same things? The answer reveals an important paradox about the death and rebirth of a consensus: to reach a new agreement, you have to have a fight. The left's argument—made volubly by Betts' old friend Michael Foot—was that real change demanded a decisive break with the old ways, through a struggle for power. With the war, the old nightmares of bankruptcy and ruin had lost a great deal of ground; but the vested interests who depended on such fears still had to be driven out. And that meant that the *Guilty Men* narrative of the recent past must be entrenched, holding those men forever to blame for what had gone wrong in the 1930s. Only once this had happened could a new settlement be established.

Foot had been hard at work on this since 1940, but now Hogg was threatening his efforts, with his emollient calls for the new Britain to be built by the Churchill-led coalition, sliding smoothly into peace-time on a slick of war-time camaraderie. So Foot went

115

on the attack. In the *Evening Standard*, he declared that building the new Britain after the war was not going to be achieved 'by the men who were quite satisfied with *their* society of 1939'. It would require 'the same awakened spirit of 1940' and 'the same over-riding authority over property which Mr Attlee sought'. Channelling Cromwell, he avowed that 'Property ... will not abdicate its throne; it must be beheaded.'[40]

For Hogg, this was all a bit much, coming from a man who, for whatever reason, had not served his country. The next day, he shot back that Foot's infantile partisanship was an insult to those who had fought and died. He agreed about the need for authority over property, and even that these were 'revolutionary times', but that only meant that national unity was more desperately needed than ever. Party squabbling would likely 'lead the country to complete frustration and disaster'.[41] When peace came, Churchill and the coalition should stand for election and keep going.

The spat between these two rising young radical tribunes ran on, dramatising the messy, fractious process through which a consensus is formed. It is not about the parties being indistinguishable or even friendly. It is about the political class settling on a shared taboo.

* * *

While Foot and Hogg kept scrapping over who should reconstruct the country, ministers and civil servants had been trying to agree on how to go about it. Three days after Mass Observation reported widespread fears of renewed mass unemployment, the government published its proposals for ensuring this did not happen.

The parliamentary debate on the new White Paper on Employment Policy was opened on 21 June 1944 by the Minister of Labour, Ernest Bevin. He had played a crucial role in marshalling the war effort; now he proposed to extend his power into peacetime. He opened with the familiar image of the 'marches of hungry men', and rejected government efforts in the 1930s as too tentative. Now the state was going to 'declare war' on unemployment. He even claimed that, when he and Churchill had recently visited soldiers about to sail off to fight, some of the men had asked: 'Ernie, when we have done this job for you, are we going back to the dole?' 'No,' replied Churchill and Bevin, 'you are not.'[42]

In the Commons, Bevin suggested that the white paper had been a hard-won compromise. Its back-room engineers were Harold Wilson's old colleagues from the Economic Section—James Meade, John Jewkes and Lionel Robbins—with Keynes himself making the case for demand management within the Treasury. Keynes' scheme had run into orthodox objections. The Treasury now accepted the need to keep demand high, and the old objection that government intervention would 'crowd out' private investment appeared to have faded; but officials remained focused on the risks of running a deficit.

Then the famous elephant William Beveridge had crashed into this delicate territory, trumpeting his own freelance plan to squash mass unemployment. In a radio talk, he had sought to reassure listeners that 'full employment of Britons doesn't mean the employment of slaves directed to jobs by a totalitarian dictator at wages fixed by him'.[43] But he seemed to be advocating a radical turn towards a heavily planned, war-style economy, complete with direction of labour. His examples of peace-time full employment were Nazi Germany and the Soviet Union. This had spurred both the Treasury and the Keynesians in the Economic Section to agree on a less alarming alternative.

The white paper was the result. It advocated swift, decisive action as a 'slump may [otherwise] develop with fearful rapidity', as in 1920–1.[44] The government accepted the fact, Bevin told MPs, that 'total expenditure on goods and services must be maintained at the level necessary to prevent general unemployment', and that, if need be, the Budget would be balanced only over a series of years. He had adopted Keynes' ideas very early, even before 1931, and now declared the white paper 'a complete reversal of the policy of the years between the wars, when it was held that the onset of industrial depression must be met by cuts'.[45]

However, the proposals balanced the end of the old economic orthodoxy with a series of warnings to workers. That 'without a rising standard of industrial efficiency we cannot achieve a high level of employment combined with a rising standard of living.' That 'it would be a disaster' if the government's promise were taken 'as exonerating the citizen from the duty of fending for himself and resulted in a weakening of personal enterprise.' That workers should be willing 'to move to places and occupations where they were needed'. 'Both sides of industry' had a duty to stop a rise in costs, and with it 'the rise in prices which is the initial step in the inflationary process'.[46] In both directions lay the risk of what Meade had called 'vicious spirals'—into depression and unemployment, and into inflation.[47]

This was a strained compromise, heavily criticised by hardliners on both sides. But it had found a way to entrench the war-time shift to the left in government policy. It did so by acknowledging the ongoing importance of the nightmares of the inter-war consensus—runaway inflation, and the total state—but subordinating them to a new taboo: mass unemployment. The 'marches of hungry men' now became the founding nightmare of the coming post-war era. What was once unavoidable was now unthinkable.

This emerging orthodoxy began to win a wide swathe of support, not least from the young Tory reformers. But it could not yet become the basis for consensus. Quite apart from Conservative back-benchers' objections, the spectacle of Churchill's coalition trying to lay claim to the cherished dream of ending unemployment raised hackles on the left. On the third day of the debate, Aneurin Bevan insisted that only socialism could bring full employment. If the white paper's Keynesian compromise worked instead, he joked, he would join Hogg and the Tory Reform Committee.

There could be no consensus on full employment without a struggle for power first. A few weeks later, Bevan's close ally Michael Foot attacked Hogg again, insisting that, as the Conservative Party hadn't cared about unemployment in the 1930s, it could not be trusted. The Tories had only changed their tune now because an election was coming. Hogg kept doggedly fighting back.[48] This is not the last time in this book that we will encounter a politician trying to get from an old consensus to a new one without a fight, nor the last time we will see such an effort fail. In the end, Foot got his climactic struggle for power, in the general election of 1945. The question was whether the left could win it.

* * *

There had been no general election since 1935, but Labour leaders did not think they would win the next one when it finally arrived.

Attlee was ready to stay in coalition with Churchill, if the government introduced social security and full employment. But at the May 1945 party conference, the mood was vehemently against this now that the war in Europe was almost won, and Labour withdrew from the government. Churchill offered a referendum on continuing the coalition, but Attlee replied that referenda had 'only too often been the instrument of Nazism and Fascism'.[49]

The 1945 election was on, and it was no festival of idealism.[50] After five years of war-time partnership against Hitler, Labour and the Conservatives prepared to fight each other. Aneurin Bevan declared the election a 'real struggle for power' between 'Big Business and the People'.[51] That struggle would be fought out—as in 1931—through a battle of nightmares: dole queues and betrayal under the Conservatives, or a Labour-led slide into totalitarianism.

With the hated coalition off his party's back, Bevan was much happier. Where once he had dismissed full employment policies as empty, he now told people not to cavil about Labour's manifesto. And it did read like a rallying cry for a power struggle. It blamed the 'great inter-war slumps' on 'the concentration of too much economic power in the hands of too few men.' It traced the blame back to 1918, when the 'hard-faced men who had done well out of the war' and 'their political friends' had 'kept control of the Government':

> They controlled the banks, the mines, the big industries, largely the press and the cinema. They controlled the means by which the people got their living. They controlled the ways by which most of the people learned about the world outside … Similar forces are at work today.

Labour invited the British people to take back control.

The manifesto cast war-time restrictions, like rationing, controls on industry and the 100% Excess Profit Tax, as a means to 'fair shares'. To keep the old powers from reasserting themselves, the Bank of England must be nationalised, and 'the operations of the other banks harmonised with industrial needs'. Old industries would be brought into public ownership. A Labour government could then use the expanded, planned state, and demand management—including, if necessary, deficits—to entrench full employment: 'No more dole queues, in order to let the Czars of Big

Business remain kings in their own castles.'[52] And the freedom of the trade unions would be restored, by repealing the restrictive Trades Disputes Act.

On 4 June, a month before polling day, Churchill sat down at Chequers to make the first of a series of radio broadcasts allotted to each campaign. He told voters that two terrible dangers awaited them, should they be tempted to choose Labour.

First, he warned of a coming 1931-style nightmare in which socialist monkeying with the credit of Britain would leave no one's nest-egg safe, leading to the debauchment of the currency. But this was a difficult case to make, after years of deficit to pay for the war, and in a speech that also made commitments to far-reaching, expensive social programmes and full employment. He would drop this angle from his second broadcast.

Second, he said:

> I declare it to you, from the bottom of my heart, that no Socialist system can be established without a political police. Many of those who are advocating Socialism or voting Socialist today will be horrified at this idea. That is because they are short-sighted, that is because they do not see where their theories are leading them. No Socialist Government conducting the entire life and industry of the country could afford to allow free, sharp, or violently-worded expressions of public discontent. They would have to fall back on some form of Gestapo, no doubt very humanely directed in the first instance.[53]

The great, unifying war leader had vanished in a puff of cigar smoke. Here again was the old Churchill: the one still remembered in the Welsh valleys.[54]

Quintin Hogg listened to the broadcast in the Carlton Club, and announced, 'That broadcast will lose us between 250,000 and 500,000 votes'. But around him, the speech went down splendidly. This, one member declared, was 'the stuff to give the troops.'[55] Bar the word 'Gestapo', it was not, as is sometimes suggested, an isolated gaffe. Churchill made much the same attack in his next broadcast, just omitting the offending term. Many Conservative candidates, along with some Liberals and Liberal Nationals, took up the totalitarian nightmare scenario with all the gusto of those listeners at the Carlton. Churchill ended that first broadcast by saying: 'On with the forward march! Leave these Socialist dreamers to their Utopias or their nightmares.' But what exactly were the 'nightmares' socialism was about to visit on Britain?

There are a remarkable number of specific warnings set out not only in Churchill's broadcasts, but in speeches by Conservative, Liberal and Liberal National candidates, including at least one minister; in anti-socialist newspaper articles; and in polemical books and pamphlets launched in the run-up to the election. The election campaign saw a barrage of publications, many belatedly designed to counter Gollancz's series of 'Victory' books that had begun with *Guilty Men*. If we bring these writings together, a scenario emerges that runs something like this:

If Labour wins, it will recall Parliament and push an Emergency Powers Bill through in a single day. This will allow socialist ministers to rule by decree, without the possibility of legal challenge. Soon Parliament will be neutered: law-making outsourced to bureaucrats, the House of Lords abolished, discussion in the Commons curtailed. The real power will lie with Labour's National Executive Committee. Attlee will be forced out.

Conformity to state diktat will be enforced by violence, with opposition treated as sabotage, or treachery. 'Sullen elements' in the civil service will be 'instantly liquidated'.[56]

The realities of trying to nationalise parts of the interconnected economy will lead to the nationalisation of all of it. The population will become 'State serfs',[57] *with youth under discipline, and compulsory state allocation of jobs and pay. The trade unions will be hobbled, losing the right to strike or bargain freely. Workers will be better fed and 'more uniformly dressed',*[58] *but no longer free. There might very well be concentration camps.*[59]

The main source material for this nightmare vision came from what Stafford Cripps had said a decade earlier, when he and Attlee had been close allies in the far-left Socialist League. In his broadcast, Churchill referred to Cripps' writing on 'Parliament in the Socialist State'. 'I have not time to read you what he said,' Churchill told his listeners, 'but perhaps it will meet the public eye during the election campaign.'[60] His candidates acted accordingly.

All this might have seemed laughable, given how heavily it was leaning on a mix of a twelve-year-old lecture and 'logical conclusions', but during the campaign two leading Labour figures managed to give the scenario fresh credence. First, Herbert Morrison was reported as saying that Labour would outsource the details of new laws to bureaucrats in government departments, and as threatening to get rid of the House of Lords.[61] This allowed junior minister Florence Horsbrugh to tell an election meeting in Dundee that Morrison's proposed parliamentary reform 'meant dictatorship'.[62] Then Harold Laski, the left-wing Chair of the Labour Party, publicly cautioned Attlee to stick to agreed policy on his visit to the Potsdam conference with Roosevelt and Stalin. This led the education minister Richard Law to warn voters in Hull that the 'Socialists were proposing to do away with the control of Parliament and substitute for it the dictatorship of the Socialist Grand Council'.[63]

Churchill alleged that the NEC would 'give the orders to the so-called responsible Ministers of the Crown', who would 'deliver orations upon which they have been instructed'. He even claimed that Cripps and some of his fellow Labour leaders 'talk of violence to be used upon us, if necessary, to make us conform sharply and promptly to the benevolent ideas of these autocratic philanthropists.'[64] Labour and its supporters in the press spied a re-run of apparently effective old 'red scares' like Philip Snowden's 'Bolshevism run mad' diatribe of 1931, and they retaliated in kind. Some of these counter-attacks deployed the ready-made rhetorical link between Nazism and unemployment. Labour ex-minister James Chuter Ede told an audience in North Shields that the means test men sent into working-class homes in the 1930s had been a form of British Gestapo.[65]

In his *Herald* column after the Gestapo broadcast, Michael Foot sought to turn the tables on Churchill. Labour's opponents clearly wanted to stop Morrison's sensible reforms in order to keep Parliament ineffective, he insinuated, while his party wanted a democratic mandate to build a better Britain. And once Labour had a majority, Foot vowed, they would not let the concentrated power of capital block their path: 'neither peers nor Press lords nor bankers nor coalowners nor cartel kings nor monopolists, nor any others shall be allowed to cheat the people of their will.' Here Foot skewered the Achilles' heel of the 'Gestapo' attacks: the only reason Cripps had once mooted a temporary dictatorship was his fear that a future socialist government would face a fascistic establishment coup. But no dictatorship would now be necessary to ram through the Beveridge plan or the employment white paper, or even nationalisation.

Churchill himself had been instrumental in this sea change. To defeat Hitler, he had championed a level of state intervention and command that *The New York Times* had labelled 'totalitarian'.[66] He now wanted to go at least part of the way back to the world before, denouncing Labour's proposals in exactly those terms. But his coalition with Labour, and the experience of war, had discredited the old nightmares of the big state as dictatorship. Labour suggested, pityingly, that Churchill's utterances were 'silly talk', a 'crazy broadcast'.[67]

Sometimes, warnings of imminent fascist nightmare are much needed. But they can also be a symptom of something else: an expression of despair at being disempowered, democratically. Labour was not proposing to seize absolute control, but it had seized the ideological initiative. The Conservatives were internally divided between a desire to shake off war-time bureaucracy and get back to the good old days of balanced budgets, low taxes and free enterprise, and acceptance of a larger state that would take responsibility for universal welfare and full employment.

One of Quintin Hogg's student campaigners in Oxford had listened to Churchill on the radio in the Junior Common Room of Somerville College. Margaret Roberts—later Thatcher—thought that with the 'Gestapo' line, Churchill had gone too far. In her memoirs, she recalls thinking that 'however logically unassailable the connection between socialism and coercion was, in our present circumstances the line would not be credible.'[68]

In present circumstances.

* * *

War having banished the old fears, Labour candidates sought to make the case to extend planning into peace-time, as a means to ensure that this would not be like the last peace. Barbara Betts had married Ted Castle of the *Mirror*, who once put her on the front page; she was now a Labour candidate in Blackburn. And so, on

13 June, Barbara Castle told the YWCA Town Club: 'Despite Mr Churchill's promises, the Tories were determined to return as soon as possible to uncontrolled private profit-making', a 'system which made poverty and unemployment inevitable.'[69] Blackburn was a cotton town that had been hit badly when the trade slumped in the Depression, with unemployment veering 'between 25 per cent and 45 per cent'.[70] Even in 1945, the town was struggling. 'One of the many things for which I shall fight', Castle told the *Mirror*, 'will be to make industry serve the people by setting up its factories where they can do most good.'[71]

Twenty miles across Lancashire, in Ormskirk, the Labour candidate, Harold Wilson, was busy making much the same case. The constituency's mining areas had been hit by high unemployment. On 14 June, he published his first book, *New Deal for Coal*, written in five weeks. Like his campaign, it set out what had gone wrong in the coal industry and how it had to be fixed. This young professional planner had no time for amateurish mining company directors who had been appointed 'solely through being the children or grand-children of the Victorian founders'. He talked of owners 'smoking expensive cigars' when they met miners' leaders 'to say that the men's wages were too high', damning their economic orthodoxy as a 'starvation philosophy' which held that 'only under conditions of mass unemployment is the industry assured of sufficient men to produce the coal required'.[72]

Wilson detected a deep mood among miners of 'sullen resentment and anger', caused by long pre-war years of 'unemployment, miserably low wages, accidents, and bad conditions of work.' They needed 'a guarantee that a new and different order of things has come to stay'.[73] That meant nationalisation, regardless of the owners' objections. Wilson's powerful ally, the miners' leader Will Lawther, came to speak for him in one of the mining villages, Skelmersdale, and extolled Wilson's plan for public ownership in the *Daily Herald*, confident that voters 'will note with glee that no Gestapo is needed to ensure security and peace in this harassed industry'.[74]

To push back against the dictatorship accusations, and to make the case for 'nationalisation', Labour argued that it was now the party of the whole nation. In his broadcast reply to Churchill, Attlee contended that the Conservatives were now the 'class Party', representing 'property and privilege'.[75] The revolutionary mood of 1940 was still a potent weapon. In its manifesto, Labour called for the 'spirit of Dunkirk and of the Blitz' to be sustained into peace-time; as David Edgerton notes, it features the word 'national' far more than 'socialist'.[76] In anticipation of the election, Gollancz republished *Guilty Men*.

In his own seat, Plymouth Devonport, the '"Guilty Men" Author', as Michael Foot was dubbed, was facing Chamberlain's old war secretary, Leslie Hore-Belisha, who had a majority of 11,000 and was happy to attack Labour as threatening totalitarianism, calling Attlee a helpless 'office boy'.[77] Foot duly cast Hore-Belisha as a Guilty Man: a friend of vested interests who had failed the troops.[78] His last *Herald* column before polling day was headlined 'Back to Tory shame—or British honour?'[79] In a flurry of new books, Conservatives scrambled to push back. Quintin Hogg hammered out a debunking of *Guilty Men*, called *The Left Was Never Right*. But it was all in vain. The battle for control of the narrative had been lost and won in 1940.

On 5 July, Labour did not consolidate its war-time reputation and come a respectable second. It won a crushing landslide. Given the choice of Labour totalitarianism or Tory mass unemployment, the voters had chosen totalitarianism. The Labour Party's general secretary detected 'a tidal wave of popular distrust which submerged the Tories'.[80] Barbara Castle won in Blackburn, once represented by Philip Snowden. In Ormskirk, Herbert Wilson watched his triumphant son hoisted up onto other men's shoulders and receiving 'a great ovation'.[81] Michael Foot learned that he was another of Labour's young surprise winners, felling one of the many ministers to lose their seat. In his first *Herald* column after the result, he was in no mood for magnanimity:

> The spirit of a new birth which swept the nation in 1940, only to be muffled by Churchill's progressive decline into the Party leader of the Right, is once again abroad throughout the land ... we are able to repudiate in the name of our great country the shameful epoch of Chamberlainism.[82]

The *Guilty Men* narrative had helped Labour to seize the flag. As the historian Philip Williamson wrote: 'What emerged was a fused

Churchillian-Labour-Keynesian interpretation dismissive towards government in the 1920s and 1930s ... This historical consensus had considerable public importance, as the real substance underlying the so-called political consensus of the 1950s.'[83]

It seemed to *The Times* that there was consensus between the parties—not on means, but on ends. For instance: 'All of them adopted the Coalition policy of accepting as a prime responsibility of the Government the maintenance of a high and stable level of employment'.[84] Likewise, the *Daily Mirror* argued as the election approached that all the main parties wanted 'to give everybody a *fairer share* of a bigger national income than we produced before the war.' The difference between them, the paper contended, 'is not about the end in view; it is about the means to the end.'[85] As Richard Toye has identified, from at least 1942 there had been talk in the press and among politicians of a cross-party 'consensus of opinion on vital issues'.[86] But Labour's victory had created a final break-point, as Michael Foot had long demanded, to draw a line under the compromises of the war-time coalition. On this new basis, a consensus could be developed—provided that enough people followed Quintin Hogg in agreeing that there could be no return to the 1930s.

The Conservatives were not yet reconciled to nationalisation; over the creation of the National Health Service, there was a huge battle coming. It was not clear how planning was going to work democratically, if it worked at all. The Bank of England was to be nationalised; it was less clear how much power was to be taken from the City. But the war-time shift of power from capital to the trade unions would now continue into peace. Looking back, the most striking thing about the Gestapo flap is what Churchill and his fellow Conservatives did *not* attack: the rising power of the trade unions. Quite the opposite. They had warned that Labour's total state would crush the right to strike.

The idea that trade unionists had more to fear from Attlee than Churchill may not have seemed convincing, but it's worth a closer look. The unions, with their faith in voluntarism and free collective bargaining, did have a fundamentally different view of power from the way the planners saw things. Even during the war, despite the ban on industrial action, there had been unofficial strikes resisting the introduction of unskilled labour into craft trades. But for the duration, everything had been held together in the enormous form of Ernest Bevin, a man big enough to embody two traditions at once. He had used his powers with restraint, consulting the unions throughout. Statutory wage controls had been resisted; in return for voluntary limits on wages, the price of essential goods had been controlled. In time, this great internal tension in the labour movement would come to loom much larger. But for now, amid the euphoria of Labour's victory, it hardly seemed to matter.

On Saturday 28 July, at the Mansion House in the heart of the City of London, Attlee appeared before the first meeting of his new MPs, who now made up two thirds of the Parliamentary Labour Party. Among them were Foot, Castle—and Wilson, who would soon receive a call from Attlee appointing him Parliamentary Under-Secretary of the Ministry of Works, with the words 'This is a planning job.'[87] He and his fellow new members hailed their new Labour Prime Minister with a standing ovation and 'thunderous volleys of cheering'.[88]

And the City outside the doors, unhappy as it was, did not trigger a run on the pound. The Labour government did not try to pass an Enabling Act, which was not blocked by the House of Lords. Attlee did not need to try to force the hand of the King or the courts, or set up a Gestapo. And no fascist militia came to drag Michael Foot or Harold Wilson in front of a firing squad, or to take Barbara Castle to a concentration camp.

A Labour-friendly City veteran would write later that the nationalisation of the Bank of England was a non-event, and that, had there been more revolutionary intent at work, something more like Cripps' old scenario might have come to pass.[89] The Attlee government was not the Socialist League, nor the revolutionary vanguard of 1940. In the first years after the war, there were still fearful scenarios to contend with: Hugh Dalton's biographer writes of 'the nightmare of collapse and mass starvation that haunted economics ministers just after the war'.[90] And, as Steven Fielding has identified, some people voted Labour as a protest while they waited for the inevitable Churchill victory, and were rather shocked when Labour actually won.

But democracy no longer seemed doomed. That paralysing, suffocating feeling—that all roads led to calamity—was gone. There was to be no return, under either party, to the miseries of mass unemployment, and the 'dismal and divided Thirties'.

PART TWO

1968–85

6

EMERGENCY GOVERNMENT

1968–9

A mile upriver from Westminster stands Millbank Tower, a 32-storey skyscraper in blue glass and stainless steel. For a short time, it was London's tallest building, and, for a little longer, an emblem of how power worked in post-war Britain. In the late 1960s, it was home to Vickers, Ferranti, the Atomic Energy Authority, and a body called the National Economic Development Council.

This had been set up in 1961 by the Conservative chancellor Selwyn Lloyd, and began meeting the following year. In the conference room on the fifteenth floor, members of the NEDC would meet to survey the nation from on high, and to try to plan its economy. To do that, it brought together leaders from government, business—and, crucially, the trade unions.

Since the end of the war, the unions had become more powerful than ever before, because the promise of full employment had actually happened. With little fear of the dole queue, workers could strike for higher pay with more confidence. That consensus on full employment had produced another one: a rough-and-ready consensus on industrial relations—governments acknowledged the unions' new power, and the union leaders generally agreed to use it sparingly, engaging with ministers and keeping wage claims under control. Around all of this, there swirled a much vaguer notion of 'consensus politics'—a sense that political catfights were more about who could best run the system than whether the system itself should be blown up.

The settlement on full employment and industrial relations was accepted by most of the Labour Party, and most of the leadership of the Conservative party. Men like Harold Macmillan had come to see the 1945 election as 'delayed punishment' for the 1930s,[1] and within two years had set to work laying out policies to keep at bay any return of mass unemployment. Many Conservatives kept faith in the old free-market orthodoxies; but they deferred to the leadership, however frustratedly, on what was now politically possible.

The party's long run of electoral success through the 1950s had doubtless helped square this political circle, just as growth had squared the economic one: an astonishingly long period of post-war expansion meant rising wages, high public spending, low inflation and full employment were all possible at once. Ministers of Labour, including Edward Heath, strove to keep industrial peace, frequently conceding to pay demands. When inflation threatened, they tried to control it not by letting unemployment rise—the old approach— but with voluntary 'incomes policy', under which the unions agreed to cap pay rises. The NEDC was meant to embody this consensual management of growth and wage restraint.

In October 1964, Harold Wilson led Labour back to power, and the NEDC was joined in Millbank Tower by a new government ministry. To run it, Wilson had coaxed the leader of the Transport and General Workers' Union, Frank Cousins, to follow his predecessor Bevin's example, and enter government. Growth was slowing; but Wilson, a man of 1945, believed he could use state planning, in concert with business and unions, to revitalise the economy. Cousins was to be Britain's first Minister of Technology, guiding the effort to modernise industry from the eleventh floor of a skyscraper piled high with executives and technocrats.

At the same time, some NEDC staff moved from Millbank to another new ministry, the Department of Economic Affairs, where they set to work drawing up a National Plan. This was how Wilson's Labour would pull off the trick of maintaining full employment and rising wages at the same time: the key was improving productivity. While the new economy was arising under the guidance of the National Plan, however, inflation had to be held down—which meant a new prices and incomes policy. The department's chief, George Brown, chivvied union leaders and bosses to sign up. For all the usual splenetic inter-party fisticuffs, the planning-plus-incomes-policy project was broadly similar to the Conservatives'. Wilson seemed to be the post-war consensus made flesh. The Conservative Party soon replaced its third Etonian leader in a row with one from a background much more like the Labour leader's: Edward Heath.

In 1966, the wind still in his sails, Wilson won a landslide. One journalist wrote that he 'had established a degree of identity with the middle vote, unequalled since Stanley Baldwin.'[2] If the government could only keep union goodwill and hold wage inflation down long enough for its National Plan to work, that would boost productivity and restore the cure-all of economic growth, securing full employment for the future.

But just weeks after Wilson's great victory, the first crack appeared in the post-war consensus. The National Union of Seamen threatened a huge pay strike, which, if successful, would shatter the government's incomes policy, and its plan to transform the economy. Wilson declared this a challenge to the state. He claimed that avoiding a strike was crucial to maintaining full employment. But the strike began, and the pound began to fall.

The post-war model rested not only on the compromise with the new power of the unions, but on another: with the enduring power of finance. Britain was now a less open, more self-sufficient economy than it had once been, but it had not become a socialist stockade. In 1944, Keynes had signed his country up for an international monetary system based on a fixed exchange rate, with the new International Monetary Fund ready to provide credit. Unlike the gold standard, the aim was to allow for the defence of the pound without sacrificing full employment. But this still left the British economy open to great pressure if international investors lost confidence in sterling—which they now did.

Wilson had trade unionists tugging at his left arm for higher pay, financiers pulling on his right to stop any such thing. This made putting the National Plan into action rather difficult. The master of compromise had to make a choice. He turned against the seamen's union, triggering emergency powers to deal with the strike, and accusing the sailors of being duped by their communist leaders. After six damaging weeks, the strike ended, but the pound kept falling, as investors worried over UK exports. The government prepared to introduce a bill to create the first ever incomes policy enforceable by law—and Frank Cousins turned his back on Millbank

Tower, and returned to the TGWU. Cousins was a very different kind of workers' leader from Ernest Bevin and the other old right-wing authoritarian union bosses who had made pay restraint work. Now he charged that the incomes policy was 'fundamentally wrong'.[3] He alleged that the Treasury had regained control over spending and planning.

Two weeks later, with the pound still tanking, a desperate government proved him right. Wilson did something he had recently called 'unthinkable',[4] and imposed a six-month wage freeze, in a bid to boost exports, reduce imports and win back the confidence of the financiers. Finally, in November 1967, in the throes of yet another sterling crisis, exacerbated by an unofficial dock strike in Liverpool, the government was forced, humiliatingly, to devalue the pound. But still the longed-for export boom was nowhere to be seen. Meanwhile, deflation had sucked the oxygen out of the expansionist National Plan, with all of its heady growth projections.

Consensus politics had stalled. The commitment to full employment was still rock-solid, even as unemployment rose past half a million; but the power of the trade unions, founded on that rock, was no longer chugging away in sync with the efforts of the Labour government. Ministers objected to strikes; unions objected to the pay freeze. The industrial relations consensus, on which the National Plan had based its hopes, was starting to crack under the strain.

In 1967 and early 1968, references in the studiously moderate *Guardian* to 'the consensus', 'consensus politics', the 'Westminster consensus' and the 'consensus society' tended to cast it as something that was strained, diminishing, exhausted, disintegrating, or just mythical. The leader of the post office workers' union declared his members tired of its failure to deliver redistribution of wealth. The consensus had depended on growth, argued the columnist Peter Jenkins, but while it might still unite experts, politicians and the head of the TUC, it 'no longer includes ordinary people'.[5] By March 1968, Jenkins judged that consensus on wage restraint was 'now absent'.[6]

* * *

As in 1931, the existing way of doing things no longer seemed to work. The Wilson government staggered from crisis to crisis, trying week by week to square the circle, bereft of its National Plan. In the wake of the seamen's strike, attention turned to the power of the trade unions, opposition to which had been slowly growing since the late 1950s. By the late 1960s, the rising number of strikes had become a pressing issue, given their apparent impact on wage inflation, the balance of payments, and confidence in the British economy. There was particular resentment at the rapid spread of 'wildcat' strikes—short, sudden, unofficial stoppages which were a plant manager's perennial nightmare. In an inter-connected economy, these could have an impact far and wide. The OECD was not alone in observing that unions seemed to be taking advantage of 'the new conditions of almost continuous full employment'.[7] To some, trade unions began to look like a concentration of power, founded on the taboo against mass unemployment. In this, if in nothing else, they resembled the way inter-war financiers' power had been built on governments' terror of deficits and inflation.

And so, as in the Thirties, with the consensus faltering, radical alternatives started to emerge. On 22 November 1967, still humiliated by the devaluation, the chancellor, James Callaghan, faced a raucous House of Commons. He complained that the government was straining to give voters both 'a perpetually rising standard of living and full employment', but that was impossible if pay claims outstripped productivity. It was taboo to use high unemployment to damp down wage demands, but the lack of a solution was breeding a dangerous cynicism. 'There is a growing view,' Callaghan warned, 'and one that is fostered in some quarters, that democracy cannot solve our problems.'[8]

One of those fostering these ideas was a former Wilson cheerleader, who had turned against him: the *Daily Mirror* supremo and Bank of England director Cecil King. He was so worried about impending economic collapse that he had taken to lobbying for an 'emergency government'—politicians from across the parties, plus responsible business leaders—to seize power. This coalition would need to impose harsh spending cuts, and an incomes policy with long, sharp teeth. But the figure most on Callaghan's mind was Sir Paul Chambers, chairman of the chemical giant ICI, and leader of a 'new big business organisation', the Industrial Policy Group (IPG), which Callaghan told MPs was 'potentially sinister'.[9] Like King, Chambers and the IPG doubted that normal democratic politics could take the necessary steps: 'drastic' spending cuts and 'action to deal with unofficial strikes'.[10] The IPG opposed incomes policy as authoritarian—yet the group would itself eventually suggest closing Parliament for a few months.[11]

Along the benches on Callaghan's own side, the maverick Labour MP Desmond Donnelly also feared that the consensus was breaking down, and was rapidly losing faith in his party's capacity to fix it. Like King, he thought a coercive incomes policy was vital; like the IPG, he wanted action to control the unions. If not, he feared worse would follow. In his pulp thriller *The Nearing Storm*, published the following April, Donnelly imagines the unions forcing a weak, Wilson-like Prime Minister to keep government spending ruinously high under threat of a general strike, while immigration stirs resentment among the 2 million unemployed. Finally, the PM is shot dead in a right-wing coup, and his body found washed up at Tower Bridge.

The notion of a non-democratic 'businessmen's government' provoked a strikingly sharp response from the right. Denouncing the idea's 'dictatorial overtones', the journalist Samuel Brittan said it was 'worse than the disease it is designed to cure.'[12] The Conservative historian Robert Blake warned that under such a government, 'liberty would soon vanish'.[13] The free-market Conservative MP Angus Maude, who was himself turning against the consensus, wrote that those who saw 'parliamentary government as a pointless waste of time' were 'fascists'.[14]

For the government, however, the problem of wages outstripping productivity—and the impact this was having on investors—threatened a more imminent nightmare: the collapse of the currency. By Thursday 14 March 1968, the pound was on the brink. The new chancellor, Roy Jenkins, told ministers: 'If we are not seen to deal strongly with wages we can't avoid a second devaluation, world monetary confusion and the destruction of this Government'.[15] Within a week, he feared Britain was about to 'plunge over the precipice into perdition'.[16] But if the businessmen's dreams of suspending democracy were anathema, what could ministers do to meet Jenkins' demand to 'deal strongly with wages', while maintaining full employment?

Over the weekend of 16–17 March, under the pressure of crisis, once-unthinkable options presented themselves. In desperation, Wilson and Jenkins asked the US government for a $6 billion stand-by loan, conscious that this would only postpone Britain's problems. At 3.30pm on the Sunday afternoon, while waiting in Downing Street for the US Treasury's answer, they convened a new, secret cabinet committee to work through what they would have to do if the Americans said no. This was 'Operation Brutus'. To stave off the collapse of sterling, Britain would have to block foreign holders of British currency from converting their money, and the pound would have to float away from its fixed rate, wrecking the international monetary system.

Brutus was a genuine last-ditch contingency plan, but in the meetings that day, Wilson let on that it was also 'some measure of blackmail' aimed at the Americans, to 'point out to them the horrors of the alternatives before us'.[17] Even when the loan came through, the threat of collapse remained, and the secret committee would continue nursing its emergency measures. The extremity of the Brutus plans just underlined the need to come up with a new way through, and fast.

* * *

What if there was no solution to be wrung from the existing shop-worn compromises? That Sunday afternoon, just up Whitehall from where the Brutus committee was meeting, a huge demonstration had been getting underway in Trafalgar Square, protesting against America's war in Vietnam. For the New Left, the horrors of napalm and slaughter, masterminded by US Democrats and abetted by Wilson, laid bare the reality of militaristic capitalism behind the moderate consensus façade. The demonstrators set off to march on the American embassy in Grosvenor Square, where they would end up fighting the police.

For these young radical leftists, the whole idea of consensus was disastrous, and had to go. Deprivation and inequality had not been fixed in the years since 1945. The problem was not that the trade

THE DEATH OF CONSENSUS

unions had too much power. It was that their leaders had been co-opted by politicians into the soft, suffocating 'consensus'.[18] Unions should be a force to transform society, yet their bosses were absorbed in making cosy deals at Millbank or the Ministry of Labour. This case was laid out in a New Left book, pointedly called *The Incompatibles: Trade Union Militancy and the Consensus*.

The sharpest weapon of 'consensus' coercion was incomes policy. The journalist Paul Foot—Michael's rebellious nephew—produced a book-length denunciation of Harold Wilson's 'new corporatism', and of the way it used incomes policy as a trick to suck union leaders 'into the network of planning'. This, the younger Foot warned, was 'drastically dangerous'. Like the Labour government's drive to merge British companies into giant national champions, incomes policy was part of a ruthless centralisation of power into unelected 'industrial and economic bureaucracies', reminiscent of the Soviet Union.[19] The New Left's *May Day Manifesto* added that, as the economy deteriorated, this would get worse. The government would have to use 'the most ruthless capitalist measures'. This would mean breaking the unions, ditching the left and 'a new kind of coalition government'—the dissent-smothering consensus taken to its logical, authoritarian conclusion.[20]

Paul Foot cheered the way Stafford Cripps had insisted, back in 1933, that an elected socialist government would have to use the 'most drastic measures to control private economic interests' as soon as it won power. Better the passionate engagement of the Thirties than Labour's squalid Sixties apathy, trying to pretend there need be no struggle for power.[21] The only real way to get rid of unemployment, he insisted, was to abandon the futility of Parliament and pragmatism, and fight for workers' control of industry.

Paul wrote much of this in his uncle Michael's house in Hampstead. This did not stop him attacking Michael's naive support for Wilson. Nor did it stop Michael from savaging his nephew in *Tribune*. The elder Foot was fiercely critical of Wilson for letting unemployment rise, and opposed the statutory incomes policy;[22] but Paul's attack spurred Michael to think back to the miserable sights that had first made him a socialist, and to defend his generation's efforts:

> Keynesian economics plus technological advance plus, above all,
> democratic pressures have changed industrial societies immensely

for the better, and if anyone tells me that the Liverpool or the Ebbw Vale or the Plymouth of 1968 are not vastly better and freer places for the mass of working people than the Liverpool etc. of, say, 1934, he is an ignorant and callous ass.[23]

But perhaps Michael Foot was just stuck in the past. To New Leftists unencumbered by nostalgia for 1945, it now seemed possible to achieve far more. When the march arrived at the American embassy, the protestors tried to break through the police lines and storm it: Britain's first violent political confrontation since the war. Capitalism, wrote one New Leftist, 'was now more seriously embattled than at any time since the thirties.' And this time the police were not facing 'exhausted men from Jarrow'.[24] If these young revolutionaries could fight and win socialism, no one would ever have to worry about sterling crises or incomes policies, or unemployment, or napalm, ever again.

If Wilson's cornered ministers could not find a solution more lasting than the loan, or less drastic than Brutus, was this what was coming next? Political violence seemed to be sweeping the world in 1968. After the 'Battle of Grosvenor Square'—the swung truncheons and thrown stones—the newspapers began to conjure up yet another possible nightmare that might follow, if the political logjam could not be broken: revolution. There were reports that leaflets had been distributed saying 'Come armed', and that 'unfired .22 cartridges' had been found in the square outside the US embassy.[25] When a reprise of the demo approached that autumn, *The Times* reported a plot by 'a small army of militant extremists' to take over 'highly sensitive installations and buildings'.[26]

* * *

On 5 April 1968, as a mutinous RAF pilot outraged by defence cuts repeatedly roared his fighter plane over Parliament, Wilson tried to recapture the initiative. Perhaps his government could still make incomes policy, and a semblance of planning, work. A new Industrial Expansion Act was already extending the use of investment grants, while ministers could claim that their interventions were boosting the rapid growth of the British computer industry. Now Wilson went further, and deployed one of his few Cabinet allies, Barbara Castle, to tackle head-on the central problem facing his administration—and the viability of the post-war settlement.

The Prime Minister took the old bastion of the industrial relations consensus—the Ministry of Labour, with its close relationship to the unions—and combined it with the remnants of the Department of Economic Affairs, which ran incomes policy. The result was the Department of Employment and Productivity, with Castle at the helm. She would have to play hard cop and soft cop at the same time: making incomes policy work, while driving up productivity to pay for wage rises. The hope was still to build a high-wage economy but, more urgently, they had to keep sterling from collapse. To stress the importance of her mission, Wilson also made Castle First Secretary of State. She was invited to join the secret Brutus committee. This gave her a bracing glimpse over the brink at what was coming if she failed. By now, the contingency plan foresaw import controls, sharp rises in both inflation and unemployment, and restrictions on the freedom of both capital and people to leave the country.[27] To steer clear of this abyss, Castle had to find a way to get the post-war model functioning again. But then came another assault on the whole idea of consensus politics—this time from the radical right.

Britain's leading free-marketeer was the maverick MP Enoch Powell, at this point the Conservatives' front-bench spokesman on defence. In the 1930s, when the orthodox Cambridge economist Dennis Robertson was losing students to the Keynesian wave, Powell had become his protégé. Three decades later, he stood out against the country built by the Keynesians. He could not abide consensus in general, or incomes policy in particular. He saw little difference between Heath and Wilson, and though no supporter of trade unions, he regarded incomes policy as 'sinister'—a smokescreen for state overspending.[28]

As Macmillan's health minister, Powell had planned with the best of them, but had now turned decisively against the whole idea. He thought it was futile, and declared himself strongly opposed to 'a policy which would like to concentrate all the economic decisions that really matter in a little group of planners at the centre'.[29] He despised the NEDC, and declared:

We are today in imminent danger of slipping unawares into that form of state Socialism which is known as fascism, whereby the control of the state over individuals is exercised largely through corporations which purport to represent the various elements of society, and particularly the employers and employees.

There is an ominous ring of the corporate state about the present relations between the Government, the TUC and the CBI.[30]

The New Left thought incomes policy was the government serving corporations; the New Right thought it was government serving itself. The New Left loathed Powell, but both sides thought that incomes policy blamed workers for government folly, that the so-called consensus was a corporatist monster that smothered radical alternatives, and had to be destroyed—and that there would have to be a struggle for power. The New Left wanted the battle to be led by militant trade unionists; the New Right seemed a little more tentative. Until Powell decided to extend his hostility to state intervention into new territory.

'Consensus politics' encompassed a tacit agreement between the main parties' front benches not to politicise 'race relations'. But public hostility to migrants from Ireland, the Caribbean and the Indian subcontinent, often expressed in crudely racist terms, began to put pressure on this. At 2.30pm on Saturday 20 April, Enoch Powell stood up in the Midland Hotel in Birmingham, and started talking about the coming black domination of Britain, and imminent racial civil strife. Powell's warning, quoted from a constituent, that 'in fifteen or twenty years' time the black man will have the whip hand over the white man' was a reversal of what was actually happening.[31] More racist intimidation and violence soon followed.

The sheer nastiness of this, however, sometimes obscures something else. This nightmare scenario was an extension of Powell's apocalyptic hostility to big government in general. As his biographer TE Utley wrote that same year, Powell saw 'the seeds of a totalitarian state in every instance of administrative control of the economy'.[32] By this logic, he was suggesting that the government's Race Relations Bill was another totalitarian seed: immigrant communities would use the new power to claim discrimination, in order 'to overawe and dominate the rest' of the country.[33]

Powell presented his speech as a populist cry of protest against this. People 'were never consulted' about immigration; now 'hundreds of thousands were saying and thinking' these thoughts, but felt that, when they wrote their MP, they had better 'omit their address' for fear of 'penalties or reprisals'. He cast the consensus elite of 1968 as careless, lying and oppressive, and likened its members to the appeasers of the 1930s, who had also 'tried to blind this country to the rising peril which confronted it'.[34] This was the rhetoric of *Guilty Men*, but directed against the very political settlement that Foot's old polemic had helped to build.

All these elements of Powell's speech expressed his crusade against the grip of polite opinion, which he saw as preventing change. Heath fired him from the Shadow Cabinet immediately, saying it was vital to prevent 'civil strife'—a position that expressed both the horror of consensus politicians at Powell's words, and their fear that not everyone would be so repulsed. The idea that Caribbean nurses or Pakistani bus drivers were somehow comparable to Nazi stormtroopers is hard to stomach; yet, as the historian Camilla Schofield has shown, the deluge of letters Powell received following the 'Rivers of Blood' speech—well over 100,000—reveals that his imagery of invasion and betrayal struck a deep chord. Despite little backing in the press, a Gallup poll in early May suggested 74% of people broadly agreed with him.[35] In part, this sprang from a sense that the hard-won post-war settlement had been a let-down.

Could Powell's rhetoric, then, break the consensus? The *Spectator* argued that 'the gap between the conventional wisdom of the consensus politicians and the attitudes of the mass of voters has become too wide', and that Powell was 'the only consistent and powerful voice of dissent'.[36] Utley wrote in his biography that Powell 'offers working class opinion not only or primarily resistance to immigration but also resistance to incomes policy'. He argued that Powell was exploiting 'the central weakness of Labour—the tension between its philosophy of state control and its dependence on the trade unions.'[37] But the difference, of course, was impact. Powell had tried to couch his criticisms of incomes policy in populist terms; but in September 1968, Utley noted that, by the time Powell had given the speech in April, it 'must have been painfully apparent to him ... that reasoned expositions of the fallacies involved in

Prices and Incomes policy ... were not likely to make him into a popular political hero.'[38] So he had found another way to lever Labour apart from at least some trade unionists. No sooner had he attacked the Race Relations Bill than thousands of dockers and porters were marching on Parliament, chanting his name.

When Frank Cousins, head of the TGWU—the dockers' union—told Castle that people were 'disillusioned with politicians', she told him sharply that the feeling was mutual. Her fellow MPs were frightened, while to her disgust, the printers' union leader said Powell 'had a lot of right on his side.'[39] One TGWU official in the London docks wrote to *Tribune* to try to repair the breach between Labour and some of his members, pointing out to the latter that, while they might like Powell's views on immigration, they should remember that the man wanted to curb union power, 'which could wreck our organisation', and that he 'believes in unemployment as an instrument of economic policy.'[40]

But even as they condemned Powell's speech, some mainstream politicians were accepting the validity of his nightmare scenario. This conception of the public as readily stirred to racial violence ratcheted up the stakes, putting consensus politics under yet more pressure by fostering the idea that it was vulnerable to rapid overthrow. And by pitting people against Parliament, it bolstered the accusation made by New Left and New Right alike: that the consensus was an elite project. What if, on top of Powell's highly effective stirring of racial tensions, the much-feared economic collapse arrived? There was much urgent speculation about whether Powell might ride his tidal wave of public support all the way to Downing Street; and about a possible lurch to the right, even into dictatorship or fascism. The underlying question was whether Powell could turn his sudden, immense, terrifying popular appeal into mass enthusiasm for market economics.

* * *

In his all-out war against consensus, on immigration and incomes policy alike, Powell looked like he might shape Britain's future; but he had blown up his front-bench career. He was not the only maverick public figure who was struggling to find a new way forward who had risked his future to force a change. A couple of weeks after Powell's speech, Cecil King, still convinced that currency collapse was imminent, took even more desperate steps. In private, he tried to recruit Earl Mountbatten, Prince Philip's uncle and former Chief of the Defence Staff, as the figurehead for an emergency government, which would need to step in and assert control as the pound went over the brink, triggering chaos and a general strike. The army, he suggested, would have to restore order, with machine-gun posts on the street corners. In public, King used the *Mirror* front page to call for Wilson to go. In the end, there was a coup—by King's own board, who seized the chance to throw the old man out. Wilson would later note with satisfaction that King 'steadfastly maintained his watch for the financial doom that never came.'[41] The vividness of King's nightmares was matched only by his lack of imagination about what might actually need to come next.

Other maverick voices were edging towards a truly unthinkable idea: ending the taboo on mass unemployment. They fared little better. A few days after the Mountbatten meeting, the Industrial Policy Group denounced full employment as 'a path to eventual ruin'. They were only suggesting that unemployment be allowed to rise from 1.5 per cent to 2,[42] but the *Mirror* declared that the IPG was confronting 'democracy in Britain with the biggest test it has faced for a generation or more'. The businessmen could not be allowed to take over, but ignoring them might 'invite chaos of an equally unpleasant kind'.[43] But in fact, the IPG soon faded away. Likewise, Desmond Donnelly, hurrying towards political oblivion, tried in 1968 to draw attention to the way full employment had entrenched union power, underpinned by 'the British psychosis regarding unemployment ... dating from the 1930s', which had 'seared deep'.[44] He was expelled by Labour and became deeply involved with a free-market think-tank, the Institute of Economic Affairs. His lonely crusade would come to an end several years later in a hotel at Heathrow airport, where he took his own life.

* * *

King and Donnelly would not be the last public figures to lose their career to the struggle to reinvent the consensus. On the day she became the most powerful woman in the history of British democracy, Barbara Castle wrote in her diary: 'I am under no illusions that I may be committing political suicide.'[45]

Her mission, as Secretary of State for Employment and Productivity, was to transform incomes policy from a constraint into a constructive tool of government. If applied fairly, and softened by controls on prices and redistributive taxation, it could be used to secure productivity deals between workers and managers. From there, the Labour government could at last achieve its dream of a high-growth, high-wage, high-skill economy, with exports thriving and inflation under control. Castle was deeply uneasy about rising unemployment, and this was an attempt to renew the promises of 1945. It was 'the only safe basis on which we can advance again to full employment and prosperity.'[46]

So why 'political suicide'? Because pulling off this balancing act would be almost impossible. The trade unions were sick of the government interfering to hold down wages. A high rate of employment was a wonderful thing, but was it really too much to ask that the jobs concerned paid decently? If the unions would not work with her on incomes policy, Castle would be left with a choice of nightmares: the Brutus scenario, or a devastating split between trade unionists and the Labour Party.

Castle had barely started at her new department that April when her former allies in the Tribune Group of left-wing Labour MPs insisted on seeing her, every bit as hostile to wage restraint as the unions were.[47] Castle did not propose to apologise: she had embraced the messy compromises of government, and had no time for purist cavilling—perhaps because she still believed, more strongly than most, in the good that government could do. Over two hours of drink-fuelled argument, she tried to get across her 'desperate sense of economic urgency', telling them grimly that 'the Government was feeling its way through two potential sources of disaster.' While somehow dodging a 'breach with the trade union movement', she had to enforce incomes policy. If she failed, there would be the dreaded second devaluation, with all the economic dislocation and disrepute that might follow. This, she warned them, 'would put social democracy out of office in Britain for the next twenty years.'[48] This prediction—that if Labour and the unions fell out, both would lose out for a very long time—would prove rather far-sighted.

All the while, Castle was straining to resolve pay disputes. Months of grinding negotiations with unions and employers, in steel, the buses, the car industry, engineering and construction, sharpened her perspective on the trade unions. She began to see them as a vested interest.[49] She persevered with incomes policy, but through 1968, as wages continued to outstrip prices, and productivity, Castle began to think the unthinkable. Perhaps she had to do what those anxious businessmen and hapless politicians had been talking about, and find a way to tackle the power of the unions itself.

This was becoming a competitive field. As the strike wave rose through the later 1960s, the Conservative leadership under Edward Heath had resolved to address union power too. The psychological difficulty of breaking post-war taboos is clear from Heath's first major policy statement, which criticises industry for being stuck in the mindset of the 1930s—yet restates the commitment to full employment. Quintin Hogg, now Shadow Home Secretary, was more decisive. For years, he had opposed party pressure for action against the unions for fear of provoking them, but by 1966, he was advocating a sweeping new law to remove immunity from several types of strike. By 1968, this had become party policy. On Castle's first day as employment secretary, Heath's Conservatives published *Fair Deal at Work*: an array of measures, developed in part by Thatcher's future chancellor Geoffrey Howe, to tackle the way 'freedom is abused by irresponsible elements to the detriment of the nation'.[50] This made it all the more urgent for Castle to come up with something new. One left-wing Labour MP thought it clearly signalled that 'the consensus really was to be broken.'[51]

There was much talk about the overweening power of the unions. But who exactly were these tyrannical ogres who had to be constrained? As the more sophisticated critics of the 'unions' identified, the word referred to a byzantine tangle of traditions, systems and power relations. Since the end of the war, the old regime of authoritarian union bosses had given way to the rise of the shop steward: an ordinary worker who volunteered to take on various unpaid duties. This included cutting 'in-the-plant' wage deals for members of his union, sometimes by calling unofficial strikes. He could do this because he was not under the direct control of union officials. This explains why the unions were at once charged with being too strong and too weak, with triggering both tyranny and anarchy. This was less a monolithic concentration of power, more its diffusion—but that meant it was uncontrollable, and the effect could feel much the same. There is a case that the unions were scapegoats for a non-existent problem. They were blamed for Britain's relative economic decline but, as the economic historian Jim Tomlinson has pointed out, much of this 'declinism' was excessively pessimistic. The British economy simply had less capacity to grow than other, more badly war-damaged countries.

As Castle was trying to decide what to do about all this, two figures brought the shop stewards' rise right to the very top of the country's two biggest unions. Hugh Scanlon, the new President of the Amalgamated Union of Engineering and Foundry Workers, and Jack Jones, General Secretary Designate of the TGWU, were stern, middle-aged, bespectacled left-wingers, who would become the public face of union power. Their opinion of the post-war consensus was closer to that of the young radical New Left than to Castle's, not least through their support for their shop stewards. Like Castle, both had been forged in the hardships of the inter-war years. Unlike her, they did not think it was the unions that should sacrifice power to protect the advances Britain had made since.

Jack Jones was a child of the Liverpool docks. This exposed him early to the grind of poverty. At 13, he helped out running messages during the general strike. He fought in the Spanish Civil War, then made his name unionising West Midlands car plants. Hugh Scanlon, seven months younger, grew up poor in Manchester. His grandfather brought him up on America's great socialist novelists like Jack London, and their tales of heroic strikers, evil capitalists and dubious union bosses.[52] At 14, like the boys in *Love on the Dole*, Scanlon became an apprentice at the great engineering factory in Trafford Park. By 22, he was a shop steward.

All this shaped Jones' and Scanlon's outlook on the new world that had emerged after 1945. True, full employment had empowered workers and their unions; but if there was a concentration of power anywhere, it was in the hands of government, not the much-maligned shop stewards. Scanlon told *New Left Review* that employers had replaced the 'heavy stick of unemployment', used to keep workers down in the 1930s, with a subtler weapon: co-opting union leaders, making them 'a recognized part of the establishment'. Jones took a similar view; his youth in the docks had given him a hatred of corrupt, tyrannical union officials cosying up to management. He and Scanlon championed the shop stewards against this elite consensus. Jones scorned the way trade unionists 'have had dunned into them the soggy post-war theme that militancy is irresponsible, even unpatriotic'. Their solution to Britain's problems was for workers to be given far more control of their workplaces. That, they argued, was a better means than incomes policy to achieve a more productive economy.[53]

* * *

Castle was stuck. She had her staff corral a group of ministers, industrialists, Labour figures, industrial relations specialists, and the head of the prices and incomes board for a weekend at a government guest-house near Ascot. They were there to work out how to rejig the balance between union power and state power. Castle's civil servants did not invite anyone from the TUC's general council.

A commission under Lord Donovan, charged three years before with examining ways forward in industrial relations, had finally reported in June 1968. It merely recommended adding a Commission on Industrial Relations—another consensual group of trade unionists and businessmen—to the quango-heavy status quo. Castle had very little time for the Donovan Report's glacial complacency. She had never been immersed in the procedural arcana of the union movement. She was, after all, a graduate of the party left, who still believed in the value of state power.

In the light of the weekend's presentations and discussions, Castle roughed out a series of policy ideas, which she presented on the Sunday morning, curled up in an armchair in the guest-house conference room. These were a handful of limited new powers that would give ministers the ability to intervene in industrial disputes for the common good. She had found a way through at last! This, she thought, would help to achieve a positive, reasonable modernisation. It just meant the Labour-run state taking a little power from its comrades in the unions. One of the ministers present, Peter Shore, applauded Castle's new idea. If 'you wanted full employment you had to have an incomes policy', he recalled, and this meant that the government had to 'find ways of limiting, or indeed stopping, the power of the strike weapon being used against our incomes policy, and frankly to stoke up inflation.'[54] The implicit alternative—reducing the unions' power by letting unemployment soar—was not an option.

By the end of the year, Castle had a draft white paper, entitled *In Place of Strife*, ready to publish early in 1969. In a December memo introducing it to Cabinet colleagues, she warned that 'there will inevitably be opposition on individual points from vested interests.'[55] Conflict was always 'unavoidable' in industrial relations, but at present it was 'in some ways out of control and damag[ing] our society and economy'. The state had long been involved in this arena, often at the request of either employers or unions, and had to step in again now—because of the effect on the wider community, on the economy, and because even small strikes could have such broad impact. She proposed a raft of pro-union reforms, but the policies that drew all the attention were the new state powers. These would allow ministers to order ballots on official strikes and 'cooling off' periods before unofficial ones, and to enforce recommendations on inter-union recognition disputes. These proposals were popular with the public. Castle told *The Sunday Times* that trade unionists 'are very important people in our society ... they must behave like important people'.[56]

* * *

In June 1968, the Trades Union Congress had marked the centenary of its foundation in Manchester, in grand style. The Prime Minister joined 100,000 trade unionists for a day of celebrations including a parade, a carnival, brass bands, a male voice choir, primary-school dancers from the Lancashire coalfield, fireworks and a pageant. The TGWU exhibited a rocket, part-designed by Jack Jones, bearing the slogan 'The Union of the Future'.[57] There could hardly have been a more ebullient expression of confidence—except perhaps the commemorative stamp, the banquet at the Guildhall for 700 guests including the Queen, and a classical concert at the Royal Festival Hall, televised on BBC1, featuring a specially commissioned piece by the composer Malcolm Arnold.[58] These festivities were a great affirmation of the unions' hard-earned rise to power. In the foreword to a lavishly illustrated commemorative book, the TUC's General Secretary, George Woodcock, argued that it had asserted its 'right to share in the government of the nation.'

Yet the theme of that Malcolm Arnold composition was not the joys of power, or the bright prospects to come, but massacre. The *Peterloo Overture* evoked in drums, brass and woodwind the notorious day in August 1819 when armed Yeomanry on horseback had charged into a mass political meeting in Manchester, killing several people. As the new commemorative book made clear, trade unionism had advanced a very long way since then, but was sworn never to forget its past struggles. Castle intended for *In Place of Strife* to help the unions embrace their post-war role in running the country, and soar into the future. But, as an assertion of state power, it brought sabre-swinging spectres galloping out of the past. Jack Jones still remembered the tight legal constraints and 'victimisation' of unions imposed after the 1926 general strike.[59] The post-war settlement was meant to have drawn a line under all that. Yet now a Labour government, already responsible for wage control by force of law, was trying to seize crucial components of union power. The employment minister's proposed changes seemed to be part of the withering of post-war ideals, leaving only a dissent-squashing elitist machine, with unions' status dependent on rights bestowed from on high.

The realisation that this was one of British politics' rare struggles for power coursed through responses to *In Place of Strife* from the unions and the left. One of the many Labour back-benchers horrified by Castle's proposal said it was an attempt to legislate class struggle away, and build a corporate state.[60] *Tribune* called her plans 'tyrannical'.[61] What would happen when Conservative ministers or biased judges got their hands on the means to restrict the right to strike? Castle insisted that trade unionists would not go to prison, but what if they refused to pay their fines? Jack Jones warned that deducting fines from wage packets would cause 'the most intense resentment', more disputes, and very likely violence.[62] The intolerable bill had to be killed. Castle's own junior minister, Roy Hattersley, thought it was 'doomed, absolutely doomed.'[63]

Right from the beginning, Castle had made things even more difficult for herself. The TUC's George Woodcock accepted that full employment gave the unions such negotiating strength that this had to be tempered through a voluntary incomes policy, or even legislation, and that otherwise, a future government would break the taboo and let unemployment rise. He understood Castle's implicit logic: her solution was a way to preserve that taboo. But then Castle picked Woodcock to run the new Industrial Relations Commission, which meant that she now faced his hostile former deputy, Vic Feather, who took over at the TUC. Feather did not seem to see any threat, present or future, to government's commitment to full employment. Plus, he had known Castle as a teenager, and could not stand her.

From there, the employment secretary hit setback after setback. After a dispute at Ford's led to management taking the unions concerned to court, and losing, TGWU shop stewards declared a victory in the battle against her foolish plan to tackle strikes by legal means. On May Day 1969, a wave of protests closed docks, car plants and the newspapers. Fifteen thousand trade unionists gathered outside TUC headquarters, where a communist dockers' leader, Jack Dash, told them that Wilson, Castle and the chancellor Roy Jenkins would 'go down in the history of the trade union movement as the people who want to turn back the clock a century'.[64]

The unions had a lot more clout than just shouting in the street; as Jack Jones took to reminding them, they also sponsored around 130 Labour MPs. Even without that pressure, some in the Parliamentary Labour Party opposed the idea of the unions coming under state control. Others thought they were strong enough to resist Castle's innovation, but that the struggle would split the labour movement. Either way, it seemed futile to tamper with the status quo. On 3 March, fifty-five of Castle's colleagues voted against her bill, and around thirty abstained. Even Michael Foot launched ferocious attacks on his old friend's proposal. 'If the public is persuaded that industrial anarchy is the cause of all the trouble,' he cried, 'they will turn to political authoritarians to cure it: in other words, the Tories.'[65] Castle snapped back that 'he had grown soft on a diet of soft options because he never had to choose'.[66]

The opposition to Castle's troublesome attempt to reorder the status quo penetrated well beyond the back benches. Her scheme was formally rejected by the Labour Party's ruling National Executive Committee, on which she sat, by sixteen votes to five. She was astonished to see the Home Secretary, Jim Callaghan, vote against his own government's policy.[67] Unlike Wilson and Castle, Callaghan had risen through the unions. Resistance to tampering with the industrial relations consensus now reached almost to the heart of power. Wilson insisted the bill was 'essential to full employment',[68] which he and Castle were trying to persuade the unions to help them defend. But the idea that the commitment to full employment could ever end did not seem to cross people's minds in 1969; without that fear on the horizon, why bother with any of this?

Castle slogged round the country, evangelising for her scheme. She flew to Glasgow and took the ferry to Rothesay to make her appeal to the Scottish TUC. Her speech next morning was couched in friendly terms, but was forthright about the issue she was trying to tackle. She told the delegates: 'Since the Industrial Revolution brought these great concentrations of power into existence—first the organisations of employers, and then the organisations of unions—society has been arguing about the limits of their rights and their obligations'.[69] Her bill was win-win, she pleaded: the unions could boost their own authority and, at the same time, bolster a Labour government. She was still out making speeches almost to the bitter end.

* * *

Castle and Wilson's struggle with union power came to a head on 1 June at Chequers, over a private dinner of roast duck. This brought together the leaders of the two opposed sides, each accompanied by their nightmares. In one camp, determined to stop the state's bid to oppress the unions, were Feather, Jones and Scanlon. In the other, Barbara Castle and their host, Harold Wilson, both of them dogged by the fear of currency collapse, and determined to stop the damage they saw strikes doing to the economy.

Something else was in the back of their minds too. Wilson knew that Scanlon had once been a long-standing member of the pro-Soviet Communist Party of Great Britain; doubtless the union leaders remembered him accusing the seamen's union of a communist plot. And, ten months before this fraught Chequers summit, the Soviet Union had led an invasion of its supposed ally, Czechoslovakia, to crush the Prague Spring—the liberalisation movement led by the reformist leader Alexander Dubček.

Feather had put together an alternative to Castle's white paper, a *Programme for Action*, under which the TUC, rather than the employment secretary, would intervene to settle industrial disputes. He had told the government that the TUC programme would be put to work, if they would only drop the penal clauses from the bill. This was Jones' and Scanlon's price for cajoling their union executives into accepting the writ of the TUC. But Wilson and Castle had refused: precisely because of Jones and Scanlon, they insisted there had to be a bill, with definite powers of sanction. Feather had requested this meeting to try to force a resolution.

In 1931, another Labour Prime Minister had held a crisis summit with the trade unions, at the start of an earlier struggle for power. Back then, Ramsay MacDonald had tried to defend the dominance of finance against the unions' pleas not to cut the dole. Now, the unions were dominant, and it was the Prime Minister who was pleading with them. Scanlon, who had come straight from a conference of his unions' activists, 'was full of dire warnings about what would happen in the factories if the Government went ahead with the intended legislation.'[70] Wilson asked if he meant strikes and protests, as on May Day. Scanlon nodded. The two union leaders were clearly determined, Wilson thought, to make the legislation 'unworkable'.

Chequers holds a collection of memorabilia from the English Civil War, and at one point in the evening, Wilson showed his guests a life mask of Oliver Cromwell, who, notoriously, had once shut down Parliament by force of arms. Perhaps it was a hint. As the conversation ran on past midnight, it became much more hard-edged. Upstairs, over brandy in the Long Gallery, Castle challenged the two union leaders on why they were manoeuvring like this. Scanlon 'cheerfully admitted' that he was not interested in dealing with the issue of strikes. He was out to defeat the bill, because once the principle of state controls had been conceded, 'there was no limit to the extent to which it could be pushed'. His people could not accept the introduction of any legal powers that could later be used against the unions by a Conservative minister. 'They thought nothing of the argument,' Wilson would note, that failing to deal with the strike issue 'would make such a Government … more likely.'

To Wilson, if the TUC 'hoped to crack their whip' over union-affiliated Labour MPs and coerce them to vote against the government, 'it would clearly mean that the TUC, a state within a state, was putting itself above the Government in deciding what a Government could and could not do.' For the Prime Minister, this raised another nightmare, even worse than economic woes. Scanlon's attitude defied the whole basis of parliamentary democracy. But Scanlon stood firm on the unions' right to assert their power. Quoting Stalin, he asked, 'How many divisions has the Pope?' He told Wilson that they did not want him to be another Ramsay MacDonald—siding with the capitalists and splitting the labour movement. The implication was clear: this time, the unions were stronger than the government, and Wilson should act accordingly.

Wilson replied that he was no MacDonald, but he also refused to be a Dubček, saying, 'I'm not going to surrender to your tanks, Hughie'—a riposte to Scanlon's crack about 'divisions'.

But, over the course of the next seventeen days, Wilson *was* slowly pushed to the point of surrender. First the parliamentary party formally folded. Then on 17 June came what Castle called 'the most traumatic day of my political life'.[71] Through the course of a day-long Cabinet meeting, her colleagues stuck, one by one, to the status quo. Even Peter Shore, who had been so convinced of the necessity of all this, now accused Castle of talking in overly militaristic terms, and threw in his hand. When the 'iron' chancellor Roy Jenkins did the same, it was all over. The next morning, the unions' tanks rolled into Downing Street. Castle and Wilson sat in another crisis meeting at Number 10, this time with Feather, Jones, Scanlon and the rest of the TUC general council. The government agreed to drop the penal clauses. In return they could not even secure a rule change, only a 'solemn and binding' undertaking.

Castle and Wilson had managed to avoid a disastrous breach with the unions, but only by giving in. Over the following year, Feather and the TUC would indeed try to settle industrial disputes, and claim some success; but the number of strikes jumped by almost half, the number of days lost more than doubled, and there was no sign of the solemnly promised disciplinary action. On television the evening after the Downing Street deal, Edward Heath observed of the Labour government that, 'although they may still wear the trappings of office, the power resides elsewhere'.[72] Castle's challenge had been doomed from the start, just like the unions' challenge to the power of finance in 1931.

But that defeat, and the splitting of the Labour government that followed, had still spelled the beginning of the end for the old economic orthodoxy—because it had drawn attention to just how powerful finance had become, and radicalised its opponents against it. Likewise, the breaking of Castle's bill drew similar attention to just how powerful the unions had become by the end of the Sixties, with similar radicalising impact.

Castle bounced back by starting to prepare another state intervention in industrial relations: what became the Equal Pay Act. But she had been right that all this was political suicide. The supposedly authoritarian minister did not break the unions. They broke her. For good or ill, she was the first person to try to reshape the post-war industrial consensus from within government, even at the cost of her career. How much this still matters is clear from the frequent claim that, had she only won, much of what followed need never have happened.

7

WITH THEIR RIFLES LOADED?

1970–4

One Saturday evening in March 1971, Edward Heath held a dinner party at Chequers. Around the fireplace in the Long Gallery, where Wilson had battled Scanlon and his tanks, Heath was hosting a few select members of his new government. They had been invited because they had served under Heath's predecessor, Harold Macmillan. And in front of the fire sat the old man himself, reflecting on things past.

In June 1970, to everyone's surprise but his own, Edward Heath had beaten Harold Wilson to become Prime Minister, bursting to get started on his comprehensive programme to modernise Britain. This was to be based on a new Industrial Relations Bill, which would constrain union power by force of law—including the possibility, if it came to it, of trade unionists going to prison. The aim was to reduce strikes, and hold down wage inflation. Heath was following in the footsteps of Barbara Castle, yet somehow he hoped for a better reception.

To Jack Jones, this was part of 'a policy of confrontation which had not been experienced since the 1930s'.[1] He and Hugh Scanlon led the fight-back. Demonstrations, factory meetings and mass rallies demanded that the government 'Kill the Bill', as militants clamoured for a general strike. A march of trade unionists, stretching 7 miles from front to back, advanced in orderly fashion through central London. On Monday 1 March 1971, Scanlon led a one-day political strike by 1.2 million workers, which shut down the Scottish shipyards, the national newspapers and almost the entire car industry.

157

That Saturday night, Heath's Attorney General, Peter Rawlinson, listened from a window seat in the Chequers Long Gallery as Macmillan delivered 'a stern, paternal warning against dividing the One Nation which the past quarter-century had created' in the wake of the two world wars:

> We must remember, said the sage, that the men from Stockton and the Yorkshire coalfields had fought and died with him at Ypres and Passchendaele and he had seen their sons march past their Sovereign in triumph in the great parade after the victory in North Africa. Here the orator flicked away what appeared by the gesture to be the ghost of an inconvenient tear. Happily only temporarily overcome, he went on gravely to reflect that we had at last become as a nation truly one people. No one and indeed no organisation of our people must be rushed. Caution, he counselled, staring into the fire, caution and, above all, restraint.

'The significance of that speech,' Rawlinson thought, was 'that the Old Guard reckoned that Ted, by giving notice that he intended to challenge the trade-union barons, was launching an abrasive initiative which threatened to blast the spirit of consensus under which the country had been governed since the end of the world war.'[2]

It appears that, in his memoir, Heath himself misremembered that evening, deluding himself that he had had Macmillan's support. As Barbara Castle once observed, Heath was a man divided against himself. This chapter tells the story of how he tried to forge ahead towards the shimmer of the future—modernising the economy, reforming industrial relations, remaking the consensus. And of how, no matter how hard he struggled, he was dragged backwards by the spectres of the past.

* * *

In the late 1930s, Macmillan's *The Middle Way* had answered the young Heath's need for a Tory solution to the scourge of mass unemployment. In the 1950s, as Prime Minister, Macmillan had made Heath his protégé, promoting him into such *Middle Way* roles as labour minister—that is, minister for conciliating the trade unions—and Secretary of State for Industry, Trade and Regional

Development. Overall, Heath had been the very model of a modernising moderate: the politician as bloodless technocrat, eyes fixed on efficiency and productivity. Yet now, as Prime Minister himself, here he was, risking his career to try to transform the consensus politics his mentor had embodied. In the run-up to the 1970 general election, he had even seemed determined to break from the post-1945 model altogether, promising to put a stop to government intervention in industry.

Within the Conservative Party, there was a rising generation of more unapologetically free-market–oriented MPs, such as Margaret Thatcher, who were more focused on present economic failure than older people's memories of the Depression, or the party's defeat in 1945. A book lauding the new Cabinet, *Here Come the Tories*, dismissed Macmillan as 'a prisoner of the 1930s'.[3] Such views chimed with the large swathe of the party who had never really accepted the post-war consensus, who increasingly wanted something done about the unions and the rising number of strikes, and who were ready to cheer on a leader who would sing their songs. And then there was Enoch Powell. His notoriety had in some ways tainted his economic ideas, but his explosive exit and sudden popularity do seem to have sharpened the feeling that something revolutionary might win wide support.[4]

Heath shared the sense that, since the war, both parties had let wages outstrip productivity—partly because of strikes—and that it was time for something new. As *The Guardian*'s Peter Jenkins wrote, Heath's line was that 'the old consensus ... had failed'. But—like Castle, unlike the Tory right—the new Prime Minister saw his move to bring the trade unions under the law not as a radical rupture, but just a sensible piece of modernisation. He appears to have thought that he could simply usher in a new version of the post-war settlement, diluting the unions' power, without a fight. But when he told the Commons that industrial relations issues would be sorted out by 'the force of argument and not the argument of force', Labour MPs laughed.[5]

Heath's whole approach is a lesson in how hard it is to break from consensus. Six months before the 1970 election, the Conservative Shadow Cabinet had held a policy conference at a hotel near Croydon called Selsdon Park. The press gleefully reported on Heath's team scoffing pheasant and quaffing claret, but did not point out that they were trying to have their cake and eat it. Heath did want to reduce the power of the unions, allowing companies to 'get rid of surplus labour', pay fewer staff more, and raise efficiency.[6] So far, so free market. But this was no ideological conversion: Heath was not desperate to get rid of the taboo on mass unemployment, any more than to declare war on the unions. It was all very pragmatic.

The press, however, was keen to detect a more decisive turn out of the decaying consensus. Keith Joseph, Heath's spokesman on trade, had been making speeches that went further towards Powell's free-market ideas, and Selsdon was written up as the birth of a new, tougher Toryism—a 'radical break ... with the past'.[7] Harold Wilson immediately spotted a way of 'rousing people's fears',[8] suggesting that Heath was now revealed as a Powellite throwback, 'Selsdon Man'. This, Wilson railed, was 'the Toryism of the Thirties', driven by 'an atavistic desire to destroy 25 years of social revolution.'[9]

Heath was cheered on, however, by many members of his party, who were delighted by his apparent revival of the old free-market faith, and he bemusedly consented to play Selsdon Man. On a manifesto promising no more bailouts for 'lame duck' firms, no more compulsory wage control, and no more untrammelled union power, he had won, hobbling Powell's plans to replace him. But as he settled in at Number 10, he remained a politician rooted in the 1930s, trained in consensus politics, and now burdened with unrealistic expectations on his own side. And Wilson's nightmare scenario about a return to the Thirties was waiting to be used against him.

* * *

At first it looked as though the new government really was going to make the radical break Macmillan feared. Just before the election, Wilson's technology minister Tony Benn had won Cabinet backing to rescue Palmer's shipyard near Jarrow, acutely aware of the 'tremendous emotional overtones' it had for Labour.[10] Benn had got the wrong yard: this was not the one that had sacked the Jarrow marchers. But it was still an area blighted by high unemployment. After losing power, he accompanied a delegation from Jarrow to his old MinTech office, hoping that his Conservative replacements would pay some heed to those memories of the 1930s.

The new technology minister, John Davies, had been the chief of the Confederation of British Industry until Heath recruited him to bring the snap of tough business expertise into government. He was unmoved by 1930s symbolism, accurate or otherwise, and refused to help. Under Heath, there would be no more funding for lame ducks. The only thing Benn and the outraged delegates received was a lecture on the free market from Davies' junior minister, Nicholas Ridley.[11]

Unlike Benn, however, Ridley—much as he was the son of a viscount—had actually worked in the Tyne shipyards, as a civil engineer, and was basing his case on eight years of first-hand experience.[12] He was only 7 at the time of the Jarrow Crusade, and his youth had been marred not by mass unemployment, but by Attlee's nationalisations. Ridley's free-market zeal sprang from the way that trade union power 'rampaged unrestricted' in those publicly owned shipyards.[13] Benn dismissed Ridley's anti-nationalisation worldview as Victorian, but the junior minister was set on turning it into the future. He and Davies scrapped Wilson's industrial strategy quangos,[14] and let the Mersey Docks and Harbour Board go into liquidation. Davies declared this approach a battle against 'national decadence.'[15]

Benn was abandoning the old ways too, but in the opposite direction. His descent in the Millbank lift, from his old department to the streets outside, marked his departure from the technocratic Wilsonian consensus. When liquidation threatened one of his own MinTech creations, the amalgamation of four unprofitable shipyards called Upper Clyde Shipbuilders, he went to Glasgow and marched alongside the communist shop stewards who had occupied the yards and instigated workers' control. Then Davies announced that UCS would indeed be liquidated, at the cost of perhaps 20,000 jobs: a brutal blow to the consensus on full employment. Benn 'attacked him violently' in the Commons.[16]

Nevertheless, by the end of 1971, Heath had some cause for confidence. The government's voluntary incomes policy had suffered a series of defeats, despite two states of emergency; but ministers had faced down a postal workers' strike, and now public-sector workers were on board. After a grinding parliamentary struggle, the Industrial Relations Act had finally passed. The trade unions vowed total non-cooperation, but Heath had succeeded where Castle had failed. In the autumn, inflation had reached 10 per cent, but had then begun to fall. The balance of payments was in surplus. Perhaps Heath really could find a way through to his vision of an efficient, prosperous economy—capped, he hoped, by admission into the European Common Market—without too much more hullabaloo.

But all through 1971, the unemployment statistics had been climbing, and were heading towards what was widely agreed to be an unthinkable figure: 1 million. From 1921, through the interwar era and even into 1940, the unemployment total had never fallen below a million. Since then, bar one blip in the winter of 1947, it had never risen back above it. Now it was about to happen again.

* * *

Fairly or not, this looked like a trail of destruction left by Selsdon Man. And if Heath's government was choosing to let unemployment rise as a matter of policy—as they had with the Upper Clyde shipyards—then there might be severe consequences. In November 1970, in the wake of John Davies' speech about national decadence, *The Observer* had warned that

> there are overwhelmingly strong social arguments against a policy which depends on high unemployment and more bankruptcies to make it work. Any free political system depends on establishing a consensus—'the mobilisation of consent', as it has been called—for effectiveness. A 'tough' policy would break this consensus and introduce a new element of social conflict.[17]

The paper's political correspondent had underlined the fear that 'the unions might resort to disruption, and even to violence, rather than submit to mass unemployment, which could be the Conservatives' last anti-inflation card.'[18]

In April 1971, Labour's barbs that the Conservatives wanted to drag Britain back to the Thirties had finally started to draw blood. In the Commons, Tony Benn had charged that 'The Cabinet has deliberately set out to destroy the whole post-war consensus based on the maintenance of a high and stable level of employment and the whole social fabric that went with it.'[19] On 5 October, Wilson had spoken at Labour's annual conference, guilt-tripping Heath with his evocation of the jobless, anxious Wilson family in 1931. There was a ready assembly of pre-war images for Wilson to prod awake. In May, for example, the BBC2 series *Yesterday's Witness* had memorialised the Jarrow Crusade, interviewing surviving marchers.

In vain, the government tried the usual Keynesian measures to drum up jobs, with promises to do more. Heath reassured the TUC that his government was committed to full employment. But just after 11.30am on 20 January 1972, the employment secretary Robert Carr confirmed to the Cabinet that, later that day, if 'the statistics for Northern Ireland were included, the total number of unemployed would be seen to exceed 1 million.' On television that evening, as Carr expressed regret that it had come to this, he looked close to tears. He issued a statement saying, 'These are figures which I had hoped never to see again'.[20] He had never forgotten how, one day in the 1930s, his father's chauffeur had driven him to Westminster School, and he had seen a contingent of hunger marchers on their way to Parliament.[21]

Carr was not the only minister round the Cabinet table that morning who had memories like this. At the side of the Prime Minister sat Quintin Hogg, now Lord Hailsham, who had once hurried home from war to cajole his fellow Tories to back full employment. Opposite Heath sat Anthony Barber, who, aged 19, had led a unit of Yorkshire miners at Dunkirk. Even those ministers too young to remember the early Thirties had inherited the folk memory. In his maiden speech in 1959, James Prior had affirmed that 'I will never work or stand for any party which would support a policy of unemployment.'[22] Likewise, Peter Walker was born in 1932, just after the eighteen months when his father had been unable to provide for the family, but this hardship had nevertheless instilled in him a 'hatred of unemployment'.[23] And Walker knew that, upstairs from the Cabinet Room in the Number 10 flat, Heath kept a painting by the Durham pitman-painter Norman Cornish, of a cloth-capped miner slumped at a bar: a reminder of the bad old days.[24]

Most of these people had come into politics in the afterglow of war-time unity, watched over by mild men like Macmillan; now they were having to deal with extremes they had thought were gone forever. With the post-war boom over, it was no longer possible to have high public spending, full employment and low inflation, all at once. Unlike lucky old Macmillan, they were going to have to make a choice between nightmares.

That afternoon, when Heath entered the Commons for Prime Minister's Questions, the chamber exploded. Labour back-benchers leapt up, chanting 'Heath out!' Two ex-miners from high-unemployment areas of Derbyshire led the way: Tom Swain orchestrated the chants, while Dennis Skinner—whose childhood memories of the 1930s included keeping debt collectors from the door—ran over to confront Heath. The Prime Minister was about to leave for Brussels, to sign the treaty taking Britain into the EEC. Skinner shook his fist in the Prime Minister's face and reportedly shouted: 'You ought to be ashamed of yourself, with one million on the dole', and: 'You are not fit to run this country'.[25] Heath, mouth tight, already badly upset about the unemployment figures, turned away. When he started to take questions over the shouting, he managed ten words before Swain was in front of him, whacking an evening paper down on the Despatch Box and bellowing, 'Here's the answer to your first bleeding question'. The headline read '1,023,583'. Heath pushed it aside, glaring at the yells of 'Fascist!' Opposite him, Wilson did nothing to stop the wall of noise. Finally, for the first time in the twentieth century, the Speaker suspended Prime Minister's Questions. The press declared that the figure was 'shameful',[26] and 'well over the limit of what is acceptable'.[27]

Heath spent the weekend in Brussels signing the treaty: his crowning achievement, and a neat expression of his ambiguous politics. From one angle, entering the Common Market was a radical break, opening Britain to a bracing gale of competition, forcing it to shake off 'decline' and stand on its own two feet. Yet from another, it simply extended Heath's technocratic view of consensus: great men meeting to sort things out in everyone else's best interests, with no more need for conflict.

On Monday 24th, back at the Despatch Box, Wilson told Heath he was running 'a Government who have been proud to tear up even the mild prospectus on full employment of Sir Winston Churchill's coalition Government, and have destroyed the consensus by which post-war Governments have governed.'[28] Jarrow's MP Ernie Fernyhough suggested that, unlike last time, the young would not put up with mass unemployment. Either work must be found, or 'the situation can lead to the end of our democracy'.[29] Tony Benn thought the Cabinet was 'very frightened' by what it had done.[30] As Labour surely knew, Heath had no desire to use mass unemployment as an economic lever; Jim Prior wrote later that it 'was counter to everything Ted believed in'.[31] But Heath was also struggling—just as Wilson had—with wage inflation.

Winding up for the government, Robert Carr promised 'all-out war' on unemployment.[32] Yet it was a war that would be fought in a series of humiliating retreats. The return of mass unemployment sent the Heath administration all the way back to the old consensus policies it had tried to leave behind. And no sooner had ministers started coming to terms with the return of an old nightmare than they found themselves confronted with a new one, courtesy of an obscure trade unionist from Yorkshire. The reverberations of these two huge shocks in rapid succession would eventually force some of Heath's colleagues to start thinking the unthinkable.

* * *

On a February Saturday night, a couple of weeks after Dennis Skinner shook his fist in Ted Heath's face, a young trade union official was on the motorway south from Barnsley, heading for the Midlands. Arthur Scargill was on the Yorkshire executive of the National Union of Mineworkers, which had been on strike for almost a month—the first official, national miners' strike since 1926. He was 34, and had been in the industry since he was 15.[33] A jazz fan too young to remember the Thirties, he had turned 18 in 1956, the year he was elected to the National Council of the Young Communist League. Now a rising star of the NUM left, he defined himself against older moderates, like the union's new president. This was Joe Gormley, born into dirt poverty near Wigan, who had gone down the pit in the depths of the Depression, and emerged as a creature of the post-war settlement: a believer in socialism won through hard negotiation and through gradual, consensual progress. But to Scargill, that was slow surrender. Since the late 1960s, the promises of 1945 had looked clapped-out. Harold Wilson may once have envisioned a *New Deal for Coal*, but in office, he had overseen swingeing pit closures as Britain moved to using oil.

Gormley's political nightmares were shaped by inter-war poverty—he endured a rotten tooth for years—but Scargill was driven by a different vision. As a teenager, like many British socialists, he had read Jack London's dystopic novel *The Iron Heel*, and later said London 'was more responsible for making me a socialist than anything.'[34] *The Iron Heel* (1908) is a vision of compromise as the road to hell. It teaches that there is a 'tacit conspiracy'—a brutal capitalist machine that enslaves or co-opts everyone, from politicians, the army and the police to trade union leaders. Only radical socialists and hard-faced businessmen can see that what really matters is power, which can be won only through an almighty trial of strength.

So, where Gormley considered political strikes out of order, and only reluctantly accepted the 1972 miners' walk-out, Scargill seized the chance to smash the discredited consensus and advance towards socialism. As he would put it three years later: 'We were out to defeat Heath and Heath's policies because we were fighting a government. Anyone who thinks otherwise was living in cloud-cuckoo land. We had to declare *war* on them...'[35]

To hold the line against wage inflation, the government was determined to ensure that the NUM did not win more than the National Coal Board had offered. But miners' pay had fallen badly behind other workers', and they wanted a 27 per cent raise. There was plenty of public sympathy for these men doing vital, underpaid, dangerous work; but at first it seemed likely they would end up giving in. Thames TV made a documentary called *The Miners' Last Stand*.

To much surprise, the strike—led by energetic, organised activists like Scargill—quickly proved effective. It became a concerted attack on the power supply system, focusing picketing effort on pressure points across the country: docks, coal depots, power stations, and the roads and railways that connected them. The miners received widespread backing from the railway workers and dockers. The TUC told union members not to cross picket lines 'in any circumstances'.[36] It also helped that so many miners now had cars: once a tip-off came through about a particular site, 'flying' pickets could be there swiftly. This unexpected creativity was of a piece with the upheavals of 1968: a revolt against stolid, technocratic consensus, driven by improvised, do-it-yourself, smash-the-old thinking. The NUM even improvised a permit process to allow supplies of coal to reach hospitals and schools, and followed lorries to make sure they did not cheat the system.

But all this was becoming a challenge to the state. At three o'clock in the morning on Sunday 6 February, Scargill arrived in Birmingham, and prepared to lay siege to a coking plant.

* * *

Curiously, the Heath government's strategy of trying to be consensual and confrontational at the same time was not proving very effective. Its voluntary 'pay norm' was in line with the gentle ways of post-war industrial relations, but it had also introduced legislation that could see trade unionists go to prison. As far as the NUM left was concerned, they were fighting the Iron Heel, or at least Selsdon Man. The NUM General Secretary, Lawrence Daly, called the Heath regime 'the most reactionary Conservative government that we've ever seen in Britain'.[37] The National Coal Board and the coal merchants demanded the police be more effective,[38] but the Ministerial Committee on Emergencies could not find a way to use the law against them.[39] The Home Office and the police were scrambling to set up communication and coordination systems to match what the NUM had already established. Meanwhile, power stations were beginning to shut, and Heath and Davies were divided over whether to call a state of emergency.

This was effectively the same struggle for power as had played out in the Long Gallery at Chequers three years earlier, pitting Wilson and Castle against Jones and Scanlon. Could union power force the government to give in once more, and give the workers what they wanted? What the developing narrative of the strike had so far lacked was a set-piece: a single confrontation to crystallise the struggle and all that was at stake, in visually compelling form.

Since six o'clock on the Sunday morning, Scargill had been hard at work with his loud-hailer and 'team of lieutenants',[40] marshalling pickets outside the West Midlands Gas Board's coking

167

plant at Nechells Place in the Saltley area of Birmingham, doing all he could to stop lorries from going in to collect coke. As the week went on, more and more miners had poured in from across the country to close the depot, and more and more police had been drafted in to hold them back. There were scuffles and skirmishes, injuries and arrests. The picket had reduced the numbers of lorries, but the gates stayed open—and more lorries kept coming, often driving at the gates in convoy without stopping. When one pushed through the crowd, two pickets were hurt, and a police officer's thigh bone snapped.

'The Battle of Saltley Gate' was not strategically crucial. It mattered because, each night on television, the nation could watch the power slowly defeating the government in action. This is what happened without some degree of consensus in industrial relations, and it left the government and the police facing an invidious choice: should force be used against pickets? It appears that the Heath government ordered the depot must be kept open 'at all costs'.[41]

At *all* costs? On Wednesday 9 February, the government was finally driven by the severe pressure on the power supply to declare the long-delayed state of emergency, imposing draconian restrictions on electricity use. But the triggering of emergency powers also meant that, in theory, the state could now deploy troops. How would the unions react to that?

Desperate to close the depot, Scargill and other Yorkshire pickets went to exhort Birmingham's trade unionists to come and support them. From 7.30am the next day, the Chief Constable of the West Midlands, Sir Derrick Capper, was at the gates in his 'full regalia',[42] having told that morning's *Times*: 'If these people come they will be here illegally and we shall take the necessary steps'.[43] The police lines were 'four deep'.[44] He had assured the Home Secretary, Reginald Maudling, that he had enough officers to keep the gates open. But then, as Scargill told it, banners appeared over the crest of the hill. Over 10,000 local trade unionists arrived to join the 2,000 pickets already on duty. In the 1930s, the non-unionised car workers of the Midlands had been unsympathetic to the distant grumbles from struggling old industries like mining. Now they were united.

In Cabinet later that morning, the industry secretary John Davies was making dire predictions about the electricity running out, the employment minister Robert Carr was saying a deal with the miners would undermine the incomes policy, and Attorney General Rawlinson was lamenting the difficulties faced by the police. At this point, Reggie Maudling was handed a note, and announced that the Saltley gates were closed. Chief Constable Capper had U-turned, and ordered the gates shut because 'his men could not keep the crowd back' to get the lorries through without 'grave risk to life and property'.[45] Heath instructed Carr, Davies and Rawlinson to work out how to stop anything like Saltley happening again. In his view, the police had been 'weak, and frightened of a scrap with the pickets'. It was 'the most vivid, direct and terrifying challenge to the rule of law that I could ever recall emerging within our own country.'[46]

This, more than any other single moment, was the point where the long post-war consensus on industrial relations was fatally wounded. Because what had happened at Saltley, ministers agreed, 'provided disturbing evidence of the ease with which, by assembling large crowds, militants could flout the law with impunity because of the risk that attempts to enforce it would provoke disorder on a large scale.'[47] Between *In Place of Strife* and the miners' strike, governments of both parties had now been publicly forced by the unions to give in. As long as their power was underpinned by the taboo against returning to mass unemployment, some unions at least were apparently invincible. And when the jobless figure had hit a million, Heath had begun to sacrifice everything to reaffirm that taboo. The Battle of Saltley Gate was one of the first struggles for power in the early stages of the death of consensus—and while that consensus favoured the unions, the struggle was always likely to go their way.

This has something in common with how the same basic process had played out in 1931. Back then, the boot was on the other foot. The unions, and elements within Labour, had tried hopelessly to hold off cuts to the dole, but had had no chance in the face of the Treasury and the banks, whose power was underpinned by the taboo against deficits and inflation. Only after that taboo was overridden could a second, much more evenly matched, struggle for power take place between the labour movement and the forces of finance. So what would it take now to override the governing nightmare of mass unemployment? As one minister who was in Cabinet when the news from Saltley arrived would recall, 'To the Left it came to assume legendary proportions. To large numbers of politicians and commentators it proved that no one could hope to stand up to the miners. Police self-confidence was shattered.'

Unlike Heath, that minister did not yearn for consensus. Like Scargill, Margaret Thatcher grasped that sooner or later, there would have to be another battle for power:

> For me, what happened at Saltley took on no less significance than it did for the Left. I understood, as they did, that the struggle to bring trade unions properly within the rule of law would be decided not in the debating chamber of the House of Commons, nor even on the hustings, but in and around the pits and factories where intimidation had been allowed to prevail.[48]

Meanwhile, the news from Saltley simply helped to breed a vivid new Conservative nightmare of government foundering against uncontrollable union power, and of what might have to be done to break it. As Heath's Private Secretary Douglas Hurd would write later in the decade, 'These weeks of the 1972 miners' dispute were the worst of all. There seemed no way through.'[49]

Pay talks had by now completely broken down, and Carr had appointed a Court of Inquiry to adjudicate. While ministers waited for it to report, and as Davies' last-ditch power cuts bit, angry Conservative MPs turned on Home Secretary Maudling. His whole attitude seemed unforgivably complacent, from the lack of planning to withstand a coal strike to the way he had strolled to the Despatch Box to declare the state of emergency. Why, they asked, had he not deployed the army to bolster the police? He retorted, 'If they had been sent in, should they have gone in with their rifles loaded or unloaded?'[50]

Maudling was a long-standing champion of consensus politics. He believed that the fruits of capitalism had to be shared by compromise, or there would be 'uncontainable resentment'.[51] His reluctance may also have been coloured by the fact that, as Home Secretary, he had been the minister ultimately responsible when British soldiers in Northern Ireland had shot thirteen people dead on Bloody Sunday, two weeks earlier. Either way, he thought that using troops at Saltley, in any form, 'could have been disastrous'.[52]

If deploying soldiers against the unions was unthinkable, so was allowing such blatant expressions of union power to become normalised. But, as Heath's government was still unwilling to break the unemployment taboo (which would be no help in the short-term anyway), ministers were forced to consider whether servicemen could provide some sort of 'way through'—specifically, a way to get coal through the picket lines before the electricity ran out. It was accepted in Whitehall that even using the army to transport coal stocks would provoke great hostility from the unions. But by the following Tuesday, 15 February, as panic buying continued in supermarkets, and with hospital power cuts coming in ten days, the Home Office and the Chief Constables even discussed the use of *armed* troops.[53]

The police chiefs advised that that would be 'the worst possible step'.[54] Nevertheless, Sir Philip Allen, the Home Office's permanent secretary—presumably under instruction from his boss Maudling—set out plans drawn up the previous year for how servicemen could be used to distribute coal. Clearly deeply worried, he attached the nightmare scenario that would likely follow. The police would need to keep a route through the pickets clear for the soldier-driven lorries, which police believed they could manage—but 'at the probable cost of great violence'. The risk that 'people could get killed would have to be accepted.' The police, Sir Philip added, stressed that deploying armed servicemen, 'with all that that implied, should be reserved as a last possible resort.'[55] The Ministry of Defence was 'adamant that under no circumstances could soldiers driving tankers force a picket line': they must be 'escorted through pickets by police'.[56]

On 18 February, a week on from Saltley, the Cabinet was told that there were plans for a 20 to 35 per cent reduction in electricity supply; and that, if it came to it, there was 'scope for using Servicemen to move stocks of coal and oil'. An operational telegram from the army's Southern Command that morning reads: 'SITUATION CONSIDERED VERY SERIOUS, LIKELEHOOD [sic] EXISTS THAT OPERATION CUTTER WILL HAVE TO BE PUT INTO EFFECT AT VERY SHORT NOTICE AND BE FULLY EFFECTIVE WITHIN 48 HOURS.'[57] At the noon meeting of the Ministerial Committee on Emergencies, Philip Allen reported that—notwithstanding the Chief Constables' and his own fears—the police had 'agreed, if the need arose, to do what they could to 'ensure' that deliveries by volunteers or servicemen 'were not interrupted by pickets.'[58]

That night, the Cabinet met by power-cut candlelight. Heath had decided to take personal charge of negotiating with the miners' leaders, and needed to agree his stance with ministers. Once again, union power confronted them with a choice of nightmares. They could give in to the NUM's demands, which would destroy the government's authority.[59] Or they could refuse, at the risk of the power supply running out, which would have much the same effect. That is, unless the servicemen on standby could keep supplies flowing—but that promised a third nightmare, of violent political unrest. Lord Hailsham came to the conclusion that they were facing the 'Abyss': government collapse. He tried to persuade the Cabinet not to 'show the white flag'; if they did, the government would last 'no more than 6 weeks.' He wanted to plough on, out of principle, with all the dangers that such a course threatened. But his colleagues were 'indecisive [and] divided'.[60] Heath finally struck a deal with the miners, but only after even more concessions.

The Spectator excoriated the government for striking confrontational poses it could not live up to: 'having created an image of hard-headedness, inflexibility and dogmatism, [it] cannot complain if a trade union uses its own strength to further its members' interests.'[61] As with Wilson and Castle's *In Place of Strife*, trade unionists had come to Downing Street to force the Prime Minister to capitulate. Back then, Heath had mocked Wilson, saying that 'power resides elsewhere'. Now, he was on television again, trying to call for a renewed consensus:

> When people said, 'the miners won a great victory' or 'the Government lost that one', what did they mean? In the kind of country we live in, there could not be any 'we' or 'they'. There was only 'us'—all of us. If the Government is defeated then the country is defeated ... We must find a more sensible way to settle our differences...[62]

But as the Prime Minister licked his wounds, Enoch Powell appeared, salt in hand, and branded the deal an 'unconditional surrender'.[63]

* * *

Heath's refusal to countenance a return to mass unemployment dragged him back to the old post-war ways. In the months that followed, he and his ministers announced retreat after retreat, to gales of laughter in the Commons. In a bid to save jobs, Trade and Industry Secretary John Davies, the supposed business hard man, resuscitated industrial policy just months after trying to kill it. The chancellor, Anthony Barber, delivered an expansionist Budget designed to turn Britain back towards full employment, even at the risk of stoking inflation.

Meanwhile, the new Industrial Relations Act took effect. It was meant to remove the need for incomes policy by reducing the unions' power, partly by banning the tactics that had helped the miners win in February. But the TUC told unions to refuse to co-operate. The legislation had created a court that was meant to settle disputes, but it ended up sending five London dockers to prison—the authoritarian nightmare which the unions would not tolerate. Dockers downed tools—as did printers, closing the national newspapers. At Jack Jones' behest, the TUC called a one-day general strike in July; within hours, the jailed dockers were released. This was not quite as dramatic as it seemed, but the unions had rendered Heath's new law unworkable.

Heath had a fourth defeat to come. With inflation burgeoning, he invited the CBI and TUC to talks to try to agree a consensus-style, voluntary prices and incomes policy; but they could not reach a deal. Instead, in November 1972, Heath had to break *another* election pledge by resorting to statutory incomes policy, as Wilson had in 1966. With his Industrial Relations Act discredited, and the mass unemployment taboo still all-powerful, this was the Prime Minister's only way to try to hold down wages, however humiliating it was to reverse course yet again.[64]

Heath remained constrained by his determination to avoid the unemployment nightmare, but in the aftermath of Saltley, different nightmare visions—of union power—were crowding into view. *The Times* denounced the dockers' breaking of the Industrial Relations Act as 'anti-democratic'. It feared that the consensus approach to politics and strikes was now giving way to 'the direct clash of power against power', warning: 'At the end of this road is the man with the bomb.'[65]

* * *

When Heath announced the statutory incomes policy, Enoch Powell enquired if he had gone mad. The only thing that could cause inflation, Powell contended, was government spending, glutting the money supply: it was not the fault of scarcity of goods, nor even of Arthur Scargill. For Heath and Barber to cause inflation and try to control it at the same time was self-deceiving nonsense, akin to banning gravity. The way out was to cut the money supply—by raising tax, cutting borrowing, or both.

This was not just a question of economic theory. Powell argued that the taboo around which Heath was contorting his government was obsolete. Inflation at 10 per cent year after year was 'an evil far more dangerous' than the temporary pain needed to deal with it. He insisted that he did not want to see unemployment used as a means to reduce inflation: unemployment and bankruptcies were just 'side-effects', and 'transitional' ones at that.[66] But he tended not to say how long the transition would take.[67]

Powell's denunciation of the overriding nightmare of inflation won him a standing ovation at the 1973 Conservative Party conference, but beyond that, his attempts to replace one governing nightmare with another ran into the sand. In Cabinet, the ghosts of the Thirties were better represented than ever: the new Secretary of State for Employment was Harold Macmillan's son Maurice. In an admiring profile of this '"consensus" man', *The Illustrated London News* noted that 'Inflation could be curbed by the abandonment of the commitment to full employment, but it would be hard to see this Government—let alone a Macmillan with folk memories of pre-war Stockton—doing so.'[68] Looking back from 1975, Lord Hailsham wrote, 'I would have felt ashamed had I supported the policy of deliberately induced unemployment favoured ... by Mr Powell'. For all his hardline stance against the abuse of union power, Hailsham was still troubled by the 'moral unhappiness' of the decade before the war.[69]

The problem for free-marketeers was that Powell was the public figure most associated with their thinking, but the prospect of him in power was easy to cast as a nightmare, because of his views on immigration. On 19 September 1973, a group of young Conservatives launched a new body to push for the kind of economic policies Powell had long championed, while rejecting racism. To demand that Heath honour the free-market promises he had supposedly once proclaimed, they held their launch at the Selsdon Park Hotel, called their new rebellious faction the Selsdon Group, and issued a 'Selsdon Manifesto'. At the launch, Nicholas Ridley, who had resigned from the front bench in disgust at the government's disastrous retreats, gave a speech attacking the middle of the road as the road to ruin. In order to change course, Ridley argued—echoing Powell—that it was vital to face down the old nightmare of mass unemployment. True, 'Some people might get hurt on the way for a time. But many people are getting hurt now; inflation is more damaging than unemployment'.[70]

The Selsdon Group's manifesto raised a second nightmare, along with inflation. In a sign of how radical the group's ideas truly were, it attacked the way power had become 'concentrated' not only in the hands of the unions but in the hands of the state, in a way that was inimical to political freedom. It lambasted the Heath government for its 'ragbag of authoritarian collectivist policies'. It argued that, if present trends continued, 'the electorate will only have a choice between two brands of collectivism at the next General Election: Socialism V. the Tory Corporate State.'[71] The post-war consensus had been founded on marginalisation of these two nightmares: of high inflation and of the authoritarian state. Now they were coming back. But those inside the state were still caught between nightmares of mass unemployment and trade union power. This was about to drive some in government to breaking point.

* * *

Ever since Saltley, officials in the Home Office, the Ministry of Defence and the new Civil Contingencies Unit had been working out how to avoid another such defeat. The agonising over using troops continued; a police 'mutual aid' system was set up, with a national co-ordinating centre to help deploy officers to anywhere they were most needed. Large coal stocks were built up. In 1973, when it looked as though the miners might go on strike again, these preparations instilled confidence—until, in October, an embargo by Middle Eastern producers sent the price of oil rocketing. Letting the miners break the statutory incomes policy was politically impossible, but at the same time, the oil shock made coal all the more vital, giving the NUM a much stronger hand, while worsening inflation. At the end of the year, Heath introduced a three-day electricity week to conserve power. The choice of nightmares— state surrender, civil strife, or no power supply—was back. And this was driving senior figures to the thought that democracy was not strong enough to survive this recurrent struggle for power.

One of the men closest the heart of government, striving to make its systems robust enough to withstand the strike, was the Head of the Home Civil Service, Sir William Armstrong; he was one of Heath's few close colleagues. Two days into 1974, he called his fellow mandarins into his office in the Old Admiralty Building, to discuss 'the longer term implications of the current economic crisis'. They considered how long they could keep the electricity on, now that the three-day electricity week had come into force on New Year's Day: for about three months, they thought. However, the economic impact of continuing the three-day week for that long would wreak 'permanent damage of the most serious kind', said Treasury mandarin Sir Douglas Allen. They also discussed the probable necessity of peace-time food rationing, the risk of a run on the shops, the prospect of 'galloping inflation.'[72] There was no sign of a settlement with either the miners or the railway workers, who were also taking industrial action.

When the meeting resumed four days later, the civil servants discussed the need, if the energy supply situation got any worse, to 'progress towards a siege economy'.[73] A plan for running the government in a severe electrical emergency was being drawn up— one in ten staff would come to work, trying to keep things going from generator-lit 'emergency suites', if they were lucky, butane-lit ones if not. Several departments had already reported that their staff refused to work by candlelight.[74]

Armstrong was no old Etonian—he was a grammar-school boy who had grown up poor in Tooting in the 1920s and 1930s. He had seen 'the restrictions imposed on people by poverty' and had 'a very great desire to help in whatever way I could to avoid the mass unemployment of the early Thirties'.[75] Early in his career, in the late 1940s, he had been a devotee of his boss, the austere revolutionary turned austerity chancellor, Stafford Cripps. Armstrong was a creature of the post-war consensus and, since the late 1960s, had been instrumental in trying to hold that economic model together. He was the Treasury civil servant dispatched to Washington in March 1968 to secure a loan at the height of the Brutus crisis. In 1972, in the wake of unemployment hitting a million, he and Heath had jointly devised the return to industrial policy and statutory incomes policy. Now, faced with a second miners' strike, he was coming under intolerable pressure. He remained committed to the taboo against mass unemployment, but this meant that his desperate search for a way out of the crisis was driving him into harder and harder stances against the miners. As the consensus was breaking down, Armstrong was starting to crack up.

On 23 January, the NUM decided to hold a pithead ballot on strike action. That weekend, Armstrong retreated to the serene confines of Ditchley Park, a country house in Oxfordshire. He was there for a weekend conference of senior British and American politicians, academics and civil servants, gathered to discuss the relative strengths of the two countries' political systems, and to await the fate of the UK, as declared by the NUM. Heath's private secretary Douglas Hurd, who was there, described the atmosphere as Chekhovian: reminiscent of the doomed world of the Russian bourgeoisie, waiting for the revolution.

Armstrong scribbled notes about Heath and Wilson's lack of charisma. Off the record, though, his own view went way beyond this. 'We sat on sofas in front of great log fires and discussed first principles while the rain lashed the windows,' Hurd would recall. 'Sir William was full of notions, ordinary and extraordinary.'[76] One Conservative Party official recalled that at this time Armstrong was impressing on the Prime Minister a 'disaster scenario of emergency'.[77] He had concluded that the miners, personified by their communist Scottish vice-president Mick McGahey, were trying to destroy the government—and democracy itself.

On the Sunday, Armstrong was called away to see Heath at Chequers where, three years before, Macmillan had sat by another fire, warning against taking on the unions. On the radio that lunch-time, Heath's energy secretary Lord Carrington said that a miners' strike might mean a two-day or even one-day electricity week.[78] This 'nightmare prospect' would lead eventually 'to the restriction of power to hospitals, sewage works, and other essential services'.[79] The next morning, 28 January, Sir William was back at his desk, instructing a permanent secretary to work out how to stop flying pickets from using coaches to move around the country. Meanwhile, a *Times* columnist laid out the government's options when the strike inevitably began: surrender, the economic devastation of a fight to the finish, or a bitter, perhaps violent, election, with the risk of a Labour government stoking higher and higher inflation.[80] *The Guardian* reported that the 'mood in Whitehall yesterday was overwhelmingly one of gloom, coupled with a kind of "Custer's Last Stand" belligerence.'[81]

That night, Heath gave Robin Day an interview. He asserted icily that it was good that it was now clear that Mick McGahey was trying to overthrow his government in favour of one which would 'toe the line'.[82] The Prime Minister had been desperate to avoid confrontation with the miners, but now he was joining battle. If Heath gave in to the hardline demands of the majority of his party, stretching from the constituencies through the special advisers to Cabinet, he would call an election. Once he had won, he would have carte blanche to do what was necessary to save the economy, including drastic new measures to deal with strikers.[83]

Two days later, a very senior Treasury civil servant, who thought himself that the government was leading the country to 'economic and social disaster', could be heard blaming the crisis on the 'clearly unbalanced' Head of the Civil Service. The problem, this man argued, was Armstrong's insistence on taking on the miners, come what may; he was blocking Treasury warnings of the folly of this from getting through to Heath.[84] From the accounts of those around him, harvested by *The Sunday Times* a couple of years later, Armstrong does seem to have been driven to a nervous breakdown. And yet 'the overall analysis by which Armstrong was increasingly gripped was rational enough.'[85] He stuck to his view of the extreme risk of the situation long after he had made a strikingly rapid and full recovery. Two years later, he would tell *Sunday Times* editor Harold Evans that the situation had almost threatened civil war.[86]

Just before he broke, Armstrong was insisting that capitulation to the miners would 'create a right-wing backlash'.[87] Amid the log fires at Ditchley Park, he had ranted about 'coups and coalitions.'[88]

On 7 February 1974, Heath finally called what became known as the 'Who Governs Britain?' election, and on 28th, he got his answer. Armstrong's ragings may have been wild talk, but he was hardly alone in fearing that the unions would break the government, only to be broken themselves by a right-wing reaction. With Labour back in office, this forbidding prospect—and the desperation for a better solution it expressed—would only grow.

8

GAUNT, TIGHT-LIPPED MEN

1974–6

Something strange had happened to Michael Foot. Here was the nemesis of 'consensus politics', passing between the policemen on his way into Number 10, clutching a ministerial red box. As Harold Wilson's new Secretary of State for Employment, he was swiftly restoring the spirit of consensus to industrial relations by settling with the miners and getting rid of the three-day week, to the applause even of the City. The *Daily Mirror*'s Geoffrey Goodman acknowledged that apprehensive readers might have seen Foot on television being 'abrasive'—the same word that was used to decry Heath's attempt to break from the past. But really, Goodman promised, they need not worry about Mr Foot.[1]

Why this curious metamorphosis? The underlying reasons were Wilson's statutory incomes policy eight years before and, in particular, the bad blood over *In Place of Strife* in 1969. Foot had furiously opposed both, and decided such a rupture must never happen again. He formed a bond with Jack Jones to restore the industrial relations consensus, at least as it had obtained between the unions and Labour. On the face of it, the Hampstead romantic with half his head in the eighteenth century had little in common with the severe Scouse powerbroker, but both had become socialists amid the poverty of the Liverpool docks between the wars, and in any case, perhaps the contrast was the point. In 1970, Jones had urged Foot to put himself forward for Labour's front bench, and in 1971 they had set up a Liaison Committee, which mixed representatives from the Shadow Cabinet, the party's national executive and the TUC.

Barbara Castle was on the committee, and had doubted that the party and the unions could settle on a joint programme. But to her surprise—and possibly envy—an 'uneasy agreement' had gradually emerged.[2] In some ways this 'social contract' was a renewal of the 1945 settlement. It was founded on the same commitment to full employment, and the union strength that flowed from that. It even revived schemes for planning and nationalisation. But it was also more consciously a deal, and one in which the unions now had the upper hand. The new committee had first met eleven days after the miners' victory at Saltley Gate in February 1972.

This new social contract, outlined in a joint declaration titled *Economic Policy and the Cost of Living*, was a voluntary incomes policy with benefits: a future Labour government would do things the unions would welcome, such as expand investment, introduce controls on British capital invested overseas, nationalise, supervise private investment, extend industrial democracy, instigate planning agreements with large firms, improve social welfare and control prices. In return for all that, the government would get ... union restraint on wage demands. With inflation climbing when Labour took office, this was the holy grail. (The idea that wages drove inflation still prevailed.) The deal gave Wilson his pitch for the 'Who Governs Britain?' election: why put up with Heath trying to fight the unions, when Labour could restore the old consensus?

So now in March 1974, as she and Foot finally found themselves in Cabinet together for the first time, Castle watched askance as her old friend held the government together around an incomes policy. As she wrote later, 'I never found what made him change his mind—it was a point on which he was bound to be sensitive.'[3] But however much Foot associated the word 'consensus' with selling out to the right, he had long supported the substantive version relating to full employment and industrial relations. His and Jones' social contract was incomes policy achieved without forcing the unions' hand by law.

For opponents of overweening union power, the new Labour government was a nightmare made flesh. Foot's deal with the miners looked not like consensus, but surrender—and the worst yet, because the unions now held sway over the state itself. He was soon pushing through a new industrial relations bill, which scrapped Heath's system and restored the unions' rights. On top of this, inflation was at 13 per cent. The old spectres that had been overridden in the 1945 settlement were rearing up once more.

A Commons debate on 18 July captured how even those who wanted to reach consensus now could not. Michael Foot and Jim Prior, soon to become his shadow, both wanted full employment, and shared a fear of approaching industrial clashes. Yet their exchange was harsh and combative, because they were so sharply at odds about how to achieve this. Foot heralded the return of conciliation to industrial relations, designed to avoid both 'the dangers of mass unemployment and the dangers of confrontation and smash-up'. A settlement was much better, he suggested, than Heath with his talk of 'battles' and 'surrender', and 'people marching in and out of Downing Street saying "The clash is coming"'. Prior shot back that Labour was letting wage inflation climb too high, and kowtowing to the 'monopoly power of trade unions', which had broken Castle's *In Place of Strife* and Heath's Industrial Relations Act alike. The country was in danger of having the worst of both worlds: high unemployment plus high inflation. This, he warned, was 'a recipe for authoritarian government and controls and loss of freedom such as we should all detest.'[4]

* * *

Peter Jay, Economics Editor of *The Times*, encapsulated the problem as many saw it. Since the war, Britain had been juggling four goals: full employment, low inflation, union-based pay settlements, and democratic government. This was no longer possible and one of the four, alas, would have to go. Democratic governments could not 'suspend the full employment commitment', nor overcome the unions; and inflation meant misery and chaos. Logically, sacrificing democratic government was the worst option, except for all the others. Jay predicted that this would come by 1980,[5] but many feared it would not take so long. In March Labour's new chancellor, Denis Healey, had warned in his Budget speech that, if accelerating inflation were not stopped, 'the political and social strains may be too violent for the fabric of our democratic institutions to withstand.'[6]

With the government struggling along with no majority, an election was likely before the end of the year. But October was the month when the winter pay round got going. If the Tories won back power at the same time, another 'winter of industrial discontent' was widely expected: Hugh Scanlon was quoted predicting 'industrial chaos this winter'.[7] Were Prior to replace Foot as employment secretary, he would be greeted by civil servants warning him that 100,000 power workers might well go on strike early in 1975.[8] If a Conservative government were then smashed by the unions yet again, and if Labour was already under their influence, neither could stop inflation and chaos. Here, as in the late 1930s, was that suffocating sense that all the exits were blocked. When this broke Sir William Armstrong, he had been left ranting about coups, right-wing backlashes, coalitions. Now his visions started to come to life.

In Chile, in September 1973, with inflation rocketing, the army had overthrown the elected left-wing government, breaking its long commitment to staying out of politics. *The Times* suggested that there was a limit 'to the ruin a country can be expected to tolerate'.[9] In *The Spectator*, the journalist Patrick Cosgrave worked through how and why a coup could happen in Britain. He argued that respect for parliamentary democracy had been corroded by government interference and compulsion, such as statutory incomes policy. This had led 'to the destruction of that spider's web of consensus on which parliamentary government of our kind depends'.[10] Add in inflation, and the unions throwing their weight around, and it was not surprising that contempt for democratic politicians was growing.

If 'industrial militancy and urban guerrilla activity became rampant', Cosgrave suggested, 'it would be impossible to avoid a military move, perhaps initially sanctioned by government, of some proportions.' With democracy discredited, a takeover might then follow, provided there was public support for it. In August 1974, Brigadier Kenneth Hunt of the Institute for Strategic Studies explained how this could, in theory, be done, by sending tanks from the Royal Tank Regiment base at Tidworth 'to the BBC, Downing Street and Parliament.' They would then have needed to install officers, Hunt thought, in about 300 vital government posts.[11] Harold Wilson worried he could face something along these lines.

But some on the right harboured the opposite fear—that the army, under-trained and over-stretched, might simply prove incapable of defeating strikes and running services themselves: they would either lose, or refuse to intervene. Through the summer, a more desperate fix emerged. In anticipation of a winter strike wave, groups of 'apprehensive patriots' appeared, ready to step in.[12] One was led by the former Commander of NATO forces in Europe, General Sir Walter Walker. In speeches, and letters to the *Telegraph*, Walker called for public action to make up for government helplessness, and received a torrent of letters from volunteers. One of the less comic-sounding groups to join Walker's new Civil Assistance organisation was the 'British Military Volunteer Forces', a mercenary outfit with combat experience in Yemen, Congo and Biafra, which claimed a membership of 1,367 ex-soldiers, officers and RAF men. Walker stressed that Civil Assistance was not a private army: just a legitimate group of civilian volunteers, ready to help the authorities in an emergency.[13] But, fulminating that 'we would seem to have a Marxist running this country, by the name of Hugh Scanlon', he did not sound like a democrat.[14]

Walker was also involved with a secretive group called the Unison Committee for Action, led by a far-right ex-MI6 officer, and organised as an underground communications network along the lines of the Special Operations Executive. This resistance network was to be activated if a strike wave shut down essential services. Should strikes close the newspapers, Unison had access to a private airport and light aircraft to distribute a news-sheet across the country.[15]

The closest thing to a private army planning to tackle union power head-on was GB75. This was the brainchild of Lieutenant Colonel David Stirling—Scottish aristocrat, founder of the SAS, and peace-time under-achiever, based at 22 South Audley Street, round the corner from MI5. He had been approached by certain individuals who were concerned about strikes hitting vital services, and thought himself that politicians were terrified of being seen as would-be strike-breakers. He had consulted lawyers, senior Conservative ex-ministers and army officers, including the Chief of the Defence Staff, and he was clear that there was no serious contingency plan for the army to break such strikes.[16] So he developed one himself.

His volunteer force was part-funded by a Jersey arms-dealer,[17] and it was rumoured that employees of the General Electric Company were signed up and ready to operate strike-hit power stations. Arnold Weinstock, GEC's Managing Director, had privately averred as early as 1971 that 'circumstances are compelling us to have an authoritarian state.'[18] He damned the anti-democratic forces behind the Labour government as far more 'sinister' than the likes of Stirling's organisation, which he dismissed, publicly at least, as 'ineffectual.'[19] Stirling's expert volunteers would be backed up by tens of thousands more in less technical roles, if GB75 could get them in and keep them there. Stirling was planning training and pilot schemes sufficient to have his volunteers ready by mid-November.[20] He intended to fly his strike-breakers into occupied factories and power stations in helicopters, and to meet any resistance from occupying workers inside, or pickets outside, by rounding them up.

Half-alarming, half-ludicrous, these organisations were as hopeless as Aneurin Bevan marching his would-be socialist militia over the Welsh hills forty years before. They expressed the desperate lack of any real new ideas about how to deal with union power. Their most likely impact would be to trigger the very chaos they claimed to oppose. The army's former chief engineer pointed out that even 100,000 volunteers would not have a chance of keeping services going. The idea of them trying to run power stations was 'a truly terrifying prospect.'[21] If the 'private armies' were a farce, they were a farce to be reckoned with.

The nightmare that most troubled the left in the summer of 1974 has since faded behind the better-remembered fears of coups and private armies. What if, when the next big strike came, there was only one way to show that parliamentary government could keep essential services running: sending troops to break picket lines by force?

As the second miners' strike approached, Mick McGahey had reportedly 'promised a personal appeal to the soldiers if troops were called in to deal with pickets'. Max Hastings suggested in the *Evening Standard* that such a deployment might need to happen. He reported that, to many army officers, 'the battle in Northern Ireland, the struggles in the ghetto streets among Woolworths and Co-ops and cornflakes billboards, have been a kind of grim acclimatisation for possible future tasks even closer to home.'[22] A government that did such things, however 'moderate', might well have to become authoritarian, if only to keep a lid on the violent unrest that would follow. *The Observer* mooted the possibility that 'the Army might also have to decide whether to obey the dictates of a legitimate authoritarian Government determined to mop up all opposition to it—perhaps by shooting on strikers.'[23]

Faced with the prospect of political strikes and uncontrollable unions on one side, and a private army-style middle-class backlash on the other, Lord Hailsham predicted that a strong government would 'seize control' and force through Parliament 'a series of authoritarian measures.' There would be 'a lot of violence one way or another'.[24] Some politicians and journalists were advocating an 'authoritarian interlude' to get a grip on the trade unions and inflation. This might involve: an 'absolute clampdown on the money supply' and a government freeze on all wages and prices;[25] the restricting or abolition of the right to strike, and preparations to withstand the general strike that these constraints might provoke,[26] including authoritarian measures to control the unions—perhaps even locking up union leaders and MPs.[27] If 'yet another British administration is wrecked by industrial power', more people would come to believe that the army should be involved in ending the crisis,[28] and might even welcome 'a period of authoritarian rule'.[29]

Alongside this, there was much talk, throughout 1974, of the need for a government of national unity. This coalition would isolate the left, just as Ramsay MacDonald had once done. As in 1931, this raised left-wing fears that such a government would be tantamount to dictatorship. This broad scenario was dramatised in *The Churchill Play*, which opened at Nottingham Playhouse that May. Howard Brenton's drama was set ten years in the future, in 1984, in a Britain ruled by an authoritarian coalition of the Conservatives and Labour's right wing. This coalition takes power in the wake of soldiers being sent to break a miners' strike, and the miners trying to kill them. In one of the many government internment camps, run by the army on an old airbase in the Lincolnshire cabbage fields, various journalists, anarchists and trade unionists are indefinitely detained. The military guards who brutalise them have been hardened by service in Northern Ireland and on picket lines.

In September, a survey from National Opinion Polls suggested that many shared General Walker and Lt-Col Stirling's nightmares: two thirds of respondents thought inflation was a menace, and 73% that the unions were too powerful, and 68% had little or no confidence in political parties. Yet 62% also thought that the private armies and their frantic, last-ditch fixes were a threat to democracy. No wonder 65% of respondents felt democracy to be in danger.[30]

On Wednesday 18 September, Harold Wilson called the year's second general election. The Conservative manifesto warned that 'no major democracy has ever survived such a catastrophic rise in the cost of living'. But Heath's only new solution was a 'national unity strategy', bringing non-party figures into government.[31] On 10 October, Labour won again, with a majority of three.

All these plans to break union power that had emerged over the course of 1974 were predicated on a climactic showdown: the much anticipated winter of industrial chaos. In December, Walker sent his Civil Assistance followers a detailed scenario for the imminent apocalypse, culminating in a general strike: 'If Parliamentary Government were to come to an end, the public, cold, hungry and confused, would probably submit fairly quickly to a new "workers'" regime of the extreme left.'[32] But with Labour back in, the winter of industrial chaos failed to happen, and many of Walker's Civil Assistance Co-ordinators began to think it never would. The general himself was beginning to despair: 'I sometimes feel that I am wasting my time and that this country deserves to be taken over.'[33] He kept trying to raise money in the City, but, ostracised by the military, he retreated into paranoia.[34]

Here was another public figure who had tried to challenge the power of the trade unions, only to wreck his own standing. Walker had done it in far cruder terms than Castle or Heath, but it is striking that he wanted to blunt the 'strike weapon' in order to restore an older post-war status quo. If he ever wanted to be a British Pinochet, it was not so that he could introduce neoliberal economics. The new Conservative MP Norman Tebbit, no fan of Hugh Scanlon, thought Walker and Stirling had simply missed the point: 'My reaction was that that was not a sensible path down which to go. That was dealing with a symptom, but one had to deal with the disease which was at the root cause of the problem, so I didn't have much sympathy with those essentially vigilante groups.'[35]

Walker was not alone in his lack of imagination. Amid all those dramas and fearful articles peering into the future, worrying about anarchy, union tyranny, Soviet infiltration, private armies, national governments and coups, no one seems to have predicted that a leading politician would have a new idea.

* * *

On 5 September, a month before Labour won its majority of three, Keith Joseph went to Preston to advocate something unthinkable.

In the wake of the February election, Heath had decided to allow his Shadow Home Secretary free rein for a re-think, and even let him set up a think-tank: the Centre for Policy Studies. Joseph had decided to see if he could find a way around the brick wall against which Heath and Castle had smashed their careers. Unlike them, he did not favour a direct attack on the unions' power. His Preston speech did not call for cooling-off periods, or industrial relations courts, or banning strikes, or threatening to break picket lines by force. He even rejected incomes policy—the one thing that had worked, the solution that Foot's social contract had now revived, and which even Joseph himself had been advocating that May.[36] That same night, Heath declared that Britain was 'teetering on the edge of a precipice' and that he could not rule out using the law to fight inflation.[37] But this, Joseph told his audience, was a fool's solution:

> Incomes policy alone as a way to abate inflation caused by excessive money supply is like trying to stop water coming out of a leaky hose without turning off the tap; if you stop one hole it will find two others. We tried incomes policy—more than once; Labour tried incomes policy. The great and the good favoured it—and many still do. But bitter experience reinforces elementary economic logic—with excess demand it will not work.[38]

But then what on earth would? It was time to break the great taboo, and sacrifice the commitment to full employment. He did not say it out loud, but ending the full employment commitment would do something else too. Without directly confronting union power, it would undermine the foundation on which that power was built.

Joseph knew the political risks of breaking the unemployment taboo; he had watched Heath reverse his entire strategy to avoid it. He acknowledged that governments were 'only free to act within the constraints set by public opinion'.[39] They would 'need for some

189

years to tread, if practicable, a narrow path between hyperinflation on the one side and intolerable unemployment on the other.'[40] He had now set himself the task of loosening the constraints on what people thought constituted 'intolerable unemployment'. To do this, he would have to chase away the post-war era's governing nightmare, and replace it with a new one.[41]

Joseph had chosen a resonant location to start exorcising the ghosts of the 1930s. Any Prestonian in their fifties or older would likely have remembered February 1931, when unemployment had doubled within a year to hit one in ten of the town's whole population. Ten miles to the east, in Barbara Castle's constituency of Blackburn, the situation had been twice as bad.[42] Forty years on, the memories were tended by oral history projects, and new books by well-known old 1930s leftists. And if, on his way to give his speech at Preston Town Hall, Keith Joseph had stopped at Brady's Record Shop in Fishergate, he might have found a copy of Alan Price's single 'Jarrow Song'. This had reached number six in the charts that May; Price's lyrics suggested that the 'Jarrow lads' were still marching in 1974, as though little had changed.

But it had, Joseph told his audience. And if politicians were still troubled by visions of the Jarrow Crusaders, they had to get over it. He acknowledged that the post-war boom had begun 'under the shadow of the 1930s' and that 'We were haunted by the fear of long-term mass unemployment, the grim, hopeless dole queues and towns which died.' The problem was that 'we talked ourselves into believing that these gaunt, tight-lipped men in caps and mufflers were round the corner, and tailored our policy to match these imaginary conditions.'

The gaunt men lived only in the memory. Mass unemployment had not come back, and pretending nothing had changed since the bad old days was just making matters worse: 'On several occasions over the past 20 years, Socialist exaggeration of unemployment levels, together with marches on Parliament, play-acting the 1930s, has stampeded us into rash over-expansion with resultant price increases and economic dislocation. We must not be stampeded again.'[43]

He delivered that last sentence with unusual force. Could it be, after Joseph's week down a Yorkshire mine in the late Thirties, that this rupture with post-war consensus needed a particular effort of will? Did he have to expunge the nagging ghosts not just from the back of everyone else's mind, but from his own? The historian Richard Vinen has noted how Joseph 'often seemed to back away from his own conclusions when ... he was faced with the human consequences of implementing his own logic'.[44]

Other figures making this intellectual leap alongside Joseph were open about the emotional difficulty of laying the gaunt, tight-lipped men to rest. Joseph's speech was largely written by Alfred Sherman, once a communist, who acknowledged that, for many, sympathy for the unemployed meant those 'outworn orthodoxies' still exerted 'powerful emotional and ideological attractions'.[45] Samuel Brittan of the *Financial Times*, who also contributed to the Preston speech, described this territory as 'an emotional minefield'. He was intellectually convinced the full employment commitment had to go, but still affirmed that he began studying economic problems through 'indignation' at the waste of unemployment in the 1930s, and added: 'This feeling persists.'[46]

Joseph presented his rejection of the old nightmares as a Damascene conversion. In April 1974, he had declared that, all along, he'd thought he was a Conservative, but now realised he had not been. In fact, his thinking had been tending this way for some years; but if his conversion drama was something of a performance, it had a clear purpose. Joseph was trying to end the consensus by creating a sharp break from the past. He therefore denounced his whole political generation as Guilty Men, starting with himself. In September, he confessed to his Preston audience that he and the rest of the Heath government had gone 'astray', and that he accepted his 'full share of the collective responsibility'. This had already become one of his regular themes.

The core of Joseph's argument was that politicians had spent too long shying away from spectral hunger marchers, frightened that 'sound money policies' would bring all that back, stoking 'intolerable social and political tensions'—yet trying to spend unemployment away had bred another, far more dangerous threat. 'Inflation', he declared, 'is threatening to destroy our society.' This 'present nightmare' was the reason why the old consensus and its obsolete fears had to go. Inflation would wreck the savings and future plans of families and businesses, bringing exactly what consensus politicians feared: 'catastrophic' unemployment and the end of 'social peace'. That was just the start. Joseph talked of Lenin, Latin America, siege economies, and the desperate need to reduce the increase in the money supply. If that was not done, we 'will destroy our monetary system; we will make all our existing problems worse—and will add as yet undreamed nightmares besides'. Specifically, a total disillusion with democratic politicians, and with that, the end of freedom: 'It could happen here. Our proud achievements, our great history, our still superb national talents do not render us immune to the processes of despair and disintegration which ultimately invite dictatorship.'

The Times made Joseph's speech its lead and reproduced the whole text, with an editorial applauding its message. This was not surprising. The paper's economics editor, Peter Jay, was a leading convert to monetarism—the doctrine Joseph was espousing, which said that inflation should be fought by constraining the money supply, not through Keynesian management of demand. Jay's Editor, William Rees-Mogg, was about to publish a book on inflation, which would join with Joseph in contending that 'We should be tearing up the full employment commitment of the 1944 White Paper'.[47]

In response, Labour ministers hurried to stoke up the old nightmare. Michael Foot called Joseph's speech 'a most insidious assault on the full employment theories so widely accepted since 1945'.[48] Raising the unthinkable prospect of unemployment surpassing 3 million, the *Mirror* warned, 'The danger of Sir Keith's policy is that it might create exactly the social tensions and unrest he seeks to avoid.' Yet Joseph had shaken the paper's faith in the consensus. If Labour's social contract failed, it conceded, 'Whatever Government was in power might be forced to adopt Sir Keith's remedy.'[49]

There were signs that the ghosts might be beginning to fade. Robert Carr, who had found unemployment hitting a million in 1972 so traumatic, told the Shadow Cabinet in July 1974 that much higher levels of unemployment seemed more acceptable to people now than ten years ago.[50] Since at least the late 1960s, a generational shift had been afoot. A working-class student at Warwick University called David Davis, for example, had been raised by his Geordie communist grandfather on stories of unemployment and protest in the 1930s. But amid the liberations of the late Sixties, Davis found it 'hard to imagine the day-to-day terrors of the people who went on the hunger marches.' Signing up to a 'gloomy, grey-skied ideology suddenly started to seem a bit unattractive'.[51] At the end of BBC2's 1971 documentary about the Jarrow Crusade, full of painful memories, the narrator had noted that young people in Jarrow were fed up with hearing about the march, which they thought gave the town a 'bad image'.[52]

And had Keith Joseph spent a bit longer in Brady's Record Shop, he might have come upon another record that had done well that summer. Monty Python's album *Live at Drury Lane* features a sketch in which rich men compete over the poverty of their inter-war childhoods, straining to trump each other's ever-more-ludicrous 'memories'. The 'Four Yorkshiremen' had been created for ITV's *At Last the 1948 Show* in 1967, largely by the Winchester-educated Tim Brooke-Taylor, and Marty Feldman, the child of a poor Jewish family in the East End of London. The sketch was certainly not intended as monetarist propaganda, but it does express a generational frustration with those who remembered the poverty of 'forty years ago' and never stopped going on about it. In his war on the ghost army from the Thirties, Joseph had a new ally: a derisive mock-Yorkshire accent bellowing 'Luxury!'

* * *

On 9 October 1974, Friedrich Hayek won the Nobel prize for economics. If Keith Joseph saw this as a sign that things were turning his way, it cannot have lasted long. The following day brought Labour's election victory, on a manifesto promising socialism. The Conservative MP Norman Lamont was one of the rising young men of the mid-1970s who grabbed onto Hayek's radical free-market ideas as a way out of the failing consensus, as zealously as an earlier generation seized on Keynes. But Lamont had to admit that he had not been beset during the campaign by voters clamouring for tighter control of the money supply—even with inflation at 15 per cent. Instead, people wanted to talk about company profits, and the unfair impact of wage restraint on workers in comparison to their bosses. 'Many times during the campaign,' he wrote shortly afterwards, 'I asked myself whether Britain was not becoming a natural socialist country.'[53]

On election night, it became clear that Heath had lost yet again and would have to go. His shadow employment secretary, Jim Prior, thought that their party was out for ten years at least, partly because of the miners' strike and 'the mess we had left behind'.[54] The press thought the Conservatives would try a warmer, more unifying version of Heath as their new leader. Could Keith Joseph and his heretical ideas seize the moment instead? On the BBC's election night coverage, the political journalist Peter Jenkins openly laughed at the idea of Joseph as leader. The Spectator's Patrick Cosgrave spoke up for a like-minded shadow minister who had had a good election: Margaret Thatcher.

Joseph often displayed a distinctive characteristic of the kind of people who try to break orthodoxies: a yen for the apocalyptic. Think of Cripps, or Beveridge, or Powell. A few days after the election, increasingly frazzled, Joseph let this tendency get the better of him. While making a speech about the 'cycle of poverty', he started talking about how 'our human stock' was 'threatened' by unfit mothers. This was misinterpreted as a call for the sterilisation of the poor. Jack Jones said it was 'very typical of the thoughts expressed by Hitler in Mein Kampf.'[55] Whether Joseph would have been a successful leadership candidate had been debatable; now it was out of the question. And so Thatcher became the candidate of those who wanted to break with consensus, and stepped forward to challenge Heath in the first round. But, like the ideas she was tentatively representing, she was very much on the outside.

The focal point of the long struggle against union power now shifted. For a few weeks, early in 1975, the battleground was the hearts and minds of the 277 Conservative MPs who would elect the party's new leader. On one side stood Heath himself, who wanted to stay in post, as the only man to lead a coalition when the crisis inevitably came. On the other side, there were Joseph's allies: men like Nicholas Ridley and Norman Tebbit. They would go on to play a key role in preparing for a struggle for power with the unions, and were now led by Margaret Thatcher, who had interpreted the Battle of Saltley Gate in precisely those terms.

Thatcher had to soft-pedal her views to woo MPs who were simply fed up with their rude loser of a leader, and the contest was not conducted on the union issue. Nonetheless, she was clearly the more 'right-wing' candidate.[56] She echoed Joseph's *mea culpa*, saying she hoped that she accepted her 'full share of collective responsibility', and that she had 'learned something from the failures and mistakes of the past'. She talked of 'opposition to excessive State power',[57] and told the *Telegraph* that 'people believe that too many Conservatives have become socialists'.[58]

To widespread shock, Thatcher knocked her boss out in the first round. The evening before the second, Tony Benn had a revealing exchange with a former diplomat during a reception at the German Embassy. Lord Gladwyn was 'very anti-Thatcher', a creature of the consensus politics that Benn, at least as much as Thatcher, thought had 'broken down'. Benn told Gladwyn that 'the soggy Centre has failed, and we're going to have a bit more Left and Right.' Gladwyn, a Liberal peer, was horrified at the idea of politics curdling into 'confrontation' between hardliners, but Benn informed him that democracy 'is about choice'. Gladwyn's reply gives a glimpse of what such men feared the coming clash might look like, hours before Thatcher became Leader of the Opposition. He asked: 'Do you want the generals to come in, do you want a military coup against the strikers?'[59] Benn does not record him saying: 'Do you want to risk a return to mass unemployment?' Perhaps, in 1975, the nightmare of strikers confronting soldiers seemed the less unthinkable of the two.

When Thatcher won, doubtless Gladwyn was aghast. Heath's former Home Secretary Reggie Maudling certainly was, gasping about a 'black day'. Lord Carrington told Heath that their parliamentary colleagues had 'gone mad'.[60]

The newspapers had not foreseen this bizarre turn of events and, ever since, her campaign manager Airey Neave has been cast as a shadowy mastermind. But at this stage, it did not seem especially likely that this slightly odd woman was going to forge a whole new political consensus—no more likely than it had when the underwhelming Clement Attlee became Leader of the Opposition forty years before. Roy Hattersley remembers that 'We thought Mrs Thatcher was beatable', that she was 'a temporary phenomenon'.[61]

195

The British economy may have been in a terrible state, with restrictions on electricity and inflation now at 18 per cent, but *The Economist* suggested that the Conservatives might be in opposition for twenty-five years. And meanwhile, the champions of the old consensus politics were all set for a late victory.

* * *

For years, the anxious great and good had been telling each other over expensive lunches that what Britain needed was a coalition to save the nation from catastrophe. On 26 March 1975, it finally arrived. In a hotel ballroom round the corner from Parliament, its leader, Labour's Roy Jenkins, sat flanked by senior politicians from all three parties: the ex-Liberal leader Jo Grimond, the Chair of the Parliamentary Labour Party Cledwyn Hughes, and leading consensus Conservatives Willie Whitelaw, whom Thatcher had beaten to the leadership, and Reginald Maudling. Jenkins' other 'vice-presidents' were to include ex-TUC chief Vic Feather and the freshly defenestrated Edward Heath. Several big businessmen had also joined Jenkins' 'executive'.[62]

This phalanx of panjandrums was Britain in Europe, the umbrella group set up to lead the Yes campaign in a referendum, scheduled for June, on whether to remain in the Common Market. It was, as *The Sun* put it, 'the most powerful all-party coalition since the war',[63] and it seized the imagination of desperate moderates. Here was a future for consensus politics made flesh. As inflation kept climbing and the pound kept sliding, the Labour government, reliant on left-wing MPs' support, was apparently unable to find solutions, while the new Conservative leadership was harbouring long-taboo ideas. Anxious moderates called for some form of national unity alliance, to push cuts through the Commons in defiance of the Labour left, and save democracy.[64] Jenkins' group was formed specifically for the referendum, but it was just too tempting to see it as the start of something more—not least as it was out to beat the Labour left, which was against the EEC.

Here again was the Labour left's nightmare: an authoritarian coalition, designed to isolate them. Left-wing MPs feared that 'a formidable combination is mustering among the political, financial and industrial establishment', perhaps involving Labour ministers, to force through a harsh deflation.[65] Alongside this, the draining of power from Parliament to the Common Market seemed designed to stymie socialist government. Shirley Williams was Labour's prices secretary, but also a leading figure in Britain in Europe. At a meeting of the National Economic Development Council, she called for a move 'away from confrontational politics', and the chancellor Denis Healey agreed, saying, 'We want a broad consensus between political parties. There may be a role for the Opposition in the NEDC'. Tony Benn retorted that to 'take industry out of politics would amount to a coalition'.[66]

All this looked rather like an establishment coup against democratic politics. As if to underline Benn's fears, *The Daily Telegraph* reported that the mining company Rio Tinto–Zinc was 'in a position to furnish a coalition government should one be required'.[67] Likewise, Wilson feared the advent of a Conservative-dominated coalition which would have terrible relations with the trade unions, to the point where, he claimed, 'I doubt if democracy could survive'.[68] But the Prime Minister blamed Benn and his fellow Labour anti-marketeers for making this more likely, through their divisive tactics in the referendum campaign.

The battle between the Britain in Europe coalition and the anti-EEC Labour left, fought out against the drumbeat of economic doom, became a kind of apocalypse Olympics. Tony Benn charged that joining the EEC two years earlier had been British capitalism's last-ditch attempt to flee the consequences of its own decline, at the expense of working people. He sketched out a full-dress nightmare scenario of a return to 'unemployment on the scale of the 1930s',[69] as the hurricane of market forces wrecked jobs, not just in the 'steel, textile, engineering and motor industries', but in 'shops and offices and … the public services'.[70] He even claimed that EEC membership had already destroyed half a million jobs. On the other side of the argument, Ted Heath, back at the Oxford Union for a televised debate against Barbara Castle, invoked the mass unemployment of the Thirties too. He insisted that Britain needed a modernising jolt of competition, and that backing out of the Common Market would bring economic collapse, food shortages, and potentially a Soviet invasion of Western Europe.[71] In another debate, on Thames TV,

Foot told Heath he had given away power to a 'superstate'. Heath sniffed that EEC membership would indeed stop Foot forging a 'siege economy', but that was a dreadful idea anyway.

The nightmare of reducing the power of Foot, Benn and the unions, it turned out, was one that the public was prepared to risk. On 5 June 1975, the UK voted to stay in the Common Market, by 67 per cent to 33 per cent. To the *Standard*, the rising power of the unions and the polarising impact of economic crisis had led to a 'flight from consensus politics', which had been working in the left's favour. It hoped that this had now been thrown into reverse: that the left's defeat in the referendum had 'helped to smooth [the] path back to consensus'.[72]

But it was no good just calling for everyone to get along without taking a clear stance on the central question of union power. The Jones–Foot alliance did have an answer: their social contract. The odd couple continued to hold things together, brokering a deal between the Treasury and the trade unions on a flat maximum pay rise of £6 a week from August 1975; this began to bring down steep wage rises, while the left put up with spending cuts. But the champions of consensus-through-coalition just wanted to wish confrontation away. The Europe referendum, as the historian Robert Saunders points out, was not the launchpad they had hoped for. It was to be their last victory for a very long time.

* * *

Keith Joseph had just as clear a view on all this as Foot and Jones. One day early in the referendum campaign, Thatcher's new Shadow Cabinet trooped into a large room at Conservative Central Office to discuss his latest paper, setting out how they could rescue Britain from its slide towards disaster. They had to abandon the full employment commitment and abjure incomes policy. Instead, they must fight the deficit and inflation by letting market competition do its work, making big spending cuts, and preparing to face down strikes against them. Joseph invited the remaining front-bench Heathites to cast themselves as Guilty Men:

> Against our better judgment, we competed with the Socialists in offering to perform what is in fact beyond the power of government. We undertook to ensure full employment in the

sense of a job for everyone of the kind, location and rewards he broadly considers right, regardless of wage-levels, productivity and the state of the economy and the world. In pursuit of this interpretation, we strained the economy to the point where jobs, living standards and the savings of millions have been jeopardised.[73]

This did not go down well. Reggie Maudling, now back as Shadow Foreign Secretary, declared: 'I do NOT agree with ONE little bit.'[74] The meeting rapidly became a tussle over the historical narrative, with many present insisting that Joseph was 'too critical of the recent past and, in particular, of recent Conservative policy'. To the moderates, the paper was a revolutionary 'recipe for disaster'. The Party 'should not repudiate its previous attempts to reach a national consensus': that was the key to winning and staying in power.[75]

This dispute within the Shadow Cabinet was taking place as Britain in Europe ascended into the light of press acclaim; in Joseph's document and the meeting itself, the possibility of working with the Labour right repeatedly reared up. Joseph wrote that coalition would be a 'fatal' compromise with the mistakes of the post-war period. But some of those defending consensus politics were ready to entertain the idea. Timothy Raison, the shadow environment secretary, said that there was 'too much misery in Keith's paper', and that 'There are matters on which we have got to operate a consensus. We must try to persuade Healey to produce a sensible budget.'[76]

The afterglow of the June referendum did not last long. Regardless of his colleagues' objections, Joseph and his allies continued to cast 'consensus', 'middle ground' and 'middle of the road' as synonyms for the complacent, self-deluding group-think that had allegedly licensed Britain's post-war 'decline', and that had to be eradicated. To prosecute his battle, Joseph had already revived the old hyperinflation nightmare—but he and Thatcher now went further, and raised that other great nightmare of the 1930s and 1940s: the total state.

In his paper, Joseph contended that 'too many discretions are given to ministers and to civil servants', to the point where the 'statute book has become an engine of near-tyranny', with too much new law 'arbitrary and outside the purview of the Courts'. But it was Thatcher who really carried this line of attack into what she called the 'battle of ideas'. Right from the start of her leadership and on into 1976, she was sounding the alarm that Britain was 'irretrievably on the path to a socialist state'.[77] Its 'steady and remorseless expansion' was stifling freedom by all sorts of methods: state ownership, coercion and control of business, taxes, bureaucracy, 'politically selective' defence of citizen's rights, and the trade union 'closed shop'.[78]

All this, Thatcher proclaimed, was leading 'to the erosion and finally the destruction of the democratic way of life'.[79] Sometimes she alleged Labour was building the corporate state, or the 'Transport House state'.[80] Invoking Alexander Solzhenitsyn, the dissident Russian novelist and former Gulag prisoner, she warned her audiences not to take freedom for granted. In one Commons speech, she suggested twice that 'the Iron Curtain State' might soon take shape in Britain.[81]

It is not an accident that, in their bid to define and destroy the 'post-war consensus', Thatcher and Joseph were using imagery from its contested beginnings. As a student in 1945, Thatcher had doubted the wisdom, in 'present circumstances', of Churchill's 'Gestapo' attack on Clement Attlee—but now circumstances had changed. What better way to attack the consensus than to revive the nightmare of the total state that its supporters thought had been banished forever? The late 1940s and early 1950s had seen a flowering of anxious near-future fictions in this vein, which were waiting to be deployed. Keith Joseph was particularly struck by a strange dystopic novel by LP Hartley, written in voluntary exile in Italy. In *Facial Justice*, Hartley satirises the horrors of statist post-war Britain by creating a society so egalitarian that anyone unusually ugly or beautiful is pressured to have cosmetic surgery. Joseph took to using what he called 'Hartley's 1984 nightmare' as an image of possible future tyranny.[82]

George Orwell's *Nineteen Eighty-Four* itself, published in 1949, was also pressed into service. In the mid-1970s, as Orwell's doom-year approached and evoked all those familiar images, references to the novel became a neat way to suggest the horrors that a left-wing Labour government could build by 1984. The Conservative MP Rhodes Boyson (once a Labour councillor) published a book of essays called *1985, An Escape from Orwell's 1984*, which offered 'A Conservative Path to Freedom' from the 'totalitarian dictatorship'

Labour would try to create 'when the crash comes'.[83] The book has an epigraph from Churchill in 1947, headed 'Set the People Free'.[84] One of Thatcher's more colourful foreign policy advisers, an ex-leftist turned 'cold warrior' called Brian Crozier, suggested one slogan she was particularly taken with: '1984 is closer than you think'.[85] To write her early, hardline foreign policy speeches, Thatcher recruited the historian Robert Conquest, a former communist who, in 1944, had witnessed Stalinists promise to uphold Bulgarian democracy, only to destroy it. In the mid-1970s, Conquest was still a Labour voter; but, repelled by the rise of Tony Benn and radical students, he had recently written a poem called '1974: Ten Years to Go'.[86]

Anxieties that Orwell's dystopia might actually be on its way flared up among the nervier sections of the right in March 1976, when Harold Wilson suddenly announced his long-planned resignation, and it looked as though Labour MPs might elect Michael Foot to succeed him as Prime Minister. In the event, however, Britain was saved from the onslaught of Foot's red terror by the election of a rather more moderate Labour leader.

* * *

At least as much as Harold Wilson, James Callaghan was the embodiment of the consensus on both full employment and industrial relations. He had risen not through Oxford and the civil service, but the trade unions, to whom he had shown more loyalty in 1969 than to his colleague Barbara Castle. In other words, he was ideally suited to inherit the social contract. But within weeks of taking office, Callaghan's ability to keep the consensus afloat was put to the test.

Both inflation and unemployment were at post-war heights, there was upward pressure on pay, and the deficit was ballooning. Investors were giving up on sterling, which was tanking faster than the Bank of England could cope with. As a new currency crisis unfolded, it fell to Callaghan to try to succeed where Castle and Heath had failed: to reinvent the consensus, balancing union power with economic pressures. On either side, Callaghan and his Cabinet were faced with a choice of nightmares. They could accept the swingeing spending cuts demanded by the Treasury and the Bank, which would kill the social contract and send unemployment even higher, and might tip Britain back into industrial unrest. Or they could face the Treasury–Bank nightmare scenario: Britain running out of money.

After two weeks of agonising, ministers managed a balancing act—agreeing to half the cuts demanded, at a cost of 200,000 jobs. The TUC would just about bear this; the City would just about buy it. But compromise was stretched to breaking point; it seemed unlikely that the government would survive another parliamentary session. By late September, it was all happening again. Callaghan told Cabinet they needed to cut another £1.5 billion. Bernard Donoughue, head of his policy unit, thought that the Treasury and the Bank of England were seizing their chance 'to try to change the whole economic stance which had characterised all British governments since the Second World War.'[87] And it looked as though they were winning.

On 28 September, amid market panic at the falling pound, Callaghan addressed the Labour conference in Blackpool. Part of the speech had been written by his son-in-law, the monetarist journalist Peter Jay, and sounded an echo of Keith Joseph's speech in Preston:

> We used to think that you could spend your way out of a recession, and increase employment by cutting taxes and boosting Government spending. I tell you in all candour that that option no longer exists, and that in so far as it ever did exist, it only worked on each occasion since the war by injecting a bigger dose of inflation into the economy, followed by a higher level of unemployment as the next step.[88]

The next day, Healey secured a desperately needed £2.3 billion loan from the International Monetary Fund, subject to negotiation of terms, and raced to Blackpool in an RAF jet, where the delegates were busy voting to nationalise the banks. The chancellor demanded that the party back him. He had to bellow over the boos of the left, who thought that capitalism was finished; but he won the vote.

This looked like surrender to the forces of finance. But all the shouting—and the tendency to reduce Callaghan's speech to that one paragraph—can easily drown out what he and Healey were trying to do. They were giving up on a Keynesian method, but not on Keynes' underlying goal. Callaghan repeatedly insisted on his commitment to full employment, saying the existing rate of unemployment 'cannot be justified on any grounds'. His case against the existing reflationary approach was that it now caused unemployment itself. His strategy for recovery was grounded on the industrial relations consensus Michael Foot had helped revive. Callaghan boasted that the number of disputes was at its lowest since 1953, praised nationalisation, and called for more worker–employer co-operation, for industrial democracy, and voluntary planning agreements. This, alongside the government's industrial strategy, itself to be developed with unions and business, was an attempt to shore up the core of the post-war approach.

Likewise, Healey—however brutal his tone—argued for, not against, incomes policy, and insisted that the IMF loan was to protect the industrial strategy from speculators' attacks on the pound. The government was absorbing monetarist methods into the consensus model, isolating the hard left but keeping the unions on-side. Tony Benn thought that Jack Jones looked 'very uncomfortable' during Healey's speech,[89] but next morning Jones was on the *Today Programme*, throwing his weight behind the chancellor's strategy in 'remarkably uncompromising terms'.[90]

To defend his attempt to rework and revive the consensus, the Prime Minister went on the attack. The only alternative, he insisted, was a nightmare. Half an hour after Healey's speech to the Labour conference, Callaghan appeared on *Tonight* on BBC1. When Robin Day asked what would happen if the government could not fix the crisis—might it mean the collapse of democracy?—he replied:

> You are right. I think this is a responsibility that falls on our Government. If we were to fall—and I don't particularly want to make any party point here—I don't think another government could succeed. I fear it would lead to totalitarianism of the Left or Right.[91]

Conference chairman Tom Bradley told the press that this meant 'the Tories would first take over and then there would be a period of confrontation with the unions which could end in the failure of Parliamentary institutions.'[92] Thatcher denounced Callaghan's fear-mongering, and over the fortnight that followed, she and her colleagues launched a series of attacks on the government, charging that it was Labour that was putting Britain at risk of totalitarianism. In a televised lecture, Lord Hailsham called the government an 'elective dictatorship'.[93] Others pointed to the power that the unions had wielded over Labour ever since *In Place of Strife*, a power which was undermining the authority of Parliament. Keith Joseph issued an open letter to Callaghan, insisting that the social contract was a 'fool's bargain' which allowed the TUC 'to dominate the economic climate and the law in field after field'. Some trade union leaders, he alleged, demanded ever more state spending because they 'want a totalitarian society'.[94] In her own conference speech, Thatcher blamed the undemocratic social contract for licensing 'a handful of trade union leaders to dictate to the government'.[95]

But without a social contract—or the kind of legal constraints on the unions that had already proved unworkable—how could the Conservatives avoid a repeat of the Heath disaster? The only other established option was incomes policy, and the party was divided over whether it really wanted to abandon that, and leap into the dark after Keith Joseph. As her authorised biographer Charles Moore makes clear, Thatcher fudged. For all its apocalyptic imagery, her speech failed to set out a convincing radical alternative. Among voters, the suspicion remained that the Conservatives would either try to enforce cuts and wage restraint through confrontation with the unions, or would even abandon the commitment to full employment and try to rescue the economy by letting unemployment climb even higher.

Both parties were now warning that the other would lead Britain into a totalitarian nightmare. For the moment, it was Callaghan's scenario—that Thatcher would trigger such a great clash with the unions that democracy would collapse—which had won out. But to sustain the consensus, he still needed a settlement with the IMF that all sides could accept.

* * *

To Tony Benn, the consensus was already dead. He lived in fear of the emergence of a 1931-style coalition of the treacherous Labour right with the Conservatives and Liberals. This option, which was stirring again among politicians and journalists, would isolate the left, appease the bankers, and kill Benn's hopes of radical change. On 5 October, Benn had lunch with the editor of *The Times*, William Rees-Mogg, and debated 'when the consensus died'. They agreed that 'there was now a pretty basic choice to be made.'[96]

A few weeks later, Benn took his betrayal anxiety north, to a by-election on the Cumbrian coast. Workington was an old industrial seat that had spent the Depression in a Distressed Area, and had been Labour forever. To Benn, the 'working men with their raincoats and cloth caps and the women in scarves' who welcomed him looked 'just like the Thirties'. In his campaign speech, he 'took them back to 1945 and the pledge that we would never have unemployment again'. The years since had not improved these people's lives nearly enough; and now, he feared, the financial crisis was going to reverse even that. They were 'going to be dropped in it again'. The only solution, Benn thought, was a sharp turn left.[97] But Workington voters made a different choice, handing Mrs Thatcher a shock victory.

Callaghan was determined to stop British politics from devolving into the divisions Benn and Rees-Mogg had agreed were coming. To keep some semblance of consensus going, the Prime Minister needed a deal that would wash with the unions and left-wing MPs on one side, the City and the IMF on the other. Callaghan and Healey told the IMF that they risked losing the confidence of the TUC if the cuts were too harsh. Keynesian ministers disputed the need for any major cuts, arguing that higher unemployment was not only bad per se, but would make the deficit worse. After weeks of Cabinet agonising, Johannes Witteveen, the Managing Director of the IMF, flew into London incognito to put last-minute pressure on Callaghan. As Bernard Donoughue recorded it, Witteveen stressed that the government 'must concede a big package of cuts—they would not accept a compromise'. To Donoughue, this was not bloodless financial logic, but a political attack.[98] Witteveen conceded unemployment would probably be higher for a time, but that the economy would then improve. Callaghan told him that mass unemployment could trigger the collapse of democracy, and if it did, he would be responsible.[99] Witteveen said Britain 'could not expect special treatment.'[100] Yet out of this shouting-match, they negotiated an agreement: not the £3 billion of cuts within a year that the IMF had been demanding, but £2.5 billion over two years. After more agony, Healey secured majority backing in Cabinet for £1 billion of cuts. The IMF demanded double that, but Healey threatened an election on the question of the IMF v. the People, and Witteveen gave in.

And so, finally, the government signed its Letter of Intent to the IMF. Like Callaghan's conference speech, this attempted to embrace monetarist thinking without allowing spending cuts to 'produce unacceptable social tensions and levels of unemployment'. It praised the trade unions, and declared the social contract and the industrial strategy the 'pillars' of the government's approach to bringing down the deficit. It promised to go at 'a pace which will not overstrain the consensus on which our policies for regenerating industry and reducing inflation must depend'.[101]

Callaghan had, apparently, adapted that consensus, and so preserved it. Where Castle and Heath had each tried to innovate on industrial relations, got caught up in a power struggle with the unions and lost, Callaghan had kept the unions on-side—and carried through a greater innovation than either of them had managed.

The economy stabilised. The Treasury's forecasts turned out to have been too gloomy. Thatcher's City adviser told her that many financiers thought a Labour government carrying out Conservative policies was probably the best solution. Many of them were quite keen on incomes policy, just as many larger companies were comfortable with the supposed horrors of the closed shop.[102] The social contract was still keeping wages under control. In time, people even began to think that Labour could win a second full term.

The likely leading figures of this new Callaghan hegemony were already emerging: smart, young, moderate ministers, concerned to keep unemployment under control, but too young to be burdened by old taboos from the Depression—like Roy Hattersley, David Owen, John Smith and Shirley Williams. As Hattersley remembers, 'My generation was the coming generation—people who'd never had it so good. ... And we thought the world was perfect and wouldn't deteriorate—so the idea of a bit more unemployment didn't frighten us in the way it would have frightened our parents.'[103] They were allied to Donoughue, a cadre of younger advisers,[104] and sympathetic media figures like the *Sunday Times* editor Harold Evans, John Birt at London Weekend Television, and *The Times*' Peter Jay.

Jay and Birt acted as informal advisers to Callaghan, but at various points in the 1970s were also in touch with Keith Joseph. As head of the Number 10 Policy Unit, Donoughue was developing policies which might yet become the hallmarks of a modernising, mildly populist second-term Labour government. He had written a controversial speech for Callaghan advocating a much greater focus in schools on equipping pupils for the world of work.[105] He developed the idea of making it possible for council-house tenants—people like his parents—to buy their homes. Such policies were pointedly designed to appeal not to middle-class left-wingers, but to pragmatic, aspirational workers: the people who were pleased that, after years of rising real wages, they could finally buy a colour telly, and not just to watch doom-laden documentaries. This was the Britain that in 1976, according to a famous 2004 study, was at its happiest. As in the Thirties, while some in politics were caught up in their heightened sense of crisis, many people could feel their lives improving.

In some ways, Callaghan's government resembles those of Baldwin and Chamberlain: a steady, middle-of-the-road affair, with one foot in the old orthodoxy, but ready to innovate; introducing mild, tentative reforms, presiding over what now looks like the lull before the breakpoint came. But at the time it was not obvious that Benn, or Joseph and Thatcher, were right. Not for the first or the last time, it seemed possible that a political party could renew itself in office, simply adapting a long-standing consensus by absorbing some new ideas, without a radical break from the past. If Callaghan could only keep avoiding a struggle for power with the unions.

9

THE ENEMY WITHIN V. THE IRON HEEL

1976–9

Margaret Thatcher was struggling: at conference, in Shadow Cabinet, in the Commons. She was already in retreat, it seemed, from Joseph's radical ideas. Callaghan's cuts combined with Foot's social contract seemed to have established a viable new normal, without the need for any more dramatic struggles. Nevertheless, Joseph continued his lonely crusade. In early December 1976, he told the Shadow Cabinet that the next Conservative government must prepare to confront trade union power. Having twice lost to the miners, that seemed suicidal. But Joseph insisted the alternative was worse. This was not just a question of wage rises, but wholesale union resistance to change, blocking economic prosperity and freedom alike. If a Conservative government flinched, it could mean that 'we shall be pushed aside by parties to our right with the stomach to resist.'[1] That summer, a young, aggressively right-wing party had risen to prominence.

The National Front, the child of Empire cranks and neo-Nazis, had come to public attention in the wake of Enoch Powell's 'Rivers of Blood' speech in 1968, with its incendiary calls for compulsory repatriation. By 1976, the party's leaders were more coy about wanting a dictatorship, insisting that they were the democratic face of nationalism, who simply thought 'the will of the majority should prevail'.[2] The violence and intimidation carried out by NF supporters was an ongoing menace to black Britons and British Asians. In response to a series of racist murders, young Asians started organising direct action.

209

As Labour struggled on with no working majority, there was much concern about whether the Front could push aside the tired old parties and make a political breakthrough.[3] In the hot summer of 1976, there appeared to be worrying signs that right-wing extremism was spreading its appeal: young punks wearing swastikas seemed 'a nightmare coming to life'.[4] A year later, the National Front would go on to win almost 120,000 votes (5.3 per cent) in the Greater London Council elections, and had done well enough in by-elections and membership, attracting support from both disaffected Conservatives and fed-up working-class Labour supporters, to become the fourth largest party in British politics. On its front page, the *Mirror* told its 12 million readers that the NF was on course to win a few seats at the next general election, after which 'We will hear, regularly and alarmingly, of Parliamentary proceedings being disrupted.'[5] And what if the uneasy industrial truce broke down? The nightmare Joseph had raised with the Conservative leadership also began to spread on the left: that renewed economic turmoil might give the National Front their chance.[6]

But how exactly? At the start of October 1976, as the Prime Minister warned that the IMF crisis could tip Britain into dictatorship, a new play was coming to the end of its first full week in Stratford-upon-Avon, in the glow of excited reviews. David Edgar's *Destiny* walked its audience through a possible NF route to power. The play follows a right-wing army veteran turned City financier, Major Rolfe, who is on the hunt for a solution to the nightmare that had tormented the establishment since Saltley: a general strike, and the collapse that would follow. What if crisis drives the powerful to do the unthinkable?

Major Rolfe despairs of the Conservative Party's weakness, even under Thatcher. He rejects the idea of intervention by private armies, or the army itself. Meanwhile Kershaw—a manufacturer driven to desperation by strikes, and receiving no help from the police—turns to the play's fascist party, 'Nation Forward', to break through the picket line outside his factory. Kershaw stiltedly justifies this to the audience, in terms we have heard before: 'Unthinkable, to use these people, but. Impossible, not to. All other options closed.'[7] Finally, the two businessmen come together to offer to finance the fascists if they will ramp up their onslaught on 'the Reds'.

210

Edgar was not the only writer confronting this scenario in 1976. In a book published while *Destiny* was running in London, Martin Walker, a journalist specialising in both the National Front and the private armies, wondered whether something along these lines was coming. 'The capitalist barons,' he wrote, 'might feel frightened enough by the spectre of trade union power to unleash a Fascist paramilitary force to destroy the unions and fragment the working class.'[8]

The return of picket-line clashes was the nightmare Michael Foot had been striving to avoid. He and Jack Jones thought they had found a workable way to resolve disputes, wherever possible, without strikes. Foot's 1975 Employment Protection Act had brought to fruition a new approach to attempting to settle industrial disputes: an autonomous, impartial Advisory, Conciliation and Arbitration Service (ACAS). This would only attempt to seek a resolution once both sides had agreed to participate.

Once again, the unions had helped Foot pull off what Castle had been told was unthinkable. They showed 'a striking new willingness ... to achieve their ends by legislation rather than by collective bargaining backed up, if necessary, by industrial action.'[9] But could ACAS extend the aspirations of the social contract, and institutionalise the renewed consensus on industrial relations? In the boiling summer of 1976, a strike broke out which would test this whole endeavour to its limits.

* * *

Grunwick was a small photo-processing firm in north-west London that embodied the virtues and the down-sides of the start-up mindset. It was intensely competitive, and successfully so; it did not recognise unions. Grievances over such things as last-minute overtime—often forced on female employees with young children—were tackled through one-to-one confrontations with a disciplinarian manager. It was a firm with no mechanism for cooling situations off and, at the height of the long hot summer, with work at its most intense, no air conditioning.

Finally, several workers, including Mrs Jayaben Desai and her son Sunil, walked out, picketed the plant, and joined the clerical union APEX, along with around sixty Grunwick staff. Soon 137 out of 490 workers were on strike, and were promptly fired. They began to campaign for Grunwick to reinstate them and recognise their union. But after campaigning and picketing all winter, the strikers had got nowhere. What happened next turned a quiet street in north London into a theatrical battleground: a stage for the next act in the epic struggle that had started eight years earlier with *In Place of Strife*.

Early on, APEX had taken the strikers' case to Foot's new Advisory, Conciliation and Arbitration Service, which did all it could to initiate a conciliation process, but was thwarted by the company at every turn. It turned out that Grunwick, led by its uncompromising boss, George Ward, was not operating alone. It was being given a helping hand by a new species of right-wing organisation called the National Association for Freedom.

The NAFF was fiercely opposed to the 'Old Gang of the Tory Party',[10] whom it saw as Guilty Men, propping up the discredited consensus because they lacked the stomach to resist union power. The Association had been set up to do just that. Its launch in December 1975 had been accompanied by a book from one of its founders, the journalist Robert Moss, which set out the organisation's credo. *The Collapse of Democracy* opens with a remarkably thorough nightmare scenario called 'Letter from London, 1985'. A wage freeze provokes a general strike, in which workers occupy factories and set up militias. The army tries to keep essential services running—but fails. As a result, a 'Working People's Government' establishes a dictatorship, complete with labour camps, a ban on the Conservative Party, and £250 gin and tonics. People needed to grasp, Moss wrote, that 'in the aftermath of the British miners' strikes of 1972 and 1974', the strike was 'a form of internal warfare'.[11] *The Times'* reviewer judged all this 'rigorous' and 'urgent', and agreed that 'It could, possibly, happen here.'[12]

These were the nightmares that had driven Civil Assistance, Unison and GB75; on the face of it, the NAFF looked like their successor. It included men who toured army bases, exhorting officers to intervene against strikes. Robert Moss was one of Britain's few cheerleaders for the Pinochet coup in Chile. And the NAFF's organiser at Grunwick was an ex-soldier called John

Gouriet, who was obsessed with Soviet subversion, and thought that the strike was part of an 'international conspiracy' to make Britain a corporate state.[13] Grunwick was the perfect vehicle for the NAFF's holy war against the perils of consensus. At the height of the strike, when local Post Office workers refused to send the company's mail to its customers, Gouriet would lead a team of volunteers in a night-time operation to smuggle out tens of thousands of envelopes from Grunwick, and post them from all over the country. But first, the NAFF helped the company use the law to maximum advantage.

When ACAS eventually recommended that Grunwick recognise APEX, the company simply refused—and ACAS had no power of enforcement. In June 1977, frustrated after forty weeks of fruitless effort, APEX and the Grunwick Strike Committee gave up on Jones' and Foot's consensual mechanisms, and decided to try confrontation. The strikers were East African Asian migrants; in the past, British Asians on strike had not exactly enjoyed much support from white trade unionists. But given Grunwick's NAFF-backed intransigence, the dispute now represented a bigger fight, over the principle of a union's right to recognition. To many trade unionists, a defeat on that issue was unthinkable. On top of that, the prospect of a pitched battle with the forces of reactionary authority also attracted the attention of the far left. The call went out for a mass picket.

And so, for the second time in the 1970s, huge numbers of people began to gather at the gates of an obscure industrial plant, ready for a power struggle. APEX was not trying to kick off a second Battle of Saltley Gate. Regardless, on the first day, 13 June, 700 people turned up, many from the Socialist Workers Party, aiming to overwhelm the police in sheer numbers and close the factory with 'aggressive picketing'.[14] George Ward claimed that some of his staff had to be physically pulled through a picket line six deep. The police responded to attempts to obstruct or intimidate Grunwick staff with 'very aggressive tactics'.[15] That first day, they made eighty-four arrests, mainly of SWP activists. To the pickets, the NAFF was the bogeyman behind the scenes, but the establishment had another fist to swing at them: the Metropolitan Police's Special Patrol Group. This was an elite unit charged with tackling industrial disputes, which had been accused of aggressive methods and of making arrests on questionable grounds.

APEX called for a daily maximum of 500 pickets; *Socialist Worker* called for another Saltley. So did Arthur Scargill, who pitched up on 23 June with a contingent of miners. They joined what became a 2,000-strong picket, up against 793 police. At the peak of the violence, one SPG officer was hit in the head by a milk bottle, and was photographed lying in an expanding pool of blood. A horrified Jayaben Desai went to visit him in hospital. One of the miners who had travelled down with Scargill said: 'I was at Saltley Gates and it was a children's Sunday picnic by the side of this.'[16] Yet the police were still managing to keep the gates open, so Scargill called for a national day of protest for 11 July, saying, 'We shall require a picket along the lines of the Saltley picket in 1972, which was way in excess of 20,000.'[17] 18,000 people showed up, to no avail.

Finally, the government set up a Court of Inquiry to try to settle the dispute, but it seemed beyond the social contract's ability to resolve. The dispute dragged on, the mass pickets petering out, until APEX and the TUC stepped back. Jayaben Desai and her comrades ended up hopelessly on hunger strike outside TUC headquarters.

Grunwick was a direct reversal of the unions' victories against Heath. As the dockers had undermined Heath's Industrial Relations Court, so Grunwick had resisted Jones' and Foot's ACAS. And Ward and Gouriet had triumphed in their struggle for power just as decisively—and as innovatively—as Scargill had at Saltley. But this was not just tit-for-tat. A hint of what might follow from the strikers' defeat was visible to anyone who took a closer look at the dispute's decisive player, the National Association for Freedom. What made the NAFF distinct from Civil Assistance and GB75 was that some of its leading figures were free-marketeers—men like Moss and Nicholas Ridley. Margaret Thatcher had attended the inaugural dinner. The organisation had positioned itself carefully, shunning General Walker and condemning the National Front as (national) socialist. It was trying to think beyond merely taking on the unions in trials of strength.

But the NAFF's free-market ideology was largely not spotted by its enemies. The left's posters simply denounced it as 'The Enemy Behind Grunwicks Management [sic]', 'the champion of sweat-shop bosses'. Former trade unionist James Undy was a Socialist Workers Party activist when he joined the picket at

Grunwick. 'We didn't appreciate they had an underlying ideology,' he says today. 'We just thought they were the bosses being bastards because that's what bosses do'.[18] The NAFF was clearly identified by the left as a serious threat, out to block the unions' advance and smash 'consensus politics in industrial relations'.[19] But no one seems to have thought that this gaggle of hardliners might be the prophets of a whole new settlement.

* * *

In the aftermath of Grunwick, as the old consensus staggered, left and right competed to take over. Each side warned that the other was a threat to democracy, and had to be stopped. The left heard the stamp of the iron heel in the writs and machinations of the NAFF, and the advance of the Special Patrol Group. In the Labour–trade union axis, the right spied the enemy within. On 24 June 1977, as Arthur Scargill headed home to Barnsley, Keith Joseph was in South Yorkshire too. In what must surely be the most ferocious oratory ever delivered in the restaurant at Doncaster race-course, he warned his audience that the siege of Grunwick had suddenly revealed 'how far we have drifted, how far power in the Labour Party and the Unions has slipped into the hands of the authoritarians, the totalitarians, the men of violence for whom law and order are dispensable.' Behind the 'façade' of moderation, he explained, 'red fascism' was spreading. The strike was 'a make-or-break point for British democracy.'[20]

In 1974, Joseph had raised the nightmare of hyperinflation; then, in 1975–6, the nightmare of a total state. Now, he was adding coercive union power, entwined with an ever-expanding state. He accused the Labour government of being the unions' political wing, with both in the grip of their most extreme elements. He lumped together everyone from Jim Callaghan to the TUC to far-left students into one enormous, malignant leviathan. On 25 July, his central accusation was bolstered by *The Sun*, which reported a Marplan poll suggesting that 80 per cent of the public thought 'union leaders have "a lot" of power and influence in governing the country'.[21]

This was an explicit attack on the consensual approach of the Shadow Employment Secretary Jim Prior, who had backed ACAS over Grunwick. Joseph was trespassing on his colleague's turf, fouling up Prior's hard-won rapprochement with the unions—but he kept at it, in terms that even Mrs Thatcher thought 'too sharp'.[22] As party conference approached, the *Evening Standard* declared a battle for the 'soul of the Tory party', between Prior and 'the Mad Monk'. It reported that the party was aiming to win 'mass support from the blue-collar trade union urban voters',[23] which meant showing that they had learnt the lessons of Heath's disastrous confrontation with the miners in 1974. The last thing party strategists needed was Sir Keith calling potential voters 'red fascists'.

But some senior Conservatives were becoming aligned with Joseph's nightmare. Lord Hailsham remained proud of his role in pulling the 1940s Conservative Party towards accepting the full employment consensus, but now condemned the unions' hold over public policy through the social contract. He warned that the Labour government's 'elective dictatorship' would 'end in a rigid economic plan' with 'a siege economy, a curbed and subservient judiciary, and a regulated press.'[24] Already, 'freedom under law' had 'moved towards a totalitarianism'.[25]

In her conference speech, Thatcher warned again that another Labour government would build a 'total Socialist state', but she was more emollient towards the unions, claiming that if she were elected, their leaders simply wouldn't use strikes to bring her down.[26] A jittery internal report, *Stepping Stones*, insisted this was not enough. The party had to break taboos in order to transform the role of the unions, or it would be unable to govern, and would be finished—as would Britain. But Prior and others were not having this. As the internal struggle raged around her, Thatcher remained strategically cautious, backing Prior for the moment, still fudging the crucial issue of whether to keep trying incomes policy.

Nevertheless, outside his divided party, Joseph's prophecies of socialist–union tyranny were finding echoing voices. An array of lectures, speeches, dramas and novels all conjured a strikingly consistent nightmare. In a December 1977 lecture on Radio Clyde, 'Us in 2000', Prince Philip foresaw something similar. As more was provided by the state and unions, people would become more dependent on keeping their jobs, and on the attendant benefits. Anything that jarred with the nation's economic policies would be gradually suppressed. The talk was abridged and included in a 1978 volume, put together by the Institute of Economic Affairs, and called *The Coming Confrontation: Can the Open Society Survive Until 1989?* It also contained essays by Hayek, the Conservative MP Nigel Lawson (who has since confirmed that he thought liberal democracy was in some danger),[27] and the former Liberal leader Jo Grimond, who warned that 1984 was approaching.

That same year, two works of fiction took all this to its logical conclusion. Between September 1977 and April 1978, the BBC broadcast two series of *1990*, a drama projecting a near-future Britain ruled by oppressive Home Office bureaucrats. Then, in October, Anthony Burgess published a novel called *1985*, which sketched a Britain ruled by a union-dominated government amid street-level anarchy, where losing your union card rendered you an un-person. In both *1985* and *1990*, Parliament is a sideshow, freedom of expression is curtailed, and dissidents are sent to re-education camps. Rather like the NAFF's nightmare scenario, laid out by Robert Moss in *The Collapse of Democracy*, Burgess imagined the House of Lords dominated by peers from the TUC.

This did not seem likely under Callaghan, but what if he won re-election, and was then eased out—or simply retired—and was replaced by Tony Benn, the champion of the left? Benn favoured a siege economy, complete with even greater state intervention, and direct union involvement in government, and had been critical of the limitations of parliamentary democracy. In 1981, an ex-MI6 operative alleged that shadow minister Airey Neave had plotted to assassinate a future Prime Minister Benn.[28] That remains unproven, but Neave was certainly worried enough to make a speech in Keighley, on 17 June 1978, in which he contended that the next election might be the last chance to stop a steep descent towards a total socialist state. This, he claimed, would take 'the same direction in terms of individual freedom' as the Nazis had.[29] Neave had escaped from the Germans' prisoner-of-war camp at Colditz, and later worked at the Nuremberg war crimes tribunal. Encountering some of the men who had administered the Holocaust had put him on high alert for totalitarian tendencies:

> In Germany, minor bureaucrats became dictators and insignificant politicians were above the law ... Economic distress, particularly unemployment, helped Hitler and his gangster government to gain

absolute power in 1933, through the ballot box. Nuremberg is there to warn us of what can happen if parliamentary democracy becomes a farce...[30]

When Robin Day suggested that likening Labour to the Nazis was a descent into 'the political gutter', Neave explained that he was not 'accusing the Labour Party of having Hitler's ideals' but that 'there wouldn't be all that difference in terms of freedom between extreme right and extreme left.'[31] He evidently meant it, but such visions were also strategically useful. They suggested that a left-wing government could only keep the economy running on socialist lines if it were ready to sacrifice democracy. To avoid this new nightmare, you might have to sacrifice another of Peter Jay's four pillars of the post-war model, and tolerate the old nightmare of mass unemployment.

On both sides, a series of overlapping anxieties coalesced around the fear of a coming authoritarian state. In 1978, a ground-breaking study called *Policing the Crisis*, co-authored by the left-wing cultural theorist Stuart Hall, took apart the right's 'construction of nightmares': its tendency to blame Britain's problems on a generalised 'enemy within', conflating pickets with other supposed subversive groups.[32] But the left was also constructing a nightmare. If the right's was based on the spectre of unconstrained union power, the left feared its mirror-image: that pickets—and other dissenters—would be crushed.

That spring, the long-running anxiety about the army breaking strikes gained new credence. *The Times* got hold of a secret report from a Conservative Party committee, led by Lord Carrington, which had been asked by the Thatcher leadership to explore what a future Conservative government could do if confronted head-on by the miners or the power workers. Denis Healey seized on this, saying that the committee's aim was 'to organise revenge for the last Conservative Government's defeat by the miners through the use of armed forces for strike breaking.'[33] A month later, a second report leaked to *The Economist*. This one, produced by a committee led by Nicholas Ridley, set out 'an anti-strike plan'.[34] Eric Varley, Callaghan's Secretary of State for Industry, said it recommended 'deliberately staged confrontation', calling it 'a blueprint for an industrial civil war'.[35]

Neither report was quite as incendiary as advertised. Nonetheless, this pair of documents made it harder to argue that a future Conservative government would not end up in confrontation with the unions. It had not escaped notice that some of the leaders of the militaristic NAFF had 'counter-insurgency' credentials. And if strikes were not broken by soldiers, what about the Special Patrol Group, as a paramilitary 'third force'? Some of those who came up against the SPG at Grunwick saw them as anti-union 'assault troops'.[36] *Policing the Crisis* itself brought these elements together with Brigadier Frank Kitson's writings on defeating insurgency— and the ongoing fear that such techniques might be applied in Britain —to critique 'the repressive state apparatus' in general.[37]

Some incorporated another hostile element: the National Front. During Grunwick, Tony Benn had written in his diary that 'Some of the police are just National Front men'.[38] Amid widespread accusations of police racism, the sight of the police protecting NF marchers prompted the anti-racist magazine *Temporary Hoarding* to rename Sir David McNee, Commissioner of the Metropolitan Police, as 'McNFE'.[39] When Labour debated law and order at its October 1978 conference, a young left-wing delegate called Jeremy Corbyn suggested the motion would be more appropriate for the National Front.[40] All this was audible at Rock Against Racism concerts, in the Tom Robinson Band's 1977 song 'The Winter of '79', which imagines an end to social security, arrests of gay people and communists, the reintroduction of National Service, SAS involvement in policing, and the National Front on the rise—all in six verses.

On 30 January 1978, Margaret Thatcher appeared on ITV's *World in Action*, and asserted that many people were 'really rather afraid that this country might be rather swamped by people with a different culture'. Thatcher was addressing Joseph's nightmare about 'parties to our right', trying to draw disillusioned voters back from the National Front, insisting that if the main political parties did not want people to go to extremes, 'we ourselves must talk about this problem and we must show that we're prepared to deal with it'.[41]

To many on the left, this put Thatcher at the heart of their growing authoritarian nightmare. Stuart Hall wrote: 'I would be happier about the temporary decline in the fortunes of the Front if so many of their themes had not been so swiftly reworked into a more respectable discourse on race by Conservative politicians'.[42] *Policing the Crisis* foresaw an authoritarian populist '"law-and-order" state', that had 'won the right … to stamp fast and hard'. It warned that 'iron times' were coming. But this prophecy had missed something. It interpreted the Iron Lady's looming law-and-order society as the consequence of increasing state intervention in the economy as consensus broke down. It saw Thatcher as part of an ongoing, long-term shift from *laissez faire* to monopoly; her economics as an 'alibi' for harsh social policies, and as an instrument of 'discipline'.[43] It did not foresee that, with the death of the old consensus, Thatcher would win huge support for forging a new one.

* * *

If you were a regular at the Royal Shakespeare Company's Warehouse Theatre in Covent Garden between 1977 and 1979, you would have seen three separate plays featuring near-future authoritarian regimes.[44] You would not have seen one imagining a free-market government letting unemployment hit 3 million. The left seemed to have lost sight of that old 1930s nightmare, which had kept free-market economics marginalised for so long. And just at that moment, late in 1977, two young historians published an arresting new study of the 1930s. In *The Slump*, John Stevenson and Chris Cook argued that, 'alongside the pictures of the dole queues and hunger marches', there 'must also be placed those of another Britain, of new industries, prosperous suburbs and a rising standard of living.'[45] Unsurprisingly, some left-wing historians were aghast. This was the turn Keith Joseph had been calling for.

In 1978, Joseph's call to chase away the old ghosts was taken up by a swathe of former left-wingers, among them the ex-Labour Cabinet minister, now a Conservative, Reg Prentice, in a high-profile collection of essays called *Right Turn*. They argued that, while the Hungry Thirties had provided Labour's great, popular moral cause in 1945, this had now been rendered obsolete by the advent of full employment and Conservative governments that no longer had 'a vested interest in the misery of the working-class'.[46]

These essayists urged readers to forget the gaunt, tight-lipped men of the 1930s, and focus on the threat of union-backed tyranny.

Paul Johnson, former editor of the *New Statesman*, decried the way the freedom-loving, unemployed-championing Labour Party of his old comrade Aneurin Bevan had turned coercive. The 'first whiff of disaster' had been the fate of *In Place of Strife*, 'destroyed by a conspiracy of cynics, defeatists and trade union authoritarians'. The final straw was the closed shop, which Johnson insisted was as wrong as imprisonment without trial. This was the road to the corporate state. Add violence, as at Grunwick, and a left-wing species of fascism was looming up ahead.[47]

The fear remained that inflicting mass unemployment on the workers of the 1970s would kick off violent social unrest. But now some Cabinet ministers sensed that 'the fears of the 1930s had very generally passed', as Roy Hattersley puts it.[48] Even some older ministers thought much the same. The Home Secretary Merlyn Rees, who was born in 1920, told Cabinet: 'I was brought up in a poor home where unemployment was bad, but it is different now. We mustn't see things through the eyes of the past.' The Northern Ireland Secretary Roy Mason, who had first gone down the pit in 1938, said, 'We have taken the heartache out of unemployment.' Tony Benn was horrified.[49]

Meanwhile, yet another collection of doom-laden essays appeared, called *What's Wrong With Britain?* One of its authors joined the calls to scrap old images, once evoked by writers like JB Priestley, of the unemployed 'hanging about the streets ... in caps and mufflers'. True, workers were still 'haunted men carrying a large chip on the shoulder' about 'past bad treatment', but things had improved; the watchword now should not be equality, but liberty.[50] The writer of this piece? JB Priestley.

In August, with Callaghan expected to call the election within weeks, it was not Labour who sought to make political use out of the imagery of unemployment, but the Conservatives. With the total out of work up to 1,608,316—a full 6.7 per cent of the working-age population—posters appeared showing a long, snaking dole queue, under the slogan 'LABOUR ISN'T WORKING'. This was a deliberate move to target Callaghan's party where it had once been strongest. Why vote Labour, and risk the nightmare of union tyranny, if they could not even stop high unemployment?

Saatchi and Saatchi's famous poster was not an attempt, however, to replicate the old imagery of the Thirties. Martyn

Walsh, the art director who designed it, says he deliberately used colour, not black and white; the 'queue' was posed by members of Hendon Conservative Association, with no attempt to dress them up in 1930s caps and mufflers. Walsh wanted it to look like 1978.[51] The poster not only reinvented the dole queue as an anti-Labour image; it replaced old left-wing clichés with a vivid new meme, evoking the frustrations of the whole country—middle-class people as much as workers.

* * *

The social contract and its voluntary incomes policy was meant to be a consensual alternative to the state-imposed limitations Barbara Castle had tried to place on union power, back in 1969. But by the late 1970s, many working people were sick to the back teeth of pay restraint, cosily sewn up between their union leaders and the Labour government. Some workers knew their employers could afford bigger raises; others were so low-paid they were struggling to manage even with in-work benefits. At his last TGWU conference before retiring, Jack Jones, the life-long champion of the rank and file, asked delegates to back another year of restraint, and was booed. His argument—that the only people to benefit from such opposition would be Thatcher's Tories—cut no ice. His successor was elected on a promise not to agree to pay limits. In the summer of 1978, Hugh Scanlon followed Jones into retirement. These two supposed communist wreckers had indeed wrecked *In Place of Strife*, but for several years they had made the social contract work. Whether even they could have sustained it for much longer is debatable; without them, it was finished.

Jim Callaghan, once their partner in thwarting Castle, was now determined not to allow inflation to rise again. In July, he set a new pay norm at the eye-wateringly low rate of 5 per cent. In September, the TUC voted against it. Even so, Callaghan delayed the election until the spring. Could the last vestiges of the consensus survive long enough to help secure Labour a majority, and somehow restore the status quo? A few days later, Ford workers were offered 5 per cent, and immediately went on strike. A BBC reporter asked one of them if they had any hope of winning. 'Well, we did in 1969,' he replied, 'against the then employment minister Barbara Castle.'[52]

At the Labour conference in early October, Castle, her ministerial career long over, watched from the platform as the union leaders waged war on Callaghan's pay policy. Turning to Michael Foot beside her, she told him that the government would never make 5 per cent stick. 'He brushed me aside irritably,' wrote Castle, 'muttering, "The unions just don't understand."'[53] Their role reversal was complete. But if anyone could persuade the unsympathetic hall to back the government, it was Foot.

To make his case that the industrial relations consensus he had rebuilt was worth preserving, Foot drew delegates' attention back to its foundations—which were his foundations, too. The party had to make sure that

> we do not make the mistake that our forebears made in 1931 when they split to atoms at the critical moment and allowed the Tories in, not only to deepen the slump but lead this country to the most dangerous moment in our history, 1940. I believe that under the Thatchers and Keith Josephs you could have an industrial crisis of that nature in Britain.[54]

He tried to get delegates to imagine what life under the next Conservative government would be like: part Thirties-style crisis, partly the horrors of the Heath regime. There would be 'massive ultra-deflation and a statutory policy as well, and you would have a nice little Industrial Relations Act 1971 thrown in again just to ease the situation.' He insisted that Labour was still better placed to tackle unemployment, high as it was, because it was more compassionate than the Conservatives.

Incomes policy had only ever been necessary because of the postwar commitment not to use rocketing unemployment to push wages down instead. But perhaps it simply seemed impossible that anything like that could happen again, or that unemployment could conceivably rise much higher. Whatever the reasons, Foot lost the vote, and Labour began its long journey into winter.

Ford management wanted to abide by the government's 5 per cent limit, but they could afford to pay their workers a lot more without raising prices. Under the pressure of weeks of strike action, they gave in, saying they wanted consent, not confrontation. The strike won a raise of 17 per cent.

The government tried to take a consensual approach too, dodging a struggle for power with the unions. When oil tanker and road haulage drivers were the next to strike, this put essential supply services at risk. Ministers had deployed troops during a fireman's strike in 1977, but this time, they resisted the calls for a state of emergency. The tanker drivers eventually settled, for 15 per cent. The hauliers, meanwhile, were using secondary picketing to block movement of food and other essential supplies: flying pickets helped stymie the Manchester and Liverpool docks, and east coast ports were heavily affected. Rather than try to use troops to replace lorry drivers, the government sought an agreement with the TGWU to maintain the movement of essential supplies: a last-ditch version of consensus, with the unions more dominant than ever. Denis Healey objected that this was 'colluding with the unions' in their attempt 'to cripple domestic road transport'.[55] In any event, Moss Evans, the new head of the TGWU, declared that his job was doing his best for his members, not running the country, and refused to intervene to stop secondary picketing.[56]

By 11 January 1979, the strike was spreading. With 'active (and effective) picketing of docks, depots and manufacturers' premises served by drivers not on strike', most ports largely shut down by backlog congestion, and chemical giant ICI saying they would have to close down within ten days, Evans and other TGWU leaders went to Number 10. Callaghan, who had evidently been spooked by the rocketing inflation four years before, asked repeatedly how he could keep it down when the 'high demands by the TGWU were making this impossible'. Evans argued that 'It was very difficult to explain to individual drivers earning only £53 for a 40-hour week that they should consider the macro-economic situation when making their demands', particularly if the driver's 'typist daughter' was earning more than him. Under the threat of calling in the troops, the union agreed to try to rein back the reach of the picketing, but control remained with local union activists.[57]

This was symbolised by the strike committees that now controlled access to ports. As in the 1972 miners' strike, permission systems were set up and run by the pickets. At Tilbury, with a picket spanning a 'multi-gate system as wide as a motorway', drivers had to visit the local TGWU office to be questioned closely by the strike committee, who turned most of them away.[58] If you wanted to move supplies through Hull, you would have to persuade a Dispensation Committee, staffed by TGWU shop stewards, that those supplies were essential. Lorry drivers had blocked the only two major access roads. You would sometimes have to wait in line all day: a different kind of queue to the one that had haunted British politics for so long.

But this time, there were no set-piece Saltley- or Grunwick-style confrontations with the police. The government had effectively accepted that the TGWU pickets were in control on the ground. Where the siege of Grunwick had seen business beat the unions, this was the unions' final blow against the Labour government. When the state allowed the road haulage employers to raise their offer, the hawkish transport secretary Bill Rodgers wrote furiously to Callaghan, objecting that this was not about pay, but 'trade union power' and 'law and order'. Despairing of the government's will to stand and fight, he protested that 'the impression was that the distribution of foodstuffs was now entirely in the control of the Transport and General Workers' Union.'[59] In February, the hauliers won a 17 per cent raise.

* * *

For Margaret Thatcher, the Winter of Discontent was a political Christmas, bringing her all she could have hoped for. She had predicted an imminent 'long hard winter of discontent' in July 1975.[60] Three years later, here it was, and with it, the chance to settle the Conservative Party's long dilemma over its stance on union power. The Callaghan government's softly-softly approach was probably wiser than sending for the troops; but once again, an attempt at consensus was just looking like surrender—and this time, Thatcher was ready to pounce. On *Weekend World* on 7 January, Thatcher said the unions 'were now too powerful and above the law, and that their position and power should now be thoroughly re-examined'.[61] She called for strike ballots, and reviews of both unions' legal immunities and the right to strike in industries 'where unions have the power to hold the nation to ransom'.[62] Ten days later, in a party political broadcast, she added a call for an end to secondary picketing. The next day, the *Daily Mail* underlined her message, talking of the 'tyranny of the pickets'.[63]

Thatcher was careful to absolve the majority of trade unionists from blame, and a poll suggested that 94 per cent of them backed her call for compulsory ballots. Instead, she pinpointed the power of the 'wreckers among us': the minority of union activists who felt entitled to pursue their interests by 'hurting others'.[64] When public-sector workers—from refuse-collectors to hospital workers and grave-diggers—went on strike at the end of January, this provided a new dramatic encapsulation of the pickets' power: the turning away of patients from hospitals. Trade unionists were now cast not just as wreckers and tyrants, but as callous arbiters of life and death. In the press, as Colin Hay puts it, strikers were 'symbolically expurgated from [the] national community' as 'the enemy within'.[65] The biggest gift the Winter of Discontent handed to the right was the new imagery it provided to illustrate its nightmares.

These were low-paid workers whose unions had embraced the social contract, only to find that public-sector spending cuts brought job losses and reduced the benefits many relied on, even in work. As recent research by Tara Martin López has shown, many of the 'wreckers' were women for whom joining trade unions, and striking for better pay, was of a piece with the emancipatory wave of the Women's Movement.[66] The young left-wing Labour activist Jeremy Corbyn was a district organiser for the National Union of Public Employees, helping refuse workers pursue their pay claims that winter. He has since emphasised the disappointment public-sector workers suffered with their 'very low pay levels' and 'very poor living standards', especially having worked hard for a Labour victory in 1974.[67] Barbara Castle, meanwhile, was in a London hospital during the strike, and wrote that those picketing outside 'were caring members of caring unions who were stirred into action by a strong sense of injustice'. She and other patients did their 'modest bit' by helping in the kitchens with the washing up.[68] But not everyone was so willing to put up with hospital workers going on strike. One paradox of union power is that if your only leverage risks extreme consequences, you may not prove to be very powerful.

The nightmare of untrammelled union power was very far from being just confected propaganda, but it also obscured quieter nightmares. One of the primary images of the strike—the unburied dead—tends to blot out the absolutely miserable lives of grave-diggers like those at Liverpool West Derby cemetery. They told a journalist that their job involved having to reopen old graves and deal with decomposed remains—a lack of washing facilities meant 'You carry the smell of death to your home'—and the daily risk of being 'trapped and smothered'. Striking for a pay rise was not something they seemed particularly keen to be doing: their picket sign read, 'SORRY FOR THE INCONVENIENCE— ONLY WAY FOR POOR PAY'. But theirs was not a nightmare many people had time for. Their strike won at least one gravedigger bricks through his windows.[69]

By the time the Leader of the Opposition had started overtly challenging the unions' power, ministers were finally reaching the same view, but too late. In Cabinet, support for the kind of measures Thatcher was advocating competed with laments on how things had swung the unions' way, especially since the NUM's flying pickets had changed the way strikes worked. If the unions would not use their power more co-operatively, it seemed likely a Conservative government would soon try to rein it in.[70] To Bernard Donoughue, the government was 'surrendering to every pressure'.[71]

There had already been a struggle for control—between the unions and the Labour government, with the Conservatives watching from the side-lines, narrating. Thatcher had managed to tell a clear story of union power. The alternative to incomes policies was letting unemployment climb even higher. But, helpfully for Thatcher, that prospect had not been to the fore, except as a possible result of the strike itself. On 15 January, *The Sun*'s headline was '3 MILLION FACE THE DOLE QUEUE'.[72] Which was perhaps more prophetic than they knew.

In the Commons on 28 March, Thatcher moved a motion of no confidence. If the government lost, it would be forced to resign. Winding up the debate for the government fell to Michael Foot. Once again, he tried to conjure images of the coming nightmare of Conservative rule. Britain must avoid a repeat of Heath's 1970–4 government, which he accused Thatcher of proposing:

Nothing more disastrous could happen to our country, not only in industrial relations, which is perhaps most strongly branded on the public's mind, but in almost all areas. It was part of the Selsdon Park policy to abandon support for British industry, drive us into the Common Market on the most disadvantageous terms, and return to the naked laissez-faire policies of [Sir Keith Joseph].[73]

Towards the end, he harked back to another momentous Commons vote: the origin story of the post-war consensus, the climax of the Norway debate on 8 May 1940. At that moment of extreme crisis, Foot said, Labour had 'saved the country', and 'Two thirds of the Conservative Party at that time voted for the same reactionary policies as they will vote for tonight.'[74]

Back then, watching the death throes of the Chamberlain government from the press gallery, the young Michael Foot had been about to write his famous denunciation of the old order, and so help to forge a new one. But thirty-nine years on, there were new candidates for the role of Guilty Men. Now it was Foot who was standing where Chamberlain had once stood, facing an Opposition who believed their time had come. He told the House that the country would soon face an election that 'will not be so dissimilar from the choice that the country had to make in 1945'.

The House divided, and the government lost, by one vote. As in 1945, the struggle for power between left and right could now be settled, through a new battle of nightmares.

* * *

Since surviving the IMF crisis, Callaghan's administration had found ways to accommodate monetarist economics without turning into Thatcher-style Conservatives. Chancellor Healey had repaid the IMF loan, and reversed the cuts made to secure it. In late 1978, the economist Vince Cable, then on his way towards leaving Labour, had nonetheless been brought in as an adviser by the new trade secretary, John Smith. Cable remembers how the intellectually self-confident figures at the top of Labour, having been in power for much of the previous two decades, were still thought of as 'the natural ruling class'; that, even after the Winter of Discontent, they 'still hoped they would win'.[75] Callaghan seemed much more obviously prime ministerial than the strange woman leading the Conservatives. Was she really the person to win working-class men away from Labour? Callaghan's pitch to voters was 'steady as she goes'. He had brought on a new generation of natural rulers: brisk, competent forty-somethings with new ideas, and a rapidly diminishing tolerance for strikes, ready to take forward his updated version of the consensus.

But Michael Foot was right that the 1979 election would have something in common with 1945—to his enemies' benefit. In the aftermath of crisis, looking like the established ruling class was no longer an advantage, especially as what had been Labour's unique selling-point in 1974—*only we can work with the unions*—was clearly broken. All Labour could do was plead that things could be changed without the need for a struggle for power, rather as Conservatives like Lord Hailsham had done in 1945.

In a speech at Cardiff City Hall on 16 April, Thatcher said: 'The Old Testament prophets didn't go out into the highways saying, "Brothers, I want consensus." They said, "This is my faith and my vision! This is what I passionately believe!"'[76] At Birmingham Town Hall three days later, she told a Conservative Party rally that Labour had once had a 'moral mission', but had degenerated into a party of 'lawful intimidation'. A country 'torn by strikes', like a country 'without law and order', could not prosper. Pickets, like muggers, demanded what they wanted, 'or else!' 'All of you,' she said, 'have suffered under the rule of pickets and the strikes this winter. We all saw at first hand that power and felt our own powerlessness.'[77] She invited the British people to take back control.

By contrast, the left's fear that Thatcher herself would usher in an authoritarian, near-fascist 'law-and-order society' barely figured in Labour's campaign. This nightmare reached its apotheosis on a smaller scale. On 28 April, five days before polling day, the National Front staged a meeting in Southall's town hall. Anti-racists, including local British Asians and members of the Anti-Nazi League, gathered to protest. The Special Patrol Group was deployed and, according to an internal police report, was almost certainly responsible for killing a protestor called Blair Peach.

The National Front was standing 303 candidates. On the BBC's election night special, when it became clear that the party had won

0.6 per cent of the national vote, this was described as an 'astonishingly bad' result—a hint of what serious commentators had been expecting.[78] It became clear that the NF's support had peaked in 1977, although without the anti-racist pressure on its base and its reputation, its defeat might have been less decisive. The front's main effect was the strikingly creative response the threat of advancing fascism provoked. The grassroots Rock Against Racism campaign had brought together anti-racists, feminists and gay rights activists in a single movement of lasting influence. Yet, outside the left, the nightmare of an authoritarian state that combined the police, the army, the NAFF, the Conservative Party and the National Front did not appear to register.

The spectre of the enemy within trounced fears of the iron heel. Thatcher had made a compelling case: that the Winter of Discontent had exposed a concentration of power that was wreaking destruction on the country, and that the unions' allies on the Labour left threatened to strangle democracy. If so, perhaps another previously unthinkable option might actually be better—a free-market government that would control inflation not by kowtowing to the unions but, if necessary, by letting unemployment climb to untold levels. Callaghan did raise the issue early on, and in his last election broadcast he claimed that 'a Tory government would withdraw financial aid to industry, leading to half-a-million more unemployed'.[79] But unemployment was already too high to make a convincing case that it would reach nightmarish new heights under the Conservatives. On 3 May 1979, Margaret Thatcher led her party back to power, with a majority of forty-four.

And so, after the various failed efforts of Barbara Castle, Edward Heath, Michael Foot and Jim Callaghan to remake the industrial relations consensus, Thatcher's willingness to take on the power of the unions had apparently succeeded. The Winter of Discontent had become her Dunkirk moment, when, as in 1940, many voters finally lost patience with a tired administration hemmed in by nightmares they no longer shared. But she still had to carry it off. Was she really prepared to break with the commitment to full employment that underpinned union power, and allow unemployment to return to the scale of the 1930s? Even if she was, could her government withstand the consequences?

10

ANOTHER TIME AND AGE

1979–85

It is relatively rare for a senior Cabinet minister to tell a journalist, on the record, that they are being moved from their job because it has 'become embarrassing' both for them and for the government. This, though, was the explanation Keith Joseph offered *The Times* in October 1981, for his departure from the Department for Industry. The Treasury was hard at work implementing the ideas he had championed, but Joseph himself had ended up reluctantly perpetuating old policies. He had been bailing out struggling companies: what *The Times* called 'the parade of investment black holes [including] Leyland, British Steel and ICL', which were deemed 'essential to the national economy'.[1] This was exactly the sort of government spending he had staked his career on bringing to an end. But in a way, it makes sense that Joseph was struggling to return to the messy compromises of office. For over five years, he had worked beyond the daily political struggle, and had successfully laid the ground for the Conservatives to face down the trade unions, and the ghosts of the 1930s. Other people would now prove better equipped to see those battles through.

Initially, the government's overriding struggle was against inflation. They were determined to manage this without resorting to incomes policy—a feat which many thought impossible. That meant finding other ways to restrain wage demands, and by the start of 1980, there was growing demand from the party itself to get on with curbing union power. As employment secretary, Joseph's old antagonist Jim Prior was trying to steer new restrictions on secondary picketing through Parliament. He was trying to pull this off without antagonising the unions: he still hoped an industrial relations consensus could be rebuilt. But he came under huge pressure to make his legislation tougher, especially when 155,000 steel workers went on strike.

At five o'clock in the morning on Valentine's Day, 1980, at least 1,000 pickets, including around 350 miners led by Arthur Scargill, marched to the gates of Hadfields steel works near Sheffield, to try to stop the firm's staff from returning to their jobs inside. Despite facing large numbers of police officers deployed in wedge formations, the mass picket worked. The nightmare was happening again: Thatcher feared this was her Saltley.[2] One picket was quoted in the *Daily Mirror* the next day, saying that 'the pay claim is second now—this is a war on her in Downing Street. She has even got some of the bobbies here facing their own fathers.'[3] Hadfields' owner telegrammed Prior to demand he legislate, telling him, 'Before long someone is going to get killed outside these gates'.[4] Thatcher's chancellor, Geoffrey Howe—architect of Heath's Industrial Relations Act—duly pushed for tighter legal controls. But still Prior resisted pressure from his right, determined not to repeat the Heath–Howe blunder of relying on one vast, provocative, unworkable new law. He refused to ban secondary picketing. His bill passed, keeping the flickering dream of consensus alive.

Thatcher, however, thought that a final showdown with union power was inevitable. At a meeting where Prior was under pressure to strengthen his bill, he warned that going too far could trigger a general strike. That, she suggested, was 'a matter of when it comes, not whether.'[5] The government wanted the coal industry to become self-financing, which meant pit closures; one member of the NUM executive declared that 'Mrs Thatcher has been out to get the miners since 1972 and 1973', and that 'If she throws down the gauntlet, I can assure her of one thing: we will pick it up.'[6] But early in 1981, when the miners threatened to strike and *The Times* declared this 'the supreme test that faces Mrs Thatcher',[7] the government backed off, to derision in the Commons. Nigel Lawson, whom Thatcher made energy secretary later that year, recalled that the only brief she gave him was: 'we mustn't have a coal strike', in the belief that the miners had brought down the last Conservative government.[8] But it was likely that the NUM's next President would be Arthur Scargill. On the basis that Scargill clearly wanted a strike, Lawson began to prepare.

* * *

At about this time, the free-market Institute of Economic Affairs published a book of think-pieces called *The Emerging Consensus?* That question mark was doing a lot of work. It was only three years since the IEA's essay collection *The Coming Confrontation*, and Thatcher and Lawson were by no means the only people who thought there was still a confrontation to come. To many, the only consensus that seemed to be emerging was that the government's radical experiment was disastrous. It had ended exchange controls, raised interest rates, and shifted the burden from direct taxation to indirect taxation; but inflation rose, and so did bankruptcies—not helped by a hike in the value of the pound, pushing up the price of exports. And unemployment, already at post-war highs, rose sharply higher. As well as Labour and the unions, businessmen were in shock at the damage being done, to the point that the chairman of ICI informed the Prime Minister that the company was thinking about leaving the UK. And yet, in March 1981, Chancellor Howe doubled down on his deflationary measures, making good on Thatcher's promise that, unlike Heath, 'the lady's not for turning'.

Looking back today, the way forward from March 1981 may seem clear: the government simply had to hold its nerve. But at the time, the emergence of a new free-market consensus seemed far from inevitable. Even after Thatcher's victory, every route still appeared to lead to nightmares.

Labour was now led by Michael Foot, but increasingly dominated by Tony Benn's radical left supporters; the party had decisively rejected the Callaghan government, denouncing the post-war consensus. The apparent failure of Thatcher's last-ditch capitalist experiment seemed to indicate that there was now no alternative but socialism, and when Benn almost won the Labour deputy leadership that September, supporters like Jeremy Corbyn believed they were 'nearly there'.[9]

But the left was haunted by the fear that a Benn government would be stopped in its tracks. A multi-authored Bennite *Manifesto* set out a scenario reminiscent of Stafford Cripps' old nightmare. A newly elected socialist government, committed to restoring full employment, would face being broken by immediate, deliberate financial crisis, and the collusion of the establishment with hostile foreign powers. To thwart this, the new government would need to impose 'a seizure of power over the City and over multinational business'.[10] In his novel *A Very British Coup*, Benn's lieutenant, the journalist Chris Mullin, fleshed out how the establishment might break a left-wing Labour government—and he soon found that three other people in his circle had been writing up the same scenario.[11] Benn's ally Ralph Miliband suggested that, even without a coup, Britain could all too easily slide gradually into an outwardly normal 'conservative-authoritarian' state, complete with 'rehabilitation centres', a much bigger role for the army in public life, and 'unpatriotic MPs' being 'temporarily detained'.[12]

The more the hard left positioned themselves uncompromisingly against all this, the more threatening they looked to Labour moderates. Bruising encounters with Benn's supporters provoked fear on the Labour right that was just as intense as the left's. In the face of sustained heckling at conference in 1980, Shirley Williams had said that party members were scared to go to meetings for fear of being yelled at and abused, declaring that her parents had both been 'on the Gestapo blacklist', so she knew something about fascism—but that there was 'fascism of the left as well as fascism of the right.'[13] Echoing Airey Neave, she said the rapid advance of Labour's extremists reminded her of a book called *The Nazi Seizure of Power*. The fight with the Bennites eventually drove Williams to break from Labour and form the Social Democratic Party with other former Labour Cabinet ministers. One of them, Bill Rodgers, was heavily influenced to leave his party by reading a biography of George Orwell, and thinking about totalitarianism.[14]

The Bennite left's 'unreality' about the dangers of their approach even began to worry the Marxist playwright Howard Brenton, author of *The Churchill Play*, and a Benn supporter himself.[15] In the summer of 1981, as the battle inside the Labour Party was at its bitterest, his play *Thirteenth Night* was staged by the Royal Shakespeare Company. Based loosely on *Macbeth*, it imagines a Labour government winning power, ousting its moderate elderly leader, and establishing a murderous revolutionary dictatorship. This regime cuts off links with America, prepares legislation for workers' control of industry—and ends in fire, as the ghost of Stalin stalks the shadows. In defeat, Labour was locked in an internal battle of nightmares.

* * *

Thatcher and her allies faced a more tangible nightmare: the return of mass unemployment. They saw letting this happen as an essential part of the cure the British economy had long needed, weakening the unions' power to drive up wages and cause disruption, and so helping to restore the country's competitive edge. But by the summer of 1981, unemployment was well on the way to 3 million, a phenomenon unseen for fifty years; and the government was at less than 30 per cent in the polls. Thatcher herself was even less popular. When Keith Joseph had talked in the 1970s of the need to abandon the full employment commitment and chase away the old ghosts, his young supporters—like the ex-student leader David Davis, and David Willetts, now a civil servant at the Treasury—had never expected unemployment to go as high as this. But then nor had Joseph himself.

The reaction provoked by the resurgence of this old nightmare threatened to drown the government's project, in two different ways. One was the fear that mass unemployment would drive the ever-more assertive working-class to riot and rebellion, to a point where the country might be ungovernable. Tony Benn told Joseph to his face that: 'I think your way will lead to a breakdown of the social fabric and that actually in ten years' time our view will prevail.'[16] Thatcher's own adviser, the journalist and Powell biographer TE Utley, had warned that Joseph's ideas could lead to civil war.

All this gave the left's nightmares about authoritarian crackdowns a new relevance. After all, why had the new government given soldiers and police officers an exceptional pay rise? In Chile, General Pinochet's military dictatorship had introduced free-market reforms. Benn wrote a foreword to a pamphlet called *Monetarism means repression*, arguing that, as in Chile, so in Britain, 'the entrenchment of market forces is completely incompatible with political democracy and free trade unionism'.[17] Some on the left saw the return of mass unemployment as a weapon deployed deliberately to break the working class, with authoritarian policing ready to suppress complaints. The visions of the late 1970s seemed to be coming to life. That April, a riot broke out in Brixton, south London. In July, more erupted in 'inner city' areas across the country: Toxteth, Moss Side, Handsworth, Chapeltown. Nothing like this had hit Britain in decades. In the face of petrol bombs, the police deployed the kind of riot gear more familiar in Northern Ireland. The post-war wisdom of keeping unemployment under control seemed to have been grimly vindicated. But it was not quite so neat as that. There were evidently other causes that had fused with unemployment to set these areas alight, like heavy-handed, racist policing. And as *The Observer*'s Labour Editor Robert Taylor wrote in *Workers and the New Depression* (1982), overall, the resurgence of mass unemployment provoked strikingly little protest. The jobless had retreated into private misery. It turned out that, as in the 1930s, being out of work for a long time imposed its own personal authoritarian regime.

This pointed to the second way in which mass unemployment endangered the Thatcher project: pity. *The Times* reported that 'the nightmare haunting the wets'—senior Tories unconvinced by Thatcher—was that the government could end up making the party appear, as in the 1930s, to be 'the spokesmen of the bosses'.[18] There were concerted efforts to draw exactly that parallel, like the TUC-organised People's March for Jobs, which set off from Liverpool on May Day 1981. One of the marchers was a retired docker called Frank Deegan, taking what the *Liverpool Echo* called a 'nightmare trip' back in time: he was retreading the route he had taken on a hunger march in 1936.[19] When Michael Foot addressed the marchers, he invoked his own conversion to socialism in the city's docks in 1935. The Conservatives were concerned enough to include questions in their private polling on how 1980 compared to the 1930s. Of 1,700 voters, 43 per cent thought unemployment was 'now worse than the 30s'; but 81 per cent thought the unemployed were 'better off than in the 30s'.[20]

That October, just before the Conservative Party conference, Edward Heath accused his successor's government of using mass unemployment to reduce inflation, and called for 'a return to consensus politics'. But things had changed since 1972: a different nightmare was dominant now. Some of the ministers round the Cabinet table with Heath when unemployment had hit a million had now left politics; others had been persuaded by the Winter of Discontent that there was, in Thatcher's phrase, 'no alternative'. She shot back that consensus was nothing but 'the process of avoiding the very issues that have to be solved'.[21]

Revisionist historians continued to chip away at the 'Hungry Thirties' imagery, arguing that, for most people, the 1930s had been positive. The Conservative MP Rhodes Boyson could claim impeccable Depression credentials: he had been 'a schoolboy in the 1930s in the centre of the Lancashire cotton belt' who was 'well aware of what unemployment, and the threat of unemployment then meant, not least to members of my own family'.[22] Even so, he argued, the National Government had rescued the situation. Similar scepticism appeared in the centre-left *New Society* and the liberal *Guardian*.[23] The labour relations specialist Robert Taylor argued that the Thirties was simply not a useful comparison anymore—a point made succinctly by a young unemployed man in Liverpool on the eve of the People's March for Jobs. He told the BBC's *Newsnight* that social security was better than it had been in the 1930s. While he still thought about the old marches, 'it doesn't seem the same in black and white'.[24] You now had to be in your 50s to remember that far back.

The process of throwing off other people's memories even appears in Alan Bleasdale's 1982 TV drama *Boys from the Blackstuff*, a great howl of anguish at the return of mass unemployment to an already-struggling Liverpool. 3.1 million people watched the first episode on BBC2, on 10 October 1982; the series generated such a strong response that it was reshown on BBC1 a few weeks later, and by the end, its audience was 7.9 million.[25] *Blackstuff* became as much a symbol for this side of the 1980s as *Love on the Dole* had been for the 1930s. In the final episode, 'George's Last Ride', an elderly woman tries to guilt-trip her trade unionist sons into not giving up by calling on her and her dying husband's efforts on the hunger marches half a century before. But, sick of hearing about all that, one son explodes, telling her that hunger marches, soup kitchens and 'standing together and fighting' belongs to 'another time and age, mam'.

Already some on the left were attempting to move on. Two Labour MPs who had lost their seats in 1979 published a book called *A Life to Live: Beyond Full Employment*, which called for a less work-centric approach to life and politics, taking advantage of automation. In the foreword, Michael Foot's protégé, the shadow education secretary Neil Kinnock, applauded the book for trying to struggle free from fixations on the past. As the Thatcher government's policies were 'ravaging the economy', there was no point trying to recreate the 'golden age of a Butskellite consensus'.[26] The book, Kinnock thought, offered 'a tangible alternative to the nightmare future of mass unemployment and social uproar'.[27]

A few weeks after the riots, Thatcher finally replaced Prior as employment secretary with a more like-minded colleague. Norman Tebbit was born in 1931 in a poor suburb of north London, where his father was an assistant shop manager until he lost his job. At conference in October, Tebbit did something higher-born Tories could not easily do, and challenged head-on the idea that mass unemployment meant unrest, saying: 'I grew up in the 1930s with an unemployed father. He didn't riot—he got on his bike and looked for work'. Joseph's maverick call seven years earlier for an end to 'play-acting the 1930s' had reached fruition. On 26 January 1982, a decade and six days after Heath's trauma in the Commons, unemployment passed 3 million. And when the government simply kept going, a forty-year taboo passed with it.

* * *

At one point early in the 1980s, a group of Conservative MPs tried to win support for a statue of Stanley Baldwin to be erected in the House of Commons lobby. His reputation had improved somewhat in recent years, but not with Michael Foot, who managed to block the monstrous idea of memorialising one of the Guilty Men. Foot's old polemic had once discredited a consensus by excoriating Baldwin and the rest, but now younger men were out to change the narrative again. Accusing eyes turned on the mandarins of the post-war civil service, who were said to have seen their role as the orderly management of decline. In 1969, a libertarian polemic endorsed by Enoch Powell had branded them *The Guilty Madmen of Whitehall*.

The whole post-war notion of a benevolent, enlightened, progressive state was increasingly presented as a sham. In attacking the subsidies pouring into inefficient industries, the free-market 'Selsdon Manifesto' declared that 'High-minded talk of the "national interest" is in these cases just a smoke-screen'. This idea was developed in 'public choice' theory, which argued that bureaucrats were just as self-interested as everyone else, and generally made decisions 'in terms of what benefits them, not society as a whole.'[28] In *Right Turn*, the historian Hugh Thomas put this in the populist language of 1940, alleging that 'there are huge vested interests in economic planning upon which the careers of innumerable fine civil servants from the best universities depend.'[29] Likewise, in the near-future TV drama *1990*, the heart of the tyranny had been the Home Office.

Early in the first Thatcher government, another TV show appeared which gave this argument much more popular expression, just as *Guilty Men* had in 1940. The comedy series *Yes, Minister* mercilessly sent up the claim that government acted to improve life for ordinary people—a basic premise of the post-war consensus. It cast democratic politicians, like its anti-hero Jim Hacker, as the hapless dupes of urbane Whitehall mandarins like Sir Humphry Appleby, who keep things running smoothly for their own benefit. The series was co-written by Antony Jay, an advocate of public choice theory, but its appeal went a long way beyond theoretical pamphlets. Like *Guilty Men*, the programme had a huge impact on how people saw politics. However accidentally, it helped to embed the Thatcher narrative about Whitehall's managers of decline, who had supposedly let their preference for consensus, self-interest and 'safety first' carry the country that had won the war to the brink of disaster in the 1970s. Thatcher liked the series so much that she took part in a skit with the series' lead actors, proposing to 'abolish economists'.

Civil servants themselves might have protested that they had strained to hold things together through crisis after crisis. But one reason *Yes, Minister* caught the imagination was that it also drew on years of frustration with Whitehall from the left. Tony Benn and his supporters shared much of Thatcher's antipathy for the Guilty Men managing the centrist consensus. The greatest irony of the series is that it drew on the experiences of ministers like Barbara Castle, who had fought civil service conservatism to build the post-war settlement. Bernard Donoughue, whose late-Seventies diaries are full of righteous rage at civil service obstructionism, was reportedly consulted by *Yes, Minister*'s writers, and Harold Wilson's radical adviser Thomas Balogh loved it, saying it reflected his own experiences.[30]

This narrative applied to another new set of Guilty Men who had allegedly acquired too much power, and led the country astray: the unions. And just as they were more exposed to criticism than they had been since the war, their power was on the wane. The end of the commitment to full employment took away the basis of their post-war strength. For a time, there were still a lot of strikes, but jobs were evaporating at an alarming speed. This made it much harder for the unions to fight back when the new employment secretary, Norman Tebbit, proposed a new law to attack some of their key immunities. As they once had against Heath, the unions organised a 'Kill the Bill' campaign. Arthur Scargill declared himself willing to defy the legislation. But Tebbit was not only in a stronger position than Heath had been: he was also a cannier operator, who had been a trade unionist himself in the early 1960s, when he was a civil airline pilot. Like Prior, he had learned from Heath's mistake, telling his officials, 'Under no circumstances will I allow any trades union activist—no matter how hard he tries—to get himself *into* prison under my legislation.'[31] Tebbit aimed not to ban the closed shop, but to undermine it, and to make unions liable for damages if they engaged in illegal secondary picketing. Unlike Prior, he was openly breaking with the old industrial relations consensus. But he made sure there was nothing for unions to refuse to comply with. This time, the campaign to 'Kill the Bill' got nowhere. When the printers' union defied Tebbit's restrictions on mass picketing, they ended up with their assets sequestrated.

In the spring of 1982, the Falklands War gave Thatcher the chance to rework some of the populist patriotic mood remembered from 1940, and to hitch it to her narrative of decline, disaster, blame and rescue. But even before that, the economy was turning up out of recession. The Conservatives' signature policy of allowing council tenants to buy their homes had taken off. In the election of June 1983, Michael Foot gave the old nightmares one last outing: mass unemployment was a prominent theme in his speeches, and one he reportedly thought was a sure-fire winner. But a new nightmare had long since overridden all that. Margaret Thatcher's 'most frequent request' during the election campaign was 'for copies of the newspaper headlines from the Winter of Discontent, to brandish as a warning of the consequences of voting Labour.'[32]

To one journalist, Foot's campaign seemed less a fight for power, more a tour of his own long past, as he slogged from Liverpool, to Nye Bevan's memorial, 'to Oxford and evocation of Munich, the Spanish Civil War and the "guilty men"', reminiscing all the while about the great victory to which Attlee had once led the party.[33] On 9 June, Labour won 27.6 per cent of the vote, and its lowest number of seats since the election when Foot had first stood for Parliament, in 1935.

* * *

In March 1984, the miners' strike that had not happened in 1981 finally began.

At one level, the strike was a traditional industrial dispute, led by miners genuinely concerned about their jobs in the face of the government's pit closures programme—especially at a time of high unemployment. After several months of an overtime ban, the National Coal Board's shock announcement that six pits were to be closed immediately triggered a strike in the Yorkshire coalfield. A further list named twenty more pits that would be shut within a year.

But the strike also had a whole other dimension. The unions had defeated Castle and Heath, then worked with Foot and Callaghan to keep the industrial relations consensus going, until all that had finally collapsed in the Winter of Discontent. In its wake, the Thatcher government had ended the full employment consensus. The 1984–5 miners' strike was the remaining, climactic confrontation: Thatcher's Conservatives against the power of the unions. Here at last was the crunch—the final, all-out battle of nightmares, much imagined throughout the 1970s.

Many miners were convinced that the government had deliberately provoked the strike to break the NUM; the government had certainly been expecting Scargill to call it, and had prepared accordingly. Nigel Lawson had appointed a hawkish head of the Central Electricity Generating Board; coal had been stockpiled, transport systems and power stations secured. The police were ready to be deployed far outside their local constabularies, to match Scargill's strategy of sending flying pickets to wherever was most effective. Where Joe Gormley had wanted to get back to the post-war settlement, Scargill wanted to go back further, to the trials of strength in the 1920s, which the victories of the 1970s had revived. For her part, Thatcher was determined to use her control over the state to purge the shame of the Conservatives' defeats in 1972 and 1974, and particularly the memory of the Battle of Saltley Gate.

Each side saw the other through the rival nightmares that had built up through the Seventies: the iron heel of the authoritarian capitalist state, pitted against the left-wing enemy within, intent on smashing democracy. In April 1984, the coal board's abrasive Scottish-American boss, Ian MacGregor, said that if the strike were prolonged, soldiers could be used to transport coal to the power stations. The Labour MP Dennis Skinner told a rally of striking miners that if Thatcher 'looks as if she's going to lose with the police and MacGregor, she'll turn to the army. And we've got to be ready. I hope you understand.'[34] As it was, the police deployed horses, dogs, roadblocks; there were many stories of bugging, spies and agents provocateurs. Scargill decried the way 'the full weight of the state' was being used to break the strike—from police 'in full battle gear' to the judges and the benefits system.[35] To many miners and their allies, this was a police state. As The Guardian pointed out during the strike, Scargill's political outlook had been formed by reading The Iron Heel, Jack London's dystopic vision of the forces of American capitalism using politicians, the army and the police to crush the socialist working class.[36] To some on the left, that scenario seemed to be coming true.

Over three weeks from 29 May 1984, the strike produced a great set-piece confrontation at a coking plant in Orgreave, South Yorkshire. Scargill explicitly saw this clash as a sequel to his great triumph at Saltley,[37] and the defeat at Grunwick too; but by the final day, the 'Battle of Orgreave' had proved far more violent. Perhaps 10,000 pickets faced at least 4,000 police. The miners were armed with projectiles—the police claimed these included 'half-bricks, spikes, ball-bearings and pieces of wood with spikes driven through them'; *The Guardian* saw 'bricks, slivers of glass as well as... containers of fuel'.[38] Besides forty-two officers on horseback, the police were armed with truncheons and long riot shields. Arrests and injuries flowed. Unlike the urban location of Saltley, as Dennis Skinner has observed, the open site was not strategically promising. This time, the mass picket did not succeed in shutting the coking plant.

On the other side of the battle lines, when Thatcher and her ministers talked about the strike, they sounded like Keith Joseph in the 1970s, lambasting the left totalitarians. Peter Walker had been a Heathite, but had now replaced Lawson as Thatcher's energy secretary. Soon after Orgreave, he condemned the 'desire to seize power through the militancy of the mob', and declared that this was 'not a mining dispute' but 'a challenge to British democracy'.[39] The next day, Thatcher told Conservative MPs that the government had defeated Argentina—'the enemy without'—over the Falklands, 'but the enemy within, much more difficult to fight, was just as dangerous to liberty'.[40] She seems to have been aiming at Scargill—who had indeed said his final goal was her government's downfall[41]—but her comment was widely interpreted to have been a reference to the striking miners as a whole.

This level of antagonism, especially the phrase 'the enemy within', caused disquiet on Thatcher's own side. In November 1984, now aged 90, Harold Macmillan finally accepted a seat in the House of Lords, pointedly choosing to become the Earl of Stockton, in memory of his unemployed constituents in Depression-era Teesside. In his maiden speech, a reprise of his unheeded warning to Heath many years before, he said:

> Although at my age I cannot interfere or do anything about it, it breaks my heart to see what is happening in our country today. A terrible strike is being carried on by the best men in the world. They beat the Kaiser's army and they beat Hitler's army. They never gave in. The strike is pointless and endless. We cannot afford action of this kind.
>
> Then there is the growing division ... in our comparatively prosperous society between the South and the North and Midlands,

which are ailing ... The old English way might be to quarrel and have battles ... but they were friendly. I can only describe as wicked the hatred that has been introduced and which is to be found among different types of people.[42]

Macmillan was far from alone in his unease at this degree of polarisation. On the trade union side, veteran deal-makers struggled in vain to make the old consensus levers work in the face of Scargill's intransigence. But if some baulked at the government's rhetoric, that did not mean that the country as a whole was desperate to see the unions recover their old strength.

The miners' strike of 1984–5 is often described as a 'war', even a 'civil war'. This captures the extreme hostility at work, from ministers' sense of defending the state against existential attack, to the feeling of invasion and occupation of families in heavily policed pit villages. But the nightmares of the 1970s—of troops sent to break picket lines—did not come true. As recently released Home Office papers make clear, plans for policing a miners' strike on a national basis had begun as far back as 1972, driven by a horror— shared by civil servants and police chiefs—at the idea of involving soldiers. There were a few reports that soldiers were used as drivers in the 1984–5 strike,[43] along with rumours about troops disguised as police officers. But in many ways this only underlines the absence of the much-predicted nightmare. The troops were not sent in, with their rifles loaded or unloaded.

Instead, the unions were defeated not in a sudden assault, but by two gradual, agonising processes: overriding the taboo on mass unemployment, and letting the law bear down on unions through their assets. The miners' strike was a last clash of nightmares; but from this distance it seems reasonable to conclude that the real struggle for power had already been won and lost.

Scargill demanded that the whole trade union movement come out in support of the miners, and there was some sympathetic industrial action. Thatcher made her 'enemy within' remark at one of the points during the strike when the government was most worried. On 10 July 1984, dockers began a strike in protest against non-union workers being used to unload coal. This, as Thatcher admitted to the 1922 Committee, was having a 'severe and immediate' impact.[44] Norman Tebbit has said that, had a national dock strike developed, the government would have lost.[45] In the event, however, the strike quickly petered out. There was one other point where a separate union might have tipped the balance the miners' way. In October 1984, it briefly looked as though the mine managers' union, NACODS, would strike, which would have forced the closure of all working pits on safety grounds—including the huge Nottinghamshire coalfield which, crucially, was still working. But the government succeeded in settling that dispute. There was no showdown between labour and capital of the kind Scargill seemed to want.

The miners' relative isolation was what many had predicted would finish them in 1972, when a documentary was made called *The Miners' Last Stand*; the shock back then was that, at the zenith of their confidence, other trade unions had helped the miners to victory, as symbolised by the Birmingham engineers marching over the hill to flood the Saltley picket line. Now, twelve years on, those predictions started to come true. By late December 1984, with the strike no nearer victory after nearly ten months, the *Guardian* columnist Peter Jenkins was able to ask:

> if the miners were doing battle not only on behalf of their own communities but on behalf of their class, rising from beneath the iron heel of Thatcherism, how was it that in the power stations and the steel works, the docks and the road and rail depots, there were so few recruits to the common cause?[46]

Scargill's answer to that question was that the rest of the unions betrayed the miners; other trade unionists pointed to the lack of a national strike ballot, and to violence on the picket lines. Either way, by 1984, there were several reasons why trying the 1972 strategy was unlikely to work again. After the Winter of Discontent, the unions had lost much public support. Now, under Thatcher—with the end of the commitment to full employment and with 3 million out of work—their negotiating strength was gone. And new legal restrictions were in place: on secondary picketing, and allowing for sequestration of a union's assets if it had defied the courts. All this had definitively buried the post-war consensus. Scargill had always opposed it, but the death of that old consensus was making it much harder for the NUM to win.

After a year of struggle and hardship, the last miners on strike marched back to work, weighed down by debt and defeat. For those who had not been sacked, their hard-won perks and rights were gone; the president of the Yorkshire NUM was soon complaining about the coal board's 'iron heel'.[47] The concentration of power that Barbara Castle had first challenged so hopelessly sixteen years earlier was nowhere to be seen. The miners had at last been defeated by the power of the state, in far more concentrated form than anything she had imagined in *In Place of Strife*. To Castle, the miners' strike 'opened the way for the further conquests a triumphant Margaret Thatcher was now planning'.[48]

The way was clear for the emergence of a new consensus, based on warding off those old 1970s nightmares of strikes, chaos, inflation. Thatcher had used the power of the state to liberate the forces of the market. Now Wilson/Callaghan-style industrial strategy was a sad old joke. Free enterprise was not to be suspected, but admired. Managers were at last at liberty to manage, and to push for productivity and profit without having to bargain with shop stewards, or face the perennial fear of strikes. Unions would never be allowed to grow so strong again. If necessary, unemployment would rise to contain inflation. Taxes fell, council tenants bought their homes, and the economy began to boom as power flowed back to a liberated City: freed from exchange controls and hide-bound old restrictions, enthusiastically helping government sell the state's utilities, thriving on the ever-more-global flow of capital, and delivering new waves of prosperity.

PART THREE

2008–22

11

THE CRASH

2008–10

'I have staked my political reputation and credibility,' wrote Tony Blair in March 1997—at which point he had a great deal of both—'on making clear that there will be no return to the 1970s'.[1] By this time, the consensus established under Margaret Thatcher—a free market, underpinned by a strong state—was accepted by most of the Conservative party, and most of the leadership of the Labour party. Men like Neil Kinnock, Gordon Brown and Tony Blair had come to see their party's repeated election defeats as punishment for the 1970s. Many Labour people kept faith in the old socialist orthodoxies, but by 1997 they had deferred to the leadership, however reluctantly, on what was now politically possible.

The old nightmares of endless strikes and soaring inflation still underpinned this new settlement, but by now Labour had decisively distanced itself from any such associations, pointedly rebranding itself as New Labour, and loosening its ties with the unions. 'Naturally,' Blair wrote, 'the Tories want to refight the election of 1979, rather than fight that of 1997. All they have left now is to try to scare people, to terrify them out of doing what otherwise people know to be right.'

Blair was not simply a neoliberal, any more than Macmillan was simply a socialist; but both leaders pursued party policies within a frame set first by crisis, then by their opponents' victory in one of British politics' rare struggles for power. After it swept into office in May 1997, New Labour introduced distinctive measures: higher investment in public services, partly paid for by 'stealth' tax rises;

a National Minimum Wage; SureStart centres to support young children and their parents; and so on. It criticised the damage it saw Thatcher's legacy doing to the social fabric. But it proposed to fix that within the 'market state' consensus, by reasserting the power of the central government without taking on the resurgent power of finance. Where Attlee had nationalised the Bank of England, New Labour restored the Bank's control over interest rates. New hospitals were built through the Private Finance Initiative. A month into his premiership, Tony Blair heralded globalisation and the 24-hour international money markets with a cry of 'New, new, new! Everything about our world is new.'[2] As chancellor, Gordon Brown continued the deregulation of the City, seeing it as the source of wealth needed to fulfil New Labour's promise of 'social justice on the foundation of a strong economy'. In 2003, he declared that 'The best industrial policy for success in a global economy is to help markets work better.'[3] Which was a long way from Harold Wilson.

But what mattered was that it worked. There was steady growth, albeit boosted by a house price bubble, with none of those old panics about rocketing inflation. If some made a lot more money than others, the taxes pouring in from the City would make up for it. If private debt grew, no matter—provided inflation was under control. The old working-class building societies were 'demutualised' and became ferociously competitive banks. From 2004, EU integration and free movement brought high levels of migration, with attendant benefits to businesses.

Alongside this economic liberalisation, the New Labour government set much store by state-led moves to liberalise society, embedding new rights in law and promoting social mobility, particularly through encouraging more and more young people to go to university. This echoed, and extended, the liberalisation of the 1960s, when the post-war consensus had created enough political head-space for a sustained period of civil liberties reform. These two periods of consensus were very different, but both the 1960s and the 1990s saw the state enshrine new personal freedoms, as well as big expansions of higher education—a vision bright with optimism and confidence, symbolised in the 1990s by the ideal of free movement, of money and people alike.

But for some, caught in this endless whirlwind of social and economic change, it felt as though things could get worse as well as better. In County Durham, in old steel towns like Consett and mining communities like Easington Colliery, this did not feel like an exhilarating race into the future. The pit closures of the Eighties and Nineties left a miserable legacy. Government-backed attempts to turn miners into entrepreneurs failed. Local economies became reliant on call centres, and were plagued by other entrepreneurs, retailing the pleasures of heroin. On behalf of his north Derbyshire constituency, Dennis Skinner managed to persuade Gordon Brown to invest £21 million to flatten Shirebrook's pit tips. The retailer Sports Direct built a huge complex on the cleared land, but Skinner found himself battling the company over its working conditions.[4] Some began to see an extreme form of liberalism—both social and economic—coming to dominate.

Looking back in 2009, Norman Tebbit, one of the architects of Thatcherism, still blamed Arthur Scargill for the miners' strike. But he regretted the damage done by the pit closures, to villages with 'good working-class values and a sense of family values'. Many former mining communities, he observed, 'were completely devastated, with people out of work, turning to drugs, and no real man's work because all the jobs had gone. There is no doubt that this led to a breakdown in those communities, with families breaking up and youth going out of control.'[5]

David Willetts, who had worked in the Number 10 Policy Unit during the strike, argues that much effort was made to try to establish new jobs for ex-miners. Critics have suggested that the Wilson government of the 1960s—which shut more pits than Thatcher's—had invested far more, with corresponding results. Either way, what has happened since casts a different light on Scargill's avowal during the strike that 'we are fighting for the survival of our communities, of our culture and of a way of life'.[6]

As the economy grew and grew through the 1990s and 2000s, all of this looked like a sad but necessary cost of progress. Until the thing that was not supposed to happen, happened. In 2007, Newcastle's Northern Rock bank, once a cautious building society with Victorian foundations, collapsed. A decade earlier, it had demutualised, and had rapidly become one of the country's leading lenders, growing its balance sheet by 500 per cent in a decade, on the back of massive wholesale borrowing. When the 'sub-prime' loans panic hit US banks, the Rock found itself hopelessly over-extended, and while the chancellor, Alistair Darling, announced that all deposits would be guaranteed by the state, the Bank of England let the bank itself fall. A year later, the global financial crisis reached its peak. Cashpoints came within hours of drying up. The consensus that had confidently prevailed since the 1980s was suddenly, literally, discredited.

So far in this book, we have traced the death and rebirth of consensus as it has played out since Britain became a mass democracy, shifting power first one way, then the other. In this final Part, let's see if those two earlier periods can help us understand the shocks Britain has been through since the Crash.

* * *

All orthodoxies have their heretics. Keynes and others had opposed the 'Treasury view' long before Attlee won power in 1945; free-market think-tanks were busy decades in advance of 'Thatcherism'. Likewise, in the 1990s, arguments began stirring which suggested that the market, backed by the state, might have become a problematic new concentration of power. Early in the decade, a young academic from London called Maurice Glasman went to visit post-communist Poland, and thought he saw a horrifying vision of the future taking shape. Under the guidance of Western experts, the state was transferring control of assets to a 'new class of managers' in the private sector—who, Glasman remembers, were in many cases just 'the old managers' with new job titles, completely bypassing the trade union–based Solidarity movement that had fought to overthrow communism in the first place.[7] Glasman concluded that this was the 'power of consensus' at work, defined as a shared understanding among 'dominant public agents' that structured the distribution of power. That consensus, he argued, had to be taken on. This meant challenging the alliance of free market and strong state, which cast itself as 'liberal democracy'.[8] Consensus, Glasman wrote, is bound by a definition of what suffering is necessary: for instance, the conclusion that unemployment is a sad business, but needed to keep inflation down. As his publisher put it on the back cover of his 1996 book, *Unnecessary Suffering: Managing Market Utopia*, the dream was of 'a world where every*thing* and every*body* can be bought and sold, a world run efficiently by managers, a world where "freedom" means the free market.' This was 'an unrealisable utopia—or a nightmare if put into practice.'

While teaching at London Guildhall University, on the edge of the City, Glasman had worked with a multi-ethnic community organising group called London Citizens. Through the 2000s, he watched a version of his 'market utopia' nightmare burgeoning in Britain, as the City grew and grew, dominating the economy, while New Labour used its taxes to patch up the losers. He was struck by the way building societies, once rooted in local communities, had turned into banks, taken more risks and got caught up in the Crash. He argued that the concentration of power in big banks and corporations was mirrored in the way the state had become disconnected from ordinary people. This line of thinking involved questioning the legacy not only of 1979 but of 1945, advocating a break from government by managerialism, in favour of trying to restore on-the-ground relationships based on solidarity and reciprocity. He argued for an economy in which a plurality of interests competed for a voice, without being drowned out by the noisy benevolence of the state, or the frenzy of the market.

Glasman was coming at this from the left, but similar arguments had also started to emerge among people who had been enthusiastic supporters of the Thatcher project. John Gray, a professor of politics at Oxford University, had championed New Right ideas since the 1970s, and was the author of *Hayek on Liberty*. Yet he spent the 1990s writing such works as *Post-liberalism*, 'The Undoing of Conservatism', and—responding to the botched launch of the free market in post-Soviet Russia—*False Dawn: The Delusions of Global Capitalism*. Thatcherism had defined itself in part against the great nightmare of Soviet oppression and military aggression. With that suddenly gone, Gray started to argue that the free market and its militant individualism were destroying the social fabric it relied on. He decried its 'creative destruction' and the 'Maoism of the Right', which imposed on people 'a regime of incessant change and permanent revolution', depleting 'the stock of historical memory on which cultural identity depends.' Markets did not function in some abstract world, as blank as an empty spreadsheet, but in real societies and communities, and the Thatcherite consensus overlooked this at its peril.

The failure to recognise this was bringing back an old nightmare. The 'dystopian prospect', Gray wrote, was that the fear and reality of unemployment would never be far away. He cast the dangers of this in even more nightmarish terms than Glasman: people would only put up with so much precariousness before they lashed back. He pointed to the rise of 'atavistic' right-wing parties in Europe, driven by 'the politically destabilising effects of structural unemployment'.[9] And he cited a 1994 essay by Edward Luttwak in the *London Review of Books* called 'Why Fascism is the Wave of the Future'. The post-war settlement had avoided such conflict through building full employment and the welfare state; now, Gray argued, it might well be up to the left to conserve the fabric of institutions and communities against the ravages of market fundamentalism.

David Willetts took Gray on, in an exchange published as *Is Conservatism Dead?* Willetts had been one of Gray's students before running the Centre for Policy Studies and, in 1992, becoming a Conservative MP, and he agreed with much of his old tutor's case about the importance of reviving society's independent institutions. But he thought that those institutions could sustain capitalism too. He was much more critical of the damage done to 'our moral and cultural environment' by the state than by the markets.[10] Even so, he found it 'hard going' making the case to his party colleagues for 'collective action', and for such independent institutions as trade unions.[11] Once again, a long, agonising slog—at the end of which British politics would look utterly different—was just beginning.

By the early 2000s, some of this started to surface in Conservative policy. Danny Kruger, then a young Conservative think-tanker, was influenced by the ideas of both Gray and Willetts, and remembers seeing similar thinking developing in the Renewing One Nation Unit at Conservative Central Office. This came to the fore after the party's new leader, Iain Duncan Smith, visited Glasgow's vast post-war Easterhouse estate in February 2002. There he had what Kruger calls a 'Damascene conversion'[12] away from pure free-market economics, towards a poverty-focused

254

social conservatism. Duncan Smith set up a think-tank, the Centre for Social Justice, to develop this.

By 2006, with Kruger writing his speeches, the new Conservative leader David Cameron was talking about social responsibility, and eventually the idea of the 'Big Society': a restoration of social bonds and institutions, with less reverence for the market, but also less reliance on the state. The Conservative Party had consciously distanced itself from Thatcherism, with Willetts, the former arch-Thatcherite, winning much of the intellectual credit. Meanwhile Cameron's 'brain', Steve Hilton, was energetically coining policy ideas, and writing speeches about decentralising the state and giving responsibility back to civil society—family, community, neighbourhood, local government.

* * *

When the Crash struck in 2008, it emerged that a toxic fusion of over-complex debt instruments, group-think and hubris had almost destroyed the global financial system. Banks, previously either admired or ignored, were suddenly exposed as wielding immense power, holding the security of national life in their hands, and taking horrendous risks with it. But the state was blamed too, for the laissez-faire regulation supported by both main parties—which suited the financial markets all too well, but failed to stop the rot.

The state switched from the banks' admiring facilitator to their guardian, bailing them out at vast cost to avert catastrophe. This was a sharp reminder of the power of government. Events unthinkable a few months before now rapidly unfolded. Like Northern Rock, the building-society-turned-bank Bradford and Bingley was nationalised. The government 'recapitalised' three bigger banks that were struggling too, then brokered the merger of two of them as HBOS was absorbed by Lloyds. Its stake in the third, Royal Bank of Scotland, would peak at 84 per cent. Meanwhile the chancellor Alistair Darling arguably saved Barclays, and much else, by stopping it from buying the US bank Lehmans shortly before it collapsed. Prime Minister Gordon Brown, once champion of light-touch regulation and New Labour ambassador to the City, now led international governmental efforts to rescue the globalised financial system.

Was this one of those rare moments, when there might be a struggle to wrest control away from entrenched power, effecting a radical break with the past? With the credibility of free-market ideas suddenly shaken, long-marginalised left-wing ideas sprang back to life. 'Occupy' protestors appeared in the City, demanding redistribution of wealth and an end to the undemocratic power of the banks. The lessons of the 1930s were invoked against the lessons of the 1970s. Comparisons with the Wall Street Crash of 1929 and the financial calamities of the early Thirties abounded, with calls for a return to Keynes, the 'Master'.[13] Gordon Brown has pointed out that he led a turn back to Keynesianism: that his government 'deliberately ran a deficit to keep people out of unemployment, to stop mortgage repossessions, to stop business bankruptcies'—even as, by the April 2009 Budget, government borrowing headed for £175 billion.[14]

The business secretary Peter Mandelson had been one of the architects of New Labour, hailing the way the party had dispelled memories of the Winter of Discontent by jettisoning old 'ideological baggage'.[15] But at party conference in 2009, he told delegates that the financial crisis demanded a total rethink: 'We need less financial engineering and a lot more real engineering ... No more saying: the market on its own will always sort it out, like some kind of dogma.'[16]

With growth and pay flat-lining after the Crash, Mandelson was driving a return to a much-derided concept from the days of Wilson, Heath and Callaghan: industrial strategy. It is telling, however, that he felt he needed to add: 'This isn't us picking winners as happened too often in the 1970s, when more often the losers were picking us.' The old nightmares of the big, blundering state of the Seventies lingered. Looking back, Brown has said he failed to communicate what his administration was doing, and why breaking post-1979 taboos was now justified.[17]

The government's rescue of the banks pointed two ways at once. It signalled that the prevailing consensus, favouring constraints on state intervention in the economy, had had to be set aside. But this was the first big shock to the consensus, and was not enough to destroy it. To some, the crucial point was that the state had let the banks grow 'too big to fail', had let them run riot, then made the tax-payer pick up the bill. Maurice Glasman was one of those who decried this as a disastrous transfer of wealth from poor to rich.

While the dust from the collapsing banks was still settling, another thinker emerged at the elbow of Opposition leader David Cameron, contending that what had just happened demanded an even bigger change of mind. In February 2009, a hitherto little-known academic called Phillip Blond made the cover of the left-leaning magazine *Prospect*, proclaiming the 'Rise of the Red Tories'. The crisis, he wrote, 'represents a disintegration of the idea of the "market state" and makes obsolete the political consensus of the last 30 years.' Like Glasman, he blamed a distant, centralised state, overly reverent towards the free market; the two together, he argued, had squashed the life out of communal bonds and institutions. Blond's answer was to break up both concentrations of power: in government through a 'new localism', and in the 'cartel of vast corporations' through ending monopolies. Instead of recapitalising the banks, as Brown had done, government should recapitalise the poor.

Blond was not the first person to make such arguments, but he was the first to have the ear of the likely next Prime Minister. Even before his article came out, he was contributing to Cameron's speeches, as at the World Economic Forum at Davos in January 2009. The speech, Blond remembers, gave a 'really involved, sophisticated account of how things could be different' by giving ordinary people economic power. It was 'quite an exhilarating time'.[18] That November, Cameron spoke at the launch of Blond's new think-tank, ResPublica.

It was noted, however, that Cameron left the launch rather swiftly.

* * *

The general election of 2010, the first since the Crash, found the electorate disaffected, with both main parties trying and failing to find a big, transformative idea. British politics had fallen into depths of uncertainty it had not experienced since the 1970s. It was no accident that the result was harder to predict than any election since the turmoil of 1974.

In Channel 4's 'chancellors' debate', the Liberal Democrats' Vince Cable tried to focus opposition on the bankers who had caused the Crash and then breezed on, coolly trousering their bonuses.

Cable denounced them as 'pin-striped Scargills'. He contended that they had now done what Scargill was once accused of doing by the Thatcherites: stretching an unaccountable concentration of power to the point where it was intolerably destructive.[19]

But in the early 1970s, when Scargill first came to prominence, attempts to tackle union power had failed. Likewise, Cable's rhetoric did not translate into a bid to wrest power from the bankers. So it seems to go when a consensus is first shaken. Indeed, the aftermath of the Crash also had something in common with 1931, when finance forced a cut in the dole, but Labour had found itself able to drum up little rage against the banks. In all three cases, the problematic vested interest had become much more visible, but no easier to bring down, because it remained shored up by the dominant nightmare of the day: in this instance, as in 1931, the fear of deficit and the spectre of financial collapse. Orthodoxies are tenacious.

The 2010 Conservative manifesto included ideas variously developed by David Willetts, the Centre for Social Justice, Steve Hilton and Phillip Blond. But the party's campaign, like Labour's, devolved instead into a partisan tit-for-tat over levels of government spending. There was one moment, towards the end, where Gordon Brown managed to point towards something quite different. On 3 May, in Westminster's Methodist Central Hall, the Prime Minister gave a heartfelt speech to an audience of community organisers. This was a hymn to duty and community, and the need for work to be valued and decently paid, drawing on his relationship with his father, a Church of Scotland minister, and his own student campaign to raise the wages of his university's cleaners. This suggested lines along which Labour could reinvent itself in the wake of the Crash. But it was all far too late.

On election night, Britain found itself with its first hung Parliament since the fall of Heath. The days and nights of weary haggling that followed dramatised the deepening flux of British politics. And then there were David Cameron and the Liberal Democrat leader Nick Clegg, striding into the Downing Street rose garden in their beautiful suits, to meet the press and launch their new government: a strikingly sunny start to the stormy decade to come. Cameron and Clegg stood beaming in confident unity at the journalists, but their new coalition faced in two directions. It wanted to break from the past and build a new Big Society. But it also looked back warmly on the last thirty years, at the economically liberal legacy of Thatcher and the socially liberal legacy of Blair, and hoped to bring them to a final, double liberal fruition.

Here was the first formal peace-time coalition since 1931. And once again, it looked like a successful compromise across party lines, ready to resuscitate the consensus after a disastrous financial crash. But it could only do that if it could make enough noise about its guiding nightmares—uncontrollable government over-spending, and the spectre of economic collapse—to drown out another sound. The low hum, audible in many parts of Britain, of a rising discontent.

12

IF ONLY

2010–15

In May 2010, the Greek government's huge deficit and debt put the country in danger of a sovereign default. This necessitated a €110 billion bail-out loan, provided partly from the IMF. In return, the government had to commit Greeks to a punishing programme of austerity. There was a general strike and huge, furious protests; riot police and tear gas. Someone fire-bombed a bank, killing three people. This was a nightmare straight out of the 1970s: a profligate government losing control. In Britain's new coalition, the Conservative chancellor George Osborne and his team were already hard at work cutting spending and striving towards balancing the books. As Osborne swiftly suggested, the Greek calamity showed the danger of not following his prudent course. Shades of Ramsay MacDonald, reminding voters of Weimar hyperinflation with his 50 billion-mark German banknote.

And so, for all the post-Crash talk of the need for Keynes-style radical heterodoxy, the Chancellor of the Exchequer stuck closer to Thirties-style orthodoxy: echoing the arguments of 1931 with his accusation that Labour had been 'maxing out the nation's credit card'.[1] This view was reasserted through austerity, which brought swingeing cuts to local authority budgets, reductions in housing benefit for council tenants found to have spare rooms, the proliferation of food banks. In some parts of Britain, spending cuts exacerbated existing problems of insecure work and failing high streets. But for the coalition, this was unavoidable, given the urgent need to reduce the deficit. The Crash—which Phillip Blond had

261

taken as the cue for a radical break from existing orthodoxy—became a reason for the government to stick to it. The international money markets needed to be convinced that Britain's economy was sound, and Blond soon found himself out in the cold. 'Cameron revealed himself,' he remembers disappointedly, 'to be just a conventional Thatcherite'.[2]

Likewise, up against pressing Treasury imperatives, the Big Society project's concerns with mending the social fabric looked intangible, and struggled for political oxygen. Amid the austerity cuts, especially as they affected local government, the idea of reviving volunteering began to look like '*noblesse oblige*', a substitute for mass voluntary movements.[3] As David Willetts recalls:

> There was a danger that, instead of us saying, 'We believe in community action and strong institutions as goods in themselves', it became instead, 'We'll cut spending and hand it over to you guys instead.' It becomes a justification of retrenchment: 'charities will pick up the slack of shrinking government'.[4]

Steve Hilton, Cameron's strategy director, was much closer than Blond ever came to the heart of power in Downing Street, but his approach to the Big Society had been developed for a pre-Crash, prospering country, and it too hit resistance. In the wake of the Crash, he seemed more engaged in a bid to recapture Thatcherite radicalism than in nurturing fragile social bonds. But his calls to break up public-sector monopolies and cut the civil service by 70 per cent ran into the sand. In government, free-market thinking was still strong, but in no mood for radical experiments.

As Barbara Castle and Ted Heath had both found, you could not change a consensus by exhortation. As Keith Joseph had shown, you had to attack its underlying taboos. And that meant a fight. But was anyone going to come up with a new approach that was convincing enough to win a new battle of nightmares?

* * *

On 22 April 2009, a few hours after Alistair Darling had told the Commons that government borrowing was heading for £175 billion, a debate had taken place at Conway Hall, in central London's Red

Lion Square. This pitched Phillip Blond against the academic who had been horrified by Poland's nightmarish market utopia, Maurice Glasman. He named his response to Blond's Red Tory ideas 'Blue Labour': a 'deeply conservative socialism that places family, faith and work at the heart of a new politics of reciprocity, mutuality and solidarity.' He called for Labour to rediscover its roots in local organising, mutual help, voluntary groups and friendly societies.[5]

This was a debate of a sort, but the ideas of both men—and the moderator, John Gray—were part of a broad move that developed in the wake of the Crash, to turn attention to the downside of relentless social and economic liberalisation. As it set out to challenge the power and ideas of the 'market–state' consensus, this new way of thinking attracted an umbrella name that echoed the title of one of Gray's 1990s books: 'post-liberalism'.

By 2010, Blond's attempt to win David Cameron over to this radical turn was already foundering. But, for a time, it appeared that Glasman was making more headway. He had advanced within Labour, getting some of the ideas he backed—like a 'living wage'—into Labour's manifesto. He had written the original draft of that heartfelt speech Gordon Brown gave at Methodist Central Hall.[6] Then, in September, Ed Miliband became leader of the Labour Party, on a platform of rejecting much of the New Labour legacy. Intrigued by Glasman's ideas, Miliband appointed him to the House of Lords. For a time, the new Labour leader seemed to run with this agenda. He took on the power of the newspaper-owners over the phone-hacking scandal. He criticised both bankers and benefit fraudsters for cheating the system, and sought to divide businesses into 'producers' and 'predators'. In May 2012, he appointed Glasman's closest ally among MPs, Jon Cruddas, to head the party's policy review. On stage at that year's party conference, Miliband pointedly praised the radical Tory Benjamin Disraeli's One Nation vision of 'a Britain where patriotism, loyalty, dedication to the common cause courses through the veins of all and nobody feels left out.'[7]

In the wake of urban riots the previous year, the need to restore a single nation in which 'nobody feels left out' seemed desperately urgent. That summer, Rowenna Davis had been completing a book on Blue Labour. She was a Labour councillor in Peckham, south

London, one of the areas where rioting had erupted. With the police fully stretched and unable to help, she had found herself trying to rescue clothes from a local woman's shop, which had been set on fire. The nightmare of pointless devastation seemed confirmation that Glasman might have a point about a lost sense of community and the worth of work. She remembers asking a young man why he had risked arrest to steal a pair of trainers.

> He said, 'My older brother went to uni. He did everything right
> and he worked really hard, and he can't find a job. And every time
> he does find a job, he certainly can't afford a new pair of trainers,
> so why bother?' There's this idea of the social contract—that if
> you work hard and play by the rules, you will get something back.
> That idea had for some young people completely broken down.[8]

Davis had been struck, too, by other local people volunteering to clean up the mess, and offering each other encouragement, and commitments to change things. But Glasman's criticism of the social changes that he thought had eroded these bonds, and his talk of family, faith, community and the dignity of work, produced a sharp reaction. Mary Creagh, then in the Shadow Cabinet, was one of many Labour figures who were 'deeply suspicious' of Blue Labour and of what she saw as its nostalgic, rose-tinted, heavily male view of working-class life. Glasman says that, having long campaigned for women's rights, these reactions caught him 'completely by surprise'.[9] But the issue that really embodied the impact of both economic and social liberalism, on which Glasman and Blue Labour found themselves most sharply confronted by a taboo, was immigration.

* * *

In 2004, ten countries, mainly in central and eastern Europe, had been admitted to the EU, and the Blair government had decided not to impose temporary migration controls. It did not expect the wave of immigration that followed. By the 2010 election, this had been a major political issue for years, fuelling the rise of the UK Independence Party, and prompting David Cameron to promise to keep immigration in the tens of thousands. During the campaign, Gordon Brown was overheard referring to a Labour-voting

Rochdale pensioner as a 'bigoted woman' after she challenged him on the issue. This served, for some critics at least, to demonstrate a chasm that had grown between the Labour leadership and many of its traditional supporters.

Blue Labour was a response to a broader discontent with the liberal market–state consensus, but immigration captured its effects, for good and ill, like no other issue. The New Labour government had seen incoming migrants as a further boost to economic growth, and an expression of Britain's confident openness to the world. But from some constituencies that had long returned Labour MPs, this could easily look like elite political administrators in distant London imposing their will and values, with little regard for the impact. In May 2010, Glasman's ally Jon Cruddas, MP for Dagenham and Rainham, argued that immigration had most affected working-class voters, becoming effectively a '21st Century incomes policy, mixing a liberal sense of free for all with a free-market disdain for clear and effective rules.'[10] The following year, Glasman was quoted making provocative comments, for which he then apologised, about how immigration should be temporarily halted, and how Labour needed to understand the point of view of members of the far-right English Defence League. Looking back, he says that his aim was to draw people back from the far right, and sees the row his remarks triggered as the cost of making a necessary challenge to the taboo on engaging with voters' concerns. It was, he says, 'a very rude awakening for me that that was going to be a hard road'.[11]

Ed Miliband soon moved away from Blue Labour's tarnished brand; but for all the discomfort it stirred, concern about immigration, on both economic and social grounds, remained an issue Labour had to address. A 2014 Fabian Society report, *Revolt on the Left*, argued that to keep long-term Labour voters away from the populist, anti-EU UKIP, the party had to acknowledge those people's concerns about immigration, which were focused partly on 'the damage done to wages, job prospects and services by "uncontrolled" immigration'. Labour should engage with voters' sense that change was 'a force beyond their control', and with their lost sense of belonging.[12] The shadow education secretary Tristram Hunt was wary of aspects of Blue Labour's politics, but could see its appeal in his Stoke-on-Trent Central constituency, which, he says, had been 'discombobulated by globalisation in 25 years'.[13] In a 2016 essay, published a month before the Brexit vote, Hunt wrote that he detected in the party an 'unnecessary metropolitan squeamishness' with any talk about English patriotism, driven by fear of association with the far right.[14] But as the political scientists Robert Ford and Maria Sobolewska point out, leading figures in Miliband's Labour who tried to engage with concerns about immigration were usually met with 'a loud chorus of condemnation' from liberals, who condemned this 'as either inherently prejudiced or designed to appease prejudice.'[15]

In the 1990s, John Gray had warned that excessive economic and social liberalism might lead to a turn towards fascism; now, the charge was that addressing this possibility might unleash nightmares in itself. Some were concerned that, for the first time in decades, economic crisis and a society in flux were driving both Labour and the Conservatives to flirt with extreme ideas.

In the Seventies, the left-wing playwright David Edgar had warned against the dangers of the far right in *Destiny*. In 2013, he revisited this theme. *If Only*, staged at the Minerva Theatre in Chichester then adapted for Radio 4 the following year, imagined the Cameron government spooked by the rise of UKIP—'running extremely scared of the far right and responding accordingly'[16]— and preparing to turn authoritarian populist, through a law-and-order crackdown, hostility to migrants, and a referendum on 'taking back power from Brussels'. As a Labour think-tanker talks in Blue Labour terms about 'faith, family and flag', Edgar has his patrician Tory desperate to stop what he calls the 'arms race to the gutter— red, white and blue in tooth and claw.' The play sees all this rhetoric as doing nothing to help the victims of the Crash, just letting them 'wrap themselves up in the flag and look around for someone poorer than themselves to blame.' It successfully predicted UKIP's victory in the 2014 European Parliament elections.

Just as left-wing objections to anything hinting at far-right ideas served to guard social liberalism, so nightmares were invoked to guard economic liberalism too. In the wake of George Osborne justifying his austerity Budgets by pointing to the near-bankruptcy of Greece, five Conservative MPs published a book that conjured up some familiar ghosts. *Britannia Unchained* (2012) was jointly written by Priti Patel, Dominic Raab, Kwasi Kwarteng, Liz Truss and Chris Skidmore. Though they had all been newly elected in 2010, their text begins and ends with images of the 1970s, from 'industrial chaos' to 'states of emergency', the three-day week to the Winter of Discontent, when 'British society was falling apart'. These old nightmares are evoked because the writers detected that, 'In the wake of the financial crisis, 1970s-style pessimism that Britain is destined to decline has returned.'[17] Like many others in the wake of the Crash, they asserted that crisis demands radical solutions. But their conclusion was that, once again, the remedy was a reassertion of free-market values. Even after a huge financial crash, there must be no going back to the 1970s—just as, amid those 1970s crises, there had been plenty of Conservatives, from Heath down, who insisted that there must be no going back to the 1930s.

In the face of these resurgent warnings, the 'post-liberal' attempts to break with economic and social liberalism were soon abandoned, by Ed Miliband and David Cameron alike. Four years on from the calamities of 2008, some maverick voices had denounced the consensus, challenged the old nightmares that underpinned it, and proposed a coherent alternative. But no one, so far, had managed to follow in the footsteps of Keith Joseph, and actually use such an analysis to win power and put a radical new approach into action. For the moment, at least, left-wing nightmares of fascism and right-wing nightmares of financial chaos marked hard limits on the politically possible.

* * *

The coalition, and Cameron's subsequent majority Conservative government, did what other governments had done when faced with a fraying consensus but no obvious replacement: they patched it up with pieces of new thinking. Post-liberal policy themes appeared here and there, but not as part of any overarching new design. The government set up a National Citizen Service, giving teenagers the opportunity to learn skills and take part in 'social action projects'.[18] In his 2015 Budget, George Osborne significantly increased the National Minimum Wage and, in the light of a major London Citizens campaign, renamed it the 'National Living Wage'.

He did not raise it to the level campaigners had been pressing for, but it did have an impact on the low pay problem. Osborne also championed the devolution of power to cities like Manchester under the Northern Powerhouse scheme, with the close involvement of his adviser Neil O'Brien, who grew up in Huddersfield and was educated in the state sector. As head of the think-tank Policy Exchange, O'Brien had co-written a report on geographical differences in voting, arguing that Conservatives could win working-class northern votes. As business secretary, the Liberal Democrat Vince Cable—scourge of the City's 'pin-striped Scargills'—laid out the case for a return to industrial strategy. This would direct procurement towards British suppliers, bolster research and development in sectors like aerospace, and bring trade unions, businesses and ministers into conference together.

Even so, the phrase 'industrial strategy', according to Cable's adviser Giles Wilkes, 'was regarded as one you couldn't put in speeches'.[19] It still had associations left over from the era when Margaret Thatcher, as Leader of the Opposition, would use it to mock Prime Minister Callaghan. When Cable finally did say it out loud, at the Confederation of British Industry's 'Industrial Future' dinner in September 2012, he felt he had to follow Peter Mandelson in warding off the ghosts, admitting to the assembled businesspeople that 'People react viscerally to industrial strategy: "Didn't we have all this stuff in the 1970s?"' He affirmed that he had been an adviser in the Department of Trade under Labour in those bad old days, so he knew what getting industrial strategy wrong looked like.

David Willetts, now Cable's science minister, found himself going through a similar thought process. He had grown up in Birmingham and remembered the bail-outs of British Leyland, when industrial strategy seemed to be 'just cheques to failing companies'. He was persuaded to set this old nightmare aside by what he saw in the United States, and in particular by the arguments of the economist Mariana Mazzucato: that behind American rhetoric about individualism was systemic state intervention. One instance of the business department's investment approach, linked to the University of Sheffield, was an advanced manufacturing research facility on the site of the old colliery at Orgreave, near the site of the famous battle during the 1984–5 miners' strike.[20] However, as Willetts ruefully observes, the regeneration took a long time. Even after the Crash, the process of edging away from old orthodoxies was proving to be achingly gradual—which led some Conservatives to take them on with a little more force.

* * *

On a hot evening in July 2013, another post-liberal grouping appeared, this time at an event held in a Victorian pub near St James's Park, not far from Westminster. The Old Star, once a watering-hole for hansom cab drivers, takes its name from its sign: an image of a standard British Army decoration from the First World War. Upstairs, bolstering the symbolism of working-class independence and institutional longevity, old Conservative posters had been stuck up, pitching the party as the builder of homes for workers, as under Macmillan. This was the launch of a think-tank called Renewal: a bid by a former parliamentary candidate called David Skelton to turn the Tories into 'the new workers' party'.[21]

Before entering politics and becoming Deputy Director of Policy Exchange, Skelton grew up in Consett, County Durham in the 1980s. 'You saw there what happened to a town when the steel works closed down,' he says. 'It had the highest level of unemployment in western Europe for a few years when I was growing up ... and there was a sense that these communities no longer had people who were listening to them in politics.' From his school, Skelton could see the empty patch of land where the works used to be. Eventually some crisp factories were built, but nothing to replace the old highly skilled, well-paid, high-status jobs. In the wake of the Crash, Skelton was struck by the rage in his home town at the bankers responsible having gone unpunished—a rage he says the London media barely noticed. He argues that while the Big Society was an important first step, it did not show 'enough of an understanding of those communities that had lost out from the past twenty or thirty years, and what the role of the state was in delivering change there.'[22] To catch up, he contended, the Conservative Party had to think much more radically.

His response was Renewal, and a book, *Access All Areas*, copies of which were piled high at The Old Star for the launch party. It featured essays by Conservative MPs focused on winning over ethnic-minority voters, the low-paid, and northerners. In his introduction, Skelton demanded that

> Conservatives must make clear that they are prepared to stand up forcefully against vested interests, whether they're public sector trade unions or rent-seeking corporations. 'Crony capitalism' should have no more of a place in today's economy than centrally controlled nationalised industries. Being the party of capitalism is not the same as being the party of big business. The Conservatives should be the party of the majority, standing up for consumers, small businessmen and hard-pressed workers.[23]

Outside the pub, Phillip Blond told a film crew from *The Guardian*: 'In ten to fifteen years, this agenda will win, and the first party to adopt a Blue Labour or Red Tory agenda will be the party that wins a new majority and governs for a generation.'[24]

This may have seemed outlandish, but away from the heart of power, there were signs that these new ideas were beginning to take. The Big Society had faded from the picture, but Conservatives were continuing to rail against the failures of supposedly free-market capitalism. The co-founder of the Centre for Social Justice, Tim Montgomerie, called for a mansion tax. Danny Kruger—Cameron's now-disillusioned former speech-writer—had left to run a charity working with ex-offenders, prisoners and young people at risk of crime; now he complained about the coalition's reliance on huge service conglomerates like G4S. Alongside the Green MP Caroline Lucas and the head of the TUC, Frances O'Grady, the Conservative MP Guy Opperman joined the advisory board of the High Pay Centre, which argued for boardroom pay restraint. Margaret Thatcher's official biographer, Charles Moore, criticised the social divisions caused by the lack of affordable housing for the young and the poor. Before the Crash, bankers and financiers had been lauded as 'masters of the universe'; now the Conservative MPs Matt Hancock and Nadhim Zahawi wrote a book which branded them 'masters of nothing'. The journalist Ferdinand Mount called such people 'a very British oligarchy'. Mount had been the co-author of the Conservatives' 1983 manifesto and a head of Thatcher's Policy Unit, and remains a conservative free-marketeer. Given all that, his 2012 book *The New Few* was a startling denunciation of gargantuan executive pay, back-scratching remuneration committees and the marginalising of private share-holders. Mount condemned the growth, in public and private sector alike, of concentrations of power—among whom the bankers stood out only, in Mount's account, because they had done the most damage.

For the moment, all these criticisms fell largely on deaf ears. At the top of government, the old market–state consensus and its underpinning nightmares remained in place. Like Keynes or Joseph, the Red Tory Phillip Blond would not see his heretical vision realised until a crisis erupted—with sufficient force to override the old nightmares with a new one.

* * *

There was only one policy area inside the government where there seemed to be a group of people willing to make a sharp break with the past: the Department of Education. A small cluster of advisers around the education secretary Michael Gove would go on to have much wider impact. The key figure here was Gove's Special Adviser and Chief of Staff, Dominic Cummings, who had been Iain Duncan Smith's strategist during his brief tenure as Conservative leader, when he played a striking role in the party's pivot to focus on the poorest and most vulnerable in society. One of the things that made Cummings a vital aide to Gove was his unusually clear and ruthless sense of how power works.

The department's flagship policy, the creation of 'free schools', was intended to devolve power to parents, teachers and community organisations who wanted to set up their own schools. The eventual aim, successful or otherwise, was to create space for a more knowledge-rich curriculum and tackle educational under-achievement. But to get there, Gove's team decided they had to break the 'stranglehold' on what schools could do.[25] This was in the hands of what they saw as the 'education establishment': the local education authorities, the teaching unions, the Department for Education itself—or, as they tended to call it, 'the Blob'.

This was a deliberate use of state power to take on and defeat what Gove's advisers saw as vested interests. On the wall of his ministerial office, Gove famously had a picture of Malcolm X, in honour of his revolutionary motto: 'By any means necessary'. For the moment, this was focused only on education policy, from within a coalition that still largely clung to the old consensus; but it was a harbinger of the much bigger struggle for power that was coming.

By 2014, having left the Department for Education, Cummings appeared at an event organised by the Institute for Public Policy Research to deliver a withering attack on the senior civil service. It is telling, given what would follow, that he cast Whitehall's 'hollow men' as part of a complacent, over-paid establishment spread across right and left alike. In a County Durham accent not so different from David Skelton's, he told his audience:

> The left won't face the scale of the debt. It won't face the problems of large bureaucracies...and it often doesn't have a very good understanding of the amazing ability of markets to solve problems. And the right also has an awful lot of blank spots—it won't face the scale of inequality, problems with financial markets, bloated pay in the private sector...and the way the rich cheat on taxes... It doesn't understand why people are resistant to the spread of markets.[26]

This sort of iconoclastic thinking had also started to rear its head within government, even if only as a statement of future intent. At the ConservativeHome website's Victory 2015 Conference in Westminster, held in March 2013, the Home Secretary Theresa May showed up to make a pointedly wide-ranging keynote speech. Until this point, no leading politician had seemed ready to take up the post-liberals' cause. Now May advocated 'breaking up the concentration of power, condemning irresponsible behaviour at all levels of society, and confronting vested interests. Reflecting the generosity that makes us a nation of volunteers, people who give to those in need.'[27]

The speech was written by May's adviser Nick Timothy, the son of a Birmingham school secretary and a factory worker who rose to become an executive. Timothy had been an ally of the Gove education vanguard, and now looked like a new candidate—in the wake of Blond and Glasman—for the role of radical maverick to lead a post-liberal breakthrough. May's speech reflected the shared political priorities she and Timothy had developed together over more than a decade.[28] Its overt focus on power came in part from Timothy's reading of Mount's *The New Few*, and also from Timothy's and May's struggle at the Home Office to take on the police. Beyond that, he says,

> Economically speaking it felt as though there were vested interests that were holding back the competitiveness of the country—big housing companies, land banking, regulating the speed with which new properties come on to the market … If you're interested in the welfare and opportunities and interests of all, you have to be interested in the distribution of power and the extent to which they have a voice or their voices matter … Working people are often exploited in markets that don't really work, but which those in power don't want to reform, because of vested interests or because of the ideologies of those regulating them.[29]

At this point, Theresa May was the figure closest to the heart of power to endorse the growing argument that the old settlement was not working any more. The speech spent five paragraphs on industrial strategy, praising David Willetts' work but promising to go further. Timothy's view was that it was not possible to rebalance the country away from the dominance of London and the south-east 'without accepting that the state needed to play a more strategic role in the economy'. Like Skelton, he thought this could help the Conservatives win 'in places we [had] never won before.'[30]

But that was not the approach David Cameron wanted to pursue, and he remained Prime Minister. At the May 2015 election, against the odds, Cameron won a majority, and it looked as though he had successfully shored up the market–state consensus. He could stay in Number 10 until his budget-cutting chancellor George Osborne took over. It would need a huge eruption to shake their governing nightmare—a profligate, deficit-hobbled state—and open up the possibility of a transformation on the scale Timothy and May wanted.

In the late 1930s, it had taken the threat of Nazi invasion to finally break the old consensus. In the late 1970s, it had taken the Winter of Discontent to force so sharp a change. This time, the fuse had been lit in the course of Cameron's strategy to stay in office. In a bid to pull back votes from UKIP, he had promised a referendum on whether Britain should remain in the European Union.

13

PROJECT FEAR

2015–17

Three months before the general election, Ed Miliband had found himself in a punch-up with a tycoon. When Stefano Pessina, the billionaire acting chief executive of Boots, pronounced that a Miliband government would be a 'catastrophe' for Britain, the Labour leader retaliated, saying he did not think 'British people would take kindly to being lectured' by a man who lived in Monaco and did not pay tax in the UK.[1] At which point the former chief executive of Marks and Spencer, the recently ennobled Conservative peer Stuart Rose, weighed in, declaring Miliband's attitude 'a Seventies throw-back'.

'For a long time,' wrote Lord Rose in the *Daily Mail*, 'we seemed to have reached a consensus about business in Britain'. Enterprise and wealth creation should not be resented, or punitively taxed, but rewarded as the foundation of a strong economy. But now, with all this talk of 'predators' and tax rises, and the stirring of resentment against business leaders, 'Ed Miliband and the Labour Party have blown that consensus apart.'[2] Rose objected to the idea that Pessina had no right to comment simply because he was not a British citizen, pointing out that over forty of the FTSE 100's chief executives were not British.

Labour had thought they were on the verge of power. They had run on a moderately left-wing manifesto, and they had still been decried by economic liberals for planning to drag Britain back to the place it must never go: the 1970s. The month after Lord Rose's attack, the Conservative Mayor of London, Boris Johnson, warned that Miliband's planned 'orgy of higher taxation and regulation' would return Britain to the grim, 'union-dominated economy' of the Seventies.[3] When the election results came through, Labour had gained only 1.4 per cent more of the vote and, in the face of a surge for the Scottish National Party, had actually lost twenty-six seats. The party was floored; Miliband immediately resigned. It seemed clear that the last thing it should do was to replace him with anyone who gave the least hint of 1970s leftism.

The main contenders to take over—Andy Burnham, Yvette Cooper and Liz Kendall—were all, like Ed Miliband, in their mid-40s, and all three followed the conventional market-attuned wisdom that what was needed was a stronger appeal to aspiration. Even Burnham, the former health secretary who was best placed to attract left-wing votes, tacked right. The Parliamentary Labour Party's beleaguered left struggled to find a candidate. They finally alighted on a back-bench MP in his mid-60s, older even than Blair and Brown. Jeremy Corbyn embodied the idea of going back to the 1970s: he had organised strikers during the Winter of Discontent. It was far from clear that he could gather the required thirty-five nominations from his fellow Labour MPs.

But then a strange thing happened. When Corbyn started appearing on hustings with his younger rivals, his old-fashioned, pre–New Labour straightforwardness struck a chord—well beyond the committed left, with people who were fed up of politicians giving cautious, calculated answers. In his account of the campaign, Corbyn's future speech-writer, the journalist Alex Nunns, argues that this reflected an appetite for real political change. Corbyn's 'outsider vibe' was rooted in the fact that he 'was the only candidate to unequivocally oppose the Thatcherite economic consensus that had failed so badly in the economic crash.'[4] Ed Miliband had been accused of blowing that consensus apart, but what if the popular response was not to draw back, but to pile the explosives higher? The other candidates had honed their skills in an era of consensus politics, which was not geared up to channel much discontent. Large numbers of people took to social media, lobbying MPs to nominate Corbyn. He managed to secure a place on the ballot—and, all of a sudden, it looked as though he might actually win.

Where Miliband had merely to contend with boilerplate 'back to the 1970s' attacks, Corbyn's candidacy attracted far greater consternation. To many in the media and politics, the idea of him as Labour leader was completely unthinkable: somehow both terrifying and ridiculous. Here was a politician of the far left who had never held a front-bench job in his thirty-two years in Parliament, and who had voted against past leaders hundreds of times. The *Mail on Sunday* ran a full-length nightmare scenario, in which David Thomas imagined the collapse of a Corbyn regime after 1,000 days of economic pandemonium: a lurid swirl of imagery from 1970s Britain, 2010s Greece, and the kind of spectres of leftist chaos that had been around since Stafford Cripps. As the Corbyn government prints money, the pound sinks and inflation hits 25 per cent. The IMF and the European Central Bank refuse to help. Taxes are hiked, and the rich flee. Black-outs and unemployment proliferate; the media is censored. Eventually, with Oxford Street and Canary Wharf boarded up, the police, long unpaid, go on strike, and riots and fires erupt, until finally Corbyn flees a burning capital in a UN peacekeepers' helicopter.[5]

On 12 September, Corbyn won the leadership by a landslide. Thomas' nightmare, among many others, had left Labour members unmoved. Helped by a rule change allowing 'registered supporters' to vote for £3, Corbyn attracted huge support among young people who, in some cases, barely remembered the 1990s, let alone the 1970s, and had far more pressing fears to contend with than a high-spending state or something called 'inflation'. Many leading political commentators had lived through Labour's long struggle back to electability after 1979: to them, Corbyn's utterly unexpected rise looked like a zombie version of Bennism, accidentally left unburied. And it is true that many of those backing Corbyn were older, ex-party members who had left during the Blair years and now returned. Nonetheless, to younger Labour members, Corbyn offered exciting new possibilities.

The economist James Meadway, who went on to advise Corbyn's shadow chancellor John McDonnell, attributes much of Corbyn's appeal to the impact of the Crash. It had shattered the promise that going to university would land you a decent job, and hit young people's earnings particularly hard, even before the coalition raised tuition fees. 'The gap,' he says, 'between what your life is really like—with very high rents, really crap places to live, and zero-hours contracts and low pay—and what you're told it should be like is very, very striking.'[6] Now, this sense of disempowerment had unexpectedly found mainstream political expression. Young activists had thrown themselves into phone-canvassing from home, using an app designed by one of Corbyn's more tech-savvy supporters.

Perhaps the shrugging off of warnings from the 1970s was helped too by a renewed fascination with a decade when, however chaotically, things seemed to have been up for grabs. Just as revisionist historians had once worked to liberate the Thirties from the ghosts of the hunger marchers, so, in turn, the Seventies were being reappraised, even before the financial crisis. In 2004, the New Economics Foundation had calculated that Britons were happiest in 1976; in 2009, as the crisis bit, books by the historian David Edgerton and the *Guardian* journalist Andy Beckett had been among those working to rehabilitate a decade that had supposedly been full of nothing but rubbish mountains, strikes, power-cuts and decline. In 2012, the National Theatre had staged *This House*, an elegy for the noble toil of Labour whips in the last years of the post-war consensus.

Even the Corbyn campaign itself, fuelled by improvised, grassroots DIY, was redolent of the kind of political activism that had been common in the candidate's 1970s youth. And in both form and substance, many involved had clearly found this empowering. As one of the new leader's close advisers told Alex Nunns: 'That phrase we used about austerity being a political choice rather than an economic necessity really resonated.' The reason for this, the adviser thought, was that 'it gave people a sense of control.'[7]

* * *

In 2014, after his revolutionary stint at the Department for Education, Dominic Cummings had been hired by a group called Business for Britain, to research what swing voters thought about the arguments over the European Union, given Cameron's pledge to hold a referendum if re-elected. He had also run focus groups with voters in marginal seats who had voted Conservative in 2010, but were having doubts about doing so next time. He was struck that, on immigration, working-class and lower-middle-class Labour voters 'were practically indistinguishable from all the Tories and UKIP people I had been talking to'.[8] Immigration, and the feeling that it was out of control, was now associated with the EU in ways it had not been a few years earlier.

But there was another, more surprising side to this anger at a loss of control. As Cummings wrote on his blog that June, contrary to the commentariat's notion that swing voters were centrist, they 'are more anti-immigration *and* anti-free market than the centre of gravity in Westminster.' Miliband was seen as weak, but Cameron was seen as standing 'just for the rich' by people who felt that 'everything's gone up except my wages'.[9] A long-standing 'anti-politics' mood had been sharpened by the financial crisis into a feeling that certain people in London had too much power. As Cummings would blog three years later, after the referendum, the Crash had

> undermined confidence in Government, politicians, big business, banks, and almost any entity thought to be speaking for those with power and money. *Contra* many pundits, Miliband was right that the centre of gravity has swung against free markets. Even among the world of Thatcherite small businesses and entrepreneurs opinion is deeply hostile to the way in which banks and public company executive pay work. Over and over again outside London people would rant about how they had not/barely recovered from this recession 'while the politicians and bankers and businessmen in London all keep raking in the money and us mugs on PAYE are paying for the bailouts, now they're saying we've just got to put up with the EU being crap or else we'll be unemployed, I don't buy it, they've been wrong about everything else...' All those amazed at why so little attention was paid to 'the experts' [warning against Brexit] did not, and still do not, appreciate that these 'experts' are seen by most people of all political views as having botched financial regulation, made a load of rubbish predictions, then forced everybody else outside London to pay for the mess while they got richer and dodged responsibility. *They are right. This is exactly what happened.*

Many Tory MPs and 'free market' pundits / think tankers are living in a fantasy world in which they want hostility to big business to end even though everybody can see that those who failed largely escaped responsibility and have even gone back to doing the same things.

He himself had argued since 2001, Cummings said, 'for big changes on executive pay to almost zero effect', and that, in the wake of the Crash, at least some of those responsible should have been jailed.[10]

Cummings had picked up on the anti-politics feeling in 2004, when he had set up a campaign to oppose the proposed North East Regional Assembly, working with conservative campaigner James Frayne; during the coalition, the two became colleagues under Michael Gove. After the Department for Education, Frayne moved to the think-tank Policy Exchange to explore similar terrain, reaching similar conclusions. Like Cummings' research, Frayne's findings drew attention to a deep disconnect between large sections of the population and those in power, running what Blond had called the liberal 'market state' from London. Frayne, who had grown up in a modest home in Nottingham, had long been frustrated by the Conservative Party's lurch in focus from the wealthy to the most vulnerable, which he thought completely missed a huge swathe of the electorate. This had also been bugging Nick Timothy.

Timothy, Frayne and Cummings had all known each other for years. By 2015, from their different starting points, they were all circling the same insight, and its political implications. Millions of working-class and lower-middle-class people in the Midlands and the north of England were widely assumed to occupy a 'middle ground', but were actually to the right on crime, immigration and welfare reform, and to the left on 'NHS funding and structure, private sector involvement in public services and the utilities, and taxation on the rich and big business'.[11] This might have seemed contradictory to Westminster analysts trying to place them on a left–right spectrum, Frayne argues, but most people do not think like that.[12] Rather, these views were rooted in a coherent set of values: family, fairness, hard work, decency. Support for 'controlling immigration and reducing the gap between rich and poor,' Frayne wrote, reflected 'the public's desire for fairness'.[13] They did not trust politicians, but they did want government to help them. He coined a phrase for these people: they were 'just about managing'.

It looked as though politicians had missed something with huge potential: these voters were not exercised by the old nightmares that still underpinned the 'market–state' consensus in Westminster. The 'just about managing' did not have a horror of a big, high-spending state. Nor did they have nightmares about authoritarianism. Their fears were insecurity, whether in terms of income or crime. Appealing to them could sweep away the old nightmares, and with them, the creaking old consensus. Either party could win these people's trust and, Frayne suggested, it would be worth their while trying. His report, published a month after Cameron won his majority, was called *Overlooked but Decisive*.

* * *

In late 2015, David Cameron was heading towards delivering on his election promise to call a referendum on the UK's membership of the European Union, in which he would campaign for the 'Remain' side, along with George Osborne. Meanwhile, Dominic Cummings was hired to run what became Vote Leave. Cummings' immersion in all those polls and focus groups—not least his identification of voters' hatred of bankers—helped to inspire the slogan he invented for the campaign. This drew directly on his focus group discoveries:

> For a lot of people, 'Take Back Control' made them think, 'Yeh, these are the guys who screwed up the economy, who drove it off a cliff in 2008, whose mates are all Goldman Sachs bankers and hedge funders on massive bonuses. Us mugs on PAYE are the ones paying the bills for this. We'll show those guys—we'll take back control from you lot in London.'[14]

The referendum, announced in early 2016 and scheduled for June, might have seemed like a tussle between right-wing Eurosceptics and the liberal centre—a competition for public support between two wings of the establishment. Instead, with 'Take Back Control', Cummings cast it as a struggle between the guardians of the governing consensus, and an insurgency of ordinary people, who were ready for radical change. This meaning of his slogan, he thought, was something Osborne and Cameron did not quite grasp.

This struggle for power also played out in the arena of high politics. In 1940, a crucial element of the struggle to oust Chamberlain, break from old taboos and radically expand the size of the state had been the insurgency within the Conservative Parliamentary Party, centred on Churchill. In 1975, a crucial element of the struggle to oust Heath, break from old taboos and radically reduce the size of the state had been the insurgency within the Conservative Parliamentary Party, led by Thatcher and Joseph. In both cases, this had toppled the party leader, and helped to lay the ground, eventually, for a whole new consensus. The question was whether there would be any such split in 2016. After much agonising, the London mayor Boris Johnson and Michael Gove, now justice secretary, broke the news to Cameron and Osborne that they would be campaigning for Leave.

Unlike the internal Conservative battles of 1940 and 1975, however, this decision played out straight away in a public vote. And, as with the great struggles for power in the elections of 1945 and 1979, the EU referendum campaign rapidly became a battle of nightmares. For Remainers, among whom were millions of ordinary people who had never been near the kind of privileges enjoyed by Johnson, Gove and Cummings, the idea of leaving the European Union was unthinkable: an act of pointless self-harm in the service of delusion, and worse. The Remain camp warned of economic calamity, including a loss to each household of £4,300 per year, and to the nation of £36 billion; of violence in Northern Ireland and the break-up of the union; and, at least as it was reported in the press, the prospect of renewed war in Europe. Alongside this was a more socially focused nightmare. Given its strong association with the immigration question, Brexit became for many Remainers a harbinger of racism, authoritarian 'post-truth'–fuelled populism, or even fascism. These two fears—economic catastrophe and domineering, harshly right-wing government—corresponded to the twin taboos underpinning the market–state consensus since Blair. The Leave campaign had to find a way to tackle them both at once.

Cummings, a student of crisis and revolution, evidently has a strong sense of the strategic importance of nightmares. He set out to neutralise the fear that leaving the EU meant economic calamity, countering with the idea that 'The euro is a nightmare, the EU is failing, unemployment is a disaster, their debts and pensions are a disaster, if we stay YOU will be paying the bills. *It's safer to take back control*'.[15] His decision to put a slogan on a red campaign bus, implying that leaving the EU would free up £350 million a week to spend on the NHS, was aimed specifically to counter Remain's economic warnings, which the Leave campaign branded 'Project Fear'.

To neutralise the other Remain nightmare—that Brexit meant a lurch into right-wing populism—he sought to distance Vote Leave from UKIP's leader Nigel Farage, to whom he thought many potential Leave voters were averse. Against this line of attack, Cummings again deployed counter-nightmares: that the 'centralisation of power in Brussels' and the Euro project were themselves fuelling the rise of extremism in Europe, and that it was 'increasingly important that Britain offers an example of civilised, democratic, liberal self-government.'[16] However, the Leave campaign has also been widely criticised for 'stoking ethnocentric voters' anxieties' by warning, with no real evidence, of Turkey's imminent accession to the EU.[17] Cummings drew on the domestic anger at vested interests that he had picked up in focus groups the year before:

> We aligned our campaign with those who were furious with executive pay / corporate looting (about 99% of the country). We aligned ourselves with the public who had been let down by the system … One of the most effective TV performances of the campaign was the day Boris hit the theme of corporate looting in a market square.[18]

As in his fight with the education establishment 'Blob', Cummings cast Vote Leave as a revolutionary campaign against an elite, which seemed to strike a chord. When President Obama announced that Britain would be at 'the back of the queue' for trade talks with the US after Brexit, Vote Leave's Henry de Zoete—another alumnus of the Gove education team—reported that the prevailing reaction among voters was that it was none of the President's business. This turn in public opinion began to trouble Remain, too. Remembering the referendum on Scottish independence in 2014, the Conservatives' Scottish secretary, David Mundell, tried in vain to warn the Remain campaign that the public 'are generally anti-business these days', and 'don't care what the CBI thinks.' Similarly, warnings of economic devastation did not necessarily have the desired impact: a Treasury projection that Brexit would lower house prices by between 10 and 18 per cent turned out to be rather attractive to young people and their parents.[19]

Both these approaches—playing with taboos, and rhetorical insurgency—seem to have helped Cummings to win the Brexit power struggle, in a way that echoes both the 1940 vanguardists such as Michael Foot, and Keith Joseph in the late 1970s. Like Cummings, Foot and Joseph were adept at identifying and disarming opponents' attacks, at understanding which nightmares worked, and at making aggressive attacks of their own. This was done partly through a conscious focus on drawing a sharp red line between past and present, and on entrenching a narrative about what had supposedly gone wrong. In 1945, Michael Foot was accused of spreading malicious lies by a ferocious but ineffective Quintin Hogg. In 1978, Saatchi & Saatchi were accused of fakery over their 'Labour Isn't Working' poster. Likewise, Cummings' £350 million for the NHS. This was challenged as a lie, on rather stronger grounds than the criticism of Saatchi & Saatchi. In concert with the voters he had been listening to, Cummings was about to create a break-point.

* * *

On 23 June 2016, Leave narrowly won the referendum, by 51.9 per cent to 48.1. Writing in the *New Statesman* just after the vote, partly in response to a spike in hate crimes that had followed, the journalist Sarah Ditum was far from alone in fearing that Britain had plunged into a 'political nightmare'. Or, in fact, two nightmares: economic calamity and a sharp, violent turn right: 'Just how bad could it be? Let's be alarmist: really bad. Twentieth-century European history bad. Recessions, pogroms, the lot. It feels impossible, but the last fortnight has felt impossible too.'[20]

Today, while still highly critical of Brexit, Ditum says she feels 'alienated' from the feelings expressed in that piece. But, she observes, it did capture the sense of a massive shock hitting 'the foundational norms of the democracy I lived in ... it did feel apocalyptic'.[21] For many Remainers, coming to terms with what had happened meant both tracking the risks Brexit presented, and trying to understand why so many people had made a choice that had seemed unthinkable.

It takes more than one shock to topple a consensus. If the first sends cracks running through the old edifice, further blows then undermine its foundations, and finally sweep it away. The events of 1931 shook the Snowden–Baldwin consensus, but it took the shock of 1940 and the election battle of 1945 to finish it off. After the Winter of Discontent, so many were sick of union power that it carried Mrs Thatcher into Number 10—but only because the fights over *In Place of Strife*, the miners' strikes and the Industrial Relations Act had gone before. Now, eight years after the Crash, here was a new and much more devastating blow to the existing order. David Cameron immediately resigned as Prime Minister. As in 1940 and 1979, it became clear that a huge swathe of the population had rejected what had, until then, seemed the dominant nightmares. The Remain campaign's warnings of economic doom and toxic populism had not stopped people voting Leave, because other troubles had become more pressing.

Looking back, Sarah Ditum reflects that she should have been more aware that there were 'pockets of neglect and indifference', of people who had been failed by mainstream politics—not least because, as a hard-up young mother, she herself had spent two years living in a run-down part of Sheffield, surrounded by 'resentment and sadness'. But in June 2016, other nightmares were too alarming to bring any of that back to mind.

Before the dust had settled, there was a surge of interest in the political worries of working-class people living in safe Labour seats in the Midlands and the north, who had just voted to Leave. They may only have been a fraction of the total; but, whether or not their votes were decisive to the referendum result, it made them more politically important than they had been in a long time—partly because they could no longer be taken for granted in future general elections. It appears from multiple studies that both 'identity conservatism' and economic disadvantage were involved, each of which intersected with issues like immigration, the sense of being forgotten or looked down on by 'financial and educated elites',[22] and the feeling of being 'cut adrift from the mainstream consensus'.[23]

In her 2020 book *Beyond the Red Wall*, Deborah Mattinson reports many expressions of loss, neglect, resentment and unfairness, alongside pride in vanished local traditions of skilled work. Voting for Brexit was seen by some of the people she spoke to as an economic cure-all, or a necessary jolt to the political establishment, or both. If the first remained an aspiration, the vote had undoubtedly achieved the second. Claire Ainsley of the Joseph Rowntree Foundation, who commissioned some of the early research on working-class Leavers' motives, argued that 'by voting leave a spotlight was shone on the condition of many parts of the UK. This should be seen as a moment to transform the prospects of the most "left behind" parts of the UK and extend prosperity to all.'[24] Phillip Blond thought this aspect of the result 'opened up the possibility of Red Toryism again'.[25]

But that would depend on who replaced David Cameron as Conservative leader, and Prime Minister. Boris Johnson seemed perfectly placed to do so—until Michael Gove suddenly decided otherwise and ran against him, wrecking both their chances. Before party members had even had chance to vote, a Remainer, Theresa May, was Prime Minister instead. Nevertheless, she embraced the idea that the result was a call for change, of the kind she had outlined in that speech back in 2013. And suddenly, Nick Timothy was in Number 10, with a chance to try to do what Phillip Blond and Maurice Glasman hadn't managed: to carry consensus-breaking, post-liberal ideas into power.

As she took office on 13 July 2016, Theresa May struck a very different note to her predecessor—with the help of a phrase from James Frayne's research three years earlier:

> If you're from an ordinary working class family, life is much harder than many people in Westminster realise. You have a job but you don't always have job security. You have your own home, but you worry about paying a mortgage. You can just about manage but you worry about the cost of living and getting your kids into a good school.
>
> If you're one of those families, if you're just managing, I want to address you directly. I know you're working around the clock, I know you're doing your best and I know that sometimes life can be a struggle. The government I lead will be driven not by the interests of the privileged few, but by yours.[26]

To Timothy, the control of immigration was a key aspect of this; but in another speech he wrote for May at this time, they focused on a different issue of control: the concentration of power in the hands of business bosses and 'transient shareholders', who didn't seem to care about their workers who had lost jobs or taken pay cuts after the 2008 Crash.[27] This speech proposed to put workers on company boards, and to change the law to push back against the 'irrational, unhealthy and growing' pay gap between workers and bosses. At the Conservative Party conference, May brought together the immigration issue with her challenge to CEO culture, presenting a picture of a powerful few—over-privileged by globalisation, breaching the 'social contract' which should have led them to train local young people before taking on 'cheap labour from overseas'. May told her audience that, 'today, too many people in positions of power behave as though they have more in common with international elites than with the people down the road ... But if you believe you're a citizen of the world, you're a citizen of nowhere.'[28]

This was reminiscent, as much as anything, of Ed Miliband's attack on billionaire tax exiles, or Vince Cable's attack on bankers as 'pin-striped Scargills'. Just as Miliband had rapidly been assailed with nightmares of a return to the 1970s, so the Thatcherite historian Niall Ferguson lambasted May's speech on the same grounds.[29] But, in the light of May's stances during her six years at the Home Office, including the much-criticised 'hostile environment' policy, the phrase 'citizens of nowhere' was also taken by some to be an attack on internationalism and immigration in general, and was even cast as a dangerous lurch to the far right.[30]

The Brexit vote appeared to hole the old consensus below the water-line, driving its last captains—David Cameron and George Osborne, whom May immediately sacked—out of politics. Post-liberals were optimistic: Maurice Glasman went to Downing Street to meet Nick Timothy and discuss how working-class interests could be protected as Brexit unfolded. But there was no guarantee that their ideas would be able to overcome the remaining forces of the status quo. Social liberals objected to May's rhetoric out of concern about migration policy; economic liberals were equally opposed to attacks on jet-setting chief executives. The question was whether this Red Tory turn could move beyond conference rhetoric into policy.

* * *

The limits to May and Timothy's power to push all this through were rapidly apparent. The education secretary Justine Greening opposed a return to grammar schools. The new Chancellor of the Exchequer, Philip Hammond, declined to fund schemes aimed at the 'just about managing'. The idea of putting workers on boards rapidly hit resistance too. But another idea redolent of the Seventies that May and Timothy had mooted back in 2013 *was* introduced: industrial strategy. In a sign of an emerging post-Crash consensus, this built on the work already done by ministers across the parties: Peter Mandelson, Vince Cable and David Willetts. Timothy recruited Cable's adviser Giles Wilkes to work on industrial and economic policy at Number 10; Neil O'Brien, George Osborne's former adviser on the Northern Powerhouse, joined them too. In the wake of May's early speeches, Wilkes says, 'It suddenly felt okay to talk about it being unfair the way some people were winners and some people were losers from this economy—that businesses were behaving in an irresponsible way at times, that corporate governance wasn't working.'[31]

May's agenda appeared to be enormously popular. With commanding poll leads over Corbyn's Labour, she decided to try and win a decent-sized majority to push through her approach—to Brexit and everything else. Given the working-class element of the Leave vote, and her willingness both to use the state to help struggling workers and to take a harder line on immigration, she seemed to stand a strong chance of persuading long-time Labour voters who had backed Leave to try the Tories. On 4 May 2017, in a sign that tacking left on economics might attract Labour voters to the Conservatives, voters in the new Tees Valley Combined Authority elected their first 'metro mayor'. This was heartland Labour territory, but the young Conservative candidate, Ben Houchen, won, promising to take the local airport into public ownership.

The general election was set for 8 June. Both main parties' manifestos signalled breaks from free-market thinking. Labour rejected austerity; it proposed ending university tuition fees and renationalising the railways, the Royal Mail and the country's energy system. There was little fear visible here of accusations about taking Britain back to the 1970s. The Conservative manifesto, largely written by Nick Timothy, rejected extreme liberalism and embraced 'the good that government can do'.[32] Talk of Red Tory and Blue Labour was back in the air. Could this be a revival to match the fall and rise of free-market economics in the 1970s—its false start under Heath, its apparent consignment to the wilderness by Labour's social contract with the unions, and then its second coming after the Winter of Discontent?

There was just one problem. The Conservative election machine could not bring itself to embrace Timothy's break with consensus, instead trying to build a presidential-style campaign around the awkward, self-conscious figure of Theresa May, selling continuity. Labour's anti-austerity platform won 40 per cent, cancelling May's majority without winning one itself. The Conservatives did make progress in their attempt to win over Leave voters and draw them from their traditional party allegiance: many Labour majorities in the Midlands and north became more marginal. But they stayed Labour.

'The tragedy of Nick Timothy and Theresa May,' Blond told BBC Radio 4 sadly, 'is that we were so much closer than we ever were with Cameron.' Like both Blond and Glasman, Timothy had failed. As suddenly as he had arrived, he was gone again, leaving politics altogether and carrying much of the blame for the defeat with him. The journalist Steve Richards, however, predicted that once the Conservatives had 'calmed down', they would need 'to revisit some of the themes in that manifesto', because it had addressed 'unavoidable demands in society.'[33]

Labour had done vastly better than expected; Corbyn declared the result a rejection of austerity. But offering a break from the old economic consensus alone had not won the party power. Reflecting a long-term shift in Labour's base of support, most of their increased vote had come from Remainers. And no one had decisively won the support of the 'just about managing'. With Parliament deadlocked, the struggle over Brexit became a rich new source of nightmares, blocking the way to any decisive change.

The morning after the election, a behavioural economics festival called Nudgestock got underway in Folkestone. One speaker was the mastermind of the Vote Leave campaign, Dominic Cummings. He readily set out the methods he had used to win the EU referendum, his analysis of crisis and voter disaffection—and how he had tapped that with the multiple meanings of 'Take Back Control'. His success was in glaring contrast with what had just befallen Nick Timothy's thwarted attempt to do something similar. 'What's happened in the last twenty four hours in the election in the Tory Party campaign,' Cummings observed, 'is another good example of how hard it has been for the bubble in SW1 to actually get to grips with what the effects of the financial crash of 2008 were'.[34] As Theresa May faced the prospect of trying to force Brexit legislation through a hung Parliament, the way was blocked to any new political settlement. Cummings' analysis would eventually become useful once again.

14

STOP THE COUP!

2017–19

Not long after Nick Timothy made his exit from Downing Street, Will Tanner, the Prime Minister's Deputy Head of Policy, left too. Timothy had recruited him to work on police reform at the Home Office, and then brought him into Number 10 when May suddenly became Prime Minister. Tanner shared Timothy's view that if the changes to British society stopped with Brexit itself, this 'would nowhere near fulfil the ambitions or the hopes and dreams of that vote' for a change in how 'society and economy operated and in whose interests.' Now all that was left was the prospect of 'a couple of years … slogging away to achieve not very much'.[1] He decided to try to set up a mental health start-up, developing digital therapeutics.

But then one of his old Number 10 colleagues, Neil O'Brien, invited him to dinner. O'Brien had made the transition from George Osborne's Treasury to May's Number 10 Policy Unit, and was now an MP. Having once run the think-tank Policy Exchange, which had started off generating ideas for the Cameron project, he now thought a new body was needed. Tanner eventually agreed to run it. The new think-tank, Onward, would become a means to incubate the thinking that they and Timothy had briefly hoped to instigate from Downing Street—ready, when the chance came, to try these ideas again. But when Onward was launched in May 2018, Westminster was descending ever deeper into its Brexit labyrinth, and for more than a year, it was not obvious that the moment would ever come.

For Theresa May, there was to be no escape from that prospect of a couple of years slogging for little reward. As the clock ran down towards Brexit Day on 31 March 2019, she tried desperately to unite the Leave and Remain wings of the Conservative Party around an EU withdrawal agreement, and to pass it into law despite lacking a parliamentary majority. Her efforts quickly foundered. May was determined to avoid the sort of hard Brexit some of her MPs demanded: leaving the single market and customs union—if need be, with few or no replacement trade deals. Those MPs included her Foreign Secretary, Boris Johnson. The likelihood of Johnson compromising was underlined by his response to Airbus, Siemens and BMW warning that a no-deal Brexit would have an impact on their UK operations. When Johnson was asked about this at an event for EU diplomats, he reportedly retorted: 'Fuck business.'[2] The next month, when May tried to forge a compromise among her sharply divided Cabinet, Johnson followed the Brexit secretary David Davis out of the door.

Jeremy Corbyn, meanwhile, was caught between those Labour MPs whose constituencies had voted to Leave, and whose majorities had shrunk alarmingly, and those whose constituencies had voted to Remain, who feared the same fate if Labour did not oppose a hard Brexit, or Brexit full stop. On 15 January 2019, the Commons rejected May's withdrawal agreement by 432 votes to 202: the worst defeat a government had suffered in decades. When she brought it back a second time, MPs rejected it again. And then again.

British politics fell back into a battle of nightmares. Leavers spied an establishment conspiracy to thwart a democratic vote, which risked triggering civil unrest. On the eve of the first vote, Johnson told the Commons that, after two and a half years since the referendum, the government could not delay triggering Article 50—which would begin the process of ending UK membership of the EU—and negotiating the deal that would take its place. If it did, 'the public would conclude that there was some plot by the deep state to kill Brexit'.[3] To Remainers, a hard Brexit, which was looking increasingly likely, threatened to usher in economic disaster, violence in Northern Ireland, and an authoritarian, nationalist, even racist Britain, utterly alien to their values. Many also thought that a hard Brexit would be more or less undemocratic, given that Vote Leave had assured the country that leaving the EU and reworking the UK's trade arrangements would be straightforward. When the Home Office tweeted on 27 December 2018 that 'EU citizens and their families will need to apply to the EU Settlement Scheme to continue living in the UK after 31 December 2020', the music journalist Pete Paphides retweeted this, adding: 'I shudder to imagine what else needs to happen for more people to realise that what happened in 2016 was an illegal far-right coup—one which the leaders of the main two political parties in this country are bafflingly determined to uphold, against the will of a rising majority.'[4]

These were the arguments of the referendum campaign. But there was now a critical difference, which made everything far worse: the referendum had at least had a single binary question, and a clear end-point. Now, with Parliament arguing over minute details of when and how, and never finding a way to back May's deal, a nightmare not raised during the campaign rose into view; an unthinkable catastrophe which terrified not only Remainers. On 27 January 2019, *The Sunday Times* reported that 'Britain is preparing to declare a state of emergency and introduce martial law in the event of disorder after a no-deal Brexit'.

A People's Vote campaign for a second referendum rapidly amassed a following in the hundreds of thousands, and twice brought roughly a million people out to march through London. Some of those involved saw a fresh vote as a democratic way to break the deadlock in Parliament, and wanted a 'confirmatory' referendum on the final deal. But other parts of this new movement saw a more severe breakdown of consensus: they regarded the referendum itself as invalid, on the basis that Vote Leave had lied and broken electoral law, and that voters were only now coming to realise what Brexit might actually involve. What amounted to a re-run of the 2016 vote, they argued, could restore consensus to an increasingly polarised country. But either way, it would be a tall order to win enough support for a second referendum, given the desperately divided House of Commons.

The suffocating sense that there was no tenable way out spread, as it had in the 1930s when people faced the choice between Nazi occupation and Armageddon under the bombs, and in the 1970s, when the future seemed to offer the rule of either the pickets or the authoritarian hard right. Now, the choice appeared to be economic collapse and authoritarianism on the one hand or, on the other, an unaccountable elite betraying the largest democratic vote in British history. All this was exacerbated by events in America, as the Trump presidency continually stoked liberal fear. Warnings first published in the era of Hitler and Stalin—like Hannah Arendt's *The Origins of Totalitarianism*, George Orwell's *Nineteen Eighty-Four* and Sinclair Lewis' *It Can't Happen Here*—were reported to be flying off the shelves. New books appeared to join them, like *How to Lose a Country: The 7 Steps from Democracy to Dictatorship* by Ece Temelkuran, and *How Democracy Ends* by David Runciman.

As the nightmare in Parliament rolled on, posters started to appear in the London Underground, promoting *The Wall*, a new novel by John Lanchester, as 'A *1984* For Our Times'. 'The book creates the fantasy of a walled-off Britain,' wrote the *Sunday Times* reviewer, 'and reveals it to be a nightmare.'[5] The novel merges Remainers' Brexit nightmare with the advancing prospect of climate breakdown. The entire British coast is now surrounded by a high concrete barrier, to protect it from rising water and from arriving migrants, or 'Others'. Everyone has a biometric chip in their arm, and everyone must be a 'Defender', serving guard duty on the wall, except those who buy their way out. If Others get in, the equivalent number of Defenders are put to sea without trial. Any Others who do make it into Britain have their children taken away and adopted, so they can become citizens. There is much boosterish patriotic rhetoric from a 'blond baby' politician about Britain being a nation of heroes.

Yet inside this authoritarian-nationalist border fortress, there are signs of a quieter dystopia trying to make itself heard. This is a story about soul-destroying shift work, and a lack of hope and agency, in a country where the tiny elite can buy their way out of the duties they impose on everyone else. But, unlike in 1940, the nationalist drive to resist invasion in *The Wall* shows no signs of sweeping away miserable work and exploitation—here, the island fortress rhetoric is a distraction which keeps people compliant.

Under the pressure of choosing between intolerable options, as in the 1930s, 1970s and early 1980s, an unusually high number of MPs decided to become independents or to cross the floor, and new parties appeared. Eight Labour MPs broke away and formed The

Independent Group. They were driven in part by antipathy to Corbyn and to some party members' aggressive anti-semitism towards Jewish Labour MPs, and by an all-out drive to stop Brexit; three like-minded Conservatives joined them. Meanwhile, Nigel Farage launched the Brexit Party, to pressure May's Conservatives from the right.

Corbyn's close comrade Andrew Murray mooted a compromise. Warning that the 'mood of impending calamity is growing', he suggested that Labour should 'offer to forge a common national position and take responsibility for delivering it in talks in Brussels.' This would deliver Brexit for Leavers, while salving Remainers' fears of no deal. Murray argued that this would be like Attlee's decisive move to enter coalition with Churchill and, as in 1940, would make Labour 'look statesman-like, confident, national, patriotic and government-ready'. Just as Labour had spent its time in the Churchill war ministry developing a radical post-war agenda, a national coalition now could afford a similar opportunity, paving the way to a promising election contest along the lines of 1945.[6]

But for many Labour figures, working with the newly nationalist Conservatives was unthinkable. The Shadow Home Secretary Diane Abbott was so aghast at what she saw as the racism and hostility to migrants inherent in the Brexit project that she dismissed Murray's whole idea. Instead, to the thwarted fury of some of those Labour MPs who had Leave-voting seats, the party edged its way towards supporting a second referendum. Corbyn's young supporters took to wearing T-shirts with the despairing slogan 'Love Corbyn, Hate Brexit'. Their problem was that many Labour voters thought the opposite—and Corbyn himself, once an outright Eurosceptic, had never come across as an enthusiastic Remainer. The Corbyn campaign team had been aware of the division between the party's northern and metropolitan bases ever since 2015. But as Ian Lavery, MP for the mining constituency of Wansbeck put it, whichever way the party turned, there would be 'blood on the walls!'[7]

There were now faltering attempts at talks between May and Corbyn and their teams, but they could not help each other. There was no solution. For both leaders, all routes led straight to disaster. In local elections that May, the Conservatives lost more than 1,300 councillors and forty-four councils, and on 24th, the

Prime Minister announced her resignation. Two days later, the Conservatives came fifth in the European elections, haemorrhaging votes to the Brexit Party, while Labour watched its Remain supporters—including some of New Labour's leading lights—turn to the Liberal Democrats. And the Independent Group, now Change UK, was dead almost before it began.

If crisis is a choice between unthinkables, the crisis breaks when something unthinkable begins to be thought. As the new Conservative leadership race began, that was exactly what started to happen.

* * *

The gridlock in Parliament—the endless permutations and procedural arcana and knife-edge votes—became a nightmare in itself: everyone running faster and faster, never getting anywhere. The only end-point was the exit date, which had been delayed. The Brexit Party's sudden success confronted Conservative MPs with an additional fear: what if Farage's candidates swept the board at the next general election—which, given the logjam in the Commons, might well be imminent? As Farage intended, the revelation of voters' willingness to turn his way added to the pressure to 'get Brexit done'. Any Conservative leadership candidate ready to do what was necessary to achieve that would have a distinct advantage.

Whatever their doubts about his other qualities, Conservative MPs began to turn to Boris Johnson, who swore to take Britain out of the EU on the new deadline day, 31 October, even if that meant leaving without a deal. But a majority of MPs were against this, and would apparently do whatever was necessary to stop it. Leavers therefore began to suggest that, to overcome this stand-off, Parliament might have to be closed—'prorogued'—until Brexit was achieved. Some leadership contenders disavowed this as an anti-democratic nightmare: Matt Hancock declared it would go against 'everything that those men who waded onto those beaches fought and died for'.[8] When Dominic Raab refused to rule it out should he become leader, his fellow Conservative MP Justine Greening tweeted that this would be 'The ultimate anti-democrat move. That's not taking back control it's taking away control.'[9] But Johnson said he would be prepared to do it. On 9 July, the

Commons decided—by a single vote—to 'make it more difficult for a future Prime Minister to prorogue Parliament'.[10]

Each side was accusing the other of trying to abuse their power to undermine democracy. Leavers insisted the referendum vote had to be honoured; Remainers retorted that the vote had been won by dubious means, and that any efforts to force it through would be taking that to new extremes. *Prospect* magazine ran a piece by the Remain campaigner Jonathan Lis, who saw all of this as part of an escalating global nightmare:

> This assault on democratic institutions and norms is not taking place in isolation. It is embedded in a far wider authoritarian movement which aims to empower the right-wing fringes of society and political opinion ... Brexit's leaders are seeking to break every guarantor of British democracy, one by one. Each month brings unprecedented outrage. If we don't end this soon, it may become too late to end it at all.[11]

Meanwhile, MPs determined to make a no-deal Brexit impossible were trying to legislate to stop funding for several government departments from the point Britain left the EU, should it do so without a deal. The former Director of Legislative Affairs at Number 10, Nikki da Costa, wrote in *The Daily Telegraph* that this was 'a significant escalation in the battle for control'. The Commons, she pointed out, 'has not voted down government spending for over 100 years'. This 'desperate rear-guard action', declared the article's headline, risked 'taking our politics to new extremes'.[12]

As all this unfolded, an epic new six-part drama by Russell T Davies had been airing on BBC1. *Years and Years*, which ran between 14 May and 18 June, begins in 2019 and follows a family fifteen years into the future, as Britain is buffeted by geopolitical and environmental turmoil, and economic strife stemming from the 2008 Crash. A new populist party rises, led by a likable, says-the-unsayable demagogue called Vivienne Rook, whom Davies has compared to Boris Johnson.[13] Rook wins power on a platform that is partly left-wing: attacks on bankers, threats to jail Silicon Valley CEOs over online pornography, deploying the army to force people with spare rooms to house the homeless. At the same time, illegal immigrants are put in concentration camps, which are outsourced to private companies;

high-crime areas are cordoned off; government critics are arrested; homeless people are, it seems, being 'disappeared'.

* * *

On 23 July, Boris Johnson won the Conservative Party leadership and duly became Prime Minister. Could this possibly be the figure to win a struggle for power, smash the old nightmares, and usher in a new politics, as Theresa May had tried and failed to do? Outside Number 10, Johnson sounded a great deal more like May than she had sounded like Cameron, promising higher wages and unleashing productive power beyond London and the south-east, talking about 'answering at last the plea of the forgotten people, and the left behind towns, by physically and literally renewing the ties that bind us together.'[14]

News broke that Johnson had appointed Dominic Cummings as his chief adviser. Three days later, the new Prime Minister gave his first big speech, in Manchester's Science and Industry Museum, where he talked about the need to 'unite our country and level up', announcing £3.6 billion in spending for Britain's towns, and sounding for all the world like Cummings explaining his 'Take Back Control' slogan:

> I am absolutely not here to tell you, Mr Mayor, that London has all the answers. Or that everywhere should be like London, or indeed like Manchester. Each place in our country has a unique heritage, a unique character, and a unique future. And indeed I recognise that when the British people voted to leave the European Union, they were not just voting against Brussels—they were voting against London too, and against all concentrations of power in remote centres.[15]

The Evening Standard noted that Cummings had 'been described as a "mad professor" and "evil genius"': shades of Keith Joseph, the 'Mad Monk'.[16] But amid all the noise, once again, a maverick had the ear of the Prime Minister. He could reportedly be heard repeating that Brexit must be achieved 'by any means necessary': shades of Malcolm X.[17] Could Cummings succeed where Blond, Glasman and Timothy had failed, and instigate a successful, democratic break from the old consensus that had tolerated inequality in the name of free markets and globalisation? Danny Kruger, last seen leaving Cameron's team in disillusion at the failure of the Big Society, now became Johnson's Political Secretary. Looking back from early 2020, he argued:

> I still think it was a great idea, and a lot of the legacy is really positive from the Big Society—but we can do it even more so. I compare David Cameron to Ted Heath, who started the privatisation agenda in 1969–70 with Selsdon Man, and then got knocked off course. I think Boris is the Thatcher to Cameron's Heath, and this time we're really going to see it: ten years, I hope, of really positive reforming government.[18]

But to get to that point, Thatcher had had to do the unthinkable: refusing to U-turn when unemployment passed 3 million, curtailing the unions' legal immunities, and defeating the mighty NUM. From where Johnson was standing, the roadblock this time was a Parliament that saw a no-deal Brexit as the overriding nightmare that had to be stopped at all costs. Would he too try to smash through his opponents' taboos, even at the cost of being condemned as an enemy of democracy?

* * *

As Johnson, Cummings and Kruger started work at Number 10, faced with a majority of MPs against no deal, more versions of that nightmare scenario were leaking out of Whitehall. Sky News obtained a 'sensitive' slide warning of what could happen in the first month after a no-deal crash-out, though it was marked 'For Discussion—Not Government Policy', and pre-dated Johnson's arrival in power. It listed such potential problems as 'consumer panic'; 'law and order challenges' in Northern Ireland; 'volatility of currency and financial markets, with potential for disruption of debt markets'; 'heightened policing resource [being] unsustainable, [such that] operational gaps continue to emerge'; and the Bank of England suggesting that the pound could fall '25% in [the] worst case scenario'.[19]

To stop the Johnson government from letting such things happen, there was much talk of a short-term national unity administration, an 'emergency government'.[20] This would have one job: to extend Article 50, delaying Britain's exit from the EU until a deal could be agreed and passed into UK law. The scenario by which this national government would take power went like this. Johnson's administration would lose a vote of confidence. MPs would then have fourteen days to try to assemble a new government that could command the confidence of the House, before an election would be called. If Corbyn could not gain majority support for an administration led by him, then perhaps a government of national unity could. Among those mooted to lead such a coalition was the former Conservative chancellor, Ken Clarke.

But this idea was doomed. The whole problem was that MPs could not agree; as the *New Statesman*'s Stephen Bush mordantly observed, this project could only happen if 'the Labour leadership, the parliamentary Labour party, the Liberal Democrats, both flavours of Change UK, the SNP, Plaid Cymru, Sylvia Hermon and 10 Tory rebels can agree on a PM.'[21] Besides, dodging one nightmare might lead straight to another: what if Johnson lost the confidence vote but refused to resign, holding out until Britain left the EU with no deal on 31 October, and only then called an election? The shadow chancellor John McDonnell said that if this happened, he would dispatch Corbyn in a taxi to see the Queen. The conservative historian David Starkey told the *Telegraph* that this would constitute a coup. The Conservative MP Dominic Grieve urged the Queen to 'dispense with Johnson's services' so that a unity government could step in. Palace aides stressed that deciding on a new government was up to Parliament.[22]

For weeks, the fever intensified. On 18 August, *The Sunday Times* revealed that someone in Whitehall had leaked the government's entire 'Yellowhammer' paper on the contingency plans for a no-deal Brexit. This was not a worst-case scenario, but Whitehall's 'most realistic assessment', predicting food, fuel and medicine shortages; three months of chaos in the ports; and a hard border with the Republic of Ireland, possibly triggering 'direct action'. The paper quoted a Cabinet Office source saying, 'Successive UK governments have a long history of failing to prepare their citizens to be resilient for their own emergencies'.[23] But James Kirkup of the Social Market Foundation argued that whoever had leaked the paper was highlighting the wrong nightmare: people would surely put up with supply problems, dried-up petrol stations and no Eurostar, evoking the 'Dunkirk spirit'. What Remainers should be warning about, he suggested, was that no deal would be a post-Brexit 'gradual slide into national mediocrity'.[24]

If leaks had insufficient impact and an emergency government was a non-starter, how else could a no-deal Brexit be blocked? The shadow Brexit secretary Sir Keir Starmer had been busy discussing a way to delay Brexit with Conservative rebels, without trying to oust Johnson. This would involve seizing control of the Commons for a day, within procedural rules, and passing a law compelling the government, if there were no deal by 19 October, to extend the deadline. Such schemes provoked a ferocious response in *The Daily Telegraph* from Allister Heath, who wrote: 'The Remainers don't realise that they are dealing with a proper, ruthless and ideologically committed operation, not the weak, dithering, dysfunctional shower of yore.' Heath, it appeared, had in mind the latter-day Lenin in Number 10: the plotting Remain MPs 'can't see that the world has changed abruptly, that they face a professional, dedicated enemy, which controls the machinery of government. There will be no pity and no quarter meted out to the dissidents.'[25]

On 28 August, it emerged that the government had royal assent to prorogue Parliament from 9 September to 14 October. In response to the news that the House of Commons would be shut for five weeks, the Speaker, John Bercow, said this would happen over his dead body. Protestors took to the streets, chanting, 'Stop the coup!' An online petition gathered over a million names in a day. Ed Davey of the Liberal Democrats said: 'This could break British parliamentary democracy. It would be a coup d'etat'.[26] Ex-Attorney General Dominic Grieve said Johnson was 'behaving like a revolutionary'.[27] The Scottish First Minister Nicola Sturgeon declared that 'Closing down Parliament' was 'dictatorship.'[28] The former head of the civil service, Lord Kerslake, judged that 'We are reaching the point where the civil service must consider putting its stewardship of the country ahead of service to the government of the day.'[29] The Lib Dem and Labour leaders, Jo Swinson and Jeremy Corbyn, asked to see the Queen. The former *Guardian* editor Alan Rusbridger said this was 'full scale revolution by Dominic Cummings, who literally holds Parliament in contempt'.[30] The journalist Paul Mason contended that this was 'a power-grab run to a script', deliberately normalising chaos.[31] But pro-Brexit Conservative MPs defended prorogation in similar terms. Mark Francois said, 'It is now the people versus the establishment and—for the sake of our democracy—the people must win.'[32] Pro-Brexit figures complained of being called fascists and harassed.

This was the latest climax in a power struggle that had been running for three years, ever since a legal challenge had won a High Court case giving Parliament the right to approve the invocation of Article 50, provoking the *Daily Mail* to call the judges involved in the ruling 'Enemies of the People'. As ever, each side had accused the other of undermining democracy.

In the face of prorogation, the long-planned cross-party move to seize control of Commons business was pressed into action, shifting the power struggle back inside the Conservative Party. Twenty-one of its MPs defied the whip and supported the motion, allowing the Commons to pass a back-bench bill to block no deal. Among the rebels were two former chancellors and a grandson of Winston Churchill; that night, they were all suspended from the party.

The back-benchers' bill passed; the Stop the Coup protests continued around the country, marching past the Commons, placards and red flares aloft. On Saturday 7 September, pro- and anti-Brexit protestors faced each other in Parliament Square. Pro-Brexit demonstrators from the Democratic Football Lads Alliance marched up Whitehall and fought the police, bringing to life something of the nightmares legible on Remainer banners and audible in Remainer speeches. One smartly dressed young Leave protestor seemed to imply that football 'firms' were readying themselves to go beyond this, if Brexit were thwarted. In the early hours of 10 September, MPs themselves protested in the Commons as prorogation began, chanting 'Shame on you!' and holding up signs saying 'Silenced'. Like Thatcher and Joseph before them, Johnson and Cummings had attacked head-on the taboos blocking their way, determined to set the country on a new track.

* * *

In 1940, it had been fairly straightforward to identify the concentration of power underpinning the old order, which had to be challenged: crudely, it was the City and its allies in government. Likewise in the late 1970s, with the unions and their allies in government. The post-liberal project of the 2010s, with its antipathy to both state and market, tended to be more amorphous. Theresa May's 'citizens of nowhere' speech had seemed to antagonise more people than it fired up. But, as two years of constitutional crisis reached an ever more piercing pitch, this offered a way of crystallising what Cummings saw as the opposition to change. On the morning immediately after prorogation, Cummings was, as usual, door-stepped by journalists outside his large house in north London. He suggested that if they wanted to understand what was happening, 'You guys should get out of London, go and—go and talk to people who are not rich Remainers.'[33]

This image of rich Remainers in the capital blocking Brexit seems to have resonated: it took two types—'those guys in London who screwed up the economy in 2008 and got away scot-free', and the 'metropolitan pro-EU establishment'—and merged them into one broad force, accused of using its power to thwart what ordinary people wanted. In 1940, Foot et al had attacked the Chamberlainites and the vested interests whose over-caution was paralysing the war effort, to the immense frustration of the public. During the Winter of Discontent, Thatcher had attacked the unions for wielding unaccountable power, and talked darkly of the 'wreckers among us' who were paralysing the country—to the immense frustration of the public. Chamberlain and the trade unions had each been sincerely motivated by other fears and concerns; likewise, in 2019, many MPs were sincerely convinced that they had to stop a no-deal Brexit. But for many voters, the prospect of the hectic Commons stasis continuing indefinitely had become a nightmare of its own. Cummings cast 'rich Remainers' as the Guilty Men and Women who were blocking Brexit—and, by extension, a move to a Britain less dominated by 'London'.

The identification of the capital with unaccountable power, the liberal metropolitan establishment, the market state, rich Remainers, citizens of nowhere and the rest had roots in real, widespread resentment at other parts of the country being neglected while the economy was managed for the benefit of the already-rich south. It was also, like all such polarising, power-struggle rhetoric, deeply unfair. Just as there were patriots in the City in 1940, and Thatcher supporters on the picket lines in 1978–9, many people living in London at the time of the Brexit referendum were neither wealthy, powerful nor indeed liberal—and there were many liberals and Remainers in the north of England.

The former Home Secretary Amber Rudd, who was not among the Conservative MPs suspended from the party, left politics in solidarity with those who had been, aghast at this 'assault on decency and democracy'.[34] But that anti-authoritarian argument was made in both directions. The MPs' seizure of the parliamentary agenda to pass their law against no deal was denounced by the historian Andrew Roberts as 'a very English form of coup d'etat' by MPs against the people.[35] Either way, Johnson was able to cast the prorogation as him taking back control from the establishment, for the people.

On 24 September, the Supreme Court ruled, unanimously, that the prorogation was illegal and declared it void. Its 'effect on the fundamentals of our democracy' it judged to have been 'extreme'. Instantly, the Commons was recalled. The Leader of the House Jacob Rees-Mogg called the Court decision a 'coup'.[36] The leading Brexit campaigner Daniel Hannan said that if the 'democracy-dodgers' kept Britain in the EU, British democracy would be 'broken'.[37]

In a fraught Commons sitting the next day, Johnson refused to stop calling the back-benchers' anti-no deal law the 'Surrender Act', even as multiple female MPs implored him to tone down his language, citing Labour MP Jo Cox's murder by a far-right activist during the referendum campaign, and their fear that something similar would soon happen again.[38] To others, however, Parliament's attempts to delay Brexit were more likely to spark trouble than Johnson's attempts to charge ahead. In the course of a Twitter exchange the night before the debate, the journalist Tim Shipman suggested that, if Brexit were blocked, it would have a 'galvanising effect' on 'people who feel their vote has been stolen from them by different branches of the establishment.' He asked: 'How can't you see how dangerous this all is?'[39]

For the post-liberals, the problem lay in an establishment resisting a democratic challenge to its power, and its taboos. Maurice Glasman argued that what had happened to Labour since the 2016 referendum was that 'there was a three-year period in which people could have shifted their position, but they couldn't shift their position.' The 'unthinkable thing' was that the referendum had brought a 'break with progressive globalisation and the legal structures that surrounded it.'[40]

Having watched all this unfold from inside Number 10, Danny Kruger argued that the prorogation was justified:

> We had a crisis because Parliament, having been elected to fulfil the referendum result, decided not to do it, and we had a majority of MPs who said they were going to run the country, not the government. In the clash between Parliament and the executive, the executive had to win—we won that battle through legitimate constitutional means. Prorogation is a prerogative power for government and it was the right time to do it. It had the great benefit of frustrating the efforts of Parliament to stop Brexit and take over the government ... The coup was the other way round![41]

Prorogation may have been thwarted, but Downing Street had long suggested that this was not the only card it was prepared to play in order to push Brexit through. Now the government resorted to breaking a different taboo, this time successfully. On 17 October, two days before the back-benchers' legal deadline for securing a deal or delaying Brexit, Prime Minister Johnson announced that he had agreed a new withdrawal agreement with the EU. The no-deal nightmare had evaporated, but at the cost of embracing another unthinkable: a de facto border in the Irish Sea, between Northern Ireland and the rest of the UK, which Johnson had promised not to accept. And then Labour and the Liberal Democrats agreed to pass the law required for a general election, which was duly called for 12 December. Each side had accused the other of trying to thwart democracy, until finally democracy was called on to resolve the situation.

* * *

While the Brexit wars raged all around, Will Tanner's new think-tank Onward had been thinking about consensus. On the face of it, this seemed rather optimistic. As in the 1970s, attempts made in the midst of confrontation to promote compromise, even unity governments, had not proved very successful. But such efforts tended to try and patch up the status quo. Instead, in a report published on 3 October 2019, Onward argued that Brexit had already provoked a sea change in British politics: 'The post-war liberalising consensus has given way to a post-Brexit consensus based on security and belonging.'[42] Only by addressing this, it argued, could we all settle on a new 'common good'. The report was written by Tanner and the Conservative peer and former minister James O'Shaughnessy; it was called *The Politics of Belonging*. This attracted a lot of attention for supposedly identifying a newly crucial species of voter, 'Workington Man', even as this was dismissed in Workington itself as a southern caricature.[43]

O'Shaughnessy was drawing on his own experience of earlier, failed attempts to develop a new common ground. As David Cameron's Director of Policy and Research, he had held to the orthodox belief in market solutions to social policy problems, through reforming the public sector. In the wake of the Big Society's failure, he eventually realised that its vision had been lacking an 'intellectually thorough-going approach' to strengthening social bonds; and that, because 'a lot of economic reform positively whittles away those facets of a society', you have to have a 'positive interventionist agenda'.[44] Working in education, and seeing the effects of poverty and unhappiness even among those in work, had led him to conclude that an economic, measurement-led approach obscured crucial problems. By 2019 this had made him much more doubtful about liberalisation as the cure for all ills, which, he says,

> works for people who have a huge amount of security in their life—whether that's financial, or emotional, or educational. If you don't have a lot of security in your life, you're not looking for more freedom, you're not looking for more exposure, you're looking for more protection. And actually the dominant narrative in politics and the media isn't that—it's always 'more freedom'—and that was badly out of tune with where people are, and you started to see that being expressed obviously through things like the Brexit referendum.

Echoing earlier post-liberal thinking, Tanner and O'Shaughnessy argued that, in the wake of both 1945 and 1979, there had been waves of social liberalisation: first in the Sixties, then in the Nineties. In each case, once the power struggle was over and a new economic consensus established, there was an opening for liberalising reform. Their report contended that this 'opening' had now run its course, and presented opinion research suggesting that, 'by a ratio of 2-to-1, voters want to live in a society that provides greater security not greater freedom'. Like James Frayne in his *Overlooked but Decisive* report four years earlier, they argued that the centre ground was not simply liberal, and that people were ready to see higher state spending and even a drop in growth if it helped reduce the gap between rich and poor. They therefore advocated a 'new and different political agenda than the one currently on offer':

> We call this 'the politics of belonging'. It is ambitious but mainstream and moderate, and is based as much on ideas of security, community and togetherness as ideas of more freedom, autonomy and choice. In the last decade, people overwhelmingly think Britain's hyper-liberalised economy and culture have moved away from their views, not towards them—especially outside London. They believe that society needs to be strengthened and that the animal spirits of the economy should be tamed, not unleashed. If the price of greater freedom is rootlessness and disconnection, voters no longer seem to think it is worth the cost.[45]

The question now was whether they were right about the nature of the struggle for power that had blown up over Brexit—and, if so, whether the election could settle it. Could 2019 be another 1945, another 1979?

* * *

The Conservatives' manifesto had much in common with the ideas Onward outlined. It was co-written by Rachel Wolf, one of those closely involved with the Gove education reforms, who has written about voters' focus on fairness, towns, local infrastructure and a sense of place, drawing on the 'just about managing' research conducted by her husband James Frayne. Having worked with both Dominic Cummings and Nick Timothy, Wolf suggests 'both of them share this basic analysis of the public', and that 'the philosophy and indeed policies that Nick has articulated were definitely a strong thread in the 2019 manifesto'.[46]

At the height of the campaign, Dominic Cummings wrote a much-pored-over blog, which drew attention to a paper called *A Resurgence of the Regions*, authored by a Remain-voting physics professor at the University of Sheffield, Richard Jones. This charted the drop in productivity that had followed the 2008 Crash, particularly outside London and the south-east. Professor Jones, who had taken part in an Industrial Strategy Commission set up under Theresa May, had ideas 'about long-term productivity, science, technology, how to help regions outside the south-east' that, Cummings wrote, 'could really change our economy for the better, making it more productive and fairer'.[47]

Cummings urged Leave supporters not to take the election result for granted, and warned them that another Parliament with no majority, unable to settle Brexit, would mean that 'the nightmare continues'. The Conservatives' election campaign declared that the time for agonising between leaving and remaining, or between Johnson's deal versus different versions of Brexit, was over; the party set out to accrue as much of the Leave vote as possible. By contrast, Labour tried to bridge the divide between its Leave and Remain supporters. Where the party's 2017 manifesto had been social-democratic, its feted creator, Andrew Fisher, had wanted ever since to offer voters something less 'transactional', more 'transformational'.[48] With its confidence massively boosted by its near-triumph last time, Labour offered such high-cost policies as universal free broadband. Corbyn's party set out to move 'beyond the old dichotomy of ownership between private sector and public sector', and develop 'new pluralistic and democratic models of ownership [which] will be vital to moving beyond neoliberalism'.[49] One argument for this was that worker ownership, for example, would boost productivity; workers joining company boards, as mooted then dropped by Theresa May, was also raised.

Corbyn supporters were confident that this was the moment of breakthrough, building on 2017. They felt they could rely on Labour's northern 'red wall' to hold, while they poured activists into places like Chingford, Iain Duncan Smith's constituency in north-east London. However, a major revival of warnings about going back to the 1970s, complete with renewed invocations of the Winter of Discontent, soon followed. The *Financial Times* suggested that Labour 'would seize £300 billion of company shares'.[50] The party had ventured beyond its successful opposition to austerity two years earlier, into a range of spending promises that many voters found implausibly grand. This damaged Labour's appeal, especially in combination with the party's ongoing scandal over anti-semitism, and the perception that Corbyn was not patriotic, particularly after his reluctance to blame Moscow for a 2018 Russian nerve agent attack in Salisbury.

When the results came in on 12 December, it became clear that Labour had lost vital Leave voters in its 'red wall' seats, without gaining sufficient Remainers to compensate. Invocations of the miners' strike, which had long made voting Tory unthinkable in some of these places, seemed to be losing their salience.

Johnson's majority was far bigger than many expected: the 'red wall' proved to be nothing of the kind, as those northern and Midlands seats that May had failed to win in 2017 turned Conservative. Workington was one such constituency. This was not only the Conservatives' first commanding majority since 1987; it was also the first such majority any party had had for a decade, and a mandate for a political programme that owed something at least to the repeated attempts since the Crash to break with old liberal orthodoxies. The Liberal Democrats' promise to revoke Brexit bombed; Labour won fewer seats than at any election since 1935. The night after the results, Maurice Glasman appeared on BBC2's *Newsnight*, mourning that Labour 'has lost its home, its heartlands'. Danny Kruger, newly elected as MP for Devizes, made his maiden speech about love of home. Talk of coups and emergency governments faded with the fear of no deal. There was a way through, once unthinkable to many. Brexit would now easily pass through the Commons.

* * *

The online magazine *Unherd* has often run articles backing the post-liberal agenda. A month after the election, it held a dinner at the Antelope pub in Belgravia, attended by post-liberals who had voted both Leave and Remain, and from both Conservative and Labour ranks. They included Lords O'Shaughnessy and Glasman, and MPs Jon Cruddas and Danny Kruger. There was excited talk that this was the start of something new. One guest, the *New Statesman* Editor-in-Chief Jason Cowley, recalls: 'The evening brought thinkers from left and right together and you sensed something important but inchoate was happening—a bit like those early gatherings of what would become the Thatcherite insurgency.'[51] There was conversation about 'the new consensus, the new politics that was emerging'; about the return of the state's role in the economy, and the role of virtue in politics.[52]

Shortly afterwards, the Onward think-tank asked Kruger and Cruddas to launch a review on 'repairing the social fabric'. Their shared aim, they declared, was to build a new post-liberal 'consensus across politics to strengthen the social fabric that binds our communities, and country, together.' A subsequent report proposed a blueprint of a new post-Brexit settlement, in line with the Conservatives' winning manifesto. Kruger detected

> a consensus among parts of my party and parts of the Labour Party that we need to strengthen local social attachments, have better pride in place, and think about quality of life in local places, rather than thinking only about structural injustice and inequality on the left or growth and globalism on the right.[53]

If a new consensus is really to bed in, it needs the side that has lost the power struggle to let go of its former nightmares—and that depends partly on the victors. Back in Parliament Square, on the evening of 31 January 2020, Leave supporters gathered again, to celebrate 'Brexit Day' as the UK formally left the EU.[54] From the stage, much of the rhetoric gestured towards reuniting the country. The journalist Julia Hartley-Brewer talked about extending the 'hand of friendship', given that 'we're all leavers now'. When the founder of the Wetherspoons pub chain, Tim Martin, declared that 'the people of Europe are our friends and allies', he was cheered.[55]

But the tone was not always so consensual. The libertarian singer Dominic Frisby gleefully performed his song '17 Million Fuck Offs'. Frisby's lyrics ridicule 'Project Fear', and the claims that voting to leave would cause food and medicine shortages and cost half a million jobs; cause riots and collapse the stock market. Frisby delivered a long list of public figures to be booed one by one as the Guilty Men and Women who had made those dire predictions, or switched parties without holding by-elections, or broken manifesto promises, or called for a second referendum. As Frisby told Radio 4 a few months later:

> The frustration built up over the course of Brexit—their trying to derail Brexit. But a lot of what happened as a result of Brexit was not about Brexit itself; it's that the curtain got pulled back and you saw how things really work, and the contempt that leaders—not just political leaders, but leaders across most institutions in the country—have for ordinary people was revealed.[56]

At the end of the night, Nigel Farage acknowledged that Tony Blair and Peter Mandelson had accepted it was all over, and said: 'The only reason we're here tonight is because Westminster became utterly detached from ordinary people ... Those people have beaten the Establishment ... The real winner tonight is democracy—democracy has won tonight.'[57] The following day, the *Telegraph* published a piece called 'The Guilty Men of Remain will never be forgiven'.

The question was whether Johnson's administration would try extending a 'hand of friendship' to reunite the country, on the basis that their huge majority was victory enough to push through their manifesto; or whether they felt they must first drive the 'Guilty Men' out of their liberal powerbases, to prevent them blocking the new government's path. The civil service was one potential target; another was the judiciary. The government's critics still harboured the nightmares of authoritarianism stirred up by the Brexit wars.

All this raised a difficult question for post-liberals, who advocate both breaking up concentrations of power, and boosting the role of independent institutions. Did taking on old concentrations of power simply require establishing a new one? Danny Kruger argued that the task was both to push power down, and at the same time to pull it back to democratic politics, away from unaccountable institutions. Outside of government, Maurice Glasman saw the new administration as trying to shift power back from ideologically liberal, ruling-class institutions to the democratic nation-state, having understood that 'all the assumptions of the previous era—that the future was global, technological, liberal rights-based, multinational—are false'. But his fellow Blue Labour thinker, Adrian Pabst, countered that he wanted to see a government that 'builds up institutions'. It should ensure they 'work properly, and in the name of democracy ... serving not just one interest but the public good'. However, those running the state should eschew a 'revolutionary approach' and what Pabst branded 'populist technocracy':[58] traits he traced back to Dominic Cummings, now installed with sweeping powers in Number 10.

Whichever path he chose—consensus-building, or perpetuating the struggle for power—Johnson could at least spend the evening of 31 January in Downing Street, celebrating getting Brexit done. His political skills had proved well-suited to breaking the taboos required to fight internal opposition. But Britain was about to come under attack from an implacable outside force, which threatened to overwhelm him.

15

LOCKDOWN

2020–22

On the evening of Friday 13 March 2020, Dominic Cummings was in the Prime Minister's study at 10 Downing Street, trying to work out how to cope with Covid-19, the highly infectious coronavirus that had reached Britain at the end of January.

At first, Boris Johnson had resisted calls for draconian restrictions on personal freedom. He insisted that public venues and events should not be shut down, and emphasised that he had been shaking patients' hands on a hospital visit. The government's initial approach was to let the virus move through the population, building 'herd immunity'. This was partly intended to avoid public 'fatigue' at restrictions when the virus' spread was peaking, as well as the threat of a second wave hitting in winter, when the NHS would not be able to cope.

But, amid reports from Italy of hospitals already struggling to deal with a wave of new patients, more and more voices argued for previously unthinkable new controls on public life to stop the virus spreading. Cummings has recounted that, on that Friday night, he suddenly realised that they had 'to ditch the whole official plan', because Britain was 'heading towards the biggest disaster this country has seen since 1940'.[1] On 23 March, just over six months after illegally shutting down Parliament, Boris Johnson's administration locked down the country, with massive public support.

Johnson was in power because Brexit had forced British politics to a break-point, apparently laying the ground for a new consensus based around a new imperative: 'levelling up'. The impact of Covid was strikingly similar to the message Westminster had eventually taken from the referendum. Namely, that there was a large swathe of the population who felt the government was failing to help them, and who wanted to see the state use its huge power and vast financial resources to make their lives feel more secure. And if that had some costs in terms of personal freedoms, so be it.

But this was a crisis of far greater urgency and scale. And this time, Johnson and Cummings were incumbents, not insurgents—on top of which, the Prime Minister was evidently chary about imposing anything as extreme as a 'lockdown'. The virus' terrifying spread created a new choice of nightmares: if the NHS was not to be overwhelmed, taboos long held by both economic and social liberals would have to be broken.

As in 1940, the crisis struck a country already in transition out of an old consensus. The shock of external attack, and the threat of seeing all that we held dear destroyed, now overrode the old nightmares that had constrained the scale of public spending and the size of the state. As government debated what to do, the financial journalist Gillian Tett thought back to the response to the Crash in 2008. She argued that, this time, the state's approach would have to be more generous towards the population, or there would be a populist revolt.[2] On 16 March, as the public was told not to go to pubs, theatres and other venues, over a million people were suddenly laid off. Next day, the former Cameron Treasury minister and ex-Goldman Sachs banker Jim O'Neill called for 'People's QE', after the 'quantitative easing' that had recapitalised the banks following the Crash.[3] Hours later, the new Chancellor of the Exchequer delivered his second Budget in a week.

Rishi Sunak is a free-market fiscal conservative, and another Goldman Sachs alumnus; but his first Budget had announced a return to the kind of government investment in infrastructure not seen for many years, in line with the Conservatives' manifesto. Now, the impending devastation of the economy forced the Treasury to go far beyond that, smashing through the limits of what was thought financially possible. This was not, Sunak said, 'a time for ideology and orthodoxy'. He suddenly sounded like Clement Attlee, telling the nation that 'This struggle will not be overcome by a single package of measures, or isolated interventions. It will be won through a collective national effort. Every one of us doing all we can to protect family, neighbours, friends, jobs'.[4] Johnson declared that 'we must act like any wartime government and do whatever it takes to support our economy.'[5] On 23 March, the government ordered all non-essential shops and venues to close, and instructed the public to stay at home.

Covid pushed economic issues, and the economic aspect of the Brexit vote, back to the fore, after years when 'identity' issues had often dominated. It drew attention to the struggles of those working in hospitals, warehouses and supermarkets, driving delivery vans and bin lorries, of many different backgrounds and ethnicities, whose low-paid, low-status labour was now visibly keeping the country running. These people were exempted from lockdown, and allowed to keep sending their children to school if no one else could take care of them, on the basis that they were now the country's 'key workers'. During the Winter of Discontent, the focus on the unburied dead rather than on the lives of the striking grave-diggers had set a pattern which had lasted for a long time; the pandemic now seemed to be forcing this into reverse. Unemployment, job security and the level of Universal Credit benefit payments became staple news stories.

The disease and the restrictions not only exposed inequality, but sharpened it—from the greater effect among ethnic minorities to the impact on the education of poorer children. The fulfilments of working from home were not obvious to those struggling to hang on to a precarious job from a small flat with rickety broadband, while trying to entertain and educate frustrated children. When Madonna appeared in her rose petal–strewn bath in an online video, rhapsodising that the pandemic had 'made us all equal in many ways', not everyone was persuaded.[6] All this put the old orthodoxies of liberal economics under further, huge pressure.

At the same time, Covid forced another transformation of the role of the state: the authoritarianism of lockdown. Yet this did not strike most social liberals as a nightmare, but as protective necessity. Here too, the impact had something in common with 1940: public willingness to embrace state compulsion was far higher than expected. Even the libertarian Conservative MP Steve Baker sorrowfully accepted the necessity of the measures—though, in a deeply felt Commons speech, he warned that the government was creating a dystopian 'command society', which should be ended as soon as humanly possible.[7] Along with this acceptance of a more activist role for the state, there was a huge surge of willingness to volunteer, with hundreds of thousands giving time to help the NHS, and the appearance of an estimated 4,300 local mutual-aid schemes.[8] This was a level of communal solidarity and reciprocity that post-liberals could scarcely have hoped for.

As in 1940, the sweeping away of old taboos on what the state could do led people to ask if a decade of austerity had left the public unnecessarily exposed. There were accusations about inadequate planning and lack of front-line equipment. On the day of Sunak's emergency Budget, the former health secretary Jeremy Hunt expressed regret at cuts made since 2010, including those to social care. This underlined the turn away from austerity that had already been happening before the pandemic—as embodied in Johnson's election victory, and his promises of a levelled-up post-Brexit Britain.[9]

But Covid cast Boris Johnson in a very different role in the political narrative. On the day that he finally announced lockdown, *The Times* suggested that Johnson risked looking less like his hero, Winston Churchill, and more like Neville Chamberlain: too hemmed in by old nightmares to combat the new one effectively.[10] After an initial surge of public support, the first-wave death toll soared. There were scandals over the commissioning of personal protective equipment, over old people initially being returned from hospitals to care homes without testing, and over the prolonged failure to set up a 'test and trace' system. As the second wave spread in the autumn and winter of 2020, Johnson was reluctant to impose renewed restrictions. On 23 December, the government announced a new 'stay at home' order for parts of England, having previously assured those affected that their Christmas Day gatherings could go ahead.

Public tolerance of all this was dependent on a sense of fairness—one of the values that James Frayne had identified as central to the worldview of the 'just about managing' voters whom Johnson had so successfully won over in 2019. But the pandemic would put that bond under huge pressure too. Dominic Cummings' cross-country journey during the first lockdown fuelled accusations that an out-of-touch elite was letting down the people, and this suspicion did not leave the government when he did. The sense of unfairness at geographical inequality that had animated the 2019 general election sprang up again over the division of the country into three different 'tiers' of Covid restrictions, amid accusations that, once again, London was treating the north of England differently.

The government's standing was transformed by the launch of its Covid vaccination programme in December 2020, in sharp contrast to the EU, whose procurement and roll-out initially faltered. The government was able to hail this as a vindication of Brexit and, in the wake of the vaccine, polling in mid-2021 suggested that voters in 'red wall' seats thought the government was handling the pandemic well. Nonetheless, the transformation wrought by the vaccine roll-out served to underline the same basic shift in British politics: towards an emphasis on fairness, decent treatment for ordinary workers, high levels of government spending and intervention, the return of industrial strategy—and national unity under the watchful eye of a protective, enabling state.

* * *

If all of this suggests the potential for a new post-Brexit, post-Covid consensus, the question remains: can either Labour or the Conservatives emulate the 1945 and 1979 governments, and actually make it happen? To do so, they will each have to address a long-standing nightmare, and embed a clear new narrative of the years since the Crash: one that makes the case for a decisive break from what remains of the pre-Crash model. In this final chapter, let's explore how this has developed so far—and ask whether, this time, there is really much chance that the divisions that have long been tearing British politics apart will settle down any time soon.

For much of the period since 2008, Labour has shunned the kind of appeal to 'red wall' voters advocated by post-liberals, because of its concerns about authoritarian populism and nationalism. For years, these centred on a deep unease about raising the question of immigration. However, since the Brexit referendum, contrary to some dire predictions, public attitudes have become more favourable, with a majority reportedly saying that 'they think the number of immigrants to Britain should remain the same or even be increased'.[11] There may now be space opening up within the party for greater consensus on this subject than there has been in two decades.

In March 2020, in the wake of the party's heavy election defeat, the pollster Deborah Mattinson convened voters representing Labour's two tribes—what she termed 'Red Wallers' and 'Urban Remainers'. This was done in conjunction with a network of activists from across the party called Labour Together, and was designed to look for common ground between the two groups. Mattinson found that Red Wallers wanted to be wooed back to the party; but that, strikingly, the Urban Remainers were now willing to compromise. However, when Labour started prominently deploying flags to symbolise its patriotism, Clive Lewis—an army veteran and one of Labour's leading ethnic-minority MPs—was highly critical. This was 'Fatherland-ism', he suggested: an unnecessary move 'down the track of the nativist right.'[12] James Meadway, former adviser to Corbyn's shadow chancellor John McDonnell, was involved in Labour Together's review of the party's election disaster. He acknowledges the suspicion of many on the left that talking about patriotism is 'going to turn far too easily into just being racist', and sees little benefit in 'just waving some of the symbols around'. However, he argues that there is a way to overcome these concerns: Labour should make patriotism a question of improving the country, by redistributing and devolving power.[13]

At the same time, media commentary on the 'red wall' has shifted, rediscovering the fact that Britain is not so simplistically polarised as was claimed during the Brexit wars. In September 2020, James Frayne contended in the *Telegraph* that the English working class in the Midlands and the north was far more liberal than 'liberal elites' gave them credit for: comfortable with gay marriage and their child marrying someone of a different ethnicity, appalled by the Windrush scandal. These voters' guiding value, he wrote, was 'not nationalism, but an obsession with fairness'.[14] The journalist James Ball, a gay, liberal-left Remainer from Halifax, tweeted: 'This reads right to me, having grown up there.'[15] Others pointed out that a third of ethnic-minority Britons had voted for Brexit. But is there enough in all this for Labour to overcome the nightmares of nationalism and authoritarian populism that have divided it against itself? Can it then win back its lost voters without losing its remaining support, and from there take ownership of a new consensus?

In April 2020, Keir Starmer was elected Labour leader, and set out to achieve this. As Corbyn's shadow Brexit secretary, he had been a prominent 'Urban Remainer', but he swiftly appointed a left-wing post-liberal as his Director of Policy. As the Executive Director of the Joseph Rowntree Foundation, Claire Ainsley had helped to fund Onward's Repairing Our Social Fabric project. In 2018, she had published a book called *The New Working Class*, a group she defined as 'multi-ethnic, comprised of people living off low to middle incomes, and likely to be occupied in service sector jobs like catering, social care or retail'; people who do not necessarily define themselves as an economic class, and are poorly understood by the political parties.[16] Ainsley's list of British values—community, family, fairness, hard work, decency—sounds very like James Frayne's. Her book is subtitled *How to Win Hearts, Minds and Votes*; she had done research work which suggested that many people felt 'let down, ignored and patronised' over Brexit, and has argued that people do not simply vote based on economic self-interest.[17] In the book, she outlines the need for strategists to think more about the need for policies to be part of a story that 'resonates with the voters' social group identification'.[18]

But what is the story Labour wants to tell about who has had power and why it should change hands? And can a party led by graduate professionals, some of whom advocated a second referendum, convincingly tell any such story to sceptical working people? In a speech in February 2021, Starmer hopefully invoked the comparisons between the Covid crisis and the Second World War, saying:

> there's a mood in the air which we don't detect often in Britain.
>
> It was there in 1945, after the sacrifice of war, and it's there again now.
>
> It's the determination that our collective sacrifice must lead to a better future.
>
> …We can go back to the same insecure and unequal economy that's been so cruelly exposed by the virus, or we can seize the

moment, and go forward to a future that's going to look utterly unlike the past.[19]

But James Kirkup of the Social Market Foundation suggested that, while the 1945 government had helped to establish a post-war consensus, its reforms 'began in contention, not consensus'. If Starmer is Attlee, Kirkup asked, 'what are the transformative, mould-breaking changes he wants that his opponents reject?'[20] In other words, Starmer would first have to declare an ideological struggle for power against the Conservatives, just as Attlee had attacked vested interests before laying the ground for a new settlement. Some frustrated voices on the left felt that Starmer's Labour had missed the chance offered by Covid to set up a narrative of what had gone wrong; to cast Conservative ministers as the new Guilty Men, whose outdated economic beliefs, elitism and loyalty to vested interests had led to unnecessary deaths.

Perhaps the closest Labour has come to a viable break-from-the-past narrative is to be found in one of the few places where it did well in the 2021 local elections. In Preston, the leader of the Labour-controlled city council, Matthew Brown, has pioneered the 'Preston Model'. This aims to revive communities hit by inequality, by intervening in the city's economy. The council encourages Preston's institutions to spend their budgets via local businesses, rather than with huge, distant corporations. In 2021, Brown published a book, co-written with Rhian E. Jones, which sets this approach in a narrative of what has gone wrong, and why power needs to change hands. In a bid to reclaim anti-vested interests rhetoric from the Leave campaign, it is called *Paint Your Town Red: How Preston Took Back Control and Your Town Can Too*.

Brown and Jones argue that 'decades of economic stagnation and political neglect have produced a volatile electorate, looking for any way out of the current failed consensus'. They cast the post-war period as having been positive for ordinary people, the 1970s included, and present the post-1979 era as negative, with outsourcing and reliance on corporations a disaster for local government. In their narrative, this culminated in the Crash and austerity, with Brexit as an expression of rage and despair. The referendum vote was, in significant part, 'an economic and anti-establishment protest by an economically neglected and politically disregarded demographic'.

Preston's democratic localism programme is 'a way of taking back control that goes beyond the superficial, and which challenges the idea that "taking back control"—a central slogan of the UK's pro-Brexit campaign—is dependent upon reactionary measures of xenophobia, racism, authoritarianism and centralisation.'[21]

Rather like Claire Ainsley, Brown believes that people's disappointment and distrust, fuelled by inequality, can be acknowledged without being turned against a scapegoated Other. He argues that there is a progressive approach to patriotism that is rooted in local pride; that says 'we want to look after everyone, and everyone can participate in producing the wealth that the nation produces'. To underline this, he draws on the memory of the 1940s:

> we have to appeal to what makes us proud of the country—the progressive ideas we have—but we need a bold programme that backs it up. In the Second World War, most people in the military supported the Labour Party, and quite a socialist vision within the Labour Party: of public ownership of industry, the welfare state, council housing. It was what people in the forces wanted. We have got to get back to that.[22]

From their different positions, Ainsley and Brown are each working to find a narrative that justifies a break from the past and a change in who holds power, without stirring left-wingers' nationalist nightmares. The Editor-in-Chief of the *New Statesman*, Jason Cowley, has argued that one answer to this has been offered by Gareth Southgate's leadership of the England football team. Cowley sees Southgate as a public figure who 'understands the need for a patriotism that is both generous and enhances national cohesion rather than undermining it.'[23]

Before the European Championship in the summer of 2021, amid a row over racism and anti-racism in football, Southgate wrote an essay for *The Players' Tribune* called 'Dear England'. This set out his sense of duty and patriotism, and its roots in his grandfather's service in the Second World War. Collectivity, inclusivity and protectiveness had already become current again, under the pressure of Covid; Southgate's team showed how these could be fused. The inclusivity was there in the players' range of ethnic backgrounds, some from deprivation; in the team captain Harry Kane's Pride armband; and in the anti-racist taking of the knee. The collectivity was there in Marcus Rashford's successful campaign to transform government policy on feeding poor pupils during school holidays. The protectiveness was there in the way Southgate hugged a young player distraught at missing a crucial penalty. Two days before England's appearance in the championship final, the journalist Sunny Hundal retweeted a clip of young fans in Wolverhampton, dancing, smiling and waving big England flags, white and British Asian alike. Hundal suggested that sport was including people in the English flag, as once it had included them in the Union Jack. Sunder Katwala of British Future noted the similarity between articles on the England team's success in *The Guardian* and the *Daily Mail*.

In May 2021, Starmer appointed a new shadow chancellor. Rachel Reeves is a former Bank of England economist on the right of the party. In 2018, she worked with the Blue Labour thinker Jonathan Rutherford developing a policy programme she called *The Everyday Economy*, which hit the familiar notes about security, stagnant wages, the importance of institutions, and the need to democratise ownership and take on technocratic elites, which have entrenched the dominance of the market and state at the expense of society. Reeves had been a Remainer, but stressed the need to reconcile Labour's social liberals and its social conservatives, and acknowledged that many Labour voters had chosen Leave in 'an expression of a deep anger at the way the governing class had ignored them and belittled their concerns about their national culture and identity'.[24] Shortly after her appointment—on the night the England team ignored the booing of Ukrainian fans as they took the knee, then won the quarter-final 4–0—Reeves announced a national version of the Preston Model approach to 'community wealth building'. Wherever possible, a Labour government would procure goods and services from British suppliers. Critics noted that, unlike the Preston Model, this did not extend to ensuring that companies would only be commissioned if they provided decent working conditions.

Then in January 2022, Labour Together published a plan for national reconstruction called *Labour's Covenant*. This was the result of eighteen months' work by a wide range of policy experts, academics and journalists, as written up by Jonathan Rutherford.

The plan advocates combining a state-led approach to economic growth with a shift of power to local institutions, like regional banks and vocational colleges, and the community wealth-building pioneered in Preston. Its aim is 'a consensus-building politics of the future that will resonate with people's everyday lives'.[25] Whether any of this is enough to resolve Labour's nightmares, however, remains to be seen. If the party's social liberals and post-liberals cannot build an internal consensus, they may struggle to make themselves the architects of a national one.

* * *

The Conservatives may have won a landslide in 2019, but they too have struggled to dispel a nightmare blocking the way to a new consensus, with a bigger role for both communities and the state: the free-marketeer's spectre of bloated government, over-spending its way towards economic disaster.

In some respects, the Johnson government appears to have broken from free-market ideology. Backed by an array of new working-class MPs from northern seats, Chancellor Sunak's March 2020 Budget increased gross capital investment in infrastructure to £640 billion over five years. This fitted with the much broader turn away from free-market orthodoxy that has been playing out since 2008. As happened in the 1930s and the 1970s, the economics profession has been rethinking. The economist Diane Coyle detects a 'steady realisation that the economy was not working in the way that the textbook models and the academic discipline had for so long assumed'.[26] Coyle argues that boundary-breaking emergency Covid measures have entrenched a change that first picked up momentum after the financial crisis. Beyond academia, the IMF has called for more to be done about inequality, and the chief of the CBI has castigated the legacy of Thatcherism. The pandemic, environmental concerns, the rise of a more aggressive Chinese state and the Russian invasion of Ukraine have all accelerated a turn away from pre-2008 style globalisation.

But even if a more interventionist state is no longer taboo, the shift still needs to be presented as part of a coherent Conservative narrative. To do this, Johnson has drawn on the analogy he made at the start of the pandemic, invoking the Churchill war ministry. In his 2020 conference speech, he said:

> In the depths of the second world war, when just about everything had gone wrong, the government sketched out a vision of the post-war new Jerusalem that they wanted to build. And that's what we are doing now—in the teeth of this pandemic.

> We're resolving not to go back to 2019, but to do better: to reform our system of government, to renew our infrastructure; to spread opportunity more widely and fairly and to create the conditions for a dynamic recovery that's led not by the state but by free enterprise.[27]

Though he still talks about 'free enterprise', Johnson has also asserted that 'The Treasury has made a catastrophic mistake in the last forty years in thinking you can just hope that the whole of the UK is somehow going to benefit from London and the south-east.'[28] There have been indications that many Conservative MPs have been happy to go along with the party's economic turn left: 'There is a rapidly growing acceptance,' one MP told the *New Statesman* in early 2021, 'that the old Thatcherite certainties just don't exist any more.'[29] Even the once arch-Thatcherite David Davis, while still sceptical about the state, has declared:

> The financial crisis of 2008 persuaded me that the financialisation of western capitalism had gone too far and was materially dysfunctional. They haven't added a great deal of social value, and they've taken a lot of money out of it. And in doing so, they've de-stabilised the economy as well.[30]

The Covid crisis has deepened his rethink, partly through its similarities with the Second World War: 'it collectivised society in those days and something like that's happened now. There's much more perception of collective risk and less of individual position, much more expectation that people will make sacrifices, and less tolerance of them pursuing their own interests despite everybody else.'

The narrative the Conservatives have been presenting is that Brexit was a sharp break with the past. This turn has since been accelerated by Covid, impelling the government to throw aside austerity, and 'build back better'. The successful development in the UK of the Oxford/AstraZeneca vaccine seemed to underline the value of industrial strategy's gradual post-Crash rehabilitation. So did the government's decision to provide a £100 million subsidy which helped to secure a new Nissan giga-factory in Sunderland, producing batteries for electric vehicles. In late 2021, labour shortages blamed on a post-Brexit lack of migrant workers led to the Thatcherite business secretary, Kwasi Kwarteng, suggesting that companies might try offering higher wages.

In September 2021, Michael Gove was appointed to head a revamped housing and communities department, with 'Levelling Up' appended to its title. Since then, he has tried to craft a narrative incorporating both Brexit and Covid. Before his appointment, Gove was already arguing that Covid had 'drawn even sharper attention to some of the inequalities in society, and therefore placed more of an onus on the government to address them.'[31] Then, in his 2021 conference speech and an accompanying interview with *The Sun*, Gove sought to set 'levelling up' within an account of the recent past, casting it as fulfilling the 'spirit of Brexit'—which, along with the 2019 election, was a vote for change from the 'old EU model' implicitly to blame for geographical and class inequality. Communities would be allowed 'to take back control of their own futures'.[32] Similarly, in his own conference speech, Johnson insisted that his government was setting to work dealing with these problems after 'decades of dither'.[33] Some suggested this was continued scapegoating of the EU for problems actually generated at home. Nonetheless, the conservative journalist Tim Stanley has approvingly declared Brexit 'the death-knell of the Thatcher project', in favour of a stronger 'nation-state', in one of many articles that appeared on this theme.[34]

The new ministerial team appointed to the 'Department for Levelling Up' gave it a distinctly post-liberal cast. This included Danny Kruger; the working-class Walsall MP Eddie Hughes; and Neil O'Brien, veteran of the Northern Powerhouse and May's industrial strategy, and co-founder of the Onward think-tank. The department's new permanent secretary was Andy Haldane, former chief economist at the Bank of England, who had served on Theresa May's Industrial Strategy Council, and who had recently given a thoughtful speech to the Local Trust about 'community capitalism', building new institutions and devolving power to 'locally-centred decision-making'.[35] Haldane has also run seminars on 'the economics of the common good' with Blue Labour's Maurice Glasman.

On 2 February 2021, Michael Gove launched the department's much-awaited white paper, *Levelling Up the United Kingdom*. Accompanied by a wide-ranging essay by Haldane, this promised a host of transformations for 'forgotten' parts of the country—to pay and to productivity, to broadband and public transport, literacy and skills training, town centres and housing quality—to be achieved in part through devolution of power from Whitehall. One of the more concrete plans Gove announced was a rise of at least 40 per cent in research and development investment spending outside London and south-east England. Critics gave the white paper some credit for at least acknowledging what had to change, and for setting out a possible basis to surpass previous attempts at such changes, which had petered out. But amid stories that the Treasury had blocked the Gove team's more radical ideas, particularly on the revival of manufacturing, many doubted how much money and power the plans could command. In the Commons, the shadow levelling up secretary Lisa Nandy contended that talk of local autonomy had not overcome the centralising forces of orthodoxy: 'we have the arrogance of a Chancellor sitting in Whitehall, drawing lines on a map, choosing which of us have earned the right to have some say on the decisions that affect not their lives, but our lives, our families and our communities.'[36] As Jessica Studdert of the New Local think-tank put it:

> Levelling up was the promise on which the last election was won, and so it will be a key issue over which the next will be fought. There is certainly still space for the main political parties to up the ante and outdo each other on who will best level up into the 2020s.[37]

If this interventionist 'new normal' is realised, it would be the direct opposite of what many Brexiteers campaigned for over decades. In December 2020, one former Conservative minister, George Bridges, complained that the 'lean state' he and others had been expecting after Brexit was nowhere to be seen. Instead, he wrote, 'a new consensus between left and right is emerging', centred round much higher spending.[38] Lord Frost would later resign as a minister and chief negotiator with the EU, citing similar objections. Leave campaigners had hoped to achieve a seismic break with the past— but not in favour of a larger state.

But then, when Churchill spent the 1930s pushing for a bigger state to fight Hitler, he did not intend to lay the ground for the decades of government interventionism that followed. Nor did Tony Benn, as he fought the compromises of the post-war consensus, intend to lay the ground for Thatcherism.

* * *

So there are routes to a new consensus, based on trying to end the nightmare articulated through the Brexit vote—of once-proud towns too long neglected, left to stagnate and grow quietly resentful. But many on the right strongly resist the idea of a more interventionist, 'protective' state, remaining focused instead on the nightmares that have shaped the last few decades: bloated government, inflation, onerous taxation. In July 2020, the former Conservative Cabinet minister David Gauke wrote sadly that, as a 'small state free marketeer' and 'one nation social liberal', he had reached the conclusion that the party had abandoned those positions.[39] Since then, the Treasury has run up colossal debts to pay for emergency Covid measures. We have seen tax rises, and the return of the cost of living as a prominent political issue.

All this has combined with growing concern about the impact of pandemic restrictions on business and personal liberty—Steve Baker's 'command society'—to create a fresh version of that familiar nightmare: the big, intrusive, over-spending state, dragging the country towards economic calamity.

In December 2021, in the face of the Omicron variant, a Conservative back-bench rebellion meant that the government had to rely on Labour support to introduce 'Plan B' Covid restrictions, suggesting the outline of a consensus that cut across party boundaries. In September, the Editor of *The Sunday Telegraph*, Allister Heath, had written a piece denouncing the government as 'no longer Thatcherite or even conservative: it is Blue Labour'.[40] Sunak had already hiked corporation tax by £45 billion to help pay for the pandemic, and national insurance to help pay for social care. In his autumn statement, he used better-than-expected growth forecasts to boost spending across government, reversing his predecessors' cuts and announcing the first grants from the new Levelling Up Fund. To Heath, all this was a 'nightmare' that risked catastrophe.[41]

Yet even as he concluded his speech, Sunak himself seemed to lament what he had just had to do, stressing the folly of over-reliance on government, and hoping to cut taxes as soon as possible. These nightmares, and the free-market ideology they underpin, remain strongly held among many of the most senior Conservatives. Memories of the 1970s may be fading, but the imagery survives: witness the former chancellor Philip Hammond warning that government subsidies to industry risked 'a fast track back to the misery of the 1970s', or the often-made observation that tax rises are 'pushing the overall tax burden to 1970s levels'.[42] In the midst of the pandemic, Sunak had affirmed that balancing the books was a 'sacred duty'.[43] His predecessor, Sajid Javid, admires the work of American libertarian novelist Ayn Rand. As business secretary, Kwasi Kwarteng abolished May's Industrial Strategy Council, even as the government published a Plan for Growth. As international trade secretary, Liz Truss championed 'Global Britain' trade deals, rather than the return of a more nationally focused economy. Kwarteng, Truss and two other co-authors of the neo-Thatcherite manifesto *Britannia Unchained* were all promoted to high office under Johnson.

At the time of writing, all this is in flux, particularly in the wake of revelations that parties were held at 10 Downing Street in May 2020, winter 2020 and April 2021, when ministers had instructed the public that social gatherings were restricted under anti-Covid regulations. As furious members of the public took to social media to recount how they had obeyed the rules, sometimes at great personal cost, polling suggested this had severely damaged Johnson's appeal among 2019-vintage Conservative voters, even before he was fined. As the political scientist Robert Ford observed in January 2022:

> Such voters have long felt disaffected from, and distrustful of, a
> political class they felt ignored their concerns and lived by its own

rules. The resentments once mobilised against the EU by the promise to 'take back control' now have a new target—an out-of-touch Downing Street team who partied while the Queen mourned.[44]

We will see whether the Partygate scandal becomes a spur to rebuild bonds with 'red wall' voters, or instead leads to Johnson's replacement by a new Conservative leader keen to turn the party back to free-market orthodoxy.

* * *

Just as nightmares of a big state trouble economic liberals, so many left-leaning social liberals find talk of patriotism and nation, of 'security' and 'belonging', deeply unsettling. They still see much to fear in the way Britain has turned since 2016. These nightmares too may make it difficult to reach a new consensus. The playwright David Edgar, who has been writing about authoritarian tendencies in British politics since the 1970s, is one of many who detect this in a long list of current issues. Edgar sees this at work in the 'anti-woke culture war baiting of the left', and in legislation to strengthen police powers to close down demonstrations, which he argues is driven by the popularity of such moves in red wall constituencies. He suggests that 'you can see the beginning of American-style infringements of the democratic process itself', citing the proroguing of Parliament, the weakening of judicial review, the government taking over the Electoral Commission, and the proposal to require voter ID, which 'will tend to reduce the anti-Conservative vote'.[45]

Likewise, Labour's Mary Creagh argues that the government's move to review EU laws incorporated into British legislation 'will be used for a massive dismantling of...rights and freedoms' which could expose consumers, victims of crime and minority groups to 'grossly unfair treatment'.[46] Other critics cite the proposal to replace the Human Rights Act with a Bill of Rights; the Nationality and Borders Bill, which includes powers to remove a person's citizenship without telling them; and the plans to send some asylum seekers to Rwanda. David Gauke, a former Conservative justice secretary, was one of the twenty-one MPs who had the whip suspended at the height of the party's civil war over Brexit, and went on to run as an independent. He has criticised his former party not only for its big-state economic turn, but for becoming authoritarian and nationalist.

Driving at least some of this is a dispute about how power should be distributed—the same basic dispute that animated the conflicts over Brexit. This is a battle between the fear of authoritarian, nationalist populism on one side, and of anti-democratic elitism on the other. The government defends their reforms on the basis that they are reasserting democratic control over an abstract system of rights imported from Europe, which has been much exploited by lawyers, regardless of the views of voters. Ministers argue these changes are necessary to achieve the security against crime and terrorism that voters have long demanded.

The underlying argument over 'authoritarianism' here is a disagreement about whether a public desire for greater security and authority should be absorbed into the mainstream, at the risk of appeasing extreme ideas—or whether it should be driven out of mainstream politics, at the risk of bolstering extremism that way.

The Onward think-tank's opinion research for its report *The Politics of Belonging* found an alarming willingness to move away from democracy altogether. This was especially prevalent, their findings suggested, among their younger respondents (under-35s), 35 per cent of whom 'believe the army would be a good way to run the country'; almost two-thirds said they would back 'a strong leader who "does not have to bother with Parliament"'.[47] The report's authors, Will Tanner and James O'Shaughnessy, argue that this is a long-run trend towards a much greater desire for security and government-led control in society, which broadly aligns with people's rising support for higher government spending. They present their argument for a greater emphasis on security rather than freedom as a way to neutralise the attractions of populist extremism, by re-connecting politicians with what voters want.

However, rather than pursuing culture wars over flags, statues and identity politics, Tanner and O'Shaughnessy suggest the way to coax people back from the temptations of authoritarian populism lies more in addressing 'the fraying social fabric, poor local transport, underfunded [further education] colleges and the dying high street' and 'building up the institutions that give meaning and strength to people in their lives—families, communities and small businesses'.[48] There are those in both parties who now see a potential consensus, built on combatting nightmares of inequality and insecurity. The question is whether either party can overcome the other fears swirling through British politics.

* * *

Economic liberals' Covid-tinged nightmares of a huge bureaucratic state, spending the country into disaster, may come to dominate politics once more. So may social liberals' Brexit-tinged nightmares of nationalist authoritarianism. Or there may never be a lasting consensus in British politics again. If so, we may see one of those nightmares come to fruition. Society may never find ways to stabilise the impact of social media on elections. If Brexit, in which such hopes have been invested, is widely felt to have failed its supporters, some fear the recriminations could trigger a frightening lurch back into populism and division. Over everything looms the gathering nightmare of climate emergency. There is no guarantee that democracy will last forever.

However, it is possible that we are nearing the end of a long, democratic process that has run since 2008, when the Crash kicked off the death of the old consensus. The question then is whether the Conservatives' stunning election victory in December 2019, followed by the pandemic, will turn out to have been the beginning of a new consensus, in the manner of Attlee's triumph in 1945, and Thatcher's in 1979. Instead, the 2019 Conservative government may prove to be yet another transitional stage: something more like the governments of Neville Chamberlain or James Callaghan, caught between attempts to modernise, and the taboos of tenacious older faiths. If so, will it be Labour that proves willing and able to complete the transition to a new settlement, and dominate any new consensus? Whoever leads the two main parties into the next election, the answer may depend on which party can come to terms with its nightmares first.

Perhaps the astonishing images of national resistance emerging from Ukraine may ease the left's doubts that patriotism, belonging and security can be progressive, pro-democratic ideas. In the wake of the Russian invasion, the willingness of some British politicians, bankers and City lawyers to take Russian oligarchs' money was suddenly cast as unacceptable, through its association with dictatorial violence. Politically, much of this carries echoes of 1940, and the left-wing nationalist fury of Orwell, Wintringham, Cassandra and Foot—and of how that fury helped to override old fears, and pave the way to a new consensus.

Meanwhile, perhaps the sudden return of the cost of living as a dominant political issue may change the right's wariness of interventionist government. The resurgence of inflation has brought yet more anxiety about how we may be 'going back to the 1970s'; in early February 2022, the Governor of the Bank of England urged workers not to push for big pay rises. But whereas, by 1979, the dominant nightmare was the power of the trade unions, forcing employers to hike their wages, the contrast with 2022 is striking. Today, the vast majority of private-sector workers are not in trade unions, and ever since the Crash, pay has been largely stagnant. The nightmare now is not of domineering pickets, but of parents having to choose between heating and eating. In the wake of Chancellor Sunak's 2022 spring statement on 23 March, some Conservative MPs were among those criticising his emphasis on higher taxation rather than higher borrowing, and his decision not to raise Universal Credit immediately in line with inflation. The following day, the pro-Johnson *Daily Express* put the plight of the 'forgotten millions' on its front page. A week earlier, the outrage across the political spectrum at the abrupt sacking of P&O Ferries workers, in apparent breach of the law on consulting trade unions, seemed to mark a similar change of mood.

If we do see a new consensus take shape, history suggests that it will be because enough of us have finally settled on a new nightmare that we agree we must ward off. And perhaps this will be neither Brexit Britain—the authoritarian-nationalist fortress—nor the bloated, over-spending state, but something less immediately frightening: depressing, hollowed-out town centres and a loss of community and pride; precarious or unrewarding work and vulnerability to disease; a feeling of being left out, and laughed at.

We may look back at the period following the 2008 Crash and see that, amid all the shock and crisis and fighting, this quieter, more ordinary, but more widely felt nightmare was struggling to make itself heard over its deafening competitors. Rather as, in the 1970s, it was all too easy for some in power to shrug off the despair induced by strikes or inflation. And, in the 1930s, it was all too easy for a dominant establishment to shrug off the despair of the unemployed. In the end, the nightmare that forms the basis of any new consensus seems more likely to be something many people have recently experienced, to which enough voters vow never to return, rather than anything merely remembered or imagined, however intensely.

Nightmares are endemic to democracy—but when they do not come true, they are easily forgotten; and next time, when they flood back, they seem terrifyingly unprecedented. Remembering the history of our old fears offers a path between panic and complacency: the kind of sceptical alertness we apply to the rest of life. Eternal vigilance is the price of liberty; but meanwhile, these periods of agony do offer one consolation.

Democracy means that any unthinkable new idea has to go through a long trial before it can be sufficiently established for a government to win power and act on it. The dispelling of an old nightmare, the destruction of an old taboo, takes a lot of back-and-forth wrangling between the established orthodoxy and the new contender. While that is happening, things look bleak, and frightening. It provokes an array of new nightmares. People decry British politics, with good reason, as a humiliating, frightening mess. But in the 1930s and 1940s, and in the 1970s and 1980s, the democratic process was able to contain these struggles for power, turning Britain significantly to the left, and then to the right, in ways that had only recently seemed unthinkable. In each case, the new consensus arrived through a series of jarring changes, but not as horrifically as the nightmares had suggested. It may not have felt like it at the time, but the death of consensus was not the death of democracy. It was democracy doing its job.

ACKNOWLEDGEMENTS

Part One of this book is shadowed by nightmares about debt. So I should try to enumerate mine.

First and foremost, I'm grateful to everyone mentioned in the source notes who generously shared their insights and memories in interviews for this book. Part Three would have been a thin business without their contributions.

Conversations with many people have helped me develop my thoughts on the themes explored here. Alongside that, I appreciate the generosity of everyone who has advised me on research questions and sources. Thanks to David Aaronovitch, Jon Alexander, Alan Allport, Matthew Bailey, Tim Boon, Georgina Brewis, Anthony Broxton, the Society of All British and Irish Road Enthusiasts, Aditya Chakrabortty, Peter Clarke, Jason Cowley, Richard Davies, David Davis, David Edgar, Steve Fielding, the Northern Mine Research Society, Maurice Glasman, Tristram Hunt, Gavin Kelly, Harry Lambert, Dorian Lynskey, Anne McElvoy, Kieran Murphy, Philip Murphy, James Noyes, Adrian Pabst, Steve Richards, Dominic Sandbrook, Sabine Schereck, Adam Smith, Peter Snowdon, DJ Taylor, Richard Toye, James Undy, James Vaughan and all who have responded to a request for help, advice or memory-dredging on Twitter. Alan Allport, Matthew Bailey, Steve Fielding and Helen Lewis read the draft in whole or in part, and offered invaluable advice, as well as much-needed encouragement. Needless to say, any mistakes are mine alone.

The thesis set out in this book started to come together in 2004, in the corners of my life not taken up with making programmes for BBC Radio; but in the last few years it has finally found its way on air. For that I have the Controller of Radio 4, Mohit Bakaya, to thank. As a Commissioning Editor, Mohit gave me the chance to explore some of these ideas, as both producer and presenter, in a

ACKNOWLEDGEMENTS

2017 edition of *Archive on 4* called 'The Thirty Year Itch'. I'm hugely grateful to him, and to his successors, Richard Knight and Daniel Clarke, for commissioning further explorations of this theme: a documentary called *Guilty Men*, and two more editions of *Archive on 4*, 'The End of the Thirty Year Itch' and 'Millions Like Us'. Making two earlier editions of the strand—'Coups and Coalitions: The Two Elections of 1974', presented by Steve Richards, and 'The Power of Political Forgetting', presented by David Aaronovitch—bolstered my enthusiasm for exploring these themes as they became topical for the first time in decades. I'm grateful to everyone who contributed to all those documentaries, and others. I could not have written this book without the lasting forbearance and support of my Editor in the BBC Radio Documentaries Unit, Philip Sellars. I'm also indebted to three of my BBC colleagues in particular—Georgia Catt, Gordon Corera and Kavita Puri—for much encouragement and sound advice.

The staff at the libraries and archives I was able to visit, before and after the worst of the pandemic, were unfailingly helpful: at the People's History Museum, the Bodleian Libraries, the UK National Archives, the British Library, the Theatre Museum and the Hull History Centre. During lockdown, other archivists kindly sent me material—from the JB Priestley Library at the University of Bradford (from their holdings of Frank Betts' *Bradford Pioneer*), the Universities of Cardiff, Keele and East Anglia, and the Hoover Institution at Stanford University. I'm much obliged to all who, in response to a Twitter plea, alerted me to Kensington Central Library's perseverance in lending out their excellent stock of biographies in the midst of a plague. And it's important no one takes for granted the labours that have built the kind of astonishingly rich, free-to-use online resources that made research and writing possible even in 2020: particularly the Internet Archive and the Margaret Thatcher Foundation.

Heartfelt thanks to my agent Andrew Gordon for guiding me from would-be author to actual author, to Tom Bromley for introducing us, and to Michael Dwyer at Hurst for giving me the chance I had sought for a long time. Many thanks too to Mei Jayne Yew for compiling the source list, to Daisy Leitch for directing production and to Emily Cary-Elwes for masterminding publicity. And most of all, thanks to this book's insightful, patient editor, Lara Weisweiller-Wu. Should you drop this book on your foot, you will have Lara to thank for it not hurting nearly as much as it would have done.

Like many people who've engaged in the gargantuan selfishness of writing a book, I owe most to my family. Sam Dowson buoyed me up even when I was far too immersed in this for anyone's good. Not only that: before this book reached the editing stage, she gave me the single most brutally effective note I had ever received. I can never thank her enough. Our children have been similarly kind and helpful. Amy advised me to show what I was trying to get across, rather than just spelling it out. Polly put her hand on my arm and told me to take a day off. My brothers, Robert and David, have proved themselves younger but wiser, as ever. And my cousin Giles Bridge not only pointed me to *If Hitler Comes*, but let me keep his copy.

My biggest debt of all, however, is to my parents, Ed and Sue: two children of the 1940s, who brought me up through the 1970s and 1980s, and taught me to value the Britain I was too young to know, as they watched it disappear. Now, as the ground is shifting again, this book is for them.

NOTES

INTRODUCTION: CONSENSUS AND NIGHTMARE

1. See e.g. Fielding, 'What Did "The People" Want?', 632; R. Eatwell, *The 1945–51 Labour Governments* (London: Batsford, 1979), 44; Williamson, 'Baldwin's Reputation', 145.
2. The Representation of the People Act tripled the size of the electorate, by giving the vote to 5.2 million working-class men, and to women over 30 if they owned property or were married to a man who did. All women over 21 won the vote in 1928, regardless of property qualifications.

1. STARVATION AND RUIN: 1931

1. *The News*, 'Harold Wilson and Frank Peace Were In the Scouts Together', 2 January 1965; Lockwood, *Colne Valley Folk*.
2. L. Smith, *Harold Wilson*, 50.
3. MS Wilson c.1613 (Herbert Wilson's press cuttings, 1946–1971), Herbert Wilson interview with the *Sunday Mirror*, 1965.
4. P. Snowden, 'Foreword', in Lockwood, 5.
5. Quoted in Laybourn, *Philip Snowden*, 165–6.
6. A. Gregory, *The Silence of Memory* (London: Bloomsbury, 2014), 59.
7. Burleigh, *The Third Reich*, 56.
8. Baldwin, *On England, and Other Addresses*, 40, 59, 66.
9. P. Snowden, *Wages and Prices* (London: Faith Press, 1920), 113.
10. Quoted in W. Citrine's unpublished diary, cited in R. Taylor, 'The revolution that never was', *New Statesman*, 11 Sept. 2006.
11. HC Deb 6 May 1926, vol 195, col 588.
12. Quoted in Skidelsky, *Politicians and the Slump*, 59.
13. MS Wilson c.1613.
14. MS Wilson c.1613.
15. Smith, *Harold Wilson*, 59.
16. Quoted in Pimlott, *Harold Wilson*, 35.
17. HC Deb 11 February 1931, vol 248 cols 447–8.
18. Snowden, *An Autobiography Vol. 2*, 892, 898.

19. D. Bradshaw ed., *The Hidden Huxley* (London: Faber, 1995), 91.
20. Ibid., 60.
21. Ibid., 66–8.
22. Quoted in *The Independent*, 23 Jan. 1994.
23. A. Huxley, 'On the Charms of History', in *Music at Night and Other Essays* (London: Chatto & Windus, 1949), 151.
24. A. Huxley, *Brave New World* (London: Flamingo, 1994), 43, 81, 133.
25. *The Clarion*, 1 Mar. 1932, 15.
26. HC Deb 28 April 1931, vol 251 col 1525.
27. HC Deb 12 February 1931, vol 248 col 691.
28. Quoted in S. Dorril, *Blackshirt* (London: Viking, 2006), 164.
29. Quoted in Clarke, *Keynes*, 67.
30. Quoted in ibid., 109.
31. Quoted in Marquand, *Ramsay MacDonald*, 608.
32. Ibid., 610.
33. Quoted in ibid., 613.
34. CAB 23 (War Cabinet and Cabinet papers, Minutes, 1916–1939) 67/16.
35. Citrine, *Men and Work*, 281.
36. Ibid., 285.
37. Quoted in Laybourn, *Philip Snowden*, 135.
38. CAB 23/67/19.
39. CAB 23/67/21.
40. M. Cole (ed.), *Beatrice Webb's Diaries 1924–1932* (London: Longmans, 1936), 283.
41. HC Deb 10 September 1931 vol 256, cols 321–44.
42. Quoted in Skidelsky, *Keynes Vol. 2*, 396.
43. Snowden, *An Autobiography Vol. 2*, 961.
44. Leith-Ross, *Money Talks*, 142.
45. Sidney Webb, quoted in H. Dalton, *Call Back Yesterday* (London: Muller, 1953), 298. Emphasis in original.
46. HC Deb 21 September 1931, vol 256 col 1299.
47. *New Statesman*, 26 Sept. 1931.
48. H. Clay, *Lord Norman* (London: Macmillan, 1957), 398; Grigg, *Prejudice and Judgment*, 260; Leith-Ross, 139.
49. Foot, *Aneurin Bevan*, 145.
50. Castle, *Fighting All the Way*, 2.
51. *Bradford Pioneer*, 16 Oct. 1931.
52. Ibid.
53. *Bradford Pioneer*, 9 Oct. 1931.
54. Quoted in Snowden, *An Autobiography Vol. 2*, 1062.
55. Ibid., 1063.
56. *New Statesman*, 24 Oct.1931.

57. *Daily Mail*, 20 Oct. 1931.
58. MS Castle 50 (Letters to her parents, Frank Betts and Annie Betts, Nov. 1929–May 1948; Mar. 1968; Oct. 1974).
59. Snowden, *An Autobiography Vol. 2*, 997.

2. WE HAVE BEEN WARNED: 1932–5

1. Castle, *Fighting All the Way*, 65.
2. Interview with Michael Foot conducted by P. Clarke, 15 Mar. 1999, for his *The Cripps Version*. I'm grateful to Professor Clarke for sharing his notes.
3. Brivati, *The Uncollected Foot*, 264.
4. Labour Party, *Labour Party Conference Annual Report* (1932), 188–92.
5. *Daily Mirror*, 27 Oct. 1932.
6. Cripps et al, *The Problems of a Socialist Government*, 38, 42–6.
7. UK National Archives, KV2/668 (The Security Service: Personal PF Series Files, Richard Stafford Cripps).
8. Griffiths, *Fellow-Travellers of the Right*, 27.
9. *Observer*, 19 Feb. 1933.
10. The Socialist League, *Forward to Socialism* (1934), 200. One young left-wing schoolmaster told BBC radio listeners that the real threat came from 'big newspapers in alliance with big business'; this plus 'a new special constabulary' was Britain's version of fascism. 'Mosley,' he added, 'is only a decoy.' Quoted in *Manchester Guardian*, 28 Feb. 1934.
11. *The Times*, 8 May 1933.
12. The character Rupert Catskill in *Men Like Gods*; Brimstone Burchell in *The Autocracy of Mr Parham*.
13. Dalton, *The Fateful Years*, 40.
14. *Manchester Guardian*, 6 June 1933.
15. Labour Party, *Labour Party Conference Annual Report* (1933), 134, 163.
16. Dalton, *The Fateful Years*, 40–2.
17. KV2/668.
18. Labour Party, *Annual Report*, 219.
19. Ibid., 162.
20. *The New York Times*, 1 Dec. 1933.
21. *The Stage*, 15 Mar. 1934.
22. S. Cripps, *The Struggle for Peace* (London: Gollancz, 1936), 40–1.
23. Castle, *Fighting All the Way*, 67.
24. Ibid., 68; MS Castle 54, 55 (both Correspondence with William Mellor, Nov. 1933–May 1942).
25. MS Castle 54, Mellor to Betts, 8 Mar. 1934; MS55, 7 Apr. 1934.
26. Allport, *Britain at Bay*, 38.

27. Clarke, *Hope and Glory*, 177.
28. Quoted in R. Self, *Neville Chamberlain* (Abingdon: Routledge, 2017).
29. Blythe, *The Age of Illusion*, 179.
30. *Western Daily Press*, 7 Feb. 1935.
31. *Manchester Guardian*, 29 Jan. 1935.
32. A. Booth, 'Britain in the 1930s?: A Managed Economy?', *Economic History Review*, 40/4 (1987), 505.
33. Todman, *Britain's War*, 43.
34. HC Deb 16 May 1934, vol 289 col 1832.
35. MS Castle 54, Mellor to Betts, 2, 27, 28 Feb. 1934.
36. Ibid.
37. S. Cripps et al, *Problems of the Socialist Transition* (London: Gollancz, 1934), 199–200, 204.
38. MS Castle 54, Mellor to Betts, 27 Feb. 1934.
39. Quoted in Pimlott, *Labour and the Left*, 50.
40. *The Times*, 8 Jan. 1934.
41. R. Postgate, *How to Make a Revolution* (London: L & V Woolf, 1934), 189.
42. Foot, *Aneurin Bevan*, 168–9.
43. Castle, 73.
44. *The Socialist Leaguer*, Oct–Nov 1934 (MS Castle 617).
45. Quoted in J. Bew, *Citizen Clem* (London: Riverrun, 2017), 188.
46. H. Dalton, *Practical Socialism for Britain* (London: Routledge, 1935), 15.
47. *Labour Party Conference Annual Report 1934*, 221.
48. *Tatler*, 20 Feb. 1935.
49. HC Deb 4 March 1935, vol 298 col 1665.
50. *Manchester Guardian*, 18 Jan. 1935.
51. Quoted in Beers, *Red Ellen*, 341.
52. Quoted in Jones, *Michael Foot*, 36.
53. *The Yorkshire Post*, 8 Sept. 2009.
54. Priestley, *English Journey*, 239.
55. People's History Museum, Box, Labour Party Archives, 329.8, *Fascists at Olympia* (London: Gollancz, 1934), 12–3.
56. *Yorkshire Post and Leeds Intelligencer*, 5 Feb. 1936, 6.
57. Foot, 170–1.
58. Quoted in Jones, 43.
59. Quoted in S. Smith ed., 'Introduction' to S. Jameson, *In the Second Year* (Nottingham: Trent, 2004), xix.

3. GAS PARALYSES: 1936–40

1. C. Mayhew, *Time to Explain* (London: Hutchinson, 1987), 20.

2. *Isis*, 20 May 1937.

3. Gillett, *Abolishing War*, 73.

4. Quoted in G. Brewis, *A Social History of Student Volunteering* (New York: Palgrave Macmillan), 102.

5. Ibid., 97.

6. Denham & Garnett, *Keith Joseph*, 31–32; Halcrow, *Keith Joseph* 5; Stacey & St Oswald eds, *Here Come the Tories*, 77.

7. HC Deb 6 February 1959, vol 599 col 782.

8. Stacey & St Oswald eds, *Here Come the Tories*, 77.

9. HC Deb 6 February 1959, vol 599 col 782.

10. *Manchester Guardian*, 9 Oct. 1936.

11. HC Deb 11 November 1936, vol 317 col 983.

12. HC Deb 17 November 1936, vol 317 cols 1652, 1659.

13. *Manchester Guardian*, 27 Nov. 1936.

14. Quoted in BBC Radio 4, 'The Thirty Year Itch', *Archive on 4*, 1 July 2017.

15. R. Thorpe, *Supermac* (London: Pimlico, 2011), 115.

16. H. Macmillan, *The Middle Way* (London: Macmillan, 1938), 8.

17. Ibid., 14, 225, 260, 299.

18. Heath, *The Course of My Life*, 18.

19. *Western Mail*, 19 November 1936.

20. *Isis*, 10 Nov. 1937.

21. Heath, 48.

22. *Isis*, 10 Nov. 1937.

23. Heath, 33, 48, 50.

24. Quoted in Skidelsky, *Keynes Volume 2*, 574.

25. Heath, 33.

26. *Daily Mail*, 15 Feb. 1963.

27. P. Rotha & R. Calder, *People of Britain* (Freenat Films, 1936), on *Land of Promise: The British Documentary Movement 1931–1950* (BFI DVD, 2013).

28. Quoted in FI Clarke, *Voices Prophesying War: 1763–3749* (Oxford: OUP, 1992), 159.

29. Overy, *The Morbid Age*, 316.

30. Nicolson ed., *Harold Nicolson's Diaries* (entry for 11 Mar. 1936); Jones, *Diary with Letters* (entry for 25 Sept. 1938); Rhodes, *Chips* (entry for 2 Sept. 1939); Gibbs, *Ordeal in England*, 113.

31. S. Cripps, *The Struggle for Peace* (London: Gollancz, 1936), 101–2.

32. *The Tribune*, 13 Aug., 19 Nov., 17 Dec., 23 Dec. 1937; 11 Mar. 1938.

33. MS Castle 550 (Speeches and lectures, 1937–48).

34. *Manchester Guardian*, 16 Nov. 1936.

35. Labour Party, *Labour Conference Annual Report 1936*, 205.

36. This was Reg Groves: see DJ Taylor, *Orwell: The Life* (London: Vintage, 2004), 152; and MS Castle 221 (Early political papers, June 1936–Sept. 1944), correspondence and papers concerning the Socialist League, June 1936–Apr. 1937.
37. Orwell, 'Spilling the Spanish Beans'.
38. G. Orwell, *Coming Up for Air* (London: Penguin, 1990), 238.
39. N. Chamberlain, *The Struggle for Peace* (London: Hutchinson, 1939), 67.
40. M. Harrison, 'Resource mobilization for World War II', *Economic History Review*, 41/2 (1988), 174.
41. Letter from Sir James Morton (founder of Sundour Fabrics), quoted in Jones (entry for 14 June 1936), 221.
42. Maiolo, *Cry Havoc*, 210.
43. CAB 55 (Committee of Imperial Defence: Joint Planning Committee: Minutes and Memoranda), 8/6 (Memoranda JP 155, 26 Oct. 1936).
44. HC Deb 20 July 1936, vol 315 col 115.
45. HC Deb 12 November 1936, vol 317 cols 1107, 1112, 1147–9.
46. HC Deb 17 November 1936, vol 317 col 1608.
47. Heath, 29.
48. Heath, *Travels*, 29.
49. M. Domarus ed., *Hitler Speeches and Proclamations 1932–45* (London: IB Tauris, 1990–2), 923.
50. Toye, 'The Labour Party and the Politics of Rearmament, 1935–1939', 307.
51. *Labour Conference*, 183–4.
52. Ibid., 206.
53. Castle, *Fighting All the Way*, 80.
54. Toye, 29.
55. CAB 24 (War Cabinet and Cabinet: Memoranda), 273/41 (TWH Inskip, *Defence Expenditure in Future Years*, 15 Dec. 1937).
56. CAB 23 (Cabinet Conclusions 1937 to 1939), 93 (6 Apr. 1938).
57. Jones, entry for 20 Mar. 1938.
58. N. Chamberlain, *The Struggle for Peace*, 238, 276.
59. CAB 23/95/6 (24 Sept. 1938).
60. Rhodes (entry for 14 Sept. 1938).
61. Quoted in Overy, *The Morbid Age*, 347.
62. Quoted in Crowcroft, *The End Is Nigh*, 139.
63. *Isis*, 17 Nov. 1938.
64. The abstainers included Wolmer, Macmillan and Sandys. (Nicolson ed., entry for 6 Oct. 1938.)
65. Heath, 31.
66. *Manchester Guardian*, 19 Oct. 1938.
67. Quoted in Lewis, *Lord Hailsham*, 56.

68. Heath, 60.
69. *The Times*, 26 Oct. 1938.
70. Heath, 61.
71. Quoted in Peden, *British Rearmament and the Treasury*, 96.
72. Nicolson ed., 398.
73. Rhodes, 194.
74. HC Deb 1 May 1939, vol 346, cols 1518–19.
75. Toye, 323.
76. *The Times*, 29 May 1939, quoted in M. Cowling, *The Impact of Hitler* (Cambridge: CUP, 1975).
77. *The Tribune*, 19 Feb. 1937.
78. Maiolo, 276.
79. Peden, 67.
80. Parker, *Chamberlain and Appeasement*, 285.
81. Peden, 103.
82. Heath, *Travels*, 55.
83. Heath, 71.
84. Wilson, *Beveridge Memorial Lecture*, 6.
85. Quoted in Crowcroft, 170.

4. IF HITLER COMES: 1940–1

1. Calder, *The People's War*, 55–6, 129.
2. Addison & Crang eds, *Listening to Britain*, 16.
3. Calder, 69, 71.
4. Addison & Crang, 21–2.
5. Calder, 49.
6. Priestley, *Postscripts*, 62.
7. Rhodes James ed. *Chips: Diaries of Henry Channon*, 300.
8. HC Deb 7 May 1940, vol 360 col 1093.
9. *The Times*, 26 April 1940.
10. HC Deb 7 May 1940, vol 360 cols 1147, 1150.
11. HC Deb 8 May 1940, vol 360 col 1321.
12. *The Times*, 9 May 1940.
13. *Manchester Guardian*, 9 May 1940.
14. He eventually developed a grisly fascination with Hitler. See Jones, *A Diary with Letters*.
15. Foot, *Armistice*, 219.
16. *Manchester Guardian*, 9 May 1940.
17. Foot, *Loyalists and Loners*, 156.
18. HC Deb 8 May 1940, vol 360 col 1279.
19. Foot, *Aneurin Bevan, Vol 1*, 315.

20. Brivati, *The Uncollected Foot*, 306.
21. *The Times*, 21 January 1927, quoted in Pugh, *'Hurrah for the Blackshirts!'*, 47; see also 43, 48, 274.
22. Brivati, *The Uncollected Foot*, 308.
23. One former Labour minister who had chafed at the gradualism of MacDonald entered not a ministerial office, but a cell in Brixton Prison. On 23 May 1940, Oswald Mosley was interned as a subversive.
24. Quoted in BBC Radio 4, 'Millions Like Us', *Archive on 4*, 3 July 2021.
25. Addison & Crang, 13.
26. Todman, 283.
27. *Daily Mirror*, 14 May 1940.
28. Calder, 102.
29. M. Foot, 'Introduction' to 'Cato', *Guilty Men* (London: Penguin, 1995), v.
30. *Evening Standard*, 31 May 1940.
31. 'Cato', 14, 16, 100, 102, 111.
32. *Nottingham Evening Post*, 21 Aug. 1940; *The Times*, 17 Aug. 1940; *Daily Mail*, 10 Aug. 1940; *The Scotsman*, 15. Aug 1940.
33. T. Wintringham, *New Ways of War* (Harmondsworth: Penguin, 1940), 116, 117.
34. Cassandra, *The English at War*, 127.
35. G. Orwell, *The Lion and the Unicorn* (London: Penguin, 1982), 103.
36. 'Cassius', *The Trial of Mussolini* (London: Gollancz, 1943), 69.
37. *Daily Herald*, 15 Jan. 1945.
38. Edgerton, *The Rise and Fall of the British Nation*, 167. Emphasis in original.
39. JB Priestley, *English Journey* (London: Heinemann/Gollancz, 1934), 278, 289, 311, 314, 325, 341, 343.
40. HC Deb 17 Nov. 1936, vol 317 col 1611.
41. Quoted in BBC Radio 4, 'Millions Like Us'.
42. Quoted in Smith, *Britain and 1940*, 50.
43. P. Davison ed., *Orwell's England* (London: Penguin, 2001), 306.
44. MS Castle 617 (Articles and reviews, Oct. 1934–Aug. 1956), various.
45. Ibid., 'Saving the Peace—Labour's Policy!', *University Forward*, 9/1 (Oct. 1943).
46. Castle, 96.
47. MS Castle 617.
48. *Evening Standard*, 13 Sept. 1940.

5. NEVER AGAIN: 1942–5

1. D. Edgerton, *Warfare State* (Cambridge: CUP, 2006), 147.
2. L. Robbins, *Autobiography of an Economist* (London: Macmillan, 1971), 166.

3. Pimlott, *Harold Wilson*, 73.
4. Sabine, *British Budgets in Peace and War*, 182, 187–8.
5. Wilson, *Beveridge Memorial Lecture*, 11.
6. Harris, *Beveridge*, 313, 315–6.
7. Ibid., 354–5.
8. Ibid., 406.
9. HC Deb 1 December 1942, vol 385 col 1044–5.
10. Jones, *The Conservative Party and the Welfare State*, 70.
11. *Daily Mirror*, 10 Dec. 1942.
12. *Daily Mirror*, 2 Dec. 1942.
13. W. Beveridge, *Social Insurance and Allied Services*, (London: HMSO, 1942), 163–5.
14. Quoted in Harris, 399.
15. Hailsham, *A Sparrow's Flight*, 204.
16. Hogg, *One Year's Work*, 52.
17. Ibid., 53.
18. Hailsham, 209.
19. Hogg, 61, 84.
20. Ibid., 43–4.
21. Ibid., 29.
22. Ibid., 44, 79, 80.
23. Quoted in Cockett, *Thinking the Unthinkable*, 61.
24. HC Deb 16 February 1943, vol 386 col 1660.
25. Ibid., col 1687.
26. Hogg, 54.
27. HC Deb 17 February 1943, vol 386 cols 1813–18.
28. *The Times*, 18 Feb. 1943.
29. Home Intelligence for Feb. 1943, quoted in Addison, *The Road to 1945*, 227.
30. Mass Observation, *The Journey Home*, 22.
31. Ibid., 71, 107, 111.
32. Perkins, 67.
33. Castle, 112.
34. Jefferys, *The Churchill Coalition*, 119.
35. C. Eade (ed.), *The War Speeches of Winston Churchill, Volume 2* (London: Cassell, 1965), 430.
36. *The Times*, 16 June 1943.
37. *Daily Mirror*, 16 June 1943.
38. MS Castle 550 (Speeches and lectures, 1937–48).
39. MS Castle 617 (Articles and reviews, Oct. 1934–Aug. 1956), 'Saving the Peace—Labour's Policy!'
40. *Evening Standard*, 22 Nov. 1943. Emphasis in original.

41. *Evening Standard*, 23 Nov. 1943.
42. HC Deb 21 June 1944, vol 401 col 213.
43. Clarke, *Beveridge on Beveridge*, 36–40.
44. HM Government, *Employment Policy* (Cmnd. 6527) (London: HMSO, 1944), 26.
45. HC Deb 21 June 1944, vol 401 col 218.
46. HM Government, *Employment Policy*, 3, 19, 20.
47. J. Meade, 'Internal Measures for the Prevention of General Unemployment', in S. Howson ed., *The Collected Papers of James Meade, Vol 1* (Abingdon: Routledge, 2005), 174.
48. *Tribune*, 14 and 28 July 1944; *Daily Herald*, 27 Mar. and 5 June 1945; Q. Hogg, *The Left Was Never Right* (London: Faber, 1945).
49. *The Times*, 22 May 1945, quoted in Toye, 'Crazy Broadcast'.
50. Fielding, 'What Did "The People" Want?'.
51. Quoted in Foot, *Aneurin Bevan*, 506.
52. Labour Party, *Let Us Face the Future* (London: Labour Party, 1945) 1–5.
53. *The Times*, 5 June 1945.
54. See Fielding, 632.
55. Hailsham, 234.
56. B. Webb, *The House Divided* (London: Hutchinson, 1945), 44, 48.
57. W. Churchill, 'Winston Churchill's Declaration of Policy to the Electors', in *1945 Conservative Party General Election Manifesto*, available at http://www.conservativemanifesto.com/1945/1945-conservative-manifesto.shtml (accessed 1/3/2022).
58. FA Hayek, *The Road to Serfdom* (Abingdon: Routledge, 1944), 205.
59. CK Allen, *Law and Orders* (London: Steven & Sons, 1945); Hayek, 88–9. Other sources for this paragraph: *Diss Express*, 1 June 1945; *The Norfolk Journal*, 1 June 1945; *The Suffolk Journal*, 1 June 1945; *The Courier* of Dundee, 2 June 1945; *Western Mail*, 14 June 1945; *South Wales News*, 14 June 1945; *The Yorkshire Post*, 16 June 1945; *The Leeds Mercury*, 16 June 1945; *The Times*, 16, 19 June 1945; *Lancashire Evening Post*, 18 June 1945; *Liverpool Daily Post*, 26 June 1945; *Hull Daily Mail*, 28 June 1945; *Truth*, 29 June 1945.
60. *The Times*, 5 June, 1945.
61. *Dundee Courier and Advertiser*, 2 June 1945.
62. *Dundee Courier and Advertiser*, 26 June 1945.
63. *Birmingham Gazette*, 21 June 1945.
64. *The Times*, 22 June 1945.
65. *Shields Daily News*, 20 June 1945.
66. *The New York Times*, 2 June 1940, quoted in Maiolo, 333.
67. *The Times*, 9 June 1945; *Daily Herald*, 5 June 1945.
68. M. Thatcher, *The Path to Power* (London: HarperCollins, 1995), 45.

69. *Lancashire Evening Post*, 13 June 1945.
70. De'Ath, *Barbara Castle*, 65.
71. *Daily Mirror*, 30 July 1945.
72. Some owners had even tried to 'starve the men into harder work by organising short-time in such a way that the men did not qualify for unemployment insurance'. H. Wilson, *New Deal for Coal* (London: Contact, 1945), 149–50, 153–4, 174.
73. Ibid., 148, 190.
74. Foot, *Politics of Harold Wilson*, 47; *Daily Herald*, 20 June 1945.
75. Toye, 674.
76. Edgerton, *Rise and Fall of the British Nation*, 219.
77. *The Times*, 16 June 1945.
78. *Western Morning News*, 4 July 1945.
79. *Daily Herald*, 3 July 1945.
80. Fielding, 'What Did "The People" Want?'.
81. *Liverpool Echo*, 26 July 1945.
82. *Daily Herald*, 31 July 1945.
83. Williamson, 'Baldwin's Reputation', 145.
84. Quoted in Lord Lexden, 'Churchill's Unexpected Election Disaster: The 1945 Labour landslide 75 years on', *Conservative History Journal*, II/8 (Autumn 2020), 48.
85. *Daily Mirror*, 21 Apr. 1945. Emphasis in original.
86. *The Times*, 25 May 1942, quoted in R. Toye, 'From "Consensus" to "Common Ground"', *Journal of Contemporary History*, 48/1 (2013), 5.
87. Foot, *Politics of Harold Wilson*, 52.
88. James Chuter Ede's diary, quoted in Jefferys, *Politics and the People*, 86.
89. Davenport, *Memoirs of a City Radical*, ch9.
90. Pimlott ed., *Political Diary of Hugh Dalton*, Introduction to Chapter 8, 468.

6. EMERGENCY GOVERNMENT: 1968–9

1. Quoted in Green, *Ideologies of Conservatism*, 236.
2. *Reading Evening Post*, 1 Nov. 1966.
3. *The Guardian*, 4 July 1966.
4. Foot, *Politics of Harold Wilson*, 168.
5. *The Guardian*, 8 Sept. 1967.
6. *The Guardian*, 12 Mar. 1968.
7. Quoted in Dorey, *Comrades in Conflict*, 16.
8. HC Deb 22 November 1967, vol 754 cols 1441–2.
9. Ibid.
10. *Daily Mirror*, 24 Nov. 1967.

11. *Coventry Evening Telegraph*, 15 Dec. 1968.

12. S. Brittan, *Left or Right* (London: Secker & Warburg, 1968), 163.

13. *The Illustrated London News*, 6 Jan. 1968.

14. Maude, *The Common Problem*, 276, 278.

15. Castle, *The Castle Diaries*, entry for 7 Mar. 1968.

16. R. Jenkins, *A Life at the Centre* (London: Pan, 1992), 235.

17. PREM 13/2051 (Economic Policy, 1 Dec. 1967–18 Mar. 1968), quoted in Davis, *Staring over the Precipice*.

18. Williams ed., *May Day Manifesto*, 143.

19. P. Foot, 315, 317–8; see also 342–4.

20. Williams ed., 130.

21. P. Foot, 321–2, 339.

22. *Tribune*, 29 Sept. 1967.

23. *Tribune*, 27 Sept. 1968.

24. David Mercer, quoted in T. Ali, *Street Fighting Years* (London: Verso, 2005), 258.

25. *The Illustrated London News*, 23 Mar. 1968; *The Times*, 19 Mar. 1968.

26. *The Times*, 5 Sept. 1968.

27. Castle, entry for 13 June 1968.

28. Quoted in Utley, *Enoch Powell*, 144.

29. Quoted in Corthorn, *Enoch Powell*, 55.

30. Powell, *Freedom and Reality*, 164.

31. Quoted in Utley, 180.

32. Utley, 138.

33. Quoted in Utley, 190.

34. Quoted in Utley, 180, 184–6.

35. C. Schofield, *Enoch Powell and the Making of Postcolonial Britain* (Cambridge: CUP, 2013), 209–10, 223–35; *The Spectator*, 10 May 1968; see Shepherd, *Enoch Powell*, 352–3.

36. *The Spectator*, 21 June 1968.

37. Utley, 172.

38. Utley, 42; Shepherd, 325.

39. Castle, entry for 23 Apr. 1968.

40. *Tribune*, 3 May 1968.

41. Wilson, *The Labour Government*, 529.

42. *Birmingham Daily Post*, 17 May 1968.

43. *Daily Mirror*, 17 May 1968.

44. D. Donnelly, *Gadarene 68* (London: Kimber, 1968), 186–7.

45. Castle, entries for 5 Apr. 1968, 15 Jan. 1969.

46. *Tribune*, 18 Oct. 1968.

47. *Tribune*, 26 Apr. 1968.

48. Castle, entries for 9 Apr. 1968, 1 July 1968.

49. CAB 129 (Post-War Memoranda 1964 to 1970), 139/31: A Policy for Industrial Relations: Draft White Paper.

50. Conservative and Unionist Party, *Fair Deal at Work: The Conservative Approach to Modern Industrial Relations* (London: Conservative Political Centre, 1968), 10.

51. E. Heffer, *The Class Struggle in Parliament* (London: Gollancz, 1973), 158.

52. *New Left Review*, I/46, (Nov.–Dec. 1967), 3.

53. Ibid.; J. Jones, 'Unions Today and Tomorrow', in Blackburn & Cockburn, *The Incompatibles*, 122–7.

54. Perkins, *Red Queen*, 279, 283.

55. CAB 129/139/31.

56. Perkins, 273.

57. Jones, *Union Man*, 199.

58. *Sunday Mirror*, 9 June 1968.

59. Jones, *Union Man*, 22.

60. Eric Heffer, in *The Guardian*, 28 Jan. 1969.

61. *Tribune*, 20 Dec. 1968.

62. *Tribune*, 14 Feb. 1969.

63. BBC Radio 4, 'The Thirty Year Itch', *Archive on 4*, 1 July 2017.

64. Quoted in ibid.

65. *Tribune*, 5 Apr. 1969; 18 Apr. 1969.

66. Castle (entry for 7 May 1969).

67. Ibid. (entry for 26 Mar. 1969).

68. Quoted in Wigham, *Strikes and the Government*, 152.

69. Quoted in BBC Radio 4, 'The Thirty Year Itch'.

70. PREM 13/2726 (Wilson, 'Note of Discussion at Dinner, Chequers, Sunday June 1, 1969'). Much of this account draws on that note; along with Castle; and Silver, *Victor Feather*.

71. Castle, entry for 17 June 1969.

72. Quoted in Jenkins, *The Battle of Downing Street*, 159.

7. WITH THEIR RIFLES LOADED?: 1970–4

1. Jones, *Union Man*, 228.

2. P. Rawlinson, *A Price Too High* (London: W&N, 1989), 248.

3. M. Harrington, 'Sir Keith Joseph', in Stacey & St Oswald.

4. S. Heffer, *Like the Roman*, ch13; *The Spectator*, 11 June 1968.

5. HC Deb 15 December 1970, vol 808 col 1138; *The Guardian*, 16 Dec. 1970.

6. Conservative Party, 'Selsdon Meeting transcript (morning session)' ['*smooth*' *transcript*], 1 Feb. 1970, Conservative Party Archive CRD 3/9/93 (Selsdon minutes, Seventh Session, 7), available at https://www.margaretthatcher.org/document/109515 (accessed 28/2/2022).

7. *The Guardian*, 26 Jan. 1970, 12.
8. Castle, *The Castle Diaries*, 178 (entry for 2 Feb. 1970).
9. *The Times*, 7 Feb. 1970; *Sunday Mirror*, 22 Feb. 1970.
10. Benn, *Office Without Power* (entries for 11–12 May 1970).
11. Ibid. (entry for 2 Sept. 1970).
12. *The Journal* (Newcastle), 30 Mar. 1959.
13. Ridley, *'My Style of Government'*, 2–3.
14. The Industrial Reorganisation Corporation, Land Commission and National Board for Prices and Incomes, seven Regional Economic Development Councils, as well as Wilson's Industrial Expansion Act.
15. HC Deb 4 November 1970, vol 805 col 1212.
16. Benn (entry for 14 June 1970).
17. *The Observer*, 8 Nov. 1970.
18. *The Observer*, 29 Nov. 1970.
19. HC Deb 29 April 1971, vol 816 col 732.
20. *The Times*, 21 Jan. 1972.
21. Author interview with David Davis, 9 June 2021.
22. Prior, *A Balance of Power*, 25.
23. P. Walker, *Staying Power* (London: Bloomsbury, 1991), 4.
24. P. Walker, *The Ascent of Britain*, 62.
25. *Daily Mirror*, 21 Jan. 1972.
26. Ibid.
27. *The Times*, 21 Jan. 1972.
28. HC Deb 24 January 1972, vol 829 col 1023.
29. Ibid., col 1069.
30. Ibid., col 1092.
31. Prior, 74.
32. HC Deb 24 January 1972, vol 829 col 1106.
33. P. Routledge, *Scargill* (London: HarperCollins, 1994), 18.
34. *New Left Review*, I/92 (July–Aug. 1975), 1.
35. Ibid., 11. Emphasis in original.
36. Darlington & Lyddon, *Glorious Summer* (London: Bookmarks, 2001), 44
37. Quoted in BBC Radio 4, 'The Thirty Year Itch'.
38. UK National Archives, HO 325/232 (Home Office: Queen's Peace QPE Symbol series Files), 'Picketing: papers relating to the coal strike of 1972'.
39. CAB 134 (Miscellaneous Committees: Minutes and Papers), 3485: Ministerial Committee on Emergencies, Meetings 1–15 (Jan–Aug 1972).
40. M. Crick, *Scargill and the Miners*, 2nd edn (Harmondsworth: Penguin, 1985), 59.
41. Holmes, *The Failure of the Heath Government*, 69.

42. FL Ffoulkes, 'The "Saltley" Incident: A Report' (British Gas Corporation, 1985), 24.
43. Darlington & Lyddon, *Glorious Summer*, 60.
44. Ffoulkes, 'The "Saltley" Incident', 24.
45. HO 325/232.
46. Heath, 351.
47. CAB 128 (Post-War Conclusions), 50/7 (Conclusion, 10 Feb. 1972).
48. Thatcher, *The Path to Power*, 218.
49. D. Hurd, *An End to Promises* (London: William Collins, 1979), 102–3.
50. Quoted from Maudling's memoirs in K. Jeffrey & P. Hennessy, *States of Emergency* (London: Routledge & Kegan Paul, 1983), 236.
51. *The Observer*, 13 Feb. 1972.
52. Quoted from Maudling's memoirs in Jeffrey & Hennessy, *States of Emergency*, 236.
53. *The Guardian*, 15 Feb. 1972; CAB 134/3485.
54. UK National Archives, HO 287/2193 (Home Office: Police POL Symbol series Files), 'Mutual aid between police forces in the event of future emergencies arising from a major industrial dispute', 1 Jan. 1972–31 Dec. 1974.
55. CAB 130/559, quoted in Hughes, *'Governing in Hard Times'*, 117.
56. Ibid., 118.
57. Ibid. 'Operation Cutter' would have involved 5000 servicemen distributing coal stocks.
58. CAB 134/3485; CAB 128/50/8 (Conclusion, 17 Feb. 1972). Allen is not specified by the minutes, but he was the only person at both this meeting and the Official Committee, which is mentioned as the source of this information.
59. CAB 128/50/9 (Conclusion, 18 Feb. 1972).
60. Churchill Archives Centre, Hailsham MSS, HLSM 1/1/4, available at https://www.margaretthatcher.org/document/111134 (accessed 6/4/2022).
61. *The Spectator*, 19 Feb. 1972.
62. Quoted in Holmes, 71.
63. Quoted in Heffer, 620.
64. A. Barber, *Taking the Tide* (Norwich: Michael Russell, 1996), 105; Prior, 73.
65. *The Times*, 28 July 1972.
66. Enoch Powell Speech Archive, POLL 4/1/9, File 3 (speeches May–Aug. 1973); PBS, *Firing Line*, 24 Feb. 1974.
67. It is clear from a survey of the typescripts of Powell's many speeches in the year after the policy was announced that he was much happier talking about inflation than unemployment. POLL 4/1/9.

68. *Illustrated London News*, 1 Sept. 1972.

69. Lord Hailsham, *The Door Wherein I Went* (London: William Collins, 1975), 296.

70. N. Ridley, 'Selsdon Park Speech', 19 Sept. 1973, reproduced at https://www.margaretthatcher.org/document/110861 (accessed 7/2/2022).

71. Selsdon Group, 'The Selsdon Manifesto'.

72. UK National Archives, BA6/ 53 (Civil Service Department: Lord Armstrong personal papers). 'Inflation Counter Measures. Energy: oil and coal.

73. Ibid.

74. CAB 165 (Committees Files), 985 (Civil Contingencies Unit: committee business, 3–31 December 1973).

75. Quoted in BBC Radio 4, 'The Power of Political Forgetting', *Archive on 4*, 5 Sept. 2015.

76. Hurd, *An End to Promises*, 131.

77. Quoted in Holmes, 114.

78. McIntosh, *Challenge to Democracy*, 64; *The Times*, 28 Jan. 1974.

79. *The Guardian*, 28 Jan. 1974.

80. Campbell, *Edward Heath*, 588–9.

81. *The Guardian*, 28 Jan. 1974.

82. *The Times*, 29 Jan. 1974.

83. *The Guardian*, 28 Jan. 1974.

84. McIntosh, 68.

85. Fay & Young, *The Fall of Heath*, 23.

86. Trewin, *The Hugo Young Papers*, 75.

87. McIntosh, 70.

88. Whitehead, *The Writing on the Wall*, 110.

8. GAUNT, TIGHT-LIPPED MEN: 1974–6

1. *Daily Mirror*, 6 Mar. 1974.

2. Castle, *Fighting All the Way*, 441.

3. Ibid., 453.

4. HC Deb 18 July 1974, vol 877 cols 708–714.

5. *The Times*, 1 July 1974.

6. *The New York Times*, 27 Mar. 1974.

7. *The Observer*, 18 Aug. 1974; *The Guardian*, 10 Aug. 1974.

8. *The Economist*, 24 Aug. 1974.

9. *The Times*, 13 Sept. 1973, quoted in J. Gittings ed., *The Lessons of Chile* (Nottingham: Spokesman, 1975), 8–9.

10. *The Spectator*, 22 Dec. 1973.

11. *The Observer*, 18 Aug. 1974.

12. Hoover Institution Archives, Kenneth Hugh de Courcy Papers, Box 2, Folder 6 (Walker, General Walter, and Burnand, P., 1973–76), W. Walker letter to de Courcy, 15 Aug. 1974.
13. Ibid.
14. W. Walker, 'Address to the 22nd Annual Study of the Association of Civil Defence Officers on the Strategic Problems of Emergency Planning at the Palace Court Hotel, Bournemouth', 6 June 1974, Papers of General Sir Walter Walker, 65/46/1–2, Imperial War Museum.
15. Private information; S. Dorril & R. Ramsay, *Smear!* (London: Grafton, 1992), 286.
16. Penrose & Courtiour, *The Pencourt File*, 243–4.
17. *The Guardian*, 24 Aug. 1974.
18. King, *The Cecil King Diary*, 1970–74, entry for 21 Apr. 1971.
19. *The Times*, 26 Sept. 1974.
20. *The Guardian*, 22 Aug. 1974.
21. *The Observer*, 22 Sept. 1974.
22. *Evening Standard*, 1 Feb. 1974.
23. *The Observer*, 18 Aug. 1974.
24. Trewin, 37.
25. Ibid., 13.
26. *The Times*, 28 Aug. 1974.
27. Benn, *Against the Tide*, entry for 28 Apr. 1974; *The Sunday Telegraph*, 20 July 1975.
28. *The Economist*, 1 June 1974.
29. *The Times*, 5 Aug. 1974.
30. *The Times*; *Evening Standard*, 17 Sept. 1974. NOP spoke to 540 people in fifty-four constituencies.
31. Campbell, 639; W. Whitelaw, *The Whitelaw Memoirs* (London: Aurum, 1989), 140.
32. De Courcy Papers 2/6, 'Civil Assistance: Appreciation of the Situation and Outline Plan by W.W.', Dec. 1974.
33. Ibid., W. Walker letter to de Courcy, 12 Mar. 1975.
34. Ibid., W. Walker letter to de Courcy, 18 Sept. 1975.
35. BBC Radio 4, 'Coups and Coalitions', *Archive on 4*, 7 Feb. 2015.
36. Joseph, *Inflation*.
37. *The Times*, 6 Sept. 1974.
38. K. Joseph, 'Inflation Is Caused by Governments', speech at Preston, 5 Sept. 1974, available at https://www.margaretthatcher.org/document/110607 (accessed 9/2/2022).
39. K. Joseph, 'This Is Not the Time to be Mealy-Mouthed', speech at Upminster, 22 June 1974, available at https://www.margaretthatcher.org/document/110604 (accessed 9/2/2022).

40. Joseph, *Inflation*.

41. Joseph, 'Not the Time to be Mealy-Mouthed'.

42. *Lancashire Daily Post*, 7 Feb. 1931; 7 July 1931.

43. The published text reads 'invoking the memory of', but in the speech, he says 'play-acting'. BBC Radio 4, 'The Power of Political Forgetting', *Archive on 4*, 5 Sept. 2015.

44. Vinen, *Thatcher's Britain*, 64.

45. A. Sherman, Editor's Foreword to S. Brittan, *Second Thoughts on Full Employment Policy* (Chichester: Barry Rose/Centre for Policy Studies, 1975), x.

46. S. Brittan, Author's Preface to *Second Thoughts on Full Employment Policy*, 11–12.

47. W. Rees-Mogg, *The Reigning Error* (London: Hamilton, 1974), 112.

48. *Daily Mirror*, 7 Sept. 1974.

49. Ibid.

50. Steering Committee: Minutes of 13th Meeting, 15 July 1974, Conservative Party Archive (SC74), available at https://www.margaretthatcher.org/document/111901 (accessed 8/4/2022).

51. Author interview with David Davis, 9 June 2021.

52. Quoted in BBC Radio 4, 'The Power of Political Forgetting', *Archive on 4*, 5 Sept. 2015.

53. *The Spectator*, 19 Oct. 1974.

54. Prior, 95.

55. *Sunday Mirror*, 20 Oct. 1974.

56. This paragraph draws on P. Cowley & M. Bailey, 'Peasants' Uprising of Religious War?: re-examining the 1975 Conservative Leadership Contest', *British Journal of Political Science*, 30 (2000), 599–629. Their detailed analysis of MPs' voting, drawing on first-hand testimony and original documentation, concludes that ideology was one indicative factor, among others. E.g. it notes that, in the first round, 85% of the right-wing 92 Group voted for Thatcher, while 71–80% of left-leaning MPs voted for Heath. See also Vinen, 73.

57. M. Thatcher, 'Speech to Finchley Conservatives', 7 Feb. 1975, available at https://www.margaretthatcher.org/document/102612 (accessed 28/2/2022).

58. Quoted in Campbell, 670.

59. Benn, entry for 10 Feb. 1975.

60. Quoted in Ziegler, *Edward Heath*, 487, 488.

61. BBC Radio 4, 'The Thirty-Year Itch'.

62. *The Times*, 27 Mar. 1975; Saunders, *Yes to Europe!*, 100.

63. Quoted in Saunders, 9.

64. See e.g. *The Guardian*, 9, 10, 15 May; 2, 4 June 1975.

65. *The Guardian*, 10 May 1975; 9 May 1975.

66. Benn, entries for 7 and 11 May 1975; *The Guardian*, 9 May 1975.
67. Quoted in Dorril & Ramsay, 284.
68. Benn, entry for 20 Mar. 1975.
69. Quoted in Saunders, 148.
70. Ibid.; *Aberdeen Evening Express*, 26 May 1975.
71. Saunders, 15, 52, 123, 148.
72. *Evening Standard*, 2 June 1975.
73. K. Joseph, *Notes towards the Definition of Policy* (Shadow Cabinet Circulated Paper, 4 Apr. 1975), available at https://www.margaretthatcher.org/document/110098 (accessed 9/9/2022).
74. Churchill Archives Centre, Hailsham MSS, HLSM 1/1/10, available at https://www.margaretthatcher.org/document/111134 (accessed 28/2/2022).
75. Churchill Archives Centre, Thatcher MSS, 'Shadow Cabinet: Minutes of 57th Meeting', 11 Apr. 1975, available at https://www.margaretthatcher.org/document/109958 (accessed 28/2/2022).
76. HLSM 1/1/10.
77. Quoted in Moore, *Margaret Thatcher*, 301.
78. A closed shop was a workplace where all employees had to be members of a given trade union.
79. M. Thatcher, 'The Historic Choice', speech to Conservative Central Council, 20 Mar. 1976, available at https://www.margaretthatcher.org/document/102990 (accessed 28/2/2022).
80. M. Thatcher, 'Speech to Conservative Central Council', 15 Mar. 1975, available at https://www.margaretthatcher.org/document/102655 (accessed 28/2/2022).
81. HC Deb 9 June 1976, vol 912 cols 1447, 1451.
82. Joseph, *Stranded on the Middle Ground?*; K. Joseph & J. Sumption, *Equality* (London: Murray, 1979), 98.
83. Boyson, Introduction to Boyson ed., *1985*.
84. HC Deb 28 October 1947, vol 443 col 703.
85. Hoover Institution Archives, Brian Crozier Papers, Box 4, Folder 1 (letter to Thatcher, 12 Nov. 1976).
86. C. Hitchens, *Orwell's Victory* (London: Penguin, 2003), 77.
87. Donoughue, *Prime Minister*, 94–5.
88. J. Callaghan, Leader's speech to Labour Party Conference, Blackpool, 1976, available at http://www.britishpoliticalspeech.org/speech-archive.htm?speech=174 (accessed 9/9/2022).
89. Benn, entry for 30 Sept. 1976.
90. *Evening Standard*, 1 Oct. 1976.
91. *Daily Mirror*, 1 Oct. 1976.
92. *Evening Standard*, 1 Oct. 1976.

93. BBC1, *The Richard Dimbleby Lecture: Lord Hailsham: Elective Dictatorship*, 14 Oct. 1976.
94. Churchill Archives Centre, Thatcher MSS 2/1/1/37 (K. Joseph, 'Open Letter to James Callaghan', 1 Oct. 1976), available at https://www.margaretthatcher.org/document/111248 (accessed 9/9/2022).
95. M. Thatcher, 'Speech to Conservative Party Conference', 8 Oct. 1976, available at https://www.margaretthatcher.org/document/103105 (accessed 28/2/2022).
96. Benn, entry for 5 Oct. 1976.
97. Benn, 3 Nov. 1976.
98. Donoughue, *Downing Street Diary*, entry for 1 Dec. 1976.
99. Quoted in Burk & Cairncross, *Goodbye, Great Britain*, 95.
100. Burk & Cairncross, 95.
101. Ibid., 229–36.
102. Moore, 344–5, 359.
103. BBC Radio 4, 'The Thirty-Year Itch'.
104. Author interview with Vince Cable, 1 Oct. 2021.
105. Donoughue, 103–13.

9. THE ENEMY WITHIN V. THE IRON HEEL: 1976–9

1. K. Joseph, 'Our Tone of Voice and Our Tasks' (Shadow Cabinet Circulated Paper, 7 Dec. 1976), 6, available at https://www.margaretthatcher.org/document/110178 (accessed 14/2/2022).
2. *The Observer*, 4 July 1976.
3. Eatwell, *Fascism*, 268.
4. Mary Harron, quoted in J. Savage, *England's Dreaming* (London: Faber, 2001), 240–1; see also e.g. S. Poliakoff, *Strawberry Fields* (National Theatre, Mar. 1977).
5. *Daily Mirror*, 4 Apr. 1977.
6. Walker, *The National Front*; Clutterbuck, *Britain in Agony*, 221.
7. D. Edgar, *Plays:1* (London: Methuen, 1997), 388; see also Walker, *National Front*, 223.
8. Walker, *National Front*, 211.
9. R. Benedictus, 'Employment Protection', *Industrial Law Journal* (5/1), 23, quoted in Rogaly, *Grunwick*, 119.
10. Ross McWhirter, quoted in R. King & N. Nugent eds, *The British Right* (Farnborough: Saxon House, 1977), 82.
11. R. Moss, *The Collapse of Democracy* (London: Abacus, 1977), 99.
12. *The Times*, 18 Dec. 1975.
13. *The Observer*, 26 June 1977.
14. Quoted in Clutterbuck, 210.

15. Geary, *Policing Industrial Disputes*, 85.
16. Routledge, 102.
17. *Evening Standard*, 24 June 1977.
18. Author interview with James Undy, 17 June 2021.
19. Dromey & Taylor, *Grunwick*, 77; Rogaly, 65, 68, 76.
20. K. Joseph, Speech at Doncaster Racecourse, 24 June 1977, available at https://www.margaretthatcher.org/document/111944 (accessed 14/2/2022).
21. Quoted in López, *The Winter of Discontent*, 149.
22. Denham & Garnett, 309–10; Rogaly, 77; K. Joseph, 'Speech at Hove Town Hall', 1 Sept. 1977, available at https://www.margaretthatcher.org/document/111945 (accessed 14/2/2022).
23. *Evening Standard*, 13 Sept. 1977.
24. Lord Hailsham, *The Dilemma of Democracy* (London: Fount, 1979).
25. Lord Hailsham, 'Elective Dictatorship', *The Richard Dimbleby Lecture*, BBC1, 14 October 1976.
26. M. Thatcher, 'Confrontation with reality' (Speech to Conservative Party Conference, 14 Oct. 1977).
27. BBC Radio 4, '1979: Democracy's Nightmares', *Archive on 4*, 27 Apr. 2019.
28. D. Campbell, 'What did a Tory MP say in the Cumberland Hotel?', *New Statesman*, 20 Feb. 1981, available at https://www.duncancampbell.org/menu/journalism/newstatesman/newstatesman-1981/what%20did%20a%20tory%20mp%20say.pdf (accessed 2/3/2022); T. Benn, *The End of an Era*, entries for 17–20 Feb. 1981.
29. BBC1, *Tonight*, 22 June 1978, quoted in BBC Radio 4, '1979'.
30. A. Neave, *Nuremberg* (London: Hodder & Stoughton, 1978), 324.
31. Quoted in BBC Radio 4, '1979'.
32. S. Hall et al, *Policing the Crisis* (London: Macmillan, 1978), 275, 277.
33. *The Guardian*, 19 Apr. 1978.
34. *The Observer*, 28 May 1978.
35. Quoted in ibid.
36. Quoted in Geary, *Policing Industrial Disputes*, 86; BBC Radio 4, '1979'.
37. Hall et al, *Policing the Crisis*, 289–90, 307, 311; T. Benn, *Conflicts of Interest*, entries for 20 Feb. 1978; 11 Jan., 22 Feb., 12 Mar. 1979. In 1971, Kitson published a study called *Low Intensity Operations: Subversion, Insurgency and Peacekeeping*, which, in the context of speculation about military intervention in strikes, attracted critical attention from the left. When Kitson was deployed to Northern Ireland, this fuelled fears that some techniques in use there might later be tried in Britain.
38. Benn, entry for 22 June 1977.
39. Gilroy, *There Ain't No Black in the Union Jack*, 165.

40. *The Times*, 6 Oct. 1978.
41. Granada TV, *World in Action*, 30 Jan. 1978.
42. S. Hall, 'The Great Moving Right Show', *Marxism Today* (Jan. 1979), 7.
43. *Policing the Crisis*, 315, 323.
44. Peter Flannery's *Savage Amusement* (1978); Howard Barker's *That Good Between Us* (1977); Howard Brenton's *The Churchill Play* (1978–9).
45. J. Stevenson & C. Cook, *The Slump* (London: Quartet, 1979), 4, 281.
46. Hough, 'Freedom in Danger', 19, in Cormack ed., *Right Turn*.
47. P. Johnson, 'Farewell to the Labour Party', in Cormack, 76–9, 86.
48. BBC Radio 4, 'The Thirty-Year Itch'.
49. Benn, entry for 6 July 1978.
50. Hutber ed., *What's Wrong with Britain?* (London: Sphere, 1978), 77.
51. Author interview with Martyn Walsh, 19 Oct. 2021.
52. Quoted in BBC Radio 4, 'The Thirty-Year Itch'.
53. Castle, *Fighting All the Way*, 508.
54. *The Times*, 30 Oct. 1978.
55. PREM 16/2124 ('Industrial Policy: Industrial action by oil tanker drivers; part 2', 18 Dec. 1978–11 Jan. 1979).
56. Ibid.
57. PREM 16/2127 ('Industrial Policy: Road haulage dispute; part 1', 22 Dec. 1978–14 Jan. 1979).
58. *The Guardian*, 30 Jan. 1979.
59. Quoted in López, 101–2.
60. M. Thatcher, 'Speech at Alnwick Castle', 30 July 1975, available at https://www.margaretthatcher.org/document/102753 (accessed 23/2/2022).
61. Quoted in PREM 16/2124.
62. Quoted in López, 99.
63. *Daily Mail*, 18 Jan. 1979, quoted in C. Hay, 'Narrating Crisis: The Discursive Construction of the "Winter of Discontent"', *Sociology*, 30/2 (May 1996), 266.
64. M. Thatcher, Conservative Party Political Broadcast (Winter of Discontent), 17 Jan. 1979, Thatcher Archive: CCOPR 71/79, available at https://www.margaretthatcher.org/document/103926 (accessed 7/4/2022).
65. Narrating Crisis', 263, citing *Daily Express*, 8 Feb. 1979.
66. López, 111–12, 116, 134, passim.
67. BBC Knowledge/Illumina, *Witness to History: The Labour Deputy Leadership Election* (2002).
68. Castle, *Fighting All the Way*, 509.
69. *Liverpool Echo*, 2 Feb. 1979.

70. CAB 128/65 (Conclusions of Cabinet Meetings 1–14 1979), 1–3 (11, 15, 18 Jan. 1979).
71. Donoughue, entry for 5 Feb. 1979.
72. Hay, 'Narrating Crisis', 265.
73. HC Deb 28 March 1979, vol 965 col 579.
74. Ibid., col 582.
75. Author interview with Vince Cable, 1 Oct. 2021.
76. M. Thatcher, 'Speech to Conservative Rally in Cardiff', 16 Apr. 1979, available at https://www.margaretthatcher.org/document/104011 (accessed 14/2/2022).
77. M. Thatcher, 'Speech to Conservative Rally in Birmingham', 19 Apr. 1979, available at https://www.margaretthatcher.org/document/104026 (accessed 23/2/2022).
78. BBC Parliament, *Decision 79: The Morning After*, 4 May 2009 (first broadcast 4 May 1979).
79. *The Guardian*, 2 May 1979.

10. ANOTHER TIME AND AGE: 1979–85

1. *The Times*, 12 Oct. 1981.
2. Moore, *Margaret Thatcher*, 512.
3. *Daily Mirror*, 15 Feb. 1980.
4. *Liverpool Echo*, 14 Feb. 1980.
5. J. Hoskyns, *Just in Time* (London: Aurum, 2000).
6. Gormley, *Battered Cherub*, 175.
7. *The Times*, 17 Feb. 1981.
8. N. Lawson, *The View from Number 11* (London: Corgi, 1992), 140.
9. BBC4, 'Battle for Labour', *Witness to History*, 30 Oct. 2002.
10. Cripps et al, *Manifesto*, 141.
11. Mullin, 'Preface' to *A Very British Coup*.
12. R. Miliband, *Capitalist Democracy in Britain* (Oxford: OUP, 1984), 154–5.
13. Quoted in Crewe & King, *SDP*, 49.
14. Ibid., 82–3.
15. H. Brenton, Preface to *Plays: Two* (London: Methuen, 1989).
16. Benn, *End of an Era*, entry for 20 Feb. 1981.
17. T. Benn, 'Foreword' to Chile Solidarity Campaign, *Monetarism means repression: economic policy in Britain and Chile*, 2nd edn (London: Chile Solidarity Campaign, 1981).
18. *The Times*, 27 June 1981.
19. *Liverpool Echo*, 1 May 1981.
20. Bodleian Libraries, Conservative Party Archive CRD 4/27 (Conservative

Research Department, Special Services Opinion Research), 86: Unemployment, 1980.

21. *The Times*, 7 Oct. 1981.
22. *Daily Telegraph*, 3 June 1981.
23. *New Society*, 8 July 1982; *The Guardian*, 1 Oct. 1980.
24. Quoted in BBC Radio 4, 'The Power of Political Forgetting', *Archive on 4*, 5 Sept. 2015.
25. D. Monaghan, 'Margaret Thatcher, and the Struggle for Working-Class Identity', *Journal of Popular Film and Television*, 29/1 (2001), 12.
26. 'Butskellite' was a mildly satirical 1950s term for the emerging post-war consensus, combining the names of Labour and Conservative chancellors: Hugh Gaitskell and RA Butler.
27. Kinnock, 'Foreword' to I. Clemitson & G. Rodgers, *A Life to Live* (London: Junction, 1981).
28. G. Tullock, *The Vote Motive* (London: IEA, 1976), 26.
29. H. Thomas, in Cormack ed., *Right Turn*, 102.
30. Morris, *The Life and Times of Thomas Balogh*, 112.
31. N. Tebbit, *Upwardly Mobile* (London: W&N, 1988), 182. Emphasis in original.
32. John Whittingdale, then head of the Conservative Research Department, quoted in López, *Winter of Discontent*, 21.
33. *The Observer*, 22 May 1983.
34. 'NUM Rally', film from Stafford & Sheffield, 1984, available at https://player.bfi.org.uk/free/film/watch-num-rally-1984-online (accessed 16/2/2022).
35. Quoted in P. Routledge, *Scargill* (London: HarperCollins, 1994), 162.
36. *The Guardian*, 4 Jan. 1985.
37. *The Guardian*, 7 Mar. 2009.
38. Quoted in Beckett & Hencke, *Marching to the Fault-line*, 96–8.
39. Quoted in ibid., 114.
40. *The Times*, 20 July 1984.
41. Routledge, *Scargill*, 149.
42. HL Deb 13 November 1984, vol 457 cols 240–1.
43. Beckett & Hencke, 94.
44. *The Times*, 20 July 1984.
45. Beckett & Hencke, *Marching to the Fault-Line*, 110.
46. *The Guardian*, 28 Dec. 1984.
47. *The Guardian*, 20 Mar. 1985.
48. Castle, *Fighting All the Way*, 570.

11. THE CRASH: 2008–10

1. *The Times*, 31 Mar. 1997, quoted in López, *The Winter of Discontent*, 186.

2. T. Blair, speech in Malmö, 6 June 1997, quoted in BBC Radio 4, 'Millions Like Us'.

3. G. Brown, 'A Modern Agenda for Prosperity and Social Reform', speech to the Social Market Foundation, Cass Business School, 3 Feb. 2003, available at http://www.smf.co.uk/wp-content/uploads/2004/05/Publication-A-Modern-Agenda-for-Prosperity-and-Social-Reform-Gordon-Brown.pdf (accessed 1/3/2022).

4. Skinner, *Sailing Close to the Wind*, 101–3.

5. Quoted in Beckett & Hencke, *Marching to the Fault-line*, 244.

6. Speech to the TUC, 22 Aug. 1984, quoted in Routledge, *Scargill*, 172.

7. Interview with Glasman.

8. M. Glasman, *Unnecessary Suffering* (London: Verso, 1996), 1–7.

9. J. Gray, *Enlightenment's Wake* (Abingdon: Routledge, 2007), 132, 134, 144, 156, 160.

10. J. Gray & D. Willetts, *Is Conservatism Dead?* (London: Profile/Social Market Foundation, 1997), 99.

11. Interview with Willetts.

12. Interview with Kruger.

13. See, for example, P. Clarke, *Keynes*; and R. Skidelsky, *Keynes: The Return of the Master* (London: Penguin, 2009).

14. S. Bush, 'Gordon Brown: "The solution to this crisis is still global"', *New Statesman*, 22 Apr. 2020, https://www.newstatesman.com/uncategorized/2020/04/gordon-brown-solution-crisis-still-global (accessed 2/3/2022).

15. Quoted in López, 23.

16. P. Mandelson, Labour Party Conference speech, 28 Sept. 2009.

17. *New Statesman*, 22 Apr. 2020.

18. BBC Radio 4, 'The Thirty Year Itch'.

19. Interview with Cable.

12. IF ONLY: 2010–15

1. See e.g. *The Guardian*, 18 Dec. 2009.

2. BBC Radio 4, 'The Thirty Year Itch'.

3. Interview with O'Shaughnessy.

4. Interview with Willetts.

5. *The Guardian*, 22, 24 Apr. 2009.

6. Rowenna Davis, *Tangled Up in Blue*, 76–7, 98–104.

7. E. Miliband, speech to Labour Party conference, 2 Oct. 2012, available at https://labourlist.org/2012/10/ed-milibands-conference-speech-the-transcript/ (accessed 2/3/2022).

8. BBC Radio 4, 'The Thirty-Year Itch'.
9. Interview with Creagh; interview with Glasman.
10. *The Guardian*, 17 May 2010.
11. Interview with Glasman.
12. M. Roberts, *Revolt on the Left: Labour's UKIP problem and how it can be overcome* (London: Fabian Society, 2014), 9, 11.
13. Interview with Hunt.
14. T. Hunt ed., *England's Identity Crisis* (Winchester: Winchester UP, 2016), 11.
15. Ford & Sobolewska, *Brexitland*, 308.
16. Interview with Edgar.
17. Kwarteng et al, *Britannia Unchained* (London: Palgrave Macmillan, 2012), 8, 114, 4, 7.
18. A. Seldon & P. Snowdon, *Cameron at 10* (London: William Collins, 2016), 154.
19. BBC Radio 4, 'Millions Like Us'.
20. Interview with Willetts; Orgreave was home to both a coking plant, the focus of the 'Battle' in May–June 1984, and a colliery, which closed in 1981. The site of the 'Battle' is visible from the new research facility. See *Guardian*, 8 July 2012.
21. *The Guardian*, 16 July 2013.
22. BBC Radio 4, 'The Thirty-Year Itch'.
23. D. Skelton ed., 'Introduction' to *Access All Areas: Building a Majority* (London: Renewal, 2013), 10.
24. *The Guardian*, 16 July 2013.
25. Interview with Frayne.
26. D. Cummings, 'The Hollow Men', speech at the Institute for Public Policy Research, 19 Nov. 2014, available at https://www.youtube.com/watch?v=GNaWPV5l4j4 (accessed 24/2/2022).
27. T. May, 'We Will Win by Being the Party for All', speech at the Victory 2015 Conference, ConservativeHome, 9 Mar. 2013, available at https://www.conservativehome.com/platform/2016/07/full-text-of-theresa-mays-speech-we-will-win-by-being-the-party-for-all.html (accessed 12/112021).
28. Shipman, *Fall Out*, xxviii.
29. Interview with Timothy.
30. Ibid.

13. PROJECT FEAR: 2015–17

1. *The Guardian*, 2 Feb. 2015.
2. *Daily Mail*, 2 Feb. 2015.

3. *The Guardian*, 31 Mar. 2015.
4. Nunns, *The Candidate*, 108.
5. *Mail on Sunday*, 22 Aug. 2015.
6. Interview with Meadway.
7. Nunns, 108.
8. Cummings, 'On the referendum #21'.
9. Cummings, 'My report for Business for Britain'. Emphasis in original.
10. Cummings, 'On the referendum #21'.
11. J. Frayne, *Overlooked but Decisive: Connecting with England's Just About Managing classes* (London: Policy Exchange, 2015), 62–3.
12. Interview with Frayne.
13. Frayne, *Overlooked but Decisive*, 9.
14. D. Cummings, 'Why Leave Won the Referendum', Ogilvy Nudgestock 9 June 2017 talk, 8 Nov. 2019, available at https://www.youtube.com/ watch?v=_Tc4bl1yZLw (accessed 24/2/2022).
15. Cummings, 'On the referendum #21', Emphasis in original.
16. Bagehot, 'An interview with Dominic Cummings', *The Economist*, 21 Jan. 2016, https://www.economist.com/bagehots-notebook/2016/01/ 21/an-interview-with-dominic-cummings (accessed 2/3/2022).
17. Ford & Sobolewska, *Brexitland*, 227.
18. Cummings, 'On the referendum #21'.
19. Shipman, *All Out War*, 192, 236, 251.
20. *New Statesman*, 1 July 2016.
21. Interview with Ditum.
22. VN Bateman, 'Brexit: two centuries in the making', UK in a Changing Europe, 23 Nov. 2016, https://ukandeu.ac.uk/brexit-two-centuries-in-the-making/ (accessed 24/2/2022). See also Select Additional Sources.
23. M. Goodwin & O. Heath, 'Brexit vote explained', Joseph Rowntree Foundation, 31 Aug. 2016, https://www.jrf.org.uk/report/brexit-vote-explained-poverty-low-skills-and-lack-opportunities (accessed 24/2/2022).
24. C. Ainsley, 'Brexit presents us with the opportunity to transform the prospects of many who voted Leave and politicians must not squander it', 24 Nov. 2016, available at https://brexitcentral.com/claire-ainsley-brexit-opportunities/ (accessed 7/4/2022).
25. BBC Radio 4, 'The Thirty Year Itch.
26. T. May, 'Statement from the new Prime Minister Theresa May', 13 July 2016, https://www.gov.uk/government/speeches/statement-from-the-new-prime-minister-theresa-may (accessed 24/2/2022).
27. T. May, 'Speech by Theresa May, launching her national campaign to become Leader of the Conservative Party and Prime Minister of the

United Kingdom', Birmingham, 11 July 2016, available at https://www.wlrk.com/docs/TheresaMayJuly11Speech.pdf (accessed 24/2/2022).

28. T. May, speech to Conservative Party Conference, Birmingham, 2 Oct. 2016, available at https://www.independent.co.uk/news/uk/politics/theresa-may-speech-tory-conference-2016-in-full-transcript-a7346171.html (accessed 24/2/2022).

29. N. Ferguson, 'Why Theresa May's Brexit class war could channel rerun of that '70s show in the UK', South China Morning Post, 11 Oct. 2016, https://www.scmp.com/comment/insight-opinion/article/2027025/why-theresa-mays-brexit-class-war-could-channel-rerun-70s (accessed 23/2/2022).

30. Shipman, *Fall Out*, 18.

31. BBC Radio 4, 'Millions Like Us'.

32. The Conservative and Unionist Party, *Forward, Together*, 2017 manifesto, available at https://ucrel.lancs.ac.uk/wmatrix/ukmanifestos2017/localpdf/Conservatives.pdf (accessed 2/3/2022).

33. BBC Radio 4, 'The Thirty Year Itch'.

34. Cummings, 'Why Leave Won'.

14. STOP THE COUP!: 2017–19

1. Interview with Tanner.

2. BBC News, 'Boris Johnson challenged over Brexit business "expletive"', 26 June 2018, https://www.bbc.co.uk/news/uk-politics-44618154 (accessed 25/2/2022).

3. HC Deb 14 January 2019, vol 652 col 905.

4. P. Paphides tweet, 28 Dec. 2018, 15:14, https://twitter.com/petepaphides/status/1078670603509555200 (accessed 25/2/2022).

5. *The Sunday Times*, 6 Jan. 2019.

6. Quoted in Maguire & Pogrund, *Left Out*, 194–5.

7. Ibid., 190.

8. Clip available via Daniel Kraemer tweet, 28 Aug. 2019, 12:37, https://twitter.com/dcakraemer/status/1166676234211905536 (accessed 25/2/2022).

9. Justine Greening tweet, 6 June 2019, 16:25, https://twitter.com/JustineGreening/status/1136655391440478208 (accessed 25/2/2022).

10. BBC News, 'Brexit: Bid to make no deal more difficult scrapes through Commons', 9 July 2019, https://www.bbc.co.uk/news/uk-politics-48930417 (accessed 25/2/2022).

11. J. Lis, 'Project fear?', *Prospect*, 19 July 2021, https://www.prospect-magazine.co.uk/politics/project-fear-the-last-three-years-have-been-

more-catastrophic-than-even-the-most-pessimistic-remainer-predicted (accessed 25/2/2022).

12. *The Daily Telegraph*, 27 June 2019.

13. D. Turchiano, 'Russell T. Davies Breaks Down Balancing Global Politics and a Multi-Year Family Saga in "Years and Years"', *Variety*, 24 June 2019, https://variety.com/2019/tv/features/years-and-years-russell-t-davies-interview-1203248705/ (accessed 25/2/2022).

14. B. Johnson, 'Boris Johnson's first speech as Prime Minister', 24 July 2019, https://www.gov.uk/government/speeches/boris-johnsons-first-speech-as-prime-minister-24-july-2019 (accessed 25/2/2022).

15. B. Johnson, 'PM speech at Manchester Science and Industry Museum', 27 July 2019, https://www.gov.uk/government/speeches/pm-speech-at-manchester-science-and-industry-museum (accessed 25/2/2022).

16. *Evening Standard*, 24 July 2019.

17. *The Sunday Times*, 28 July 2019.

18. Author interview with Kruger, 12 March 2020.

19. Sam Coates Sky tweet, 1 Aug. 2019, 19:07, https://twitter.com/SamCoatesSky/status/1156989930477953025 (accessed 2/3/2022).

20. Chuka Umunna, quoted in *Evening Standard*, 13 Aug. 2019.

21. Stephen Bush tweet, 6 Aug. 2019, 15:58, https://twitter.com/stephenkb/status/1158754271459979264 (accessed 25/2/2022).

22. H. Yorke, 'John McDonnell threatens to march on palace', 7 Aug. 2019, https://www.telegraph.co.uk/politics/2019/08/07/john-mcdonnell-threatens-march-palace-tell-queen-taking-boris1/ (accessed 25/2/2022); R. Nikkhah et al, 'Queen: Our politicians can't govern', *The Sunday Times*, 11 Aug. 2019, https://www.thetimes.co.uk/article/queen-our-politicians-cant-govern-twjmp657f (accessed 25/2/2022); J. Murphy, 'Jeremy Corbyn undermining vote of no confidence to block no-deal, claim Tory rebels', *Evening Standard*, 13 Aug. 2019, https://www.standard.co.uk/news/politics/jeremy-corbyn-undermining-vote-of-no-confidence-to-block-nodeal-claim-tory-rebels-a4212006.html (accessed 25/2/2022).

23. *The Sunday Times*, 18 Aug. 2019.

24. *The Times*, 20 Aug. 2019.

25. A. Heath, 'Tory arch-Remainers will soon find they have no place left in their party', *The Daily Telegraph*, 14 Aug. 2019, https://www.telegraph.co.uk/politics/2019/08/14/tory-arch-remainers-will-soon-find-have-no-place-left-party/ (accessed 25/2/2022).

26. Ed Davey MP tweet, 28 Aug. 2019, 11:29, https://twitter.com/edwardjdavey/status/1166659116791717888?lang=en (accessed 25/2/2022).

27. G. Heffer, 'Queen approves PM request to suspend parliament', 29 Aug.

2019,SkyNews,https://news.sky.com/story/pm-boris-johnson-plans-to-ask-queen-to-suspend-parliament-from-mid-september-11795978 (accessed 25/2/2022).

28. Clip available via Channel 4 News tweet, 28 Aug. 2019, 14:44, https://twitter.com/channel4news/status/1166708206992875520 (accessed 25/2/2022).

29. Quoted in J. Elgot, 'MPs call for drastic action against prorogation of parliament', *The Guardian*, https://www.theguardian.com/politics/2019/aug/28/mps-call-for-drastic-action-against-prorogation-of-parliament (accessed 25/2/2022).

30. Alan Rusbridger tweet, 28 Aug. 2019, 22:56, https://twitter.com/arusbridger/status/1166831896472563712 (accessed 25/2/2022).

31. P. Mason, 'Chaos is being normalised', *The Guardian*, 11 Sept. 2019, https://www.theguardian.com/commentisfree/2019/sep/11/chaos-normalised-boris-johnson-pernicious-plan-democracy (accessed 2/3/2022).

32. Clip available via Channel 4 News tweet, 29 Aug. 2019, 19:22, https://twitter.com/channel4news/status/1167140491277848576 (accessed 25/2/2022).

33. Clip available via BBC Politics tweet, 10 Sept. 2019, 10:40, https://twitter.com/bbcpolitics/status/1171357844073000960?lang=en (accessed 25/2/2022).

34. Amber Rudd tweet, 7 Sept. 2019, 21:11, https://twitter.com/amberrudduk/status/1170429481879842817 (accessed 25/2/2022).

35. *The Mail on Sunday*, 21 Sept. 2019.

36. J. Doyle et al, 'Jacob Rees-Mogg accuses the Supreme Court of a "constitutional coup" over its stunning ruling', *MailOnline*, 24 Sept. 2019, https://www.dailymail.co.uk/news/article-7500543/Jacob-Rees-Mogg-accuses-Supreme-Court-constitutional-coup-stunning-ruling.html (accessed 25/2/2022).

37. D. Hannan, 'If the Establishment's coup against Brexit succeeds, our institutions will never recover', *Daily Telegraph*, 21 Sept. 2019, https://www.telegraph.co.uk/politics/2019/09/21/establishments-coup-against-brexit-succeeds-institutions-will/ (accessed 25/2/2022).

38. HC Deb 25 September 2019, vol 664, cols 774–806.

39. Tim Shipman tweet (@ShippersUnbound), 24 Sept. 2019, 21:19, https://twitter.com/ShippersUnbound/status/1176591987241365512 (accessed 2/3/2022).

40. BBC Radio 4, 'The End of the Thirty Year Itch'.

41. Author interview with Danny Kruger, 12 March 2020.

42. W. Tanner & J. O'Shaughnessy, *The Politics of Belonging* (London: Onward, 2019), 6.

43. T. Burrows, 'So farewell, then, Workington man', *The Guardian*, 22 Nov. 2019, https://www.theguardian.com/commentisfree/2019/nov/22/workington-man-voter-caricature-essex-man (accessed 25/2/2022).

44. Interview with O'Shaughnessy.

45. Tanner & O'Shaughnessy, *Politics of Belonging*, 4, 5.

46. BBC Radio 4, 'The End of the Thirty Year Itch'.

47. D. Cummings, 'On the referendum #34', *Dominic Cummings's Blog*, 27 Nov. 2019, https://dominiccummings.com/2019/11/27/on-the-referendum-34-batsignal-dont-let-corbyn-sturgeon-cheat-a-second-referendum-with-millions-of-foreign-votes/ (accessed 25/2/2022).

48. Quoted in Maguire & Pogrund, *Left Out*, 38.

49. James Meadway & Matthew Lawrence, quoted in *Financial Times*, 4 Sept. 2019.

50. *Financial Times*, 1 Sept. 2019.

51. Author email exchange with Jason Cowley, 21 Jan. 2022.

52. Interview with Glasman.

53. Author interview with Kruger, 12 March 2020.

54. This began a one-year transition period, during which the UK would remain in the single market and the customs union.

55. Author audio recording from the event, 31 Jan. 2020.

56. BBC Radio 4, *Guilty Men*, 27 July 2020.

57. Clip available via *The Telegraph*, 'Nigel Farage: This is the greatest moment in the history of our modern nation', YouTube, 31 Jan. 2020, https://www.youtube.com/watch?v=gK6Z5X7D3Fo (accessed 25/2/2022).

58. BBC Radio 4, 'The End of the Thirty Year Itch'; A. Pabst, 'Power without purpose: how the Tories don't have a national plan', *New Statesman*, 12 Feb. 2020, https://www.newstatesman.com/world/uk/2020/02/power-without-purpose-how-tories-don-t-have-national-plan (accessed 2/3/2022).

15. LOCKDOWN: 2020–22

1. Heath and Social Care Committee and Science and Technology Committee, 'Oral Evidence: Coronavirus: Lessons learnt', HC 95, 26 May 2021.

2. BBC2, *Newsnight*, 16 Mar. 2020.

3. BBC Radio 4, *Today*, 17 Mar. 2020.

4. R. Sunak, 'Chancellor of the Exchequer, Rishi Sunak on COVID19 response', 17 Mar. 2020, https://www.gov.uk/government/speeches/chancellor-of-the-exchequer-rishi-sunak-on-covid19-response (accessed 25/2/2022).

5. *The Guardian*, 18 Mar. 2020.

6. *The Times*, 14 Apr. 2020.

7. HC Deb 23 March 2020, vol 674 col 142.

8. Anne Power and Ellie Benton, 'Where next for Britain's 4,300 mutual aid groups?', https://blogs.lse.ac.uk/covid19/2021/05/06/where-next-for-britains-4300-mutual-aid-groups/.

9. *Newsnight* (BBC2), 17 March 2020.

10. *The Times*, 23 Mar. 2020.

11. L. McLaren, 'Immigration', in UK in a Changing Europe, *Brexit and Beyond*, 64–5.

12. *The Guardian*, 2 Feb. 2021.

13. Interview with Meadway.

14. *The Daily Telegraph*, 6 Sept. 2020.

15. James Ball tweet, 6 Sept. 2020, 15:00 (tweet since deleted).

16. C. Ainsley, *The New Working Class* (Bristol: Policy Press, 2018), 2–4, 27–9.

17. C. Ainsley & A. Menon, 'We asked people from deprived areas what matters to them after Brexit', *i*, 31 July 2019, https://inews.co.uk/opinion/comment/we-asked-people-from-deprived-areas-what-matters-to-them-after-brexit-this-is-what-they-told-us-320219 (accessed 2/3/2022).

18. Ainsley, 44.

19. K. Starmer, 'Full text of Keir Starmer speech on A New Chapter for Britain', 18 Feb. 2021, https://labour.org.uk/press/full-text-of-keir-starmer-speech-on-a-new-chapter-for-britain/ (accessed 25/2/2022).

20. Kirkup, 'Why Starmer is no Attlee'.

21. M. Brown & RE Jones, *Paint Your Town Red* (London: Repeater, 2021), 10, 34.

22. Interview with Brown.

23. *New Statesman*, 8 June 2021.

24. Reeves, *The Everyday Economy*, 8.

25. Labour Together, *Labour's Covenant* (London: Labour Together, 2022), 9, passim.

26. Interview with Coyle.

27. Quoted in BBC Radio 4, 'Millions Like Us'.

28. Payne, *Broken Heartlands*, 356.

29. *New Statesman*, 5 Feb. 2021.

30. BBC Radio 4, 'Millions Like Us'.

31. Payne, 369.

32. *The Sun*, 1 Oct. 2021.

33. Johnson, 'Keynote Speech', 6 Oct. 2021, https://www.conservatives.

com/news/2021/boris-johnson-s-keynote-speech————we-re-getting-on-with-the-job (accessed 25/2/2022).

34. *The Spectator*, 16 Oct. 2020.
35. A. Haldane, 'The Second Invisible Hand', inaugural Community Power lecture, the Local Trust, 6 July 2021, available at https://localtrust.org.uk/wp-content/uploads/2021/07/Andy-Haldane_Community-power-lecture_6-July.pdf (accessed 25/2/2022).
36. HC Deb 2 February 2022, vol 708 col 316.
37. J. Studdert, 'A White Paper fit for Groundhog Day', New Local, 2 Feb. 2022, https://www.newlocal.org.uk/articles/a-white-paper-fit-for-groundhog-day/ (accessed 1/3/2022).
38. *The Spectator*, 17 Dec. 2020.
39. D. Gauke, 'I fear the Conservative Party is lost...', ConservativeHome, 4 July 2020, https://www.conservativehome.com/thecolumnists/2020/07/david-gauke-i-fear-the-conservative-party-is-lost-for-small-state-free-marketeers-and-one-nation-social-liberals.html (accessed 2/3/2022).
40. *The Daily Telegraph*, 9 Sept. 2021.
41. *The Daily Telegraph*, 27 Oct. 2021.
42. *Financial Times*, 31 Aug. 2020; *The Daily Telegraph*, 22 July 2021.
43. *The Guardian*, 3 Oct. 2021.
44. *The Guardian*, 15 Jan. 2022.
45. Interview with Edgar.
46. Interview with Creagh.
47. Tanner & O'Shaughnessy, *The Politics of Belonging*, 4, 20.
48. Ibid., 5.

SELECT ADDITIONAL SOURCES

Limitations of space prohibit a full bibliography. This is a list of sources that were particularly helpful in researching this book, and which are not cited in the Notes, or which informed the text more broadly than a brief citation suggests.

PART ONE
1931–45

Bodleian Libraries, Archive of Barbara Anne Castle (MS Castle).
Bodleian Libraries, Archive of (James) Harold Wilson (MS Wilson).
UK National Archives, CAB (Cabinet Papers).
Addison, P. *The Road to 1945: British Politics and the Second World War* (London: Pimlico, 1994).
Allport, A. *Britain at Bay, 1938–1941: The Epic Story of the Second World War* (London: Profile, 2020).
Aster, S. '"Guilty Men": The Case of Neville Chamberlain', in Boyce, R. and Robertson, E.M. *Paths to War: New Essays on the Origins of the Second World War* (Basingstoke: Macmillan, 1989).
Baldwin, S. *On England and Other Addresses* (Harmondsworth: Penguin, 1937).
Beers, L. *Red Ellen: The Life of Ellen Wilkinson, Socialist, Feminist, Internationalist* (Cambridge: Harvard University Press, 2016).
Benton, N. *Naomi Mitchison: A Biography* (London: Pandora, 1990).
Beveridge, W. *Social Insurance and Allied Services: Report by Sir William Beveridge* (London: HMSO, 1942).
Brivati, B (ed.). *The Uncollected Foot: Essays Old and New 1953–2003* (London: Politico's, 2003).
Brooke, S. *Labour's War: The Labour Party During the Second World War* (Oxford: Clarendon, 1992).
Butler, D. and Butler, G. *Twentieth Century British Political Facts 1900–2000* (London: Macmillan, 2000).

Cairncross, A. and Watts, N. *The Economic Section, 1939–1961: A Study in Economic Advising* (London: Routledge, 1989).

Calder, A. *The People's War: Britain 1939–1945* (London: Pimlico, 1992).

Campbell, J. *Edward Heath: A Biography* (London: Pimlico, 1994).

Cassandra [William Connor]. *The English at War* (London: Secker and Warburg, 1941).

Castle, B. *Fighting All the Way* (London: Pan, 1994).

Citrine, W. *Men and Work* (London: Hutchinson,1964).

Clarke, JS (ed.). *Beveridge on Beveridge: Recent Speeches of Sir William Beveridge* (London: Social Security League, 1944).

Clarke, P. *Hope and Glory: Britain 1900–2000* (London: Penguin, 2004).

————— *Keynes: The Twentieth Century's Most Influential Economist* (London: Bloomsbury, 2009).

————— *The Keynesian Revolution in the Making* (Oxford: Clarendon, 1988).

Cockett, R. *Thinking the Unthinkable: Think Tanks and the Economic Counter-Revolution, 1931–1983* (London: Fontana, 1995).

Cole, GDH. *A Plan for Britain* (London: Labour Book Service, 1932).

Cowling, M. *The Impact of Hitler* (New York: Cambridge University Press, 1975).

Cripps, S. et al. *Problems of a Socialist Government* (London: Gollancz, 1933).

Crowcroft, R. *The End is Nigh: British Politics, Power and the Road to the Second World War* (Oxford: Oxford University Press, 2019).

Davenport, N. *Memoirs of a City Radical* (London: Weidenfeld and Nicolson, 1974).

Davison, P (ed.). *Orwell's England* (London: Penguin, 2001).

————— (ed.). *The Complete Works of George Orwell, Vol. 11* (London: Secker and Warburg, 1998).

De'Ath, W. *Barbara Castle: A Portrait from Life* (London: Clifton, 1970).

Denham, A. and Garnett, M. *Keith Joseph* (Chesham: Acumen, 2001).

Edgerton, D. *Britain's War Machine: Weapons, Resources and Experts in the Second World War* (London: Penguin, 2012).

————— *The Rise and Fall of the British Nation* (London: Penguin, 2019).

Fielding, S. 'What Did "The People" Want? The Meaning of the 1945 General Election', *The Historical Journal*, 35/3 (1992), 623–39.

Foot, M. *Aneurin Bevan, A Biography, Volume 1: 1897–1945* (London: MacGibbon and Kee, 1962).

SELECT ADDITIONAL SOURCES

———— *Armistice, 1918–1939* (London: Harrap, 1940).

———— *Harold Wilson: A Pictorial Biography* (Oxford: Pergamon, 1964).

———— *Loyalists and Loners* (London: Collins, 1986).

Giles, D. *An Analysis of the Parliamentary Opposition to the National Government's Handling of the International Situation November 1935–May 1940*, unpublished PhD thesis (University of Nottingham, 1976).

Gillett, N. *Abolishing War: One Man's Attempt* (William Sessions, 2005).

Gow, R. and Greenwood W. *Love on the Dole (edited by Ray Speakman)* (Oxford: Hereford Plays/Heinemann, 1986).

Gracchus [Tom Wintringham], *Your MP* (London: Gollancz, 1944).

Graves, R. and Hodge, A. *The Long Weekend: A Social History of Great Britain, 1918–1939* (London: Penguin, 1971).

Greene, LS. 'Industrial Location and Reconstruction in Great Britain', *The Journal of Land & Public Utility Economics*, 17/3 (1941), 333–43.

Greenwood, W. *Love on the Dole* (London: Vintage, 2014).

Griffiths, R. *Fellow-Travellers of the Right: British Enthusiasts for Nazi Germany, 1933–9* (London: Constable, 1980).

Hailsham. *A Sparrow's Flight* (London: Fontana, 1991).

Halcrow, M. *Keith Joseph: A Single Mind* (London: Macmillan, 1989).

Hannington, W. *The Problem of the Distressed Areas* (London: Gollancz, 1937).

Harrington, W. and Young, P. *The 1945 Revolution* (London: Davis-Poynter, 1978).

Harris, J. *William Beveridge: A Biography* (Oxford: Clarendon, 1997).

Harris, K. *Conversations* (London: Hodder and Stoughton, 1967).

Heath, E. *The Course of My Life: My Autobiography* (London: Hodder and Stoughton, 1998).

———— *Travels: People and Places in my Life* (London: Sidgwick and Jackson, 1977).

Hogg, Q. *One Year's Work* (London: Hurst and Blackett, 1944).

Hoggart, S. and Leigh, D. *Michael Foot: A Portrait* (London: Hodder and Stoughton, 1981).

Hopkins, C. *Walter Greenwood's 'Love on the Dole': Novel, Play, Film* (Liverpool: Liverpool University Press, 2018).

Jefferys, K. *Politics and the People: A History of British Democracy since 1918* (London: Atlantic Books, 2007).

———— *The Churchill Coalition and Wartime Politics, 1940–1945* (Manchester: Manchester University Press, 1995).

Jones, H. *The Conservative Party and the Welfare State 1942–1955*, unpublished PhD thesis (London School of Economics, 1992).

Jones, M. *Michael Foot* (London: Gollancz, 1994).

Jones, T. *A Diary with Letters, 1931–1950* (London: Oxford University Press, 1954).

Kandiah, M. and Jones, H (eds.). *The Myth of Consensus: New Views on British History, 1945–64* (Basingstoke: Macmillan, 1996).

Kelly, S. '"The Ghost of Neville Chamberlain": Guilty Men and the 1945 Election', *Conservative History*, 5 (2005), 18–24.

Kowol, K. 'The Conservative Movement and Dreams of Britain's Post-War Future', *The Historical Journal*, 62/2 (2019), 473–93.

Laing, M. *Edward Heath: Prime Minister* (London: Sidgwick and Jackson, 1972).

Laybourn, K. *Philip Snowden: A Biography 1865–1937* (Aldershot: Temple Smith, 1988).

Lewis, G. *Lord Hailsham: A Life* (London: Pimlico, 1998).

Liepmann, H. *Death from the Skies: A Study of Gas and Microbial Warfare*, translated from the German by Eden and Cedar Paul (London: Secker and Warburg, 1937).

Maiolo, J. *Cry Havoc: The Arms Race and the Second World War, 1931–1941* (London: John Murray, 2011).

Marquand, D. *Ramsay MacDonald* (London: Cape, 1977).

Mass Observation. *The Journey Home: A Report prepared by Mass-Observation for the Advertising Service Guild* (London: Murray, 1944).

McCallum, RB. and Readman, A. *The British General Election of 1945* (Basingstoke: Macmillan, 1999).

Middleton, R. *Towards the Managed Economy: Keynes, the Treasury and the Fiscal Policy Debate of the 1930s* (London: Methuen, 1985).

Mitchison, N. *We Have Been Warned* (London: Constable, 1935).

———— *You May Well Ask: A Memoir, 1920–1940* (London: Gollancz, 1979).

Moggridge, DE. 'From Theory to Policy: The "Keynesian Revolution" in Britain', *Monetary Theory and Thought*, 1 (1993), 109–45.

Morgan, KO. *Michael Foot: A Life* (London: Harper Collins, 2007).

Mowat, CL. *Britain Between the Wars, 1918–1940* (London: Methuen, 1968).

Nicolson, N (ed.). *Harold Nicolson's Diaries 1930–1939* (London: William Collins, 1966).

Norwich, JJ (ed.). *The Duff Cooper Diaries* (London: Phoenix, 2006).

Orwell, G. *Nineteen Eighty-Four* (London: Penguin, 1989).

Overy, R. *The Morbid Age: Britain and the Crisis of Civilization, 1919–1939* (London: Penguin, 2010).

Parker, RAC. *Chamberlain and Appeasement* (Basingstoke: Macmillan, 1993).

———— *Churchill and Appeasement* (London: Papermac, 2000).

Peden, GC. 'The "Treasury View" on Public Works and Employment in the Interwar Period', *Economic History Review*, 37/2 (1984), 167–81.

———— *British Rearmament and the Treasury 1932–1939* (Edinburgh: Scottish Academic Press, 1979).

Perkins, A. *A Very British Strike: 3 May–12 May 1926* (London: Macmillan, 2006).

———— *Red Queen* (London: Macmillan, 2003).

Perry, M. *Bread and Work: Social Policy and the Experience of Unemployment* (London: Pluto, 2000).

———— *The Jarrow Crusade: Protest and Legend* (Sunderland: University of Sunderland Press, 2005).

Pimlott, B. *Harold Wilson* (London: Harper Collins, 1992).

———— *Labour and the Left in the 1930s* (London: Allen and Unwin, 1986).

———— (ed.). *The Political Diary of Hugh Dalton 1918–40, 1945–60* (London: Cape, 1986).

———— (ed.). *The Second World War Diary of Hugh Dalton, 1940–45* (London: Cape, 1985).

Priestley, JB. *English Journey* (London: Heinemann in association with Gollancz, 1933).

———— *Postscripts* (London: Heinemann, 1940).

Pugh, M. *'Hurrah for the Blackshirts!': Fascists and Fascism in Britain Between the Wars* (London: Cape, 2005).

———— *Lloyd George* (Harlow: Longman, 1988).

———— *We Danced All Night: A Social History of Britain Between the Wars* (London: Bodley Head, 2008).

Renwick, C. *Bread for All: The Origins of the Welfare State* (London: Penguin, 2018).

Rhodes James, R (ed.). *Chips: The Diaries of Henry Channon* (London: Weidenfeld and Nicolson, 1993).

Roth, A. *Heath and the Heathmen* (London: Routledge and Keagan Paul, 1972).

Sabine, BEV. *British Budgets in Peace and War, 1932–1945* (London: Allen and Unwin, 1970).

Searle, GR. *The Quest for National Efficiency: A Study in British Politics and Political Thought, 1899–1914* (Oxford: Blackwell, 1971).

Skidelsky, R. *Keynes, Volume 2: The Economist as Saviour, 1920–1937* (London: Papermac, 1994).

——— *Keynes, Volume 3: Fighting for Britain, 1937–1946* (London: Macmillan, 2000).

——— *Politicians and the Slump: The Labour Government of 1929–1931* (Harmondsworth: Pelican, 1970).

Smart, N. *Chamberlain* (Abingdon: Routledge, 2010).

Smith, L. *Harold Wilson: The Authentic Portrait* (London: Hodder and Stoughton, 1964).

Smith, M. *Britain and 1940: History, Myth and Popular Memory* (Abingdon: Routledge, 2000).

Snowden, P. *An Autobiography, Volume Two: 1919–1934* (London: Nicholson and Watson, 1934).

Stacey, T. and St. Oswald, R (eds.). *Here Come the Tories* (London: Tom Stacey, 1970).

Stewart, G. *Burying Caesar: Churchill, Chamberlain and the Battle for the Tory Party* (London: Phoenix, 2000).

Thorpe, A. *Britain in the 1930s: The Deceptive Decade* (Oxford: Blackwell, 1992).

Thorpe, DR. *Supermac: The Life of Harold Macmillan* (London: Pimlico, 2011).

Timmins, N. *The Five Giants: A Biography of the Welfare State* (London: William Collins, 2017).

Todman, D. *Britain's War: Into Battle, 1937–1941* (London: Penguin, 2017).

Tomlinson, J. *Employment Policy: The Crucial Years, 1939–1955* (Oxford: Clarendon, 1987).

Toye, R. *The Labour Party and the Planned Economy, 1931–51* (Woodbridge: Royal Historical Society/Boydell Press, 2003).

——— 'The Labour Party and the Politics of Rearmament, 1935–1939', *Twentieth Century British History*, 12/3 (2001), 303–26.

——— 'Winston Churchill's "Crazy Broadcast": Party, Nation, and the 1945 Gestapo Speech', *The Journal of British Studies*, 49/3 (2010), 655–80.

Weldon, D. *Two Hundred Years of Muddling Through: The Surprising Story of Britain's Economy from Boom to Bust and Back Again* (London: Little, Brown, 2021).

Williamson, P. 'Baldwin's Reputation: Politics and History, 1937–1967', *The Historical Journal*, 47/1 (2004), 127–68.

Wilson H. *The Beveridge Memorial Lecture 1966* (London: Institute of Statisticians, 1966).

Ziegler, P. *Harold Wilson: The Authorised Life* (London: Weidenfeld and Nicolson, 1993).

PART TWO
1968–85

UK National Archives, PREM 13 (Prime Minister's Office, Harold Wilson 1964–70).

UK National Archives, PREM 16 (Prime Minister's Office, James Callaghan 1974–9).

Aims of Industry, *Halfway to 1984…1979* (Council of Aims of Industry, 1979).

Adeney, M. and Lloyd, J. *The Miners' Strike: Loss Without Limit* (London: Routledge and Kegan Paul, 1986).

Allen, VL. *The Militancy of British Miners* (Shipley: Moor Press, 1981).

Andrew, C. *The Defence of the Realm: The Authorized History of MI5* (London: Penguin, 2010).

Barker, H. *That Good Between Us: Credentials of a Sympathizer* (London: Calder, 1980).

Barnett, A. 'Class Struggle and the Heath Government', *New Left Review*, 1/77 (1973).

Baston, L. *Reggie: The Life of Reginald Maudling* (Stroud: Sutton, 2004).

Bateman, D. ILP pamphlet—'In Place of Strife'—Means In Place of Trade Unions (London: Independent Labour Party, 1969).

BBC Radio 4, 'The Thirty Year Itch', *Archive on 4*, 1 July 2017.

Beckett, A. *Pinochet in Piccadilly: Britain and Chile's Hidden History* (London: Faber and Faber, 2003).

———— *When the Lights Went Out* (London: Faber, 2009).

Beckett, F. and Hencke, D. *Marching to the Fault-line: The 1984 Miners' Strike and the Death of Industrial Britain* (London: Constable, 2009).

Benn, T. *Office Without Power: Diaries 1968–72* (London: Arrow, 1989).

———— *Against the Tide: Diaries 1973–76* (London: Arrow, 1990).

———— *Conflicts of Interest: Diaries 1977–80* (London: Arrow, 1991).

———— *The End of an Era: Diaries 1980–90* (London: Arrow, 1994).

Birt, J. *The Harder Path: The Autobiography* (London: Time Warner, 2002).

Blackburn, R. and Cockburn, A. *The Incompatibles: Trade Union Militancy and the Consensus* (Harmondsworth: Penguin/ New Left Review, 1967).

Boyson, R (ed.). *1985, An Escape from Orwell's 1984: A Conservative Path to Freedom* (Enfield: Churchill Press, 1975).

Burk, K. and Cairncross, A. *Goodbye, Great Britain: The 1976 IMF Crisis* (London: Yale University Press, 1992).

Callaghan, J. *Time and Chance* (London: Collins, 1987).

Campbell, J. *Edward Heath: A Biography* (London: Pimlico, 1994).

Castle, B. *Fighting All the Way* (London: Pan, 1994).

———— *The Castle Diaries, 1964–70* (London: Weidenfeld and Nicolson, 1984).

Clegg, H. *How to Run an Incomes Policy and Why We Made Such a Mess of the Last One* (London: Heinemann, 1971).

Clutterbuck, R. *Britain in Agony: The Growth of Political Violence* (Harmondsworth: Penguin, 1980).

Coates, K. and Topham, T. *The Law versus the Unions* (Nottingham: Institute of Workers' Control, 1969).

Cockett, R. *Thinking the Unthinkable: Think Tanks and the Economic Counter-Revolution, 1931–1983* (London: Fontana, 1995).

Conservative and Unionist Party, *Fair Deal at Work: The Conservative Approach to Modern Industrial Relations* (London: Conservative Political Centre, 1968).

Conservative Party, *The Right Approach* (London: Conservative Central Office, 1976), available at https://www.margaretthatcher.org/document/109439 (accessed 14/3/2022).

Cormack, P (ed.). *Right Turn: Eight Men Who Changed Their Minds* (London: Cooper, 1978).

Corthorn, P. *Enoch Powell* (Oxford: Oxford University Press, 2019).

Cowling, M (ed.). *Conservative Essays* (London: Cassell, 1978).

Crewe, I. and King, A. *SDP: The Birth, Life and Death of the Social Democratic Party* (Oxford: Oxford University Press, 1997).

Cripps, F., Griffith, J., Morrell, F., Reid, J., Townsend, P. and Weir, S. *Manifesto: A Radical Strategy for Britain's Future* (London: Pan, 1981).

Crozier, B. *Free Agent: The Unseen War, 1941–1991* (London: Harper Collins, 1993).

Darlington, R. and Lyddon, D. *Glorious Summer: Class Struggle in Britain, 1972* (London: Bookmarks, 2001).

Davis, J. *'Staring over the Precipice into the Abyss': An Anatomy and an Analysis of 'Operation Brutus', November 1967–July 1968*, unpublished MA thesis (Queen Mary University of London, 1999).

Denham, A. and Garnett, M. *Keith Joseph* (Chesham: Acumen, 2001).

Donoughue, B. *Downing Street Diary: With James Callaghan in No. 10* (London: Pimlico, 2008).

———— *Prime Minister: The Conduct of Policy under Harold Wilson and James Callaghan* (London: Cape, 1987).

Dorey, P. *Comrades in Conflict: Labour, the Trade Unions and 1969's 'In Place of Strife'* (Manchester: Manchester University Press, 2019).

Dromey, J. and Taylor, G. *Grunwick: The Workers' Story* (London: Lawrence and Wishart, 1978).

Eatwell, R. *Fascism: A History* (London: Chatto and Windus, 1995).

Edgerton, D. *The Rise and Fall of the British Nation* (London: Penguin, 2019).

Fay, S. and Young, H. *The Fall of Heath* (Sunday Times, 1976).

Ferris, P. *The New Militants: Crisis in the Trade Unions* (Harmondsworth: Penguin, 1972).

Foot, P. *The Politics of Harold Wilson* (Harmondsworth: Penguin, 1968).

———— *The Rise of Enoch Powell: An Examination of Enoch Powell's Attitude to Immigration and Race* (Harmondsworth: Penguin, 1969).

Friend, A. and Metcalf, A. *Slump City: The Politics of Mass Unemployment* (London: Pluto, 1981).

Geary, R. *Policing Industrial Disputes* (Cambridge: Cambridge University Press, 1985).

Gilroy, P. *There Ain't No Black in the Union Jack* (London: Routledge, 2002).

Gormley, J. *Battered Cherub* (London: Hamilton, 1982).

Green, EHH. *Ideologies of Conservatism: Conservative Political Ideas in the Twentieth Century* (Oxford: Oxford University Press, 2002).

Hailsham, Lord. *A Sparrow's Flight* (London: Fontana, 1991).

Harris, K. *Conversations* (London: Hodder and Stoughton, 1967).

Hattersley, R. *Who Goes Home?: Scenes from a Political Life* (London: Little, Brown, 1995).

Heffer, S. *Like the Roman: The Life of Enoch Powell* (London: Weidenfeld and Nicolson, 1998).

Holmes, M. *The Failure of the Heath Government* (London: Macmillan, 1997).

Hughes, RA. *'Governing in Hard Times': The Heath Government and Civil Emergencies - the 1972 and 1974 Miners' Strikes*, unpublished PhD thesis (Queen Mary University of London, 2012).

HM Government, *In Place of Strife: a policy for industrial relations (Cmnd. 3888)* (London: HMSO, 1969).

Ingham, B. *Kill the Messenger* (London: Harper Collins, 1991).

Jenkins, P. *The Battle of Downing Street* (London: Knight, 1970).

Jones, H. *The Conservative Party and the Welfare State 1942–1955*, unpublished PhD thesis (London School of Economics, 1992).

Jones, J. *Union Man: An Autobiography* (London: Collins, 1986).

Joseph, K. *Inflation* (Shadow Cabinet Circulated Paper, 1 May 1974), Conservative Party Archive LCC 1/3/1, https://c59574e9047e61 130f13–3f71d0fe2b653c4f00f32175760e96e7.ssl.cf1.rackcdn.com/ DD328A79735D4C4CA8DCCEADDF6807CF.pdf (accessed 9/2/ 2022).

———— *Stranded on the Middle Ground? Reflections on circumstances and policies* (London: Centre for Policy Studies, 1976).

————, Maude, A. and Percival, I. *Freedom and Order* (London: Conservative Political Centre, 1975).

King, A (ed.). *Why is Britain Becoming Harder to Govern?* (London: BBC, 1976).

King, C. *The Cecil King Diary 1965–70* (London: Cape, 1972).

———— *The Cecil King Diary, 1970–75* (London: Cape, 1975).

Lewis, G. *Lord Hailsham: A Life* (London: Pimlico, 1998).

López, TM. *The Winter of Discontent: Myth, Memory, and History* (Liverpool: Liverpool University Press, 2014).

Maude, A. *The Common Problem* (London: Constable, 1969).

McIntosh, R. *Challenge to Democracy: Politics, Trade Union Power and Economic Failure in the 1970s* (London: Politico's, 2006).

Moore, C. *Margaret Thatcher: The Authorized Biography, Volume One* (London: Penguin, 2014).

Moran, M. *The Politics of Industrial Relations: The Origins, Life and Death of the 1971 Industrial Relations Act* (London: Macmillan, 1977).

Morgan, KO. *Callaghan: A Life* (Oxford: Oxford University Press, 1997).

———— *Michael Foot: A Life* (London: Harper Collins, 2007).

Morris, J. *The Life and Times of Thomas Balogh: A Macaw Among Mandarins* (Brighton: Sussex Academic Press, 2007).

Mullin, C. *A Very British Coup* (London: Politico's, 2001).

Paynter, W. *My Generation* (London: Allen and Unwin, 1972).

Peak, S. *Troops in Strikes: Military Intervention in Industrial Disputes* (London: Cobden Trust, 1984).

Penrose, B. and Courtiour, R. *The Pencourt File* (London: Secker and Warburg, 1978).

Perkins, A. *Red Queen* (London: Macmillan, 2003).

Phillips, J. 'The 1972 Miners' Strike: Popular Agency and Industrial Politics in Britain', *Contemporary British History*, 20/2 (2006), 187–207.

Pickard, T. *Jarrow March* (London: Allison and Busby, 1982).

Pimlott, B. *Harold Wilson* (London: Harper Collins, 1992).

Powell, E. *Freedom and Reality (edited by John Wood)*, (Kingswood: Elliott Right Way Books, 1969).

Prior, J. *A Balance of Power* (London: Hamish Hamilton, 1986).

Ridley, N. *'My Style of Government': The Thatcher Years* (London: Fontana, 1992).

Rogaly, J. *Grunwick* (Harmondsworth: Penguin, 1977).

Sandbrook, D. *White Heat: A History of Britain in the Swinging Sixties* (London: Little, Brown, 2006).

———— *State of Emergency: The Way We Were: Britain, 1970–1974* (London: Allen Lane, 2010).

———— *Seasons in the Sun: The Battle for Britain, 1974–1979* (London: Allen Lane, 2012).

———— *Who Dares Wins: Britain 1979–1982* (London: Allen Lane, 2019).

Saunders, R. *Yes to Europe!: The 1975 Referendum and Seventies Britain* (Cambridge: Cambridge University Press, 2018).

Seldon, A. 'The Postwar Consensus', *Contemporary British History*, 2/1 (1988), 16.

Selsdon Group. 'The Selsdon Manifesto', 19 September 1973, available at https://www.margaretthatcher.org/document/110860 (last accessed 7/2/2022).

Selway, D. *Collective Memory in the Mining Communities of South Wales*, unpublished PhD thesis (University of Sussex, 2017).

Shepherd, R. *Enoch Powell: A Biography* (London: Pimlico, 1997).

Silver, E. *Vic Feather, TUC* (London: Gollancz, 1973).

Skinner, D. *Sailing Close to the Wind* (London: Quercus, 2014).

Taylor, R. *Workers and the New Depression* (London: Macmillan, 1982).

———— *The Trade Union Question in British Politics: Government and Unions since 1945* (Oxford: Blackwell, 1993).

Taylor, R. and Seldon, A. 'Symposium: The Winter of Discontent', *Contemporary Record*, 1/3 (1987), 34–43.

Trewin, I (ed.). *The Hugo Young Papers: A Journalist's Notes from the Heart of Politics* (London: Penguin, 2009).

Tyler, R. *'Victims of Our History'? The Labour Party and in Place of Strife, 1968 to 1969*, unpublished PhD thesis (Queen Mary University of London, 2004).

Utley, TE. *Enoch Powell: The Man and His Thinking* (London: Kimber, 1968).

Vinen, R. *Thatcher's Britain: The Politics and Social Upheaval of the 1980s* (London: Simon and Schuster, 2009).

Walker, M. *The National Front* (London: Fontana/Collins, 1977).

Walker, P. *The Ascent of Britain* (London: Sidgwick and Jackson, 1977).

Ward, G. *Fort Grunwick* (London: Temple Smith, 1977).

Weldon, D. *Two Hundred Years of Muddling Through: The Surprising Story of Britain's Economy from Boom to Bust and Back Again* (London: Little, Brown, 2021).

Wheatcroft, G. *The Strange Death of Tory England* (London: Penguin Allen Lane, 2005).

Whitehead, P. *The Writing on the Wall* (London: Michael Joseph, 1986).

Whitelaw, W. *The Whitelaw Memoirs* (London: Aurum, 1989).

Wigham, E. *Strikes and the Government, 1893–1981* (London: Macmillan, 1982).

Williams, R (ed.). *May Day Manifesto 1968* (Harmondsworth: Penguin, 1968).

Wilson, H. *The Labour Government 1964–1970: A Personal Record* (London: Weidenfeld and Nicolson and Michael Joseph, 1971).

Ziegler, P. *Edward Heath: The Authorised Biography* (London: Harper Press, 2010).

PART THREE

2008–22

Author interviews:

Danny Kruger, 4 Nov. 2021.
David Edgar, 12 Oct. 2021.
David Willetts, 13 Oct. 2021.
Diane Coyle, 4 Oct. 2021.
James Frayne, 23 Sept. 2021.
James Meadway, 9 Dec. 2021.

SELECT ADDITIONAL SOURCES

James O'Shaughnessy, 1 Nov. 2021.

Mary Creagh, 9 Dec. 2021.

Matthew Brown, 1 June 2021.

Maurice Glasman, 14 Dec. 2021.

Nick Timothy, 11 Oct. 2021.

Sam Freedman, 3 Dec. 2021.

Sarah Ditum, 1 Dec. 2021.

Tristram Hunt, 10 Dec. 2021.

Vince Cable, 1 Oct. 2021.

Will Tanner, 13 Oct. 2021.

BBC Radio 4, 'Millions Like Us', *Archive on 4*, 3 July 2021.

———— 'The End of the Thirty Year Itch', *Archive on 4*, 28 Mar. 2020.

———— 'The Thirty Year Itch', *Archive on 4*, 1 July 2017.

Bale, T., Ford, R., Jennings, W., Surridge, P. *The British General Election of 2019* (London: Palgrave Macmillan, 2021).

Beckett, A. *When the Lights Went Out* (London: Faber and Faber, 2009).

Berry, C. '"A Mood in the Air ... Like 1945": Democratic Socialism and the Post-Corbyn Labour Party', *Political Quarterly*, 92 (2021), 255–63.

Beynon, H. and Hudson, R. *The Shadow of the Mine: Coal and the End of Industrial Britain* (London: Verso, 2021).

Blond, P. 'Rise of the Red Tories', *Prospect*, 28 Feb. 2009.

Cable, V. *Free Radical: A Memoir* (London: Atlantic Books, 2009).

Cummings, D. 'My report for Business for Britain on the dynamics of the debate over the EU, and a small but telling process point on the EU', *Dominic Cummings's Blog*, 30 June 2014, https://dominiccummings.com/2014/06/30/my-report-for-business-for-britain-on-the-dynamics-of-the-debate-over-the-eu-and-a-small-but-telling-process-point-on-the-eu/ (accessed 24/2/2022).

———— 'On the referendum #21: Branching histories of the 2016 referendum and the "frogs before the storm"', *Dominic Cummings's Blog*, 9 Jan. 2017, https://dominiccummings.com/2017/01/09/on-the-referendum-21-branching-histories-of-the-2016-referendum-and-the-frogs-before-the-storm-2/ (accessed 24/2/2022).

Curtice, J. *The vote to leave the EU* (London: NatCen Social Research, 2016).

D'Arcy, C. *Low Pay Britain 2018* (London: Resolution Foundation, May 2018).

SELECT ADDITIONAL SOURCES

Davis, R. *Tangled Up in Blue: Blue Labour and the Struggle for Labour's Soul* (London: Ruskin, 2011).

Edgerton, D. *The Rise and Fall of the British Nation* (London: Penguin, 2019).

Fielding, S. 'Keir Starmer needs to find his own Guilty Men', *Spectator*, 6 July 2020, https://www.spectator.co.uk/article/keir-starmer-needs-to-find-his-own-guilty-men (accessed 1/3/2022).

Fletcher, M. 'How People's Vote destroyed itself', *New Statesman*, 20 Nov. 2019, https://www.newstatesman.com/politics/2019/11/how-peoples-vote-destroyed-itself (accessed 1/3/2022).

Ford, R. and Sobolewska, M. *Brexitland: Identity, Diversity and the Reshaping of British Politics* (Cambridge: Cambridge University Press, 2020).

Geary, I. and Pabst, A. *Blue Labour: Forging a New Politics* (London: I.B. Tauris, 2015).

Glasman, M. *Unnecessary Suffering: Managing Market Utopia* (London: Verso, 1996).

Goodhart, D. *The Road to Somewhere: The Populist Revolt and the Future of Politics* (London: Hurst, 2017).

Kirkup, J. 'Why Starmer is no Attlee', *UnHerd*, 20 Feb. 2021, https://unherd.com/2021/02/whats-the-point-of-starmers-labour/ (accessed 1/3/2022).

Lambert, H. 'Dominic Cummings: The Machiavel in Downing Street', *New Statesman*, 25 Sept. 2019, https://www.newstatesman.com/long-reads/2019/09/dominic-cummings-the-machiavel-in-downing-street (accessed 14/3/22).

Lanchester, J. *Whoops!: Why Everyone Owes Everyone and No One Can Pay* (London: Allen Lane, 2010).

López, TM. *The Winter of Discontent: Myth, Memory and History* (Liverpool: Liverpool University Press, 2014).

Mattinson, D. *Beyond the Red Wall: Why Labour Lost, How the Conservatives Won and What Will Happen Next?* (London: Biteback, 2020).

Mount, F. *The New Few, or A Very British Oligarchy* (London: Simon and Schuster, 2013).

Nelson, F. 'The real father of Cameronism', *Spectator*, 24 June 2006.

Nunns, A. *The Candidate: Jeremy Corbyn's Improbable Path to Power* (London: OR Books, 2018).

Payne, S. *Broken Heartlands: A Journey Through Labour's Lost England* (London: Macmillan, 2021).

386

SELECT ADDITIONAL SOURCES

Pogrund, G. and Maguire, P. *Left Out* (London: Vintage, 2021).

Reaction, 'David Gauke & Tim Montgomerie on what they got wrong on Brexit', Rapid Reaction 17, 23 June 2021, available at https://www.youtube.com/watch?v=kMNwVJ4LNxE (accessed 2/3/2022).

Reeves, R. *The Everyday Economy* (Leeds: Labour, 2018).

Sayers, F. 'Meet Claire Ainsley, Keir Starmer's intriguing new Head of Policy', *UnHerd*, 23 April 2020, https://unherd.com/thepost/meet-claire-ainsley-keir-starmers-intriguing-new-head-of-policy/

Shipman, T. *All Out War: The Full Story of Brexit* (London: William Collins, 2017).

——— *Fall Out: A Year of Political Mayhem* (London: William Collins, 2018).

Skinner, D. *Sailing Close to the Wind* (London: Quercus, 2014).

Tooze, A. *Crashed: How a Decade of Financial Crises Changed the World* (London: Penguin, 2019).

UK in a Changing Europe. *Brexit and Beyond* (London, 19 Jan. 2021).

INDEX

Abbott, Diane, 295
Abyssinia, 68
Access All Areas (Skelton), 269–70
Admiralty, 71
Advisory, Conciliation and
 Arbitration Service (ACAS),
 211, 212, 213, 214
Age of Illusion, The (Blythe), 47
Ainsley, Claire, 286, 319, 321
Air Ministry, 71
Air Raid Precautions, 84
Airbus, 292
Alexander, AV, 102
All-Party Parliamentary Action
 Group, 88
Allen, Douglas, 176
Allen, Philip, 171
Amalgamated Union of
 Engineering and Foundry
 Workers, 147
Amery, Leo, 84, 88–9, 91, 92
Anderson, John, 111
Anderson shelters, 87, 103
Antelope pub, London, 309–10
Anti-Nazi League, 229
anti-Semitism, 295, 309
APEX, 212, 213, 214
Arendt, Hannah, 294
Argentina, 240, 243
Armstrong, William, 176–9, 184
Arnold, Malcolm, 150

Arrival of the Jarrow Marchers, The
 (Dugdale), 53
Article 50, Treaty on European
 Union, 292, 300, 302
Asian immigrants, 211–12, 213,
 214, 229
AstraZeneca, 325
Atomic Energy Authority, 131
Attlee, Clement, 1, 37, 80, 161,
 195, 241, 252, 314, 320
 Bank of England nationalisation
  (1945), 126, 127, 250
 general election (1945), 1, 118–
  27, 200, 284, 317, 320
 re-armament debate (1930s),
  69–70
 referenda, views on, 119
 Second World War (1939–45),
  88, 90–91, 92, 116
 Socialist League (1932–7), 37,
  50, 121
Auden, WH, 55
austerity
 1930s, 15, 16–17, 18, 19, 20,
  21–7, 30, 47, 96
 2010s, 261–2, 266, 278, 316,
  320
Austria, 48, 76, 83
authoritarian nationalism, 292,
 294–5, 321, 330, 331

INDEX

INDEX

INDEX

Liberal Party, 13, 19, 31, 35, 36, 48, 54–5, 89, 91
  general election (1945), 120
  National Government (1931–40), 23–32, 34, 39, 41, 45, 50, 88
  Oxford by-election (1938), 78
Life to Live, A (Clemitson and Rodgers), 238
Lincolnshire, England, 90
Lindsay, AD, 78–80
Lion and the Unicorn, The (Orwell), 99
Lis, Jonathan, 297
Live at Drury Lane (Monty Python), 193
Liverpool Echo, 236
Liverpool, Merseyside, 54–5, 147, 181, 224, 227, 236
Lloyd George, David, 13–14, 19, 48, 52, 89–90, 95, 97, 106
Lloyd, Selwyn, 131
Lloyds Bank, 255
Local Trust, 326
localism, 257, 320–23
Locarno Treaties (1925), 57
London
  Battle of Grosvenor Square (1968), 139
  Blitz (1940–41), 86, 102–4, 125
  Brixton riot (1981), 236
  City of London, *see* City of London
  Guildhall University, 253
  hunger marches (1930s), 36, 37, 51, 53, 59, 61, 236
  Jarrow Crusade (1936), 53–4, 61, 139, 160, 163, 190, 193

  Metropolitan Police, 39, 213, 215, 219, 229
  Orwell and, 92
  public corporations, 47
London Citizens, 253, 267
London Review of Books, 254
London School of Economics, 105, 106
London Weekend Television, 207
London, Jack, 166, 242
López, Tara Martin, 226
Lord Haw-Haw, *see* Joyce, William
Loss of Eden (Brown and Serpell), 96–7
Love on the Dole (Greenwood), 42–3, 51–2, 53, 102, 147
Lucas, Caroline, 270
Luttwak, Edward, 254

MacDonald, James Ramsay, 21–31, 35, 42, 56, 78, 95, 114, 153, 154, 187, 261
MacGregor, Ian, 242
Macmillan, Harold, 62–3, 65, 67, 73, 74, 109–10, 157–9, 163, 249, 269
  Chequers dinner party (1971), 157–8
  general election (1945), 132
  Lords accession (1984), 243
  Middle Way, The (1938), 62–3, 65, 67, 74, 109–10, 158, 249
  miners' strike (1984–5), 243–4
  Norway debate (1940), 91
  Oxford by-election (1938), 80

INDEX

Weekend World (1979), 225

Winter of Discontent (1978–9), 225–6, 227–8, 229, 241, 303

World in Action (1978), 219

theatre, 41–3, 50, 51–4, 210–11, 220, 234–5, 266, 278

Thirteenth Night (Brenton), 234–5

This House (Graham), 278

Thomas, David, 277

Thomas, Dylan, 102

Thomas, Hugh, 239

Tidworth, Wiltshire, 184

Tilbury, Essex, 224–5

Times, The, 89, 112, 126, 139, 168, 173, 178, 184, 192, 205, 218, 231, 232

Timothy, Nick, 272–3, 280, 286–90, 291, 307

Today Programme, 203

Todman, Daniel, 48

Tom Robinson Band, 219

Tomlinson, Jim, 147

Tonypandy riots (1910–11), 91, 120

Tooting, London, 176

Tory Reform Committee (1943–7), 111, 115–16, 118

Toxteth riot (1981), 236

Toye, Richard, 75–6, 82

trade unions, 2, 4, 13, 15, 21, 22, 28, 29

Attlee government (1945–51), 120, 126

Callaghan government (1976–9), 202, 205, 209, 211–28, 229

Heath government (1970–74), 157–62, 164, 165–79

In Place of Strife (1969), 149–55, 167, 181, 183, 201, 204, 212, 221, 222, 246, 285

Industrial Relations Act (1971), 157, 161, 173, 183, 214, 223, 232

Second World War (1939–45), 89, 92, 110, 115

strikes, _see_ strikes

Thatcher government (1979–90), 232, 233, 235, 236, 240–46

Wilson government, first (1964–70), 132–55

Wilson government, second (1974–6), 181–9, 194–5

Trades Disputes Act (1906), 120

Trades Union Congress (TUC), 15, 22, 23, 141

centenary (1968), 149–50

financial crisis (1931), 22, 23

general strike (1926), 15, 78, 91, 150

general strike (1972), 173

Grunwick dispute (1976–8), 214

Heath and, 163

In Place of Strife (1969), 148, 151–4

Liaison Committee (1971–6), 181–2

Macmillan on, 63

People's March for Jobs (1981), 236, 237

Second World War (1939–45), 92

Socialist League, relations with, 41

421